CONTENDING REPRESENTATIONS III   *Questioning Republicanism in Early Modern Genoa*

Contending Representations III

Questioning Republicanism in Early Modern Genoa

Edited by Enrico Zucchi and Alessandro Metlica

BREPOLS

DUNAMIS Studies in the empowerment of early-modern representations

Series Editors
Ralph Dekoninck
Agnès Guiderdoni
Alessandro Metlica

This book received funding from the European Research Council (ERC) under the European Union's Horizon 2020 Research and Innovation programme (G.A. 758450 – ERC-StG2017 "Republics on the Stage of Kings. Representing Republican State Power in the Europe of Absolute Monarchies, late 16th–early 18th century")

Language correction: Kate Delaney, Amanda Swain
Editorial assistance: Laura Armillotta

ISBN 978-2-503-60521-0 (book); 978-2-503-60522-7 (e-book)
D/2024/0095/141
DOI 10.1484/M.DUNAMIS-EB.5.132881

Copyright © 2024 Brepols Publishers, Turnhout, Belgium

This is an open access publication made available under a CC BY-NC 4.0 International License: https://creativecommons.org/licenses/by-nc/4.0/. No part of this publication may be reproduced, stored in a retrieval system, or transmitted, in any form or by any means, for commercial purposes, without the prior permission of the publisher, or as expressly permitted by law, by licence or under terms agreed with the appropriate reprographics rights organization.

Designed by Paul van Calster

Printed in the EU on acid-free paper.

CONTENTS

I EARLY MODERN GENOA IN CONTEXT
1528–1700   6

1

Enrico Zucchi and Alessandro Metlica
Piecing the Puzzle: Liberty, Identity, and Crisis
in the Republic of Genoa   8

2

Manuel Herrero Sánchez
The Representation of Genoa in a Monarchy
of Urban Republics: Between the Integration of Private Genoese
and the Limits of the Model of Full Sovereignty   20

3

Matthias Schnettger
'Camera et civitas nostra imperialis':
The Republic of Genoa in the Imperial Perspective   34

II THE AGE OF LIBERTY 1528–1620   46

4

Laura Stagno
The Gift of Concord and Freedom:
Images of Andrea Doria in Late Sixteenth Century Art   48

5

Wouter Kreuze
Perspectives on a Republic:
The Genoese crisis of 1575 in Italian avvisi   64

6

Benoît Maréchaux
Contending Republicanisms: Pamphlets, Liberty,
and Political Uses of the Past in Genoa, Venice, and Rome
at the Time of the Interdict (1606-07)   76

7

Fiorenzo Toso
'Versci, morte dro tempo': Civil Commitment
and Celebratory Rhetoric in Genoese Literature
in the Sixteenth and Seventeenth Centuries   89

III THE NEGOTIATION OF GENOESE IDENTITY
1620–1660   96

8

Valentina Borniotto
Personifications of the Republic in Genoa:
Before and After Cesare Ripa's Iconologia   98

9

Sara Rulli
Continuity and Renewal of the City Image:
The Enhancement and Strengthening of Public Architecture and
Infrastructure as an Instrument for Political Communication   114

10

George L. Gorse
A 'Royal Republic':
The Virgin Mary as 'Queen of Genoa' in 1637   124

11

Simona Morando
'Vera pace godeste in mezzo all'armi': The Commitment of Theatre
and Literature in the Latter Half of the Seventeenth Century   132

12

Giorgio Tosco
'I più savij politichi di tutte le nazioni del mondo': The Political Use
of the Dutch Model in Seventeenth-Century Genoa   140

IV THE AGE OF CRISIS 1660–1700   148

13

Luana Salvarani
'Nelle varietà proprie della Città nostra':
Giovan Francesco Spinola's Instruttione famigliare between
Genoese Identity and the Renaissance Pedagogical Tradition   150

14

Emilio Pérez Blanco
Neutrality in Question:
Genoa, the Embassy of Spain, and the Consequences of 1684   160

15

Michael Paul Martoccio
Touring 'the Peru of Italy:' The Bank of Saint George
and the Endurance of the Genoese Republic
in the English, French, and German Press, 1684–1797   168

List of Abbreviations   176
Bibliography   177
Notes on Contributors   195

EARLY MODERN GENOA IN CONTEXT

1528–1700

Enrico Zucchi
Alessandro Metlica

PIECING THE PUZZLE

*Liberty, Identity, and Crisis
in the Republic of Genoa*

Among the few republican states that survived in the Europe of absolute monarchies, i.e., between the late sixteenth and early eighteenth centuries, the Republic of Genoa held a position that was both prominent and peripheral. On the one hand, Genoa was an exemplary case because of its longevity: born as a free commune in the eleventh century, in the late Middle Ages Genoa asserted itself as a naval power with a republican system that survived until the Napoleonic occupation – although it was deeply reformed under the guidance of Andrea Doria in the sixteenth century, when Genoa was consolidated into a full-fledged oligarchy.[1] On the other hand, the Genoese republic strongly differed from other political entities flaunting more definitive republican identities, such as Venice, which stood out for its constitutional 'myth', or the Dutch Republic, where that 'myth' was consciously replicated and re-contextualised. Of course, Genoa's republican order was flaunted as well. As early as the sixteenth century, however, its close relationship with the Spanish monarchy was also considered a source of pride – a privilege extended to certain families that reverberated throughout the entire state, enriching its coffers and enhancing its political role in the European arena. The pride of being a republic independent from the surrounding monarchies was not a value universally shared in Genoa, but rather was the claim of a particular political faction: the *repubblichisti*.[2] Other factions, supported by families that were far more politically influential, aligned with either Spain or France.

Thus, in Genoa even some key republican motifs, like the concept of liberty, were less undisputed than elsewhere. The bitter conflicts between Genoa's pro-French and pro-Spanish factions, as well as the very structure of the Republic – a pyramid topped by eminent figures belonging to one or the other party, who monopolised power – made the idea of liberty there more nuanced, if not openly ambiguous. Indeed, most treatises and debates in early modern Genoa revolved around the freedom of trade or safeguarding of private property, instead of the freedom of citizens.[3] This affected both the self-representations produced by the Genoese state[4] and external perception of its republican status, which was deemed opaque and devoid of actual autonomy. Consequently, in the political imagination of late-Renaissance Europe Genoa was often presented as the counterpart to Venice: if, according to its 'myth', Venice was a Serene Republic marked by political harmony, Genoa was depicted as turbulent, contentious, and troubled by constant infighting.

We find an example of such depictions in the *Ragguagli di Parnaso* ('News-Sheets from Parnassus', 1612–1615) by Traiano Boccalini, a satirical writer who fiercely attacked the 'most serene Liberty of Genoa'.

> For many years now, the most serene Liberty of Genoa has not been admitted to the visits and domestic conversation of the noble Venetian Republic and the other most virtuous Liberties, in Italy and in Europe. Although in the past she lived in Parnassus with the highest reputation for her perfect modesty, over the past few years her credit has been greatly diminished by the domestic conversation that she has held with the deceitful Spain. To the great detriment of her reputation, the Liberty of Genoa has not only accommodated the noblest flat of her house, but has even allowed the most distinguished subjects of her nobility to serve.[5]

In line with his notorious anti-Spanish positions, Boccalini portrays Genoa's liberty as a prostitute unworthy of sitting at

Detail of 1.2
Anthony van Dyck, *Portrait of Agostino Pallavicino.*
Los Angeles, Getty Center, c. 1621.

1.1
Bust of Giano Bifronte (detail).
Genoa, Pozzo di Giano in
Piazza Sarzano.
Photo: Matteo Bimonte.
Reproduced with permission.

the council of republics. A later author, Gasparo Squarciafico – who unlike Boccalini came from a noble Ligurian family – chooses a different but equally unflattering metaphor to describe his homeland. In *Le politiche malattie della republica di Genova e loro medicine* ('The Political Diseases of the Republic of Genoa and their Remedies', 1655), Squarciafico argues that

> the current state of the Republic is not dissimilar to its ancient institutor, Janus the Fabulous King. The political state has one body but two faces. One face, resembling a venerable old man, looks back to past ages, and is made up of old nobles, who regard the power of their elders and are eager to have it back. The other face, born with the new year, has youthful cheeks, and is made up of new nobles enrolled in the book of government. Having forgotten the past, the latter jealousy preserve the present authority and boldly nourish new hopes.[6]

As a novel embodiment of two-faced Janus, the mythological father of the city (fig. 1.1), Squarciafico portrays Genoa as a monstrous republic, harshly internally divided. Questioning republicanism in early modern Genoa, as this volume does, means taking these basic contradictions into account. Such an analysis must confront motifs and ideas that, like Squarciafico's 'old nobles' and 'new nobles', not only clash but also contend for cultural and political influence. The challenge is therefore to bring these contrasting pieces together, into a coherent composite image.

Questioning the state of the art

This volume aims to shed new light on representations of republican power in Genoa between the reconquest of the city by Andrea Doria in 1528 and the crisis that followed the French bombardment in 1684 – when Genoa was definitively reduced to the status of a minor piece on the European chessboard. Of course, our inquiry builds on a solid historiographical tradition. The peculiar features of the Republic of Genoa within the context of early modern Europe have been illuminated by several seminal studies, published between the 1970s and the 1990s by historians such as Claudio Costantini, Edoardo Grendi, and Carlo Bitossi. These studies have focused on matters as varied as trade practices and investments in charitable works, the hotel and banking systems, aristocratic networks and the conflicts among political factions.[7] Both edited volumes and research monographs considered Genoese literature, painting, and architecture, providing extensive lists of texts and works of art and discussing the role that politics played in cultural production. These studies have effectively demonstrated how rich, multi-layered, and even conflicting this cultural production was, and opened up space for further, more comprehensive investigation.[8]

The novelty of this volume consists in its intersecting and cross-disciplinary perspectives. Our first goal is to survey and compare the many modes of representing republican power, regardless of media type or rhetorical tropes. We achieve this by examining a wide variety of documents: paintings, statues, and palaces, but also texts as diverse as political treatises and propaganda pamphlets, dialectal poems and pedagogical writings, books on iconology and ephemeral prints. In spite (and indeed because) of its array of sources, this corpus conveys an image of the Republic of Genoa that is both historically accurate and more pluralist than previously imagined.

Our second goal is to offer a broader methodological framework that enhances communication between academic fields focused on cultural production (art history, literary and theatre studies) and some critical perspectives instead pertaining to intellectual history. In this respect, this volume builds on the work of Thomas Allan Kirk, Matthias Schnettger, and Manuel Herrero Sánchez, which paved the way for comprehensive reconsideration of republicanism in early modern Genoa. Kirk first emphasised the never-ending negotiation constituting Genoa's identity in the Mediterranean throughout the late Renaissance and Baroque periods; Schnettger and Herrero Sánchez placed this dialectic within the European context, by interpreting Genoa not as a self-sufficient entity but as a particular *civitas imperialis* – a province of the Habsburg Empire enjoying some advantages in exchange for a more or less formal profession of subjection – and as one of the peripheral centres of the polycentric Spanish monarchy.[9]

These volumes successfully challenged the rhetoric of early modern republicanism to the extent of catalysing a paradigm shift. In the past this rhetoric was presented as a synchronic repertoire of symbols and ideas, which stood out throughout all of Western civilization for its high intellectual coherence. In the wake of the loose historiographical movement ushered in by the Cambridge School, influential studies began asserting the existence of a resilient republican model, rooted in the ancient Greece and Rome, which was revived in Italy during the fifteenth and sixteenth centuries and subsequently revitalised in the United States by the American revolution. This model was considered the shared foundation of modern liberal democracies; it was therefore framed in opposition, or even in stark contrast, to monarchical culture. Deemed impervious to any external political influence, republican tradition was considered to be common to both Machiavelli's Florence and Cromwell's Commonwealth.[10]

This idea of republicanism was the result of a sophisticated theorization. Locating such a clear-cut discourse or political tradition in the republican states of the early modern era, however, is a whole other matter. The cultural representations that were actually produced and displayed in these republican contexts – in Genoa, Venice, and the Dutch republic, but also in smaller European republics like Lucca and Ragusa – were far from unambiguous. Instead of merely repelling monarchical iconographies and ideas, these representations often exploited them; besides drawing on the republican canon of Livy, Cicero, and Machiavelli, they also absorbed and repurposed absolutist authors like Jean Bodin, Justus Lipsius, and Thomas Hobbes.[11]

Indeed, seventeenth-century Europe boasts a richer heritage than we often suppose. Early modern republicanism offers an alternative repertoire of concepts to the one we usually associate with the ancien régime. However, this should not lead us to believe early modern Europe was characterised by a series of black-and-white binary oppositions heralding the transition towards modern democracy. This volume shows that such dichotomies should instead be jettisoned. Like the Genoa that emerges in the work of Squarciafico, early modern Europe was itself a Janus-faced entity divided between monarchies and republics. Yet, the metaphor that best represents early modern conceptions of power is a mosaic – an assemblage of interlocked values and identities in which all the pieces nonetheless contribute to the meaning of the whole.

Liberty

The contributions by Manuel Herrero Sánchez and Matthias Schnettger, together with the pages that you are reading (chapters 1–3), serve as an overall introduction to the volume and are intended to put early modern Genoa into historical context. Updating and revamping the seminal studies that we discussed above, chapters 2 and 3 stress how a comprehensive, pan-European perspective foregrounds the self-presentation of Genoa as an autonomous republic as neither singular nor consistent. Rather, Genoa's showcasing of independence was the result of political mediation which balanced patriotic pride with the need not to lose the privileges granted to a subject city.

The second section of the volume (chapters 4–7) focuses on the so-called *Age of Liberty*, the period extending from 1528, when Andrea Doria rejected the offer of lordship, to 1637, when doge Agostino Pallavicino was publicly crowned (fig. 1.2–1.3).

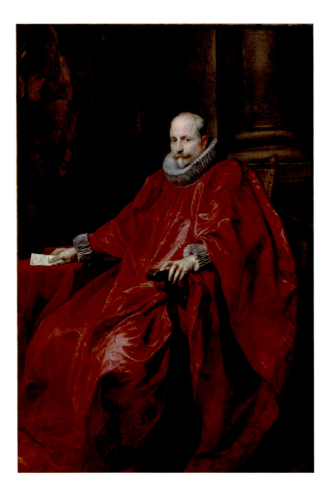

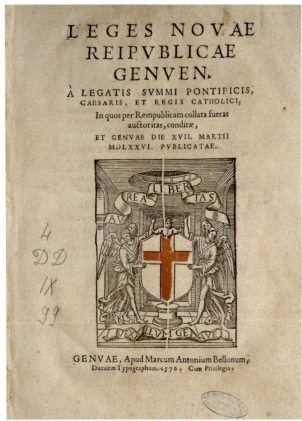

1.2
Anthony van Dyck, *Portrait of Agostino Pallavicino*. Los Angeles, Getty Center, c. 1621. Photo: Open Content Program.

1.3
Copy of Domenico Fiasella, *Portrait of Agostino Pallavicino, doge from 1637 to 1639*. Genoa, Galleria Nazionale di Palazzo Spinola, early 18th century. Reproduced with permission from the Italian Ministry of Culture – Musei Nazionali di Genova.

1.4
Title page of *Leges novae Reipublicae Genuensis a legatis summi Pontificis Caesaris et Regis catholici*, Genuae, Apud Marcum Antonium Bellonum, 1576.

1.5
Diego Velázquez, *The surrender of Breda*.
Madrid, Museo Nacional del Prado, 1634–1635.
Oil on canvas, 307 × 371 cm (P001172).
Photo: © Photographic Archive Museo Nacional del Prado.
Reproduced with permission.

This timespan was marked by several major achievements and upheavals, as the age of liberty saw the strengthening of the republican government in the wake of Doria's actions. The consolidation process peaked in 1576 with the Casale agreements, which redefined the Republic's elective practices, management of power, and distribution of offices (fig. 1.4).[12] The liberty of Genoa, however, remained a disputed concept. Indeed, during the same period, Genoa's relationship with the Spanish monarchy also tightened, confirming both the economic and the political subordination of Genoa to the Spanish crown – as evidenced by its repeated bankruptcies. The figure of Ambrogio Spinola (fig. 1.5), for instance, shows that the agreements of Casale did not effectively address the Ligurian aristocracy's lack of a strong republican identity. An eminent Genoese general who fought successfully for the King of Spain, Spinola expended little energy protecting the interests of his homeland republic and was inclined to seek the favour of his powerful patron instead.[13]

The Casale agreements also failed to curb the factional conflict within the Genoese government, which intensified in the 1620s and led to the siege of the city by a joint Franco-Savoyard army in 1625. On this occasion, competing pro-French and pro-Spanish conspiracies pushed Genoa to the brink of civil war.[14] The painting by Antonio de Pereda on the cover of this volume, *The Relief of Genoa by the second Marquis of Santa Cruz* (1634–1635: fig. 1.6), effectively depicts the political

1.6

Antonio de Pereda y Salgado, *The Relief of Genoa by the second Marquis of Santa Cruz*. Madrid, Museo Nacional del Prado, 1634–1635. Oil on canvas, 290 × 370 cm (n. P007126). Photo: © Photographic Archive Museo Nacional del Prado. Reproduced with permission.

1.7

Detail of 1.6.

compromises that this double-dealing politics entailed. The canvas shows the entry into Genoa of the Spanish fleet's commander Álvaro de Bazán, who has just relieved the city of the Franco-Savoyard siege. His meeting at the gates of Genoa with doge Federico De Franchi Toso, however, is not depicted as a military alliance, but rather as an act of homage and subservience. Pereda imagines the doge as an old man, hat in hand, bowing his head to welcome the city's liberator. The latter, who instead wears a smile of condescension on his face, stands proudly in his black and gold armour, and thereby appears taller than the doge. The details of this image serve as a visual transposition of the political hierarchies at play (fig. 1.7).

Such a bold representation of Genoa's (lack of) liberty is not itself surprising. Pereda painted the scene for display in the Hall of Realms, i.e., the hall of the royal throne in the Buen Retiro Palace in Madrid: commissioned directly by the Spain crown, *The Relief of Genoa* belonged to a propaganda campaign that celebrated the military power and geographical vastness of the Spanish empire in resounding tones.[15] Yet, this representation was also made possible by the inconsistency of Genoese republican culture. Repeatedly sacrificed to international alliances and private wealth, the concept of liberty was mainly invoked in Genoa by actors – such as the *repubblichisti* Andrea Spinola and Ansaldo Cebà – who were peripheral and without influence. The ruling factions, on the other hand, were willing to sacrifice this symbolic capital in the name not only of political contingency but also of private interest.

Chapter 4 by Laura Stagno investigates the figure of Andrea Doria as the symbolic pivot of an ideal (and to some extent chimerical) representation of the Republic grounded in the values of concord, unity, and freedom. In the works of art portraying his life and deeds, Doria comes to embody a distinctive political myth: the man who put the state ahead of personal gain. This results in a rather peculiar conception of liberty: liberty not as a virtue rooted in a social class or political system – as it was in Venice, at least after the *serrata* (closure) of the Great

Council in 1297 – but a gift granted by a superhuman or demigod, whose exceptional merit constituted the sole guarantee against tyranny.

In chapter 5 by Wouter Kreuze, the focus shifts from art history to history and from effective to conditional liberty. The 1575 *avvisi* ('newssheets') overturn the image of unity symbolically evoked by Doria's figure, instead underscoring the polarisation of Genoa's political life (old and new nobles, pro-French and pro-Spanish factions). Still, even behind these contrasts lurked an idea of liberty. The liberty of Genoa, the 1575 *avvisi* suggest, needed to be conditional to be preserved: political and commercial alliance with one of the two great foreign monarchies was essential to survival of the Republic. Liberty in Genoa was therefore conditional, and it was only the extent of these conditions that could be discussed.

Chapter 6 by Benoît Maréchaux delves into the contest over the meaning of republican liberty between Genoa and Venice, which shows why the Cambridge school paradigm does not concretely apply to early modern Europe. Indeed, in this case the ideological opposition was not between republican and monarchical states but two rival republics. By examining what he calls a 'war of writings', made up of both published pamphlets and unauthorised manuscripts that circulated widely during the conflict between the Papal State and the Venetian Republic (1606–1607), Maréchaux sheds new light on the indeterminacy inhering in the very concept of republican liberty: whereas Venice, according to Genoa, was not entirely free because of the tribute paid to the Turks, Genoa, according to Venice, lacked full sovereignty and was not even a republican state but a city subject to the King of Spain.

In chapter 7, Fiorenzo Toso addresses what we may call the quest for linguistic liberty. Starting with Paolo Foglietta's *Lamento de Zena*, between the late sixteenth and the mid-seventeenth century Genoese poetry used the vernacular as the language of politics. The vernacular thus emerged in opposition to the Tuscan language as the idiom of political independence. Consistently employed in celebrations of the doge, such as in the verses composed by Barnaba Cigala Casero and Gian Giacomo Cavalli, the vernacular was also used to celebrate the coronation of Agostino Pallavicino in 1637. It thereby contributed to a radical shift in representations of the state, which shifted away from focus on the offered lordship embodied by Doria toward emphasis on a new royal status (though merely allegorical) symbolised by the crowned doge. Ligurian poets played a part in this process by vehemently justifying the royal status of Genoa and the Republic's control over the Kingdom of Corsica.

Identity

The 1637 coronation marks the beginning of a new era, as well as a new section of our volume. The contributions collected in this third section (chapters 8–12), which is entitled *The Negotiation of Identity*, survey cultural production in Genoa from 1625 – when the definitive edition of Cesare Ripa's *Iconologia* was printed – to 1660, the year that Giovanni Andrea Spinola's *Perfidia fulminata da Sansone* was published. All the chapters centre on the representation of the state, which during this period of Genoa's history proved to be increasingly elusive and multi-faceted. On one hand, after overcoming the turmoil of the 1620s, Genoa became an international Baroque capital, thanks in part to the ambitious literary program championed by Anton Giulio Brignole Sale and the revival of the navalist project.[16] On the other hand, this international 'launch' was quickly followed by an 'eclipse' foreshadowing the crisis of the Republic.[17] These contradictions were vividly reflected in Genoese cultural production, with textual and figurative representations depicting the continual search for a more consistent political identity. Indeed, the attempt to portray Genoa as an imperialist power with key possessions in the Mediterranean (e.g. the Kingdom of Corsica) deeply affected the coherence of any republican representation and led to even more frequent evocation of symbols and figures from the monarchical repertoire.

In chapter 8, Valentina Borniotto studies the evolution of allegorical representations of Genoa between the sixteenth and seventeenth centuries. Previously embodied by several local heroes, such as the medieval general Guglielmo Embriaco, Genoa acquired a fixed identity after the publication of Cesare Ripa's *Iconologia* – which canonised the image of a lean, manly-looking female figure whose helmet and corselet were adorned with allegorical elements referring to the Ligurian virtues of prudence and industriousness. The lasting and vast purchase of this depiction, which was also reproduced in Joan Bleau's *Theatrum Orbis Terrarum* (1640), once again highlights the hybridization of the political codes of the time: unlike liberty, a virtue belonging to the symbolic field of republicanism, prudence was considered the distinctive quality of a good sovereign by all major theorists of the absolutist state, from Justus Lipsius to Thomas Hobbes.

Chapter 9 by Sara Rulli investigates public architecture as an instrument of political communication. Also in this respect the late 1620s were a turning point, since the project of building an independent fleet and strengthening the Genoese defence system found concrete realisation in the construction of the walls. Throughout the following decades (1630–1650), the walls became a distinguishing symbol of the city. As such, they were reproduced in what we might consider a republican manifesto: the frontispiece of *Il genio ligure risvegliato* ('The Awakened Ligurian Genius') by Giovan Bernardo Veneroso (1650). They were also recalled and celebrated in such masterpieces of Genoese Baroque fiction as Bernardo Morando's *Rosalinda* (1650) and Anton Giulio Brignole Sale's *Instabilità dell'ingegno* ('The Unstable Intellect', 1635). As Rulli points out, the role played by the walls in these works was not merely descriptive, but rather took on a precise political value. They were intended to offer a new image of the city as a strong, pacified republic: no longer quarrelsome or divided, but calm and reunited.

Chapter 10 pivots upon another, and seemingly opposing representation, dating from the very same years: the portrayal of Genoa as a divine monarchy. Indeed, in this chapter George Gorse focuses on the coronation of the Virgin Mary as the Queen of Genoa in March 1637, an event which was considered in parallel to the aforementioned coronation of doge Agostino Pallavicino. A direct response to the political and military crisis of the mid-1620s, the coronation aimed to strengthen the Genoese identity using the cultural influence and diplomatic prestige associated with royal status. However, according to Gorse, this monarchical image should not be understood as conflicting with contemporary republican imagery. As proof of this, Gorse points to the belt worn by the Virgin Mary, which resembles the pattern of the recently constructed walls – a key symbol, as clarified in chapter 9, of Genoa's independence and republican identity.

In chapter 11, the focus shifts from figurative works to literary texts. Simona Morando provides convincing evidence of why many novels and plays from the period should be read in light of their political allusions, since their characters and narrative situations hint at the chronicle in a very subtle and targeted way. Despite their seemingly light-hearted plots, for instance, the musical dramas of Giovanni Andrea Spinola build on explicit political allegories: in *Ariodante*, a work based on Ariosto's *Orlando furioso*, anti-Spanish references unfold beneath the love story, while *Europa*, a mythological tale taken from Ovid, openly addresses the ongoing conflicts in Europe by proposing a matrimonial policy.

The last chapter of the third section, chapter 12, is by Giorgio Tosco. Tosco addresses the adoption of the political model of the Dutch Republic in the Republic of Genoa, arguing that Amsterdam served as a republican exemplar for commercial reasons but was limited on an ideological level. The Genoese East India Company, for instance, was established as a concrete strategy for economic growth: though the measure was taken up within the navalist framework, it did not mirror an abstract republican ideal. Indeed, the Genoese East India Company was soon opposed by the Dutch East India Company, which was unwilling to accept an alliance that would have threatened its own interests.

Crisis

Tosco's point leads to the fourth and last section of the book, which is dedicated to the *Age of Crisis* (1660–1700). The navalist project presented in Veneroso's *Genio ligure risvegliato* called for a strong solidarity among Venice, Genoa, and the United Provinces that would offer mutual economic and military support and foster a republican network in the Mediterranean. However, the second half of the seventeenth century was instead marked by republican competition. As discussed in chapters 6 and 12, with respect to the Republic of Venice and the Dutch Republic, the state rivalry prevailing during this period disregarded the form of government. Thus, Veneroso's ambitious political program was only implemented on paper: the increasing crisis led to the Republic of Genoa's rapid deterioration, until it reached a point of no return in 1684.

In chapter 13, Luana Salvarani focuses on a lesser known text that proves fundamental for exploring this topic: Giovan Francesco Spinola's *Instruttione famigliare* ('Family Education'), which was published in the same year as the *Genio ligure risvegliato* (1650). While the latter may be seen as the last attempt to represent Genoa as a political model and a naval power, Spinola's book offers a private counterpoint to this public image. Underlining the widespread concern of the Genoese nobility, as early as 1650, about the fate of the Republic, the *Instruttione famigliare* greatly undermines the trust in republican institutions that Veneroso suggests was shared by the patrician families. In this respect, as Salvarani argues, the book marked a shift in the history of aristocratic pedagogy: the *humanae litterae* were no longer deemed essential for noble education, as had previously been the case, and were dismissed in favour of mathematical and commercial training. The virtue at the centre of this pedagogical system was once again prudence, but the concept as outlined in Ripa's allegory (and investigated in chapter 8) had undergone a sea change. Because of the instability of the Genoese political situation, Spinola urged young people to be prudent, but his warning no longer referred to absolutist ethics and instead exclusively applied to the ability to save and invest in reliable businesses.

Chapter 14 by Emilio Pérez Blanco frames the year of the collapse: 1684, when the French bombardment of Genoa took place. Studying how tensions between Genoa and Madrid led to the defeat, Blanco offers a two-fold historiographical perspective. On one hand, the chapter shows how the decline of the Spanish monarchy, confirmed by the Treaty of the Pyrenees in 1659, facilitated the growth of Genoese independence and conceptions of the navalist project. On the other hand, it argues that the navalist project itself laid the groundwork for the events of 1684. From that moment on, as the documentation gathered by Blanco shows, the Republic was

1.8

Burning of the Golden Book in the Piazza d'Acquaverde on 14 June 1797, print s.a. and s.d., paper engraving 43,8 × 21 cm, inv. St/3322. Photo: © Istituto Mazziniano – Museo del Risorgimento. Reproduced with permission.

no longer the master of its own choices: relations between Genoa and Spain in the 1680s and 1690s remained ambiguous, but the path of neutrality pursued by the Republic was more the result of fear of French retaliation than an autonomous political choice.

Chapter 15 by Michael Martoccio, the last chapter of the volume, broadens our perspective on this age of crisis. It examines how Northern European countries saw and interpreted Genoa between the French bombardment of 1684 and the collapse of the Republic in 1797. Despite the difficulties Genoa experienced during this timespan, surprising data emerging from Martoccio's analysis confirm the resilience of republican symbolism. Foreign travellers who arrived in Liguria and expected to find a civilization in decline, instead reported encountering a flourishing city, an extremely wealthy aristocracy, and an avant-garde public health system. Years of neutrality and financial capitalism led by the Bank of Saint George had allowed Genoa to experience a new prosperity. The fall of the Republic in 1797, when Genoa was annexed to France following the Napoleonic invasion, still seemed a long way off (fig. 1.8).

This volume is dedicated to the memory of Fiorenzo Toso, a distinguished scholar of Genoese literature and language, who passed away while this book was taking shape.

1 See the seminal study by Savelli, *La Repubblica oligarchica*.

2 On this political group, including literary authors such as Andrea Spinola and Ansaldo Cebà, see Bitossi, *Il governo dei magnifici*, pp. 207–50, and Bitossi, 'Due modelli di educazione'. Most of Spinola's works were not published at the time, but a modern edition edited by Bitossi is available. See Spinola, *Scritti scelti*. A strong republican identity, near to that of the *repubblichisti*, inspired the manifesto of the Accademia degli Addormentati ('the Sleepers'), which was published in 1587 and also made available in a recent edition with extensive commentary. See Beltrami, ed., *Leggi e ordini*. On the afterlife of these ideas within the navalist party in the late seventeenth century, see Lo Basso, 'Diaspora e armamento'.

3 See Bitossi, 'Città, Repubblica e nobiltà' and Costantini, 'Politica e storiografia'.

4 See Ceccarelli, *'In forse di perdere la libertà'*.

5 'Sono già molti anni che la serenissima Libertà di Genova non è ammessa alle visite e alla domestica conversazione dell'inclita Republica veneziana e delle altre castissime Libertadi italiane e oltramontane, percioché, ancorch'ella per il passato sia vissuta in Parnaso con somma riputazione d'una perfetta pudicizia, in questi ultimi anni nondimeno grandemente le ha scemato il credito la troppo domestica conversazione ch'ella ha sempre tenuta con la fallace nazion spagnuola, alla quale, e con grandissimo detrimento della sua riputazione, ella non solo ha accomodato il più nobile appartamento della sua casa, ma fino ha permesso che i più insigni soggetti della sua nobiltà la servino'. Boccalini, *Ragguagli di Parnaso*, II, p. 6. Unless noted otherwise, the translations are all ours.

6 See Squarciafico, *Le politiche malattie*, p. 34: 'Lo stato odierno della Republica non è ponto difforme dall'antico suo istitutore, Giano Re favoloso. Un sol corpo e due volti costituiscono lo Stato politico. Quello che, simile a un venerabile vecchio, risguarda l'età passate, è formato da Vecchi Nobili, che la potenza de' loro Maggiori rimirano, e impatienti la riattendono. L'altro, che nato co 'l nuovo Anno, ha giovanili le guancie è composto da Popolari scritti nel libro del Governo, che poste in oblio le cose andate, la presente autorità gelosi conservano, e novelle speranze audacemente nutriscono'.

7 See Constantini, *La Repubblica di Genova*; Grendi, *Introduzione alla storia moderna*; *La Repubblica aristocratica* and *I Balbi*; and Bitossi, *Il governo dei magnifici*.

8 For a comprehensive perspective, see Puncuh, ed., *Storia della cultura ligure*. On sixteenth- and seventeenth-century painting and architecture, see the books by Pesenti, *La pittura in Liguria* and Magnani, *Il Tempio di Venere*; the volume by Gavazza, Lamera and Magnani, eds, *La pittura in Liguria*; and the most recent inquiry by Bober, Boccardo, and Boggero, eds, *A Superb Baroque*. Also see chapters 4, 8, 9, and 10 in this volume.

9 See Kirk, *Genoa and the sea*; Schnettger, 'Principe sovrano'; Herrero Sánchez and others, eds, *Génova y la Monarquía*; Albareda and Herrero Sánchez, *Political representation*. Also see chapters 2 and 3 in this volume.

10 See Pocock, *The Machiavellian Moment*; Bock, Skinner, and Viroli, *Machiavelli and Republicanism*; Skinner, *Liberty before Liberalism*; Viroli, *Repubblicanesimo*; Van Gelderen and Skinner, eds, *Republicanism*.

11 This conclusion is one of the major achievements of the project RISK – *Republics on the Stage of Kings* (GA 758450 – St G2017), in the context of which this very volume, as well as the whole *Contending Representations* series, was conceived (see Oddens, Moorman, and Metlica, *Contending Representations I* and Florio and Metlica, *Contending Representations II*). On the conceptual hybridization of republican and monarchical sources, see in particular Metlica, 'Magnificence and Atticism', *Lessico* and Zucchi, 'Republic in Comparison', 'Alessandro Tassoni', 'Contesting', 'Repubblicanesimo'. More broadly, on Lucca and Venice respectively, see Gallucci, *Recitar cantando* and Florio, *Micropolitica*.

12 For more on the Casale agreements, also from a legal perspective, see in particular Assereto, *Le Metamorfosi* and Savelli, *Che cosa era il diritto patrio?*.

13 A comprehensive portrait of Ambrogio Spinola is presented in the recent volume by Garcia Garcia, Lo Basso, and Mostaccio, eds, *Ambrogio Spinola*.

14 On this key historical juncture, see Ceccarelli, 'Tra sovranità e imperialità'. For a more accurate account of these events in the context of the Thirty Years' War, see Ieva, 'Il Principe di Piemonte' and Pizzorno, 'Il cannone e l'eversione'.

15 See Hermoso Cuesta, 'The Hall of Realms' and Metlica, *Lessico*, pp. 20–22.

16 On the latter, see Lo Basso, 'Diaspora e armamento'.

17 We take the metaphor from Graziosi, *Lancio ed eclissi*.

2

Manuel Herrero Sánchez

THE REPRESENTATION OF GENOA IN A MONARCHY OF URBAN REPUBLICS

Between the Integration of Private Genoese and the Limits of the Model of Full Sovereignty

The interpretive paradigm around republicanism put forth by the Cambridge school does not seem to leave room for the Republic of Genoa. Freedom understood as the absence of any form of domination whatever, martial sobriety in defence of the community, and austerity as the best antidote for the corrupting effects of trade are among the main pillars of the Anglo-Saxon (with a Tuscan touch) form of republicanism advocated by John Pocock.[1] Genoa's limited ability to defend its independence from external threats and its strong links with the Hispanic Monarchy after the *condotta* agreement reached by Andrea Doria and Charles V in 1528 explain the relative disdain suffered by a republic which its contemporaries often compared with that of Venice. Against the Venetian myth, archetype of mixed and balanced form of government, capable of guaranteeing its own political independence with its commercial resources and a state galley fleet,[2] Genoa was presented as a weak republic, exposed to the whim of personal interests. According to Giovanni Botero's famous adage, the good governance and defence of the collective interest represented by Venice stood tall against Genoa, whose stability was totally reliant on a wealthy oligarchy interested only in consolidating their private financial transactions with the Spanish king and in getting richer by leasing out their galleys:

> There are in Italy two great republics, Venice and Genoa. There is little doubt that Venice overtakes Genoa by a long way, and if we look for the reasons for this, we shall find that Venetians have gained only mediocre wealth when trading individually, and much more when doing so together. In Genoa, in contrast, we see them immoderately attending their individual business, while undermining public revenue.[3]

This argument, as we shall see, was adopted by the so-called *repubblichista* party from the late sixteenth century onwards,

in their attempt to review Genoa's links with Madrid and follow a policy of active neutrality, with a view to recovering the former commercial impetus, now playing second fiddle to financial transactions. While in the late sixteenth century Paolo Foglietta encouraged the Genoese youth to 'live in Venice at least for a couple of years so that we could rule our republic like the Venetians',[4] in the opening years of the seventeenth century Ansaldo Cebà and Andrea Spinola openly argued in favour of adopting a new institutional set-up inspired by the Venetian model.[5] These notions are fully in line with nineteenth century romantic-liberal traditions according to which the agreement with Charles V was one of the most tangible expressions of the beginning of foreign domination in Italy. According to this perspective, following the agreement the dynamic commercial groups of the Republic, and main agents of the Genoese naval expansion in the Middle Ages, became paralysed, while the values of sobriety and republican virtue were fatally undermined.[6]

Indeed, one of the main reasons behind Genoa being neglected by the prevailing views on republicanism is its close links with the Hispanic Monarchy, which is often presented as the counterpoint of that model of government.[7] In a recent collective volume, we have endeavoured to redress this unilinear narrative, while emphasising the polysemic nature of the concept of republicanism and the tight bonds that entangled monarchic and republican systems.[8] In said volume, I present the Hispanic Monarchy as a polycentric imperial

2.2
Peter Paul Rubens, *Marquis Ambrogio Spinola.*
Saint Louis, Saint Louis Art Museum, c. 1630.
Oil on canvas, 117.8 × 85.1 cm,
33:1934. Reproduced with permission.

DOI 10.1484/M.DUNAMIS-EB.5.142031

structure formed by a complex aggregation of urban republics under the jurisdiction of a single ruler, which was held to be the guarantor of their respective privileges and liberties. This imperial structure included some of the most thoroughly urbanised regions in Europe, and the power of the sovereign was consolidated by the foundation of new cities, as shown by the process of expansion overseas.[9] Said cities were highly autonomous and had a close relationship not only with the court in Madrid, but with one another and with other cities outside of the system, such as Genoa, whose elites were interested in the profits to be made in such wide and lucrative markets. The Spanish imperial system was built upon a complex framework of overlapping aristocratic, bureaucratic, military, religious, and mercantile transnational networks, which pivoted around urban centres. This made the system extremely adaptable and, to a large extent, explains its survival over time. This was a heterogeneous space that facilitated the operation of mercantile diasporas capable of thriving within a mosaic of multiple jurisdictional and monetary contexts, acting as connectors between disperse territories and offering a wide variety of resources that were essential for the operation of the system; this proves the importance of private initiative for the governance of the Hispanic Empire and the key part played by local agents in channelling goods and capital. The Genoese were to be among the leading agents in these transnational networks.

Spanish-Genoese symbiosis and the integration of republican citizens in the Spanish imperial system

It is not coincidental that the aspect of Spanish-Genoese relations that has received the most attention to date concerns the financial activities of Genoese financiers. The notion of 'the century of the Genoese', coined by Felipe Ruiz Martín and made popular by Fernand Braudel, has become a commonplace, supporting a voluminous bibliography that demonstrates that no understanding of the operation of the Hispanic Monarchy is possible without taking sufficiently into account the central role played by businessmen who seemed to be everywhere and to hold the very fate of the imperial system in their hands.[10] The presence of the Genoese in the main cities under the Catholic King's jurisdiction in Castile, Aragon, Naples, Sicily, Milan, the Low Countries, and the American colonies, and the control they had over both the king's finances and local transactions, marked the image and the representation of the Republic in the Monarchy's structure.[11] Genoese businessmen enjoyed a relative advantage over other mercantile communities and found promotion within the Spanish system comparatively easy. Their control over international capital flows and their wide-ranging networks were compounded, vis-à-vis the competing Portuguese, by their unimpeachable 'purity of blood',[12] and vis-à-vis the English and the Dutch, by their firm Catholicism. This came on top of an aristocratic veneer that other foreign mercantile communities lacked, which was consolidated by the 'oligarchisation' of the Genoese elite in the early sixteenth century, in the same year, in fact, in which the Republic decisively sided with the Habsburgs in their conflict with the Valois.[13] These aristocratic credentials allowed the Genoese to acquire local offices that were reserved for the aristocracy, facilitating their social promotion and giving them privileged access to royal patronage. Although many became citizens and merged into their local societies, following shrewd matrimonial policies that saw them joining hands with the most conspicuous members of the local elites, they often preferred to keep a distinct Genoese identity, which allowed them to enjoy the numerous prerogatives and concessions granted by the Crown in its Iberian, Italian, and Flemish dominions.[14] In order to reinforce this privileged position and undermine the competition posed by other mercantile communities, the Genoese adopted a policy of corporate protection. This not only safeguarded their interests, but also strengthened their collective identity through the foundation of confraternities, hospitals, chapels, churches, and cemeteries for the exclusive use of community members.[15] Consulates, established in all the main harbours of the Hispanic Monarchy, played a central role in this framework, monitoring that the privileges awarded to the Genoese were upheld and arbitrating possible intra-community conflicts.[16]

In line with Edoardo Grendi's pioneering work on the Balbi family,[17] studies on the shifting strategies of some of the main Genoese families in the dominions of the Catholic King have recently proliferated. Combining private documents and records from Spanish, Italian, and Belgian archives, Carmen Sanz traced the personal steps of one of Philip IV's foremost bankers, Ottavio Centurione.[18] In the same vein, Antonio Álvarez-Ossorio and I have followed the spectacular rise of the heirs of Ambrogio Spinola to the top of the Monarchy's decision-making bodies, their ability to place their investments in the right place, and their complex matrimonial policy, which combined endogamic ties with the old Genoese nobility, like the Doria, and high-flying aristocratic alliances in Castile (Guzmán, De la Cerda) and Italy (Colonna).[19] For her part, Yasmina Ben Yessef has published an impeccable study of the strategies mobilised by the Serra family to offer financial services and galleys to the Spanish Crown over three generations, from the late sixteenth to the first half of the seventeenth century. She also analysed their ability to straddle three loyalties simultaneously – to the Republic, the Catholic King, and their own family – and to shift resources between the Monarchy's Iberian and Italian dominions depending on the circumstances.[20] It must not be forgotten that the burgeoning debt and recurrent defaults of the Hispanic Monarchy led to a profound transformation of Genoese investment strategies and social status. In exchange for their loans, the Genoese ended up hoarding prebends of all stripes and the Crown's and the local governments' most lucrative rents. Families like the Balbi, the Centurione, the Spinola, the Doria, and the Serra greatly increased their assets by creating *mayorazgos*, making massive investments in real estate, and hoovering up the best public bonds (*juros*), while easily being granted the attributes of military orders and patents of nobility. Their managerial skills, their links with the most prestigious families, and their wide social networks earned them places in the government of the most prosperous cities in the Monarchy, whose public offices they purchased systematically. The Genoese not only entered local governments, but also gained lofty positions at court, taking active part in the main councils and government *juntas*. Although there is little doubt that the increasing volatility of their business affairs with the Crown prompted them to shift investment towards sumptuary goods, patents of nobility, fixed rents, and real estate, the Genoese never ceased to take advantage of their complex mercantile networks and highly efficient information systems. This has been recently illustrated by Alejandro García Montón's study of Domenico Grillo's control of the slave *asiento* between 1663 and 1674, which reveals the dynamism of Genoese financial and mercantile structures despite the ongoing tensions in Spanish-Genoese relations.[21]

As well as providing valuable financial services, the Genoese played an irreplaceable role freighting people, troops, supplies, cereals, and money between the different territories of the Monarchy in the western Mediterranean, where the Spanish naval system was heavily reliant on the services provided by private Genoese galley contractors (*asentistas de galeras*). Despite its obvious relevance, this naval structure has received little attention to date, a fact probably explained by the dispersion and complexity of the relevant sources. To this, we might add the fact that the transnational character of these galley fleets is an awkward fit with the strongly nationalist nature of traditional approaches to military studies, which have created a false correlation between the military revolution and the consolidation of the modern and fully sovereign state. Although Thomas Kirk and de Luca Lo Basso have taken a more balanced approach to the study of Genoa's naval system, they looked at private fleets only tangentially, focusing instead on the government's attempts to build a state galley fleet similar to Venice's.[22]

In recent years, Benoît Maréchaux has masterfully combined the records in the *Archivo General de Simancas* and the *Archivio di Stato de Genova* with private archives pertaining to some of the main families in the business. This has allowed him to present a novel perspective of the management and evolution of this polycentric naval system based on the hire of private naval entrepreneurs by the Spanish monarch. From the outset, in 1528, the fleet led by Andrea Doria specialised in shifting resources between the different territories of the Hispanic system. His twelve galleys, increased to twenty in 1539, became the core of the various squadrons deployed by the Catholic King in the Mediterranean. During the sixteenth century, these forces grew with the squadrons commanded by Agostino and Giorgio Grimaldi, Visconte Cicala, Antonio Doria, Bendinelli Sauli, Stefano de Mari, Marco Centurione and Nicolò and Agostino Lomellini. According to Maréchaux's data, between 1566 and 1580 the fleet had a minimum of 24 galleys, and between fourteen and fifteen towards the end of Philip II's reign.[23]

Genoese galleys played an even more important role from the 1570s onwards, when the Dutch revolt and the conflict with England made it harder to sail in the Atlantic, forcing the Monarchy to use the Mediterranean as the logistic platform to bring resources to northern Europe. As pointed out by Alejandro García Montón in his work on the slave *asiento* and the Grillo-Lomellino company, Genoese companies were still essential for the operation of the Atlantic system in the second half of the seventeenth century, and also created a series of mechanisms that allowed the entry of capital into the, theoretically closed, Castilian commercial monopoly in the Atlantic. The Grillos established an impressive, and markedly transnational, network of agents in the main Caribbean harbours, while enjoying important concessions and the appointment of *jueces conservadores* (privative judges for the *asiento*) to facilitate their transactions.[24] The Genoese progressively moved away from the Crown finances, but this does not mean that their communities became less important in the Catholic King's main harbours. Sheltering behind the neutrality of the Republic in the wars that shook Europe in the late seventeenth and early eighteenth centuries, Genoese mercantile communities flourished, skillfully channelling all sorts of illicit goods, and reinforcing their role as middlemen.[25]

The Genoese also played a crucial part in the control of information. The Spanish imperial structure depended on the effective circulation of news between the different hubs of the system and the court. Apart from the always unreliable overland route, it was essential to have a maritime route connecting the Iberian Peninsula and Genoa, which was the main node of communication between the different territories of the Crown. Official postal networks[26] were complemented by private channels. For instance, the network operated by Gian Andrea Doria from 1576 until his death in 1606

2.1
Jan Cornelisz Vermeyen, The map from the tapestry series of *The Conquest of Tunis*. Sevilla, Real Alcázar, 1546. Reproduced with permission.

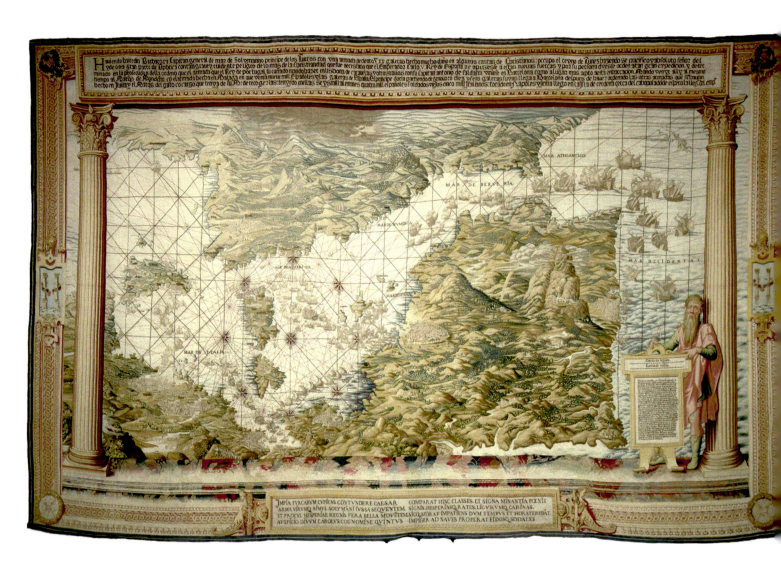

was an alternative link between Madrid and Genoa, sometimes more reliable and informative about conditions inside the Republic than the reports sent by the king's ambassador.[27] As analysed by Johann Petitjean, this was compounded by the news that circulated among Genoese consular networks.[28] As illustrated by the tapestry that commemorates the conquest of Tunis in 1535 (fig. 2.1), which depicts an inverted map of the Mediterranean, with Genoa at the top, the Republic became the nerve centre of the Spanish imperial system. It was not only 'la llave de Italia' ('the key to Italy') and the central node of communication between the Crown's Iberian and Italian dominions: as the natural harbour of the Duchy of Milan, it also was the main vector of communication with the imperial territories of the Habsburgs and the first link in the Spanish Road to Flanders.[29]

The ambivalent image of the Genoese within the Hispanic Monarchy

The solid foundations of the Spanish-Genoese alliance did not shelter it from criticism, especially concerning the monopolistic position of Genoese bankers in the king's financial affairs, a dominance that did nothing but increase after the acute crisis suffered by the Republic in 1575 and 1576. The civil strife that fractured the ranks of the Genoese nobility coincided with the pressure posed by Castilian cities for the king to break the hold of Genoese *asentistas* over the Crown's finances. Philip II's default in 1575, however, forced members of the old nobility, which were among the most grievously affected by the measure, to accept a settlement. This was later to be endorsed by the publication of the *Leges Novae* in 1576, which were to restore stability to the Republic until the late eighteenth century. The following year, the *Medio General* negotiated by the king and Genoese bankers not only frustrated the aspirations of Castilian *Cortes* to replace Genoese financers with local businessmen, but actually increased the number of Genoese financial companies interested in making their enormous resources available to the Catholic King.[30] The bonds between Republic and Monarchy were stronger than ever, while the Genoese old nobility – the Doria, Spinola, Grimaldi, Pinelli or Lomellino – and the new – the Balbi, Invrea, Giustiniani, Durazzo or Sauli – became an increasingly close-knit elite. Using the records in the Archivo General de Simancas, Carmen Sanz Ayán has estimated that, in the years between 1598 and 1609, Genoese influence in the Spanish imperial system reached its apex, when Ligurian *asentistas* entirely monopolised the Monarchy's money supply, and they shipped to Flanders an eye-watering 38 million ducats, with net profits of nearly 5 million.[31]

The Castilian *Cortes*'s complaints about the role played by the Genoese in the Crown's financial system and about their widespread infiltration of local finances were replicated in harsh terms by the *arbitristas*. Most proposals put forth to alleviate the demographic and productive crisis into which the formerly dynamic cities of interior Castile had plunged blamed foreign, especially Genoese, businessmen, for ruining the kingdom. As late as 1650, in line with arguments presented early in the century by Sancho de Moncada and Francisco Murcia de la Llana, Francisco Martínez de la Mata launched an aggressive diatribe against the Genoese:

> Genoa's feigned trade and friendship was and is a knife that keeps Spain poor and on its knees […] because its profits and growth are based on another's loss; Your Majesty's royal coffers, and those of your vassals, have been prey to their greed, because they have no other God but their interest, and no other Law but their convenience.[32]

The resentment against the Genoese was made worse by the conflict triggered by the seizure of Finale's ships off the Ligurian coast, followed in 1654 by the seizure of the assets of Genoese private citizens in the dominions of the Catholic King in Italy, which caused a deep commotion.[33] In this context, Juan Bautista Cicardo revived Martínez de la Mata's diatribe to accuse the Genoese of pillaging the Monarchy's precious metals and controlling trade with the Indies:

> Time has shown the great harm that the Genoese have caused, not to these kingdoms alone, but also to Naples, Sicily and Milan, as nobody wanting to send goods to the Indies goes there any longer, as they used to, because the Genoese take so many of theirs to Cádiz to dispatch to the Indies that they have drained the outgoing traffic from Spain and from those realms and states.[34]

This negative view was, however, not universal, as illustrated by Francisco de Quevedo's ambivalent attitude. Like most Castilian *arbitristas*, he did not hesitate to call Genoese leeches of Spanish wealth and American treasure. Quevedo criticised the inefficiency of republican governments, which he accused of being under the thumb of a closed oligarchy that put their own interests ahead of those of the collective:

> That freedom reigns! The Genoese said, in a rage. You must be mad, and because you have not been a citizen of the republic you are unaware of its misery and slavery. Reasons of state will not make us agree […] If the senate sits many, everything is chaos; if few, this only breaks the back of unity […] Genoa has so many republics as she has noblemen, and so many miseries as she has plebeians, and all these personal republics meet in a palace to count our money, and when they see it on us, they squeeze it out.[35]

However, Quevedo rightly pointed out that the interests of Genoese private citizens in the Monarchy's markets were like a golden chain that limited their room for manoeuvre, binding them to the interests of the Catholic King. In *Lince de España* or *Zahorí* (1628), he not only praised the services lent by galley entrepreneurs, such as the Doria, and great generals, such as Ambrogio Spinola (fig. 2.2), but acutely noted that:

> Many of the victories that Your Majesty owes that state were the house of Doria's, and his country the freedom; and in these services you owe a very enlightened emulation in Flanders to the house of Spinola. How much Genoa's friendship to Spain means, only the one who pays for it can say […] The gold and silver go to Genoa, this is true; but then they use it to buy bonds, rents, estates, and titles in your kingdoms of Spain, Naples, Milan, and Sicily […] This should remove the fear that the *asientos* will be left untaken, or that contracts will be broken, and encourages us to take what measures we will, as they are chained to loyalty.[36]

This was the same argument used once by Andrea Spinola, one of the main critics of the private transactions that kept the main members of the Genoese elite bound to the Spanish king's wishes, making the Republic dependent on Madrid and preventing the development of an autonomous naval policy: 'It makes the purchase of fiefdoms an easy matter, which our citizens do for the sake of vain appearances, but then licences to sell them are very hard to come by. If you give them a cross, they will give generously, and His Majesty

2.3

Cornelius Bloemaert after Domenico Fiasella, *The Genius of the Republic of Genoa Summoned by Fame*. Frontispiece of Giovan Bernardo Veneroso, *Genio Ligure Risvegliato, Genoua, sotto la direttione di Giovan Domenico Peri*, 1650. Photo: Genoa, Biblioteca Civica Berio. Reproduced with permission.

is happy to give a finger of red cloth for a subject, even if he comes from a free city'.[37]

As suggested by these words, the honours bestowed by the Catholic King upon the most eminent members of the Genoese aristocracy in exchange for financial and naval services opened a rift in the Genoese nobility, breaking its theoretical unity and triggering a deluge of criticism of the dangerous double loyalties that they implied. From the late 1630s, with the key positions in the Republic in the hands of the group which defended limiting ties with Madrid, the animosity against the families that had therefore acted as main links with the Monarchy became especially acute. They were, in addition, accused of a lifestyle that was at odds with the principles of sobriety and frugality that should characterise republican *mediocritas*. The triumphal reception enjoyed by Ambrogio Spinola in August 1629, when he was about to take office as governor in the Duchy of Milan, was one of the latest shows of deference towards this kind of outstanding mediator.[38] The increasing tension put these connectors under growing pressure, as clearly pointed out by the Spanish envoy, Antonio Ronquillo, when he wrote to Madrid in late 1649: 'the aim of this republic is to bring down the houses of the Prince Doria, the Duke of Tursi and the Marquis of Los Balbases, because they cannot suffer them being better than the rest'.[39] Ronquillo denounced the prevailing feeling in the republican government and their attacks on the Dorias and Spinolas who served the king: '[it is said] that their greatness is nothing compared to the Genoese citizens, and they harass them daily, telling them that their greatness is of no value in Genoa, being subject to the same measuring rod as the rest'.[40] For his part, the Republic's diplomatic delegate in Madrid, Stefano de Mari, did not hesitate to criticise the Duke of Tursi and the Marquis of Los Balbases for not having 'other purpose than to base their estimation in the oppression of the Republic and to show in Spain that everything they do is carried by their authority'.[41] It is clear that the social leverage of these figures depended on their ability to play with a fluid identity, to easily straddle the Iberian and Italian dominions of the Crown. The second Marquis of Los Balbases, Filippo Spinola, who in his letters to the Spanish ambassador to The Hague, Antoine Brun, defined himself as a Castilian,[42] suffered all the same the seizure of Genoese assets in his numerous properties in the Kingdom of Naples

in 1654.[43] The structure of his property, spread across Castile, Genoa, Milan, and Naples, illustrated the cosmopolitan outreach of the Genoese families in the service of the Catholic King, the main connectors of a hybrid and transnational cultural model on which elements from all the Crown's dominions converged, and which is most eloquently reflected in Rubens's and Van Dyck's portraits.

The Spanish Monarchy's reaction to Genoese sovereign policies and the limits of international republicanism

The Spanish-Genoese conglomerate that led the Republic to lend its naval and financial services to the Catholic King in exchange for military protection seemed to peak when the troops under the Marquis of Santa Cruz succoured Genoa in 1625. This episode was commemorated, along with other resounding victories, like the surrender of Breda to Ambrogio Spinola also in 1625, in the iconographic programme designed by the Count-Duke of Olivares for the Palace of Buen Retiro in Madrid.[44] However, Pereda's and Velázquez's paintings were carried out ten years after these events, by which time the alliance was under fire. The default of 1627, which had hit Genoese *asentistas* hard, unlike their Portuguese counterparts (who were converts of Jewish stock), reinforced the position of the so-called *repubblichista* party. As rightly pointed out by Claudio

2.4

Luis Góngora Alcasar e Pempicileón, *The Republic of Genoa Crowned on a Chariot*. Frontispiece of *Real grandeza dela serenissima republica de Genova, en Madrid por Ioseph Fernandez de Buendia, 1665 et in Genoua per Gio. Battista Tiboldi, 1669*. Photo: Real Academia de la Historia de Madrid. Reproduced with permission.

Costantini and Carlo Bitossi, the *novatori* argued for Genoa arming itself and reinforcing its administrative and government apparatus, so that it could loosen ties with Madrid and guarantee its neutral position with its own forces.[45] Between the election of Agostino Pallavicini as doge in 1637 and the severe outbreak of plague in 1657, which decimated the families of the elite, the *repubblichisti* came to monopolise the main magistracies in the Republic. In line with Bernardo Veneroso's famous discourse, published in 1650 (fig. 2.3), the plan was to 'awaken the Ligurian genius' and renovate Genoa's glorious past so that the Republic could regain its ancient freedom.[46] While Veneroso was inclined to resuscitate Genoese naval power by keeping close ties with Venice against the Ottoman Empire and encouraging trade in the Levant, other proposals argued for a monopolistic company model similar to that followed by the Dutch Republic, as reflected by an anonymous essay published in the early 1640s:

> who with great profit have traded with their eastern and western Indies and northern companies, which uphold the republic and with this profit have made such a long war against the Spanish ... trade with the Levant will replace that with the Spanish, which will therefore miss the comfort they get from trading with the Genoese.[47]

Giorgio Tosco's recent works have demonstrated that, in the second half of the seventeenth century, boosted by the end of the conflict between Madrid and The Hague, monopolistic commercial companies and the ground-breaking naval technology deployed by the Dutch Republic became a model for Genoa.[48] In any case, the cooperation between friendly republics was nothing but a mirage. Commercial interests overruled any form of solidarity between republics that vied for the same markets. Genoese attempts to wean themselves from Madrid by reactivating the naval sector and encouraging commercial colonialism in the 1640s and 1650s were undermined by the United Provinces, which had made peace with the Catholic Monarch in 1648. This led to a swift expansion of their lucrative markets and to a new role as primary naval suppliers of the Hispanic Monarchy.[49] Also in 1648, the brand new *Compagnia Genovese delle Indie Orientali* saw with dismay that their ships, purchased in the Amsterdam shipyards, were seized in Batavia by the VOC, which was unwilling to surrender an inch of their mercantile monopoly in Asia.

Far from acting as allies, the republics competed ferociously with one another, even fighting over protocol issues of precedence just like monarchic regimes. Genoa's pretension to regal status was rejected not only by the Catholic Monarch and the Pope, but also fell flat in the Dutch Republic, defying expectations. As bitterly pointed out by the Genoese consul in Amsterdam, Stephano d'Andrea, the Dutch did not allow the Ligurian representatives to keep their hats on before the Assembly of the States General.[50] Enrico Zucchi has rightly argued that, throughout the seventeenth century, European republics, as they increasingly struggled to clearly define the *locus* of sovereignty, were forced, in order to survive in a Europe dominated by princes, 'to negotiate a strong identity, and even constitutionally adopt monarchic qualities'.[51] As it had had on Genoa, Bodin's model of full sovereignty had a significant impact on the Dutch Republic after the death of William II of Nassau in 1650. According to Thomas Maissen, the Great Pensionary Johan De Witt and the De La Court brothers, the main ideologues of the first Stadtholderless period, brought about a model of republican absolutism that questioned the supremacy of mixed forms of government and the balance between the dynastic components provided by the House of Orange and the republican-aristocratic models of the regent elite.[52]

The decision to Crown the Virgin Mary as Queen of Genoa in 1637 was presented as an act of affirmation of the Republic's full sovereignty and autonomy.[53] This was put in categorical terms by the Genoese Jesuit Carlo Speroni, writing under the pseudonym Luis de Góngora Alcasar e Pempicileón, in a diatribe entitled *Real grandeza dela serenissima republica de Genova* (fig. 2.4). Before arguing why the Republic deserved a regal title, he wrote that:

> These titles are not attached to the names of King and Kingdom, excluding Republics; owing to their antiquity, freedom, and independence; to the Royal and Imperial Nobility of the blood of their children; to the Kingdoms and Estates that they possess and have possessed; to their illustrious deeds; to the prominence and privileges bestowed by the greatest Monarchs; they deserved the honours enjoyed by other Kings and Kingdoms'.[54]

This memorandum, published in Madrid in 1665, was the culmination of the vain efforts deployed by the Republic to convince the Catholic Monarch to recognise regal rights in the absence of a royal title. During his embassy to Philip IV in 1646, Anton Giulio Brignole Sale, one of the most conspicuous members of the *repubblichisti*, requested for Genoa the same treatment that the king gave some of its citizens: 'Why is it that the royal rights granted to citizens who are no more than private citizens of the Republic, my republic, which possesses kingdoms, cannot be bestowed on the ambassador who represents it?'[55]. The most striking thing about Brignole Sale's arguments is that, in contrast with the concept of liberty advocated by *repubblichisti* such as Andrea Spinola earlier in the century, now the stress was put on the sort of behaviour that characterised authoritarian princes:

> What use is there in consulting ministers and councils? Is not Your Majesty the master of all? Is your authority not absolute? Cannot you do as you will? Is this not to be done, when reason and interest so clearly demand it? It is, also, a prudent thing for princes to, every now and again, do something by themselves, if only to show the will and sovereignty of their power.[56]

Despite Anton Giulio Brignole Sale's regret, by 1646 the Spanish Monarchy was veering towards a model that ruled out all forms of authoritarianism. The failure of Olivares's centralising policies, which had triggered revolts in Catalonia and Portugal, and which soon led to rebellion also in Naples and Sicily, recommended returning to the path of consensus with the regional elites and the urban republics that constituted

2.5

Massimo Stanzione (attributed), *Marianna of Austria embarks at Finale*. Naples, Palazzo Reale di Napoli, Hall of the Ambassadors, c. 1653–1659. Reproduced with the permission from the Italian Ministry of Culture – Palazzo Reale di Napoli.

the monarchy, a policy of exquisite respect for local privileges and rights. In the opinion of the Catholic King, relations with Genoa should not change in any way that questioned the king's role as protector of the liberty of the Republic. In 1649, during the journey to Spain of Philip IV's future wife, Marianna of Austria, the delegates of the Republic expressed their wish to remain covered in her presence, generating a diplomatic fracas. This explains why the queen's entourage embarked in Finale, instead of Genoa, as was the custom (fig. 2.5). The tensions with the Republic made it convenient to reaffirm the sovereignty of the Catholic King over an enclave which, as we have pointed out, was a constant source of tension due to the activity of Finale-based corsairs and issues with the salt supply. This was a highly symbolic act, and was, not by accident, chosen to decorate the ambassadors' hall in the royal palace in Naples.[57]

The Habsburgs and the defence of the Republic's freedom. French military expansionism as an obstacle for the return to the Spanish–Genoese alliance

The catastrophic effects of the plague of 1657 and the failure of the sovereign policies launched by the *repubblichisti* facilitated the normalisation of Spanish-Genoese relations. Meanwhile, Louis XIV's wish to project France's full autonomy vis-à-vis the mercantile republics crystallised in aggressive policies that culminated in 1672 with the invasion of the United Provinces. This attitude was diametrically opposed to the Hispanic Monarchy's, which saw the sovereign models advanced by France in these republics with suspicion, and which still depended on their naval and financial services.

By then, despite the marked improvement of diplomatic relations with the Hispanic Monarchy and the presence in Madrid of eminent mediators, such as the third Marquis of Los Balbases, Paolo Spinola Doria, and Domenico Grillo, who was responsible for Genoa's embassy when there was no official delegate, the Republic never managed to fully restore the breadth and scope of its former networks. The recurrent seizure of Genoese assets in the Crown's Italian dominions, for instance in the Duchy of Milan in 1685, explains the gradual withdrawal of Genoese capital from the territories under the Catholic King and its flight to more lucrative markets.[58] This situation was especially acute in Castile, where, as shown by Carmen Sanz, the formerly ubiquitous Genoese financial *asentistas* became a rarity from 1680 onwards, being involved in less than 10% of the silver loans negotiated by the Crown.[59]

The Peace of Nijmegen (1678) did not bring French expansionist policies, or France's wishes to consolidate its Mediterranean position, to an end. The Habsburgs had tried to present themselves as the defenders of the freedom of

imperial free cities, like Strasburg, which was annexed by France in 1681, as well as the main guarantors of the autonomy of republican systems. However, their ability to respond to France was limited without the English-Dutch naval support, which would remain unavailable until the Glorious Revolution of 1688 made the Stadtholder William III of Orange king of England. The dramatic events in Genoa between 1678 and 1685 illustrate this situation most eloquently. As pointed out by Carlo Bitossi, the French bombardment of San Remo and Sampierdarena in 1678 made the Republic fear an invasion from the French and the Duke of Savoy.[60] In reality, the bombardment was only the preamble of a diplomatic and military offensive aimed to sever the remaining ties between the Republic and Madrid. Pidou de Saint Olon's embassy to Genoa in 1682, which broke the former Spanish diplomatic monopoly, triggered numerous complaints, owing to the imperative nature of his demands, which were a direct attack upon the freedom of the Republic.[61] The Venetian ambassador in Paris, Sebastiano Foscarini, expressed this most eloquently in his report to the senate, when his time in office was drawing to an end in 1683:

> The French want to reduce the Genoese to a position of precarious freedom, if not of declared servitude [...] The pretensions aroused by the Darsena, the differences in salutations, the requests for warehouses for salts in Savona, the virtual command to disarm the galleys, were all traps set up to disturb and dismantle the protection of the Spaniards, which was as profitable to them as it was to the Genoese, and to take over the predominance of the Genoese.[62]

The rejection of these draconian demands was the pretext the French needed to shell the city.[63] On 16 May 1684, an imposing French fleet under Admiral Duquesne and the Marquis of Seignelay deployed off Genoa. According to a detailed English report, the fleet included '20 Galleys, 10 Galliots, carrying each 2 Mortar-pieces for Bombes, 14 Men of War, 6 Fly-Boats, 18 Tartanes, 20 Chaloups, and 40 great Fisher-boats'.[64] After a futile attempt at negotiation, the fleet brought the city to its knees in ten days of intense shelling, in which 13,000 rounds were shot (fig. 2.6). Only the strong military reinforcements sent by the Count of Melgar from Milan and the local militia could frustrate several French attempts to land foot soldiers and keep public order.[65]

The Hispanic Monarchy's traditional role as protector of the freedom of the Republic was, in the event, only a mirage. The fall of Luxemburg into French hands and the Dutch Republic's unwillingness to get involved in the new conflict forced Charles II to sign a truce in Ratisbon in 1684. Louis XIV did not accept including Genoa in the truce's guarantees, pushing the Republic to sign a separate bilateral agreement with France in February 1685, in which Genoa not only accepted all the French demands but agreed to send the doge and a delegation of four senators to prostrate themselves before Louis XIV. This ceremony, held on 15 May 1685 in the Hall of Mirrors, Versailles, was duly reproduced in paintings and commemorative medals in honour of the *Le Roi Soleil*, expressions of his policy to publicly suppress the freedom of urban republics (fig. 14.1). Two years earlier, France had also bombarded Algiers, and would carry on doing so to the main cities of a monarchy of urban republic such as the Spanish. The French shelled Brussels in 1695 and Barcelona in 1697, the same year in which they sacked Cartagena de Indias. The War of the Spanish Succession followed the death of Charles II in 1700; the dynastic clash between Habsburgs and Bourbons was a struggle between two antagonistic models of sovereignty. In this conflict, Genoa remained neutral, although the main aristocratic families sided with the new Bourbon dynasty, which was regarded as more capable of avoiding the disintegration of the Spanish imperial structure within which they enjoyed lucrative rents and demesnes, and of which they had been one of the most important pieces.[66]

2.6
Simon Fokke, *Bombing of Genoa*.
Amsterdam, Rijksmuseum, 1684.
Reproduced with permission.

---

* This work was undertaken within the framework of project ATLANREX "Una monarquía policéntrica de repúblicas urbanas ante la rivalidad europea en el Atlántico ibérico (1640–1713)" (PID2022-14501NB-I00), funded by MCIN/AEI/10.13039/501100011033 and FSE+, and Fulbright Scholarship Program for researchers and university lecturers Ministerio de Universidades de España (PRX21/00263), which took place at the History Department, University of Pennsylvania in 2022.

1 Pocock, *The Machiavellian Moment*.
2 Haistma-Muiler, *The Myth of Venice*.
3 'Abbiamo in Italia due republiche floridissime, Venetia e Genova. Di queste senza dubbio, che Venetia avanza di gran lunga Genova, e di Stato e di grandezza, e, se ne cercaremo la ragione, trovaremo ciò essere avvenuto perché Venetiani, attendendo alla mercatantia reale, si sono arricchiti mediocremente in particolare, ma infinitamente in commune; all'incontro i Genovesi, impiegandosi affatto in cambii, hanno arricchito immoderatamente le facoltà particolari, ma impoverito estremamente l'entrate publiche'. Botero, *Della Ragione di Stato*, p. 28. Botero seems to adopt the Machiavellian vision that compared the efficient management and governance of the Banco di San Giorgio and political disorder in the republican government: 'E s'egli avvenisse, che col tempo in ogni modo avverrà, che S. Giorgio tutta quella città occupasse, sarebbe quella una Repubblica più che la Vineziana memorabile' ('Should it happen, and it will happen in due course, that S. Giorgio takes over the whole city, this will be a true Republic, and not the memorable Venice'). Machiavelli, *Istorie fiorentine*, VIII, p. 28. This was a contrast between 'eccellenza finanziaria e mediocrità politica' ('financial excellence and political mediocrity') which, as rightly argued by Carlo Bitossi, glossed over the fact that the Banco

di San Giorgio was managed by the same group that led the Republic, Bitossi, 'Il governo della Repubblica', p. 92.

4 'Andar ad abitar almeno un par d'anni a Venezia per imparar a governar bene la nostra Repubblica da quella de' Venetiani'. Foglietta, *Il barro*, p. 360.

5 Maréchaux, 'Cultiver l'alternative', p. 660.

6 About anti-Spanishness as a basic feature of Italian national identity particularly in Genoa, see Bitossi, 'Lo strano caso del antispagnolismo'.

7 About the marked opposition between republics and monarchies see Van Gelderen and Skinner, eds, *Republicanism*.

8 Herrero Sánchez, *Repúblicas y republicanismo*.

9 See Cardim and others, *Polycentric Monarchies*; Herrero Sánchez, 'Urban republicanism' and Díaz Ceballos, *Poder compartido*.

10 For an overview considering the classic works by Ramón Carande, Enrique Otte, Felipe Ruiz Martín, Giovanni Muto and Enrica Neri, see Canosa, *Banchieri genovesi*. The study of the quasi-monopolistic role played by the Genoese in imperial finances and of the scope and impact of the successive defaults remains a fruitful field of study, as shown by the recent works by Sanz, *Los banqueros y la crisis*, and the gripping debate about the relationship between debt, taxes, and financial crisis, between Drelichman and Both and Álvarez Nogal and Chamley in *The Economic History Review*.

11 The special issue that I edited for the journal *Hispania* in 2005 focused for the first time on outlining the diachronic evolution of the Spanish-Genoese relationship in the sixteenth and seventeenth centuries (works by Pacini, Kirk and Herrero), without neglecting the important role played by the Genoese as bankers and administrators of the royal finances (works by Álvarez Nogal and Sanz). Similarly, the introduction underlined the need to present overviews capable of linking the numerous partial studies about the Genoese presence in certain cities, and to study the galley *asientos* more in depth. A few years later, in the company of Bitossi, Ben Yessef and Puncuh, we edited two large volumes in which the main specialists on the matter were offered the opportunity to debate and thus open new avenues of analysis. See Herrero and others, eds, *Génova y la Monarquía Hispánica*. Not coincidentally, recent years have witnessed a deluge of doctoral theses about Spanish-Genoese relations, such as Yasmina Ben Yessef's, Alejandro García Montón's, Rafael Girón's and Benoît Maréchaux's, to name but some of the most outstanding among them.

12 In 1655, while tensions with the Crown were running high owing to the issue of Finale, Giambattista Raggio published an essay entitled *Varie considerazioni per le prattiche, che s'hanno con Spagna, e per la miglior direttione delle cose publiche*, whose forty-second point openly accused the

Spaniards of having dirty blood: 'I spagnuoli sono un composto del sangue de' mori, cioè di Maomethe, e di Moisè, gente vile, et abierta' ('The Spaniards' blood is a mixture of Moors, that is of Muhammad and Moses, open, vile people'). Taken from Bitossi, 'Un oligarca antispagnolo del Seicento', p. 290.

13 For the constitutional reform launched in 1528, aimed at ending the factional strife that had facilitated foreign interference in the internal business of the Republic, and its relationship with the agreement between Andrea Doria and Charles V, see the essential Pacini, *I presupposti politici del 'secolo dei Genovesi'*. A more recent study in Salonia, *Genoa's Freedom*.

14 For Castile, see for instance the recent work by Girón Pascual, *Comercio y poder*; for Italy see Muto, 'La presenza dei Genovesi'; for the Low Countries see Beck 'Éléments sociaux et économiques'.

15 Herrero Sánchez, 'Génova y el sistema imperial hispánico', pp. 536–37.

16 For a historiographically balanced study of this issue, with emphasis on the Genoese consulate in Messina see Calabrese, *Figli della città*. For Naples, see Brancaccio, 'Nazione genovese'.

17 In this study, Grendi argued that Genoese families must be seen as 'le vere protagoniste della storia genovese, una storia più privatistica che statuale' ('the true protagonists of Genoese history, a history that is more private than institutional') and pushed for case studies capable of merging the reconstruction of their way of life, habits, social practices, personal relations, and ties of friendship and cooperation with other Genoese families and the territories in which they operated, Grendi, *I Balbi*, p. IX.

18 Sanz, *Un banquero en el Siglo de Oro*.

19 Herrero Sánchez, 'La red genovesa Spínola'; Herrero Sánchez and Álvarez-Ossorio, 'La aristocracia genovesa'; Álvarez-Ossorio, '¿El final de la Sicilia española?'.

20 Ben Yessef, *Los Serra entre la República de Génova y la Monarquía Hispánica*.

21 García Montón, 'Trayectorias individuales durante la quiebra del sistema hispano-genovés'.

22 Kirk, *Genoa and the Sea*; Lo Basso, *Uomini di remo*.

23 Maréchaux, 'Los asentistas de galeras genoveses'; Maréchaux, 'Business organisation in the Mediterranean'. His doctoral dissertation, carried out under the supervision of Carlos Álvarez-Nogal, Universidad Carlos III, and subsequent research will form the basis of a monograph to be published by Routledge under the title Maréchaux, *Genoese Galley*.

24 García Montón, *Genoese Entrepreneurship and the Asiento*. Luca Lo Basso has emphasised the globalisation of Genoese transactions in the second half of the seventeenth century, by linking the renovation of naval production, their leading role in Atlantic trade, under the

umbrella of the *asiento*, and the penetration into the Ottoman Levant following the Dutch withdrawal. Lo Basso, 'De Curaçao a Esmirna'.

25 For the consolidated position and dynamism of Genoese merchant communities in the Iberian Atlantic space during the eighteenth century, see Brilli, *Genoese Trade and Migration*.

26 Yasmina Ben Yessef has analysed the role played by the Serras in the control of the office of the *Correo Mayor* of Milan, Ben Yessef, 'Entre el servicio a la Corona'.

27 Carpentier and Priotti, 'La forge instable d'une domination'. Rafael Vargas Hidalgo has published the full correspondence between Gian Andrea Doria and Philip II in *Guerra y diplomacia en el Mediterráneo*.

28 Petitjean, 'Gênes et le bon gouvernement de l'information' and Petitjean, *L'intelligence des choses*.

29 See the essential Pacini, '*Desde Rosas a Gaeta*', p. 75 and Pacini, 'Poiché gli stati non sono portatili'.

30 About the 1575 default and the *Medio General* of 1577 see, from different perspectives, Drelichman and Voth, *Lending to the Borrower from Hell* and Álvarez-Nogal and Chamley, 'Debt Policy under Constraints'.

31 Sanz, 'La triple red diplomática', p. 34.

32 'El comercio y amistad fingida de Génova ha sido y es el cuchillo de España y la tiene pobre y desacreditada. […] porque funda sus medras, creces y aumentos en el daño ajeno; y ha sido y es la Real Hacienda de Vuestra Majestad y la de los vasallos despojo y presa de su codicia; porque no tienen otro Dios que su interés, ni otra ley que su conveniencia'. Martínez de la Mata, *Memoriales y Discursos*, pp. 267–68.

33 Herrero Sánchez, 'La quiebra del sistema hispano-genovés', pp. 139–43.

34 'El tiempo ha mostrado el gran daño que los genoveses han causado no tan solamente a estos reinos sino también al de Nápoles, Sicilia y estado de Milán que no negocian ni nadie va a dichos reinos a comprar como lo solían hacer los que tratan de embarcar mercaderías para las Indias porque los genoveses llevan tanta abundancia de las suyas a Cádiz y las embarcan para dichas Indias que han quitado tráfico y salida de las de España y dichos reinos y estados'. ASG, Lettere dei Ministri di Spagna, leg. 2450, Memorandum by Juan Bautista Cicardo, 1656.

35 '¡Qué la libertad reina! dijo dado a los diablos el genovés. Tú debes de estar loco y como no has sido repúblico, no sabes sus miserias y esclavitudes. No bastará toda la razón de Estado a concertarnos […] Si el senado repúblico se compone de muchos, es confusión; si de pocos, no sirve sino de corromper la firmeza y excelencias de la unidad […] Génova tiene tantas repúblicas como nobles y tantos miserables esclavos como plebeyos y todas estas repúblicas personales se juntan en un palacio

a sólo contar nuestro caudal y, en viéndonos abultados de caudal, nos exprimen para sí'. Quevedo, *La hora de todos*, cap. XL. The Spanish ambassador in Genoa, Antonio Ronquillo, used a similar argument when, in 1648, he sent a memorandum to Madrid accusing the republican government of aloofness and vanity, concluding: 'De donde nace que juzgan por la mayor grandeza ser ciudadanos de Génova y no se avergüenzan de decir delirios, antes aplaudiendo una proposición que Rafael Torre hizo en un memorial para pedir la Sala Regia de que era más debida a la embajada de la república que a la de ningún rey porque los embajadores de los reyes son vasallos de quien los envía y los de la república parte del mismo príncipe'. ('This means that they think that being born in Genoa confers the highest greatness, and applaud the memorandum in which Rafael Torre asked for the Sala Regia, as becoming more the embassy of the Republic than any king, because the ambassadors of kings are also their vassals, and those of the Republic part of the prince himself'). AGS, Estado, leg. 3604, Letter from Ronquillo to the King, Genoa, 13–12–1648.

36 'Grande parte de las victorias que os dieron aquellos estados debe Vuestra Majestad a la casa de Doria y su patria la libertad; y en estos servicios debéis emulación muy esclarecida en Flandes a la casa de Espínola. Cuánto importa la amistad de Génova a España, nadie lo dice mejor que lo que le cuesta [...] El oro y la plata llevan a Génova, es verdad; mas de allí lo pasan a emplear en posesiones, juros, rentas, y estados, y títulos en vuestros reinos de España, Nápoles, Milán y Sicilia [...] Esto quita el miedo de temer no se retiren los asientos, o nos levanten el contrato, y da ánimo para disponer lo que convenga con satisfacción de obediencia encarcelada'. Quevedo, *Lince de Italia u Zahorí español*, p. 101. For Francisco Quevedo's views on Italy, see Ceribelli's doctoral dissertation, 'La literatura italiana en la obra de Quevedo'.

37 'Dà facilità grande alle compre de' feudi, che fanno i nostri cittadini invaniti d'apparenze e de' titoli; ma fatte che sono, è difficilissima cosa ottener licenza di venderli. Li abiti o siano croci si danno a furia, parendo a Sua Maestà gran guadagno per un dito di pagno rosso acquistare un suddito anche siamo in una citta libera'. BNM, ms 995, Andrea Spínola, *Osservationi intorno al governo di Genova*, p. 216. See Carlo Bitossi's compilation of Andrea Spinola's writings in Spinola, *Scritti scelti*.

38 See Luca Lo Basso's recent article, which focuses on the final years of the first Marquis of Los Balbases, an eloquent testimony of the growing Spanish-Genoese estrangement following the issue of Montferrat and the Crown's relations with the dukes of Mantua and Savoy, Lo Basso, 'To Lose One's Honour'.

39 'el fin de esta república es bajar estas tres casas del Príncipe Doria, Duque de Tursi y marqués de los Balbases no pudiendo sufrir su grandeza ni que haya desigualdad de ellas a las demás'. AGS, Estado, leg. 3604, Letters from Ronquillo to the King, Genoa, 12–12–1649.

40 'son menos por grandes que por ciudadanos genoveses y ha muchos días que procuran mortificarlos y que se entienda que el grado de grandeza no les hace valer nada en Génova y que han de pasar por la medida de los demás ciudadanos'. AGS, Estado, leg. 3604, Letters from Ronquillo to the King, Genoa, 13–12–1649.

41 'altro fine che di fondare la loro estimatione nell'opressione della Repubblica e di ostentar in Spagna che quanto si opera tutto è portato dalla loro autorità'. Stefano de Mari's report to the Genoese embassy in Spain, 29–2–1652 (ASG, Istruzioni ai ministri, 6/2713, n. 82) taken from Ciasca, ed., *Istruzioni e relazioni*, III, p. 275. The Genoese delegate in Milan was of a very different opinion, decrying the negative effect that the excesses against these families in Genoa was having on Genoese interests in the Duchy. ASG, AS, Lettere dei ministri a Milano, leg. 2302, Letter my Minister Spinola about 'le innovationi seguite con le case delli Signor Marchese Spinola e duca Doria', Milan, 25–12–1652.

42 Filippo Spinola's (who was to become the right-hand-man of Philip IV's *valido*, Don Luis de Haro) opinion about negotiations between the Dutch Republic and England, in a letter written from his country retreat in Rossano, near Tortona, was that: 'Así yo juzgo que se acomodarán porque tenemos un refrán en Castilla que dice: donde uno no quiere dos no barajan.' ['they will reach an agreement, because, as the saying we have in Castile, has it: two don't fight if one of them doesn't want to'. AGS, Estado, Embajada de España en La Haya, leg. 8710, Letter from the 2nd Marquis des Balbases to Antoine Brun, Rossano, 28–7–1652.

43 The Viceroy of Naples, Count of Castrillo, wrote a concerned letter to his colleague in the Council of State: 'La novedad de haberse secuestrado por vía de represalias todos los bienes de genoveses en este Reino en virtud de una orden que para ello he tenido de Su Majestad originada de las molestias que genoveses hacen en el Final impidiendo aquellos vasallos el comercio [...] dígame Vuestra Excelencia si también ha sido comprendido en esta orden pues ya se ve que como tan verdadero servidor de Vuestra Excelencia no pudiera yo dejar de sentirlo'. ('The news of the seizure, in retaliation, of Genoese assets in this Kingdom following a Royal Order, because of the trouble that the Genoese are stirring in the Final, and impeding their trade [...] let me know if this also applies to you, because as a true servant of

Your Excellency I would be willing to forfeit said order'). ASN, Segreteria dei Viceré, Scritture diverse, leg. 181, Letter by Count of Castrillo to the Marquis of Los Balbases about the seizure of Genoese assets, Naples, 5–5–1654.

44 Brown and Elliott, *A Palace for a King*.

45 Costantini, 'Política e storiografia'; Bitossi, *Il governo dei magnifici*; Bitossi, 'Navi e política nella Genova del Seicento', which presents an excellent overview of the *novatori* and their proposals, some of which came to fruition, such as the construction of a new wall, an aqueduct and a pier.

46 Veneroso, *Il Genio ligure risvegliato*. As pointed out two years earlier by Ronquillo, this aspiration clashed with the Spanish interests of the Genoese elite: 'El dictamen general es conservar la neutralidad e imaginar esta república tan poderosa como la de Venecia para mantenerla y son pocos los que se libran de esta aprensión, pero en inclinarse a Francia son los menos y los de menos caudal y obligación y los más y de porte siguen la inclinación a la corona de España o por su afecto o por sus intereses'. ('The general idea is to think and imagine a republic as powerful as Venice, so they can keep themselves, and few escape this notion, but fewer, and only the poorest, lean towards France, while the great still look to Spain, following their inclination or their interest'). AGS, Estado, leg. 3603, Letter from Antonio Ronquillo, Genoa, 28–4–1648.

47 'Che con gran loro profitto hanno eretto le negoziazioni e compagnie dell'Indie Orientali e Occidentali e del Settentrione che sono quelle che mantengono la loro Repubblica e la somministrano le spese eccesive che hanno fatto e fanno in una guerra tanto lunga contro gli spagnoli... nei traffici di Levante tralasceranno quelli di Spagna e per conseguenza verrano gli spagnoli a mancar di quelle comodità che cavano dal danaro de Genovesi'. ASCG, MBS, ms 105–B-7 BS, fols. 327–344.

48 Tosco, 'Importing the Netherlands'. For the mutual influences of these republics see Haitsma Mulier, 'Genova e l'Olanda'.

49 Herrero Sánchez, 'Republican Monarchies, Patrimonial Republics'.

50 'E solamente nel honorifico le permettono il coprirsi avanti i tribunali degli borgomastri e degli schiavini pero non nell'Aya avanti l'Asamblea de Gli Stati Generali che viene ad esser l'estesso che costi avanti il Senato Serenisimo' ('They only allow them to cover before the Burgomaster and his aldermen but not the Assembly of the States General, which is the equivalent to the Most Serene Senate'). ASG, AS, 2657, Lettere consoli Olanda, Amsterdam, 12–2–1671. Herrero Sánchez, 'La quiebra del sistema imperial hispano-genovés', pp. 137–39.

51 Zucchi, 'Republics in Comparison', p. 369.

52 Maissen, 'Liberty and Liberties in Europe'. In this regard, Enrico Zucchi reproduces Galeazzo Gualdo Priorato's criticism of the rights and privileges accrued by the prince of Orange, which made him just like a king, and of the fact that in Genoa the authority of the Republic fell to aristocratic families dependent on the Catholic Monarch. For these reasons, in his view, these two republics did not compare well to Venice, Zucchi, 'Republics in Comparison', pp. 370–72.

53 Julia Zunckel has indicated that this ceremony had no precedent among the states that had chosen the Virgin Mary as protector: 'La repubblica di Genova non si limitava ad attribuire a lei lo status di protettrice, ma l'incoronazione genovese fu il primo caso d'investitura di regalità terrene alla Regina del Cielo, al quale seguì una vera marea d'intitolazioni analoghe da parti di quasi tutti i potentati cattolici' ('The Republic of Genoa did not limit itself to appointing the Virgin as its protector; the coronation was the first time the Virgin Mary was given an earthly royal title; this was followed by a tide of similar titles by almost every other Catholic ruler'). Zunckel, 'Tra Bodin e la Madona', pp. 179–80.

54 'No están vinculados los honores regios de tal suerte al nombre de Rey y Reino que excluyan las Repúblicas, que por su antigüedad, libertad y independencia, por la Nobleza Real y Imperial de la sangre de sus hijos, por los Reinos y Estados que poseen y han poseído, por las hazañas ilustres, por las preeminencias y privilegios de los mayores Monarcas, merecieron gozar los honores concedido a otros Reyes y Reinos'. Góngora Alcasar, *Real Grandeza*, p. 2.

55 '¿Por qué las honras reales que han podido alcanzar ciudadanos que no eran más que caballeros particulares de mi república, mi república, que posee reinos, no podrá alcanzarlos de Vuestra Majestad en su embajador que la representa?'. ASG, AS, Leg. 2447, Memorandum by Anton Brignole Sale to Philip IV, Madrid, 8–4–1646.

56 '¿Qué menester son aquí más consultas de ministros, ni de Consejos? ¿No es Vuestra Majestad soberano señor de todo? ¿No tiene absolutísima autoridad? ¿No puede hacer lo que quiere de por sí solo? ¿No lo debe hacer cuando es tan clara la razón y las conveniencias? Por lo demás es grandísima fineza de la real prudencia que el príncipe de cuando en cuando haga resoluciones totalmente de por sí solo para mostrar y ejercitar enteramente el brío de su voluntad y la soberanía de su poder'. ASG 2003, AS, leg. 2447, Memorandum by Anton Brignole Sale to Philip IV, Madrid, 8–4–1646.

57 Carrió-Invernizzi, 'Génova y España en la pintura', pp. 763–66. For Ambassador Ronquillo's failed attempt to have the queen travel through Genoa see his report in BNM, ms 2380, Letter from Antonio Ronquillo y Briceño on the reception of the Queen in Genoa, Genoa, 23–7–1649.

58 As bitterly pointed out by Juan Carlos de Bazán in a report issued in 1693, when he left his post as ambassador in Genoa, 'que habiéndose comenzado a practicar los medios de la represalia en diferentes tiempos y ocasiones contra los pactos expresos de sus contratos, comenzaron algunos a vender sus montes y otros a hacer sus nuevos empleos en Francia, Polonia, Venecia y Roma y ahora últimamente en el Imperio' ('reprisals being practised in various places and the breach of contracts brought some to sell their loans and others to seek lending in France, Poland, Venice, and Rome, and lately also in the Empire'). AGS, Estado, leg. 3636, Don Juan Carlo Bazán's account of his time in Genoa between 20–2–1684 and 1–7–1693.

59 Sanz, *Los banqueros de Carlos II*, p. 296.

60 Bitossi, 'La circulación de la información'. AGS, Estado, leg. 3616, Letter by Manuel Coloma on the French bombardment of San Remo, Genoa, 3–9–1678.

61 AMAER, Gênes, Fonds Divers, 20MD/24, 1682–1684, Mémoire adressé au roi par M. de Saint Olon sur son ambassade à Gênes de 1682 à 1684.

62 'Inviluppar vorrebbe la Francia nelle soggezioni d'una precaria libertà, se non ne' titoli di una servitù dichiarata, li genovesi […] Le pretese suscitate della Darsena, le differenze per saluti, le richieste dei magazzini per Sali in Savona, il virtuale comando del disarmo dell'accresciute galee, furono insidie tese per disturbare e rompere la tutela de' spagnuoli tanto a loro proficua, quanto a' genovesi salutare, e subentrar nel predominio'. Firpo, ed., *Relazioni di ambasciatori veneti*, VII, pp. 349–437.

63 As noted by Vitale, in 1681, the Genoese ambassador in Madrid, Gian Andrea Spinola, had arranged for a Spanish squadron to remain in the Tyrrhenian Sea in 1683. However, the French demand to keep the Duke of Tursi's galleys in the Genoese harbour forced the Spanish to withdraw, creating the conditions for the bombardment in 1684. Vitale, *La diplomazia Genovese*, pp. 316–19. See also Bitossi, '"Il piccolo sempre succombe al grande"'.

64 *A true relation of the actions of the French fleet before Genova*, p. 1.

65 Another of the memoranda that circulated about these events, which sent shocked ripples across the whole continent, emphasised the efficiency of Milanese and Neapolitan contingents: 'et l'on donna la main aux secours que les ministres d'Espagne offrirent et présentèrent avec toute sorte de générosité pratiqué en particulier par Monsieur le comte de Melgar Gouverneur de Milan avec la dernière finesse et manière obligeante ayant été fait par Don Jean Charles Bazan, envoyé de SM Catholique, le quel dans cette occasion il s'est fait connaître un ministre aussi attentif que plein d'affection' ('and we were helped by the generous assistance lent by Spanish ministers, especially Melgar, governor of Milan, and the obliging manners of Don Juan Carlos de Bazán, ambassador of His Catholic Majesty, who in this occasion behaved with great affection to us'). KC, ms Codex 955, Lettre de rèsponçe sur les hostilitéz que les François ont fait contre Gennes, Genoa 1684, p. 5v. See also the doge's letter to the Madrid government expressing his gratitude for 'los socorros que se han servido mandar y ponderando la puntualidad y fineza con que los ministros de Italia han obrado en esta ocasión' ('the succour that you sent, and the finesse and punctuality with which your Italian ministers have acted'). AGS, Estado, leg. 3620, Letter from the doge, Genoa, 7–7–1684.

66 Asseretto, 'La guerra di Successione spagnola'.

3

Matthias Schnettger

'CAMERA ET CIVITAS NOSTRA IMPERIALIS'

The Republic of Genoa in the Imperial Perspective

Research on the foreign relations of the Republic of Genoa in the early modern period has often focused on the relationship of the *Superba* with the Spanish Crown, and to a lesser extent with France.[1] But the Republic was also almost continually represented diplomatically at the Viennese or Prague court of the Austrian Habsburgs – long before Austria attained a position of supremacy on the Italian peninsula in the eighteenth century.[2] In the sixteenth and seventeenth centuries, the necessity of having a representative at the Imperial court was rather due to the fact that the Holy Roman Empire of the German Nation and its Emperor still held numerous feudal territories and legal titles in the so-called Imperial Italy (*Reichsitalien*), reminiscences of the medieval *Regnum Italiae*.[3] The Republic of Genoa and the Genoese nobility were in possession of several Imperial fiefs whose affairs had to be negotiated again and again at the Imperial court.[4] But the Imperial claims to supremacy also extended to the *Superba* herself, and posed a latent threat to the freedom of the Republic, which was so central to the Genoese self-image.[5] Against this background, the article outlines the relationship of the Republic of Genoa to the Holy Roman Empire and especially to the Emperor in the sixteenth and early seventeenth centuries, with an emphasis on the Imperial perspective on the Republic. The first section deals with Genoa's relationship with the Emperor and the Empire in the early sixteenth century. Special attention will be paid to the Imperial privileges and infeudations in favour of the 'Imperial City' of Genoa, which formed the legal basis for the relationship of the Republic to the Emperor and the Empire. Though the two sides interpreted their legal relationship very differently, they generally ignored this discrepancy in a dissimulating manner. The following sections are devoted to two specific moments in the history of Imperial-Genoese relations in order to show, by way of example, how the differing views of Genoa's legal status vis-à-vis the Emperor and

the Empire had a decisive influence on their diplomatic relations. What could happen when dissent over the legal status of Genoa escalated into open conflict will be illustrated in the second section. The dispute over the Margraviate of Finale (1558–1564) offers a most illustrative example for the potential of conflict caused by the Imperial claims on jurisdiction, which not only affected the disputed *Marchesato*, but Genoa herself. It took considerable effort to calm the conflict once it had escalated. Finally, the former state of affairs was restored, which allowed both sides to cultivate their own ideas about the Genoese-Imperial relationship. The third section turns to the 1630s, when the Genoese aspirations to obtain full sovereignty or respectively equality with the European monarchies for their Republic led to a substantial change in the Imperial-Genoese relations. For it was no longer possible for a royal Republic to slip into the guise of an Imperial City, even if only in certain contexts. At the Imperial court, the Genoese striving for sovereignty and the resulting damage to the Imperial claims of supremacy over the Republic were taken very seriously. Indeed, thanks to the difficult situation of the House of Austria in the final phase of the Thirty Years' War the Genoese *Signoria* managed to obtain some concessions from Emperor Ferdinand III, which considerably weakened the Imperial legal position. This didn't mean, however, that the Imperial claims had been given up definitively. Rather, they were maintained until the end of the eighteenth century.

3.1

Tiziano Vecellio, *Emperor Charles V at Mühlberg*. Madrid, Museo Nacional del Prado, 1548.
Oil on canvas, 335 × 283 cm, n. P000410.
Photo: © Photographic Archive Museo Nacional del Prado. Reproduced with permission.

The Republic of Genoa and the Holy Roman Empire in the early sixteenth century

While in the late Middle Ages the relations between Genoa and the Holy Roman Empire had loosened notably,[6] a certain rapprochement took place during the reigns of Maximilian I (1493–1519) and especially of Charles V (1519–1556; fig. 3.1). When Maximilian visited Genoa in 1496, he granted a diploma in favour of the Republic, which confirmed every privilege Genoa had ever received from the hands of a Holy Roman Emperor.[7] With a second diploma, issued in 1513, Maximilian confirmed the pretended Genoese monopoly on the salt trade in the Ligurian Sea.[8] However, for the present these Imperial-Genoese rapprochements were merely interludes; in general the French influence continued to prevail until the 1520s. Only in 1528, when Andrea Doria (fig. 3.2) switched from Francis I of France to Emperor Charles V, did the relations between the Republic and the Holy Roman Empire change fundamentally. Charles V, who combined the eminent dignity of the Holy Roman Emperor with the enormous means of the Spanish Empire, became the protector of Genoa. With his reign, the long-lasting affiliation of the Republic to the Spanish Empire began.[9] Also the relationship of Genoa with the Holy Roman Empire was consolidated notably. Charles V confirmed the Genoese privileges and possessions in Liguria even more generously than had Maximilian I with three diplomas of 1529 and 1536.[10] Each single diploma reflected the result of intense diplomatic negotiations, but Charles's concessions took the form of an Imperial grace towards the 'Camera et civitas nostra imperialis' – the Imperial chamber and city – of Genoa.

Indeed, Genoa was usually addressed as 'Civitas imperialis' in every Imperial diploma or letter of this period, which clearly stated an overlordship of the Emperor and the Empire. As a matter of fact, in the hierarchy of the Holy Roman Empire there was no other position for a free Republic than that of an Imperial City. Hence, in the Imperial perspective, the liberty of Genoa was the same liberty that the German Imperial Cities like Cologne, Frankfurt or Augsburg possessed: an extensive autonomy that included the privilege to regulate their own affairs both internally and externally independently, but all under the Emperor's supremacy. According to this view, Genoa not only owed the Emperor respect and obedience, but was also subject to his jurisdiction.[11]

The Genoese understanding was completely different: their liberty had never been conferred on the Republic by any temporal authority but was innate to Genoa. Thus, the Imperial privileges did not create the Genoese liberty, but merely confirmed it. As the highest secular ruler of Christendom, the Emperor deserved respect; but he was not recognised as Genoa's overlord.[12]

Both sides were aware of this divergence. Since neither the Emperor and the Empire nor the Republic of Genoa were in a position to assert their view of the mutual legal relationship, both sides tended to dissimulate.[13] They overlooked the view of the other side as if their own position was undisputed. However, in certain situations the Republic was forced to accept the position of an Imperial City or to slip into the role of an Imperial City if it aspired to certain Imperial privileges or graces.

The three diplomas of Charles V and the one of Maximilian I that confirmed the Genoese monopoly of the salt trade formed in a certain manner the legal basis of the relationship between Genoa and the Holy Roman Empire even in the period when, following the abdication of Charles V in 1556, the personal union of the Holy Roman Emperorship and the Spanish crown was dissolved. These four privileges were so important to the Genoese government that it asked each new Emperor for their confirmation and usually received it.[14]

In addition to these privileges, the Republic also received investments in the Imperial fiefdoms that Genoa acquired over time.[15] Thus, from an Imperial point of view, the Republic of Genoa was in a double legal relationship with the Emperor and the Empire: Genoa herself was an Imperial City, and for her above-mentioned Imperial fiefdoms she was an Imperial vassal.[16]

A question of jurisdiction: The conflict over Finale (1558–1564)

The conflict over the Margraviate of Finale turned out to be most illuminating for the dissent over the status of the Republic within or vis-à-vis the Empire.[17] Since the Middle Ages, Finale had been one of the Republic of Genoa's expansion targets. The Margraves of the House of Del Carretto sought to secure themselves with Imperial privileges against their over-powerful neighbours. In 1451, the Republic achieved partial success when it forced Giovanni I Del Carretto to take a part of his Margraviate from the *Superba* as a fiefdom. When in 1558 the subjects of Finale revolted against the Marchese Alfonso II Del Carretto, the Republic took the opportunity to strengthen its grip on the Margraviate. In the autumn of 1558, it forced the Marchese to sign an armistice treaty. Among other conditions, he had to leave the fortress of Castel Franco to the Republic and to quit the Margraviate until the conflict would be settled definitively. Alfonso, however, revoked his agreement to the treaty and travelled to the Imperial court to defend his cause. He directed his accusations against the Republic, whose plans to seize Finale were a manifest violation of the Emperor's feudal supremacy. Despite the opposition of the Genoese envoys at the Viennese court, Emperor

3.2

Agnolo Bronzino, *Portrait of Andrea Doria as Neptune*. Milan, Pinacoteca di Brera, 1540. Reproduced with permission.

Ferdinand I revoked the treaty of 1558 and, by decree of 19 May 1559, 'as Emperor and Lord of the fiefdom' ('tanquam Imperator & feudi dominus'), claimed jurisdiction in the case.[18] He decidedly rejected the Genoese proposal to entrust the decision of the case to arbitrators to be appointed by himself and the Republic: if the Republic itself were not under the supremacy of the Empire, this might have been a way out. However, Genoa was designated in numerous Imperial privileges as 'our and Holy Empire's Chamber and City of Genoa' ('nostra & sacri Imperii Camera & Civitas Genuae'), possessed many Imperial fiefs and owed the restoration of its freedom to Emperor Charles V. The Genoese proposal might lead Ferdinand to suspect that Genoa was trying to free herself from the Empire, thus taking the path not only of inequity but also of the greatest ingratitude. At the same time, Ferdinand declared that he did not want to deprive the Genoese of the freedom they enjoyed like many other cities in Italy and Germany – a freedom under Imperial supremacy, of course.[19]

The Genoese were not inclined at all to recognise the Imperial jurisdiction, even when Ferdinand I modified his position in so far as he declared his willingness to allow settlement negotiations at his court. Only when the Emperor let it be understood that there would be no confirmation of the Genoese privileges if the Republic did not appoint a representative to the negotiations,[20] did the *Signoria* decide to send a new envoy, Ottaviano Di Negro, to the Imperial court.[21] However, Di Negro refused to answer on behalf of the Republic before the court commission, appointed by the Emperor, because he asserted that it first had to be clarified whether Finale was an Imperial fief at all. Subsequently, the Finale affair transformed from a conflict between the Marchese Del Carretto and his subjects into a conflict between Genoa and the Emperor. In the end, no longer just the question of the Imperial jurisdiction over Finale was at stake, but rather that of the freedom of Genoa herself. The Genoese *Collegi* emphasised this point in a letter to the Emperor in January 1560.[22] Their representative di Negro went even further when, in March 1560, he presented a memorandum which, in the strongest terms possible, protested against all measures taken by the Emperor that could lead to the 'prejudice to the free State' ('praeiudicium liberi status') of the Republic and declared them annulled, for they were contrary to the privileges granted to the Republic and the 'form of law and sacred canons' ('formam juris et sacrorum canonum'). Instead, di Negro appealed to the Pope.[23] Ferdinand I rejected the memorial and had it returned to the Genoese envoy. Since his actions at the Imperial court had made him *persona ingrata*, di Negro was finally recalled. But his successor Bartolomeo Fiesco was not more successful either.[24]

Finally, on 13 March 1561, an Imperial judgement in *contumaciam* was passed against Genoa, which invalidated the appeal to the Pope, rejected the treaty between Alfonso II and the Republic as forced and ordered the latter to return the Margraviate to Del Carretto and to reimburse him for all costs incurred and income lost.[25] In this way, Ferdinand I put into practice his position that Genoa was an Imperial City and thus under the Emperor's jurisdiction, but the *Signoria* did not submit to the Imperial judgement. Rather, it refused to accept the Imperial letter and had its bearer expelled.[26]

Ferdinand reacted to this manifest disregard for his Imperial dignity by seeking to implement an Imperial execution against the Republic. Since he had no forces of his own in Italy, he assigned the execution to Philip II of Spain. But the Spanish king treated the Imperial request dilatorily, so that Ferdinand finally sent the Imperial herald John Francolin to Genoa to proclaim new Imperial patents, but Francolin had to leave Genoa without having achieved anything and according to his own testimony at the risk of his life.[27] Ferdinand took the events as a further manifest disregard for his Imperial dignity.

In view of Philip II's dilatory attitude, the Imperial court began to explore the possibility of an execution against the Republic without Spanish help. To this end, it established contacts with Aurelio Fregoso, a descendant of the former Genoese doge family, who was in Florence and who, in the event of a seizure of power in Genoa 'while safeguarding due and competent freedom, as well as immunities, prerogatives, privileges and rights' ('salvis tamen debita et competenti libertate, ac immunitatibus, praerogativis, privilegiis et iuribus'), promised to remain 'in faith, devotion and obedience' ('in fide, devotione et obedientia') with Emperor Ferdinand and his successors.[28]

In view of the Imperial decisiveness, Philip II sent a special envoy to Vienna to mediate a settlement between Ferdinand and the Republic. In 1563 the following conditions were agreed: Genoa submitted herself to the Emperor's judgement as *Dominus directus* of Finale and returned the Margraviate to Del Carretto. However, the even more delicate question of the Emperor's jurisdiction over Genoa herself was left in limbo by the declaration that neither the Imperial judgments, on the one hand, nor their non-acceptance by the Republic, on the other, nor the restitution of Finale or any other event connected with this dispute would affect any right of the Empire or of Genoa, but that everything would remain as it had been at the time of Charles V.[29] The decision on certain factual issues was delegated to Philip II in his capacity as Duke of Milan.

In the spring of 1564 an epilogue of the affair took place, which is very illuminating for the perception of the Republic at the Imperial court. The dispute concerned the wording of the imperial decree announcing the settlement of the Finale conflict. A first decree stated that Ferdinand had granted an audience to the new Genoese *orator* Bernardo Spinola, at the insistent request of the latter and in accordance with his promise to the Spanish envoy Don Martino de la Nuza. The following passage in the decree was offensive from a Genoese perspective: the Republic and Imperial City of Genoa could have put an end to the lengthy discussions and excuses long ago had she obeyed the Imperial judgement as she should have done. Since it was not possible to undo what had happened, however, and since the Republic had now obeyed the Imperial order, the Emperor, through the intercession of Philip II, had graciously decided to grant her clemency from the punishment she deserved for her disobedience, to absolve her from her transgressions and to accept her once again to the Imperial grace. Ferdinand also promised to preserve the former liberty of the Republic and that his son and successor, the King of the Romans Maximilian (II), would adopt the same attitude.[30]

The Genoese considered this decree to be highly dangerous, as it was an infringement of the liberty of the Republic, which the settlement had been intended to repel.[31] Although Bernardo Spinola thought it would be appropriate to accept the decree, he recognised the problem that lay in the Imperial concept of the Genoese liberty, since for Ferdinand I and his ministers it was the same freedom which the German Imperial Cities possessed.[32]

The complaints of the Genoese orator had a counterproductive effect: a second Imperial decree was issued, which confirmed the first one. The new decree made it clear that neither Ferdinand I nor his son Maximilian had ever doubted the services in favour of the Emperor, the Empire and the House of Austria which the Republic had repeatedly rendered.

However, the decree also recalled that Genoa, in her capacity as *Civitas Imperii*, had been rewarded for her services with extensive privileges, rights, freedoms and graces. Ferdinand and Maximilian had been prepared to follow the example of their predecessors. But then the Republic had violated the name and dignity of the Emperor and the Empire not only by occupying Finale, but particularly with the disregard for the Imperial envoy and the Imperial herald. Therefore, Ferdinand felt himself obliged to protect the rights, honour, authority, and jurisdiction of the Empire. The first decree could not be changed under any circumstances, as it in no way contradicted the settlement reached. The Emperor had never intended to harm the Genoese liberty. If the Republic wished to protect its liberty, it should be careful not to give the impression that, on the pretext of this liberty, it was violating the name, dignity and authority of the Emperor and the Empire and prescribing to the Emperor how to respond to the Genoese envoy.[33] The new decree thus constituted a clear rebuke to Spinola and confirmed in clear terms Ferdinand's view of his overlordship over the Republic. Finally, a new Genoese envoy, Giambattista Lomellino, managed to obtain an assurance from Ferdinand, that neither the Imperial decrees nor the answers he would give to Lomellino at his future audience would affect the liberty of the Republic and its 'immunities, exonerations, rights and privileges' ('immunitates, exemptiones, iura et privilegia').[34] In his reply, Lomellino affirmed the 'devotions and usual compliance' ('devozione ed osservanza solita') of the Republic to the Emperor and the Empire. He thus used wording of homage as it was customary for a lower-ranked person to a higher-ranked one or for a client towards his patron. The Republic of Genoa and the Genoese envoys used the same wording towards monarchs other than the Emperor, too. In contrast, Lomellino carefully avoided expressions such as 'loyalty' ('fedeltà') or 'deference' ('ossequio'), which would have indicated subordination of the Republic to the Emperor.[35]

With the submission of the Republic, Ferdinand I achieved a prestigious success. This does not mean, however, that he succeeded in establishing once and for all the Imperial supremacy he claimed over the Republic of Genoa. On the contrary, the *status quo ante* was in principle restored. The question of the Imperial supremacy over Genoa remained open, and both sides had maintained their respective positions.[36] This is also reflected in the evaluation of the affair of Finale by later generations: while the Genoese historiographer Francesco Maria Accinelli interprets the agreement as a recognition of the Genoese independence by Ferdinand I,[37] Andrea de Andreis alias Gerolamo Maria Del Carretto speaks of a complete submission of the Republic to the Imperial judgement.[38]

In the following decades, the question of the Emperor's supremacy, and in particular his jurisdiction over Genoa, was occasionally raised, sometimes in a quite fundamental way, such as in the context of the Genoese constitutional conflict of 1575/76,[39] but also when the Republic, on its own behalf, attributed the title 'Serenissimus' to its doge.[40] In the end, however, the situation remained open: both sides insisted on their views on the legal nature of the Republic's relationship with the Emperor and the Empire and overlooked the divergent positions by dissimulation. This remained so until the 1630s, when the Republic was about to reject even the slightest appearance of Imperial supremacy.

From liberty to sovereignty: The 1630s as a turning point

In Genoese history, the 1630s represent a decade of renaissance. At least, the so-called *repubblichisti* aspired to the rebirth of the Republic's greatness. An important element of this revival was the consolidation of Genoese liberty. Therefore, the aims of the *repubblichisti* had an anti-Spanish impetus because in their opinion the Spanish king acted more as a master than as an ally of the Republic. But the *repubblichisti* were not only concerned to free the Republic from its dependence on Spain, but also to make clear its complete freedom from any temporal authority.[41] Meanwhile, the concept of sovereignty had become established for this kind of freedom and had been widely adopted in Italy.[42] The Genoese striving for sovereignty was also connected with a shock to the hierarchy of the European powers, which had started from papal Rome in 1630. At that time Pope Urban VIII, Maffeo Barberini, issued a decree with which he wanted to secure the rank of the cardinals – and especially of his cardinal-nephews. According to this decree, the cardinals were to directly follow the kings in rank but precede all other princes. By placing the cardinals, so to speak, between the kings and the non-royal princes and powers, the latter were implicitly devalued in rank. This papal decision had considerable impact beyond Rome, so that the non-royal powers – including Genoa – had to fear the most damaging consequences for their position in the hierarchy of the European princes and powers. The courts and governments concerned were ultimately left with only one option to avert the damage: they had to become royal or obtain recognition from the Pope, Emperor and kings as being equal to the kings and thus deserving equal honours. But only Venice succeeded in doing so. Others achieved this goal only after a considerable time delay, such as the Duke of Savoy when he received the Kingdom of Sicily in the Peace of Utrecht in 1713; others did not achieve it at all.[43]

In Genoa, the efforts to secure the royal rank of the Republic converged with the efforts of the *repubblichisti* to renew the Republic's greatness. In 1637, several decisions and measures were taken and implemented in rapid succession to secure the royal rank for the Republic and to remove any semblance of foreign sovereignty.[44] In March 1637, the Blessed Virgin was crowned Queen of Genoa and Liguria, which was a first step towards establishing that Genoa was a kingdom. A few months later, in November 1637, the new Doge Agostino Pallavicino became the first Genoese Doge to be crowned with a royal crown. Some accompanying measures deserve special mention in our context. In particular, the customary inscription 'Conradus Rex' on Genoese coins, which referred to the privilege of minting issued by King Conrad III in 1138, was replaced by the image of the Blessed Virgin as Queen of Genoa.

However, to secure royal rank for the Republic, it was crucial that it be recognised by the other powers. And here, in addition to a few others, such as the Pope and the Spanish king, the Emperor played a most important role. For it was above all his claims to supremacy that stood in the way of Genoese sovereignty. The adoption of royal rank by the Republic of Genoa coincided with the death of Emperor Ferdinand II and the accession of his successor Ferdinand III to the throne in 1637. It was customary for Genoa to send a high-ranking envoy to congratulate the new head of the Empire and at the same time to obtain for the Republic the confirmation of the Imperial privileges and investitures by the new Emperor.

With Giambattista Negrone, the Republic also sent a congratulatory envoy to the Imperial court in 1638, whose legation was prepared by the long-time Genoese resident in Vienna Gerolamo Rodino. It was nothing new that questions of rank and ceremonial also played an important role in such legations. Against the background of the Genoese increase in rank, however, they were of particular importance, because were Genoa of royal rank, its ambassador had to be received with royal honours.[45]

With regard to the renewal of the investitures with the small Imperial fiefs of the Republic continuity was observed. The resident Rodino asked for them and received them on behalf of the Republic in 1638. However, for the first time the Republic did not ask for confirmation of her Imperial privileges in the usual manner. In fact, as early as 1637, the resident Rodino had declared himself in favour of asking only for the renewal of the two privileges, which confirmed in general terms to the Republic all the privileges, rights, and possessions dependent on the Empire, or respectively the property of the *Oltregiogo*. On the other hand, Rodino judged the renewal of Maximilian I's privilege of 1513 on the salt trade and especially that of Charles V of 1 November 1536 to be unnecessary. In his opinion, the latter only contained the confirmation of the Genoese liberty, which would not need further confirmation. The *Collegi* followed this recommendation. Hence, a fundamental change in the Genoese attitude to Imperial privileges is evident. They were no longer seen as advantageous but as a potential interference with Genoese liberty.[46]

Meanwhile, the Imperial court had become suspicious, knowing that the Genoese had elevated themselves to a higher rank on their own authority and being dismayed that the renewal of the investiture had not been accompanied by a request for confirmation of the Imperial privileges. Against this background, Giambattista Negrone started his legation under difficult conditions. Gerolamo Rodino had already noticed this when, in 1638, in the run-up to Negrone's legation, he asked for a change in the Emperor's title of the Republic which should be addressed as 'Doge, governors, and procurators of the Genoese Republic' ('Duci, Gubernatoribus, et Procuratoribus Reipublica Genuae') – thus with omission of the 'Civitas imperialis' – from now on and for the royal honours to be granted to the Genoese representative. Several ministers made it clear that the Emperor disapproved the Republic's arbitrary increase in rank.[47]

An advisory on the Genoese claims, issued by the Imperial Aulic Council the 19/20 April 1638, is of the greatest interest to our question.[48] While a minority of the councillors were of the opinion that the wishes of the Republic should be met in something, but 'given the superiority of the Caesarian Majesty and that of the Holy Roman Empire' ('salva superioritate Maiestatis Caesareae et Sacri Romani Imperii'), the majority felt that one could not wonder enough that Genoa was making such unseemly demands aimed at her 'total exemption' from the Empire.

Both parties agreed that the Republic should continue to be regarded as 'a state and member' of the Empire. This would be supported by the term 'Civitas et camera imperialis', which had hitherto been used for the Genoese, the signing of letters addressed to the Emperor by the Genoese as 'very devoted' ('devotissimi'), the granting and confirmation of the Imperial privileges, the fact that the Emperors continued to exercise their jurisdiction over Genoa even after having granted and confirmed the liberty of the Republic, and the image of King Konrad on the Genoese coins. The majority felt that the Emperor would renounce his supremacy should he change the title of Genoa in the desired manner. In their opinion, the Republic invoked the kingdom of Corsica in vain in support of its request, because this island was not really a kingdom. And even were one to accept the argument, one would have to ask whether the Imperial supremacy did not extend to Corsica. Genoa had also long been in possession of the island, without having derived such claims from it.

The improvements concerning the title granted by former Emperors were not admitted as an argument either. The claim to parity or even priority over Venice was rejected. While the Venetians also enjoyed the honours of a royal power at the papal and other courts, the Genoese had received it only from France, the enemy of the Emperor and the Empire, obviously 'in odium et aemulationem Imperii', whereas the Pope had refused it to them. The argument that the Genoese Doge, unlike the Venetian, was not elected for life, but only for two years and was then 'private' again was also important. If the Genoese wishes were to be honoured, the Republic would claim precedence not only before the Prince Electors but also before Austria. In the final analysis, the councillors judged the Genoese approach to be close to a *crimen laesae Maiestatis*.

Accordingly, the majority vote was in favour of completely rejecting the request for a change of the Genoese title. The Genoese ambassador should be granted the same ceremonial treatment as his predecessors. Furthermore, it was suggested that the Genoese resident Rodino or respectively the ambassador be asked straightforwardly what the requests were actually aimed at. In addition, the Prince Electors should also be asked for their opinion.

This vote shows, on the one hand, that the Imperial Aulic Council had clearly recognised the direction of the Genoese innovations in ceremonial matters, and, on the other hand,

its determination to maintain the supremacy of the Emperor and Empire over Genoa – which not even the minority willing to compromise questioned. The Privy Council and the Emperor largely followed the majority vote of the Imperial Aulic Council when they decided to give a negative reply to the Genoese resident. Thus, the hope that Negrone could move into Vienna as a royal ambassador with all the corresponding honours was not fulfilled. Even during Negrone's presence in Vienna, neither he nor the resident Rodino managed to achieve a breakthrough on the question of the title and ceremonial status to be granted to the Republic.[49]

After Negrone's departure a further scandal occurred when, on 7 June 1638, an Imperial decree was issued in which Ferdinand III not only rejected the Genoese demands for ceremonial revaluation of the Republic but also qualified the Republic as *Civitas imperialis*, a title which was no longer acceptable to the Genoese. As a result, the resident Rodino refused to accept the decree. When the Emperor consulted the Prince Electors on this question, they replied in the negative, as had been expected.[50]

Further irritation at the Imperial court was caused by Genoa's action on the question of privileges. Shortly before his departure, Giambattista Negrone asked for confirmation of the two privileges of 29 June 1529 and 10 November 1536, in order to give the Imperial ministers a favourable opinion and to facilitate Rodino's further negotiations. In this matter the Imperial Aulic Council avoided an open conflict but dissimulated. It took the decision to confirm all four privileges and had the confirmation diplomas drafted. Rodino was informed that, if he wished to have the privileges confirmed, he would have to submit a new memorial to the Imperial Aulic Council based on the model of the previous ones. At the end of August 1638, the leading Imperial minister Maximilian von Trauttmansdorff explained to the Genoese resident how irritated the Emperor was at the fact that the confirmation of the privileges had not been requested in the usual manner and that this irritation was preventing any concessions on the question of the title, which was of particular interest to the Republic.

As a result, the *Signoria* revised its position on the question of privileges, and on 9 November 1638 Rodino presented a new memorial in which he requested the renewal of all four privileges. However, due to the irregularities that had occurred, the issue could not be handled as a matter of routine by the Imperial Aulic Council, but needed to be dealt with by the Imperial Privy Council, too. In fact, at that time no decision at all was taken regarding Genoese affairs.[51]

Only in 1640, did the negotiations start moving again – not because one side had changed its positions, but because the Genoese side changed its strategy. In view of the enormous financial requirements of Emperor Ferdinand in the final phase of the Thirty Years' War, attempts were made to achieve the desired concessions as an act of Imperial grace with a substantial sum of money.[52]

In view of the financial benefits promised by Rodino, Ferdinand III set up a small deputation of councillors to discuss this offer and Genoese affairs in general.[53] Apparently the Emperor took this path because he expected greater flexibility from these hand-picked councillors than from the entire Imperial Aulic Council. On 26 March 1640 the deputation submitted its report:[54] The councillors referred to the vote of the Imperial Aulic Council of 1638 and to Rodino's uninterrupted efforts, but also recalled the Genoese refusal to accept the Imperial decree of 7 June 1638, the irregular request for the renewal of privileges and the rejection of the Genoese demands by the Prince Electors. However, the councillors saw a change in favour of Genoa in comparison to spring 1638 in the fact that 'since then she has recognised her initial mistake to such an extent that she has ceased to penetrate her demands as a legal title, and has also accepted the submission to the Holy Roman Empire'. Genoa would now 'so fervently seek this grace from Your Imperial Majesty' and also the confirmation of the privileges. Thus, the most important reasons why the Imperial Aulic Council had advised the Emperor against granting the Genoese requests in 1638 were no longer valid. However, the councillors still regarded the arbitrary acceptance of the royal insignia and the changes to the coins as problematic. It would be desirable that the Genoese 'repair the usurpation committed' before granting the requested Imperial graces. This would, however, be 'difficult' to enforce. Moreover, it was to be feared that, 'since one wanted to seriously continue the shown severity', the Republic might be 'seduced to [...] even more dangerous decisions'. Above all, Genoa had shown her willingness to grant the Emperor 'the due gratitude and appropriate devotion', and could well offer a considerable benefit (of money). Accordingly, the councillors recommended that the Genoese wishes 'should be met in something', however, 'in such a way that the supremacy of Your Imperial Majesty and of the Empire is confirmed and no one else is prejudiced'. Specifically, they proposed to use the following address in future writings to Genoa: 'Serenissimo Duci et Gubernatoribus Reipublicae nostrae Genuensis'. The title 'Serenissimus' would put the Republic on an equal footing with the higher ranks, while the word 'nostrae' would confirm the Imperial supremacy.[55] The councillors saw this formula as the outermost limit of Imperial concession. If possible, one should even try to maintain the terms 'camera' or 'imperialis' in the address to express the Imperial supremacy more clearly. Furthermore, the decree to be issued should expressly state that it would not affect the precedence of the Prince Electors and of the House of Austria. Since it was to be expected that the Republic would offer considerable payments only if all her wishes were granted, the councillors also recommended that all Genoese privileges should be confirmed.

By following this advice, the Emperor's decision of principle in favour of Genoa was made. However, a diplomatic tug-of-war unfolded over the exact implementation of the concession. Only in autumn 1641 were the negotiations finally concluded.[56] The decree in which Ferdinand III with reference to the 'amplitudo' and 'gloria' of Genoa, her merits towards the Empire and the House of Austria, in particular the 'great financial help' ('egregium subsidium pecuniarium') provided in the present wartime period, and the example set by his predecessors as Roman Emperors, stipulated that the Republic was to receive the following address from him and his successors in word and writing in future 'to the most serene doge, our dearest prince, and to our beloved and famous governors of the Genoese Republic' ('Serenissimo Duci Principi nostro charissimo, ac Illustribus Gubernatoribus Reipublicae Genuensium nostris dilectis').[57] The desired royal honours, however, were not granted to the Republic. Although the deputised councillors and other decision-makers at the Imperial court verbally emphasised that this improvement of the title granted to the Genoese Republic did not detract anything from the supremacy of Emperor and Empire over the city and Republic of Genoa, it did so, of course – and should do so from the Genoese perspective. In fact, for the sake of short-term financial gains, the Emperor and his ministers now accepted what only a few years before had been castigated as Genoese arbitrariness, yes, even crime of lèse majesté against the Emperor. Indeed, by renouncing the 'civitas nostra imperialis' in the correspondence with the Republic, the Emperor substantially weakened his own legal position. However, neither he nor his ministers abandoned it at all.

The question of the Genoese privileges remained open, too. After the decision in principle had been made to confirm them, neither side pursued the matter with any particular commitment, and it fell gradually into oblivion in the face of more urgent business. Thus, it happened that the Genoese resident Rodino left Vienna in 1643 without the privileges having been confirmed.[58]

Conclusion

The question of Genoa's position vis-à-vis the Emperor and the Empire remained open throughout the early modern period. While the Genoese conception of liberty categorically excluded interference by foreign powers in the internal affairs of the Republic, and thus conceded the Emperor and the Empire only a primacy of honour, but not real supremacy, the hierarchical system of the Holy Roman Empire did not acknowledge any place for a free, sovereign Republic beyond the subordinate position of an Imperial City. In the sixteenth century, the opposing Genoese and Imperial views were still somewhat concealed under the ambiguous name of 'liberty'. But the developments of the 1630s changed Genoa's relationship to the Emperor and the Empire. After the Republic had explicitly insisted on its sovereignty and royal rank, it became much more difficult to reconcile the conflicting positions, or rather, to overlook them in a dissimulating manner.

The Emperor, the Imperial institutions and the Imperial jurists persistently held on to the idea that Genoa was an Imperial city and, from time to time, conflicts arose, e.g. regarding the Imperial privileges, the Imperial jurisdiction over Genoa and its possessions, and the financial obligations of the Republic towards the Emperor and Empire.[59] However, apart from several phases of escalation, the relations between Vienna and Genoa remained largely unaffected by these differences. This was due to the fact that the strictly Imperial view increasingly appeared to be more of a fiction, which also lost credibility because the Emperors themselves, when they did not act as heads of the Holy Roman Empire but as representatives of the Habsburg dynasty or as rulers of the great power of Austria, preferred a more pragmatic approach and tended to treat Genoa de facto as a sovereign, albeit not royal power. As more time passed, the view of the Imperial jurists and institutions fell out of force. As a latent threat, however, it remained a source of concern for the Republic of Genoa to the very end.

---

1 For Spain, Herrero Sánchez and others, eds, *Génova y la Monarquía Hispánica (1528–1713)*; for France, Bottaro Palumbo, ed., *Genova e Francia al crocevia dell'Europa (1624–1642)*; Boccardo and others, eds, *Genova e la Francia*; Gorse, 'A question of sovereignty'.

2 Vitale, *Diplomatici e consoli della Repubblica di Genova*, pp. 107–30.

3 Schnettger and Verga, eds, *L'Impero e l'Italia nella prima età moderna*; Cremonini and Musso, eds, *I feudi imperiali in Italia tra XV e XVIII secolo*; Taddei, Schnettger, and Rebitsch, eds, *'Reichsitalien' in Mittelalter und Neuzeit*.

4 Schnettger, *'Principe sovrano'*, pp. 413–529; Zanini, *Strategie politiche*; Zanini, 'Feudi, feudatari ed economie nella montagna ligure'.

5 Schnettger, *'Principe sovrano'*. The article is based on the results of this monographic study. Also Schnettger, 'Libertà e imperialità'.

6 In the fifteenth century, Genoa was instead under the rule of the King of France and the Duke of Milan for long periods of time (1421–35, 1458–61, 1466–76). Favreau-Lilie, 'Genua und das Reich am Ausgang des Mittelalters (14./15. Jh.)'.

7 The diploma of 20 September 1496 has been printed in Johann Christian Lünig, *Codex Italiae diplomaticus*, II, col. 2147–2149; and [Senckenberg], *Imperii Germanici Ius*, pp. 272–75. See Schnettger, *'Principe sovrano'*, pp. 62–63.

8 The diploma of 4 April 1513 has been printed in: Lünig, II, col. 2149–2151; [Senckenberg], *Imperii Germanici Ius*, pp. 282–85.

9 This combination of Imperial legal titles and Spanish means of power became dangerous for Genoa's independence, especially after the Fieschi uprising of 1547, which, however, ultimately ended without harm to the Republic. For Genoa's position towards Charles V, Pacini, *La Genova di Andrea Doria nell'Impero di Carlo V*; Pacini, 'Genoa and Emperor Charles V'.

10 The diploma of 29 June 1529 (Lünig, *Codex Italiae diplomaticus*, II, col. 2151–2153; [Senckenberg], *Imperii Germanici Ius*, pp. 293–94) confirmed all privileges, rights and possessions of the Republic. The diploma of 1 November 1536 ([Senckenberg], *Imperii Germanici Ius*, pp. 300–03) again confirmed every liberty of the Republic and granted the Genoese doge the right to make use of the ducal insignia. The diploma of 10 November 1536 ([Senckenberg], *Imperii Germanici Ius*, pp. 297–300) confirmed the Genoese possessions in the *Oltregiogo*. Schnettger, *'Principe sovrano'*, pp. 64–69.

11 Schnettger, *'Principe sovrano'*, pp. 170–71.

12 For the republican concept of liberty, Koenigsberger, 'Republicanism, monarchism and liberty'; Mackenney, *The City-State, 1500–1700*; Van Gelderen and Skinner, eds, *Republicanism*, esp. II, part I: 'Republicanism and Political Values'; Maissen, 'Républiques et républicanismes en époque moderne'.

13 Recently, 'dissimulation' has been discussed primarily as a practice to manage confessional diversity. Zagorin, *Ways of Lying*; Stollberg-Rilinger, 'Einleitung'. But dissimulation was a fundamental practice in other fields of politics, too. Villari, *Elogio della dissimulazione*. Dissimulation was facilitated by ambiguities, as were also inherent in the term 'liberty'. Indeed, dissimulation and ambiguity may be regarded as signatures of the early modern period. Von Thiessen, *Das Zeitalter der Ambiguität*.

14 As mentioned above, the privileges also confirmed the territorial possessions of the Republic. They were confirmed by Maximilian II, Rudolph II, Matthias and Ferdinand II. Schnettger, *'Principe sovrano'*, pp. 77–84.

15 Ponzano (1541/62), Montoggio, Varese and Roccatagliata (1547/65), a part of Savignone (1581), Sassello (1611/14), a part of Carosio (1614), Zuccarello (1624/32), one half of Campofreddo (1636). Later the Republic acquired Finale (1713) and Buzalla (1738). Schnettger, *'Principe sovrano'*, pp. 413–96; Zanini, *Strategie politiche*.

16 Schnettger, *'Principe sovrano'*, pp. 73–168.

17 Manca, 'Ingerenze genovesi e spagnole'. Most studies of the Finale conflict focus on the later events and neglect the phase up to 1564, which is usually treated very briefly. For example, Edelmayer, *Maximilian II., Philipp II. und Reichsitalien*, pp. 7–13; Calcagno, 'La puerta a la mar', pp. 427–28.

18 Decree of Ferdinand I, 1559 V 19, OSW, HHS, Judicialia Latina (Jula) 198, printed in: [Senckenberg], *Imperii Germanici Ius*, pp. 310–14 (misleadingly labelled as 'Litterae Ferdinandi I. ad Genuates').

19 [Senckenberg], *Imperii Germanici Ius*, pp. 313–14. Schnettger, *'Principe sovrano'*, pp. 244–46.

20 Ferdinand I to the Signoria of Genoa, Augsburg 1559 VI 23, OSW, HHS, Jula 198.

21 Power of attorney for Ottaviano Di Negro, Genoa 1559 IX 11, OSW, HHS, Jula 198.

22 The Signoria of Genoa to Ferdinand I, Genoa 1560 I 4, OSW, HHS, Jula 198.

23 Memoriale of Ottaviano Di Negro, presented 1560 III 12, OSW, HHS, Jula 198, printed in: [Senckenberg], *Imperii Germanici Ius*, pp. 318–19. A detailed exposition of the Genoese position, 1560, [Senckenberg], *Imperii Germanici Ius*, pp. 321–26.

24 Schnettger, 'Principe sovrano', pp. 246–48.

25 Decree of Ferdinand I, 1561 III 13, HHStA W, Jula 198, also in OSW, HHS, Jula 199, printed in: [Senckenberg], *Imperii Germanici Ius*, pp. 326–28. Schnettger, 'Principe sovrano', p. 249. Lucchini, 'Genova e Finale nella seconda metà del sec. XVI', pp. 47–48; Lucchini, *Dominio e Sopravvivenza*, p. 62, misleadingly speaks of the Emperor having again taken jurisdiction over the Finale case in April 1561.

26 Claudio de Luna to Philip II, Vienna 1561 IX 14, in Ramirez de Arellano and others, *Colección de documentos inéditos para la historia de España*, pp. 242–43; Marengo, 'Alfonso II° Del Carretto Marchese di Finale e la Repubblica di Genova', pp. 45–46; Lucchini, 'Genova e Finale nella seconda metà del sec. XVI', and Lucchini, *Dominio e Sopravvivenza* does not mention this dramatic escalation of the dispute.

27 Schnettger, 'Principe sovrano', pp. 249–50.

28 Aurelio Fregoso, 'Obligatio super reductione civitatis Genuae ad obedientiam', Freiburg i. Br. 1563 I 5, OSW, HHS, Jula 199; Fregoso to Ferdinand I, Freiburg i. Br. 1563 I 3. Schnettger, 'Principe sovrano', p. 251.

29 'The formula of the oration given by the Genoese orator, thirdly corrected, was presented by Don Martino della Nuzza, December 17, 1563' ('Formula orationis habendae per oratorem Genuensem tertio correcta exhibita per Don Martinum della Nuzza 17 decembri 1563'). OSW, HHS, Jula 199. There are several revisions of the 'formula', which shows how difficult it was to find a solution to which finally the Emperor gave his approval. Schnettger, 'Principe sovrano', pp. 251–53.

30 Decree of Ferdinand I, Vienna 1564 III 10, ASG, AS 256, printed in: [Senckenberg], *Imperii Germanici Ius*, pp. 330–32. Schnettger, 'Principe sovrano', pp. 253–54.

31 The *Collegi* to Bernardo Spinola, Genoa 1564 III 30, ASG, AS 2521.

32 Bernardo Spinola to the *Collegi*, Vienna 1564 V 3, ASG, AS 2521.

33 'It was not even the intention of His Majesty, nor is it now, to diminish, undermine or overthrow the liberty of the Republic of Genoa by the same decree, but it is fair and just for the Republic of Genoa to protect and preserve its liberty in such a way that it does not appear to be acting under the pretext of its alleged liberty. injures and attacks the name, dignity, and authority of His Imperial Majesty and the Holy Empire, by prescribing the law and manner of His Imperial Majesty, according to which he shall answer the same speaker' ('[…] Neque etiam animus fuit, neque nunc est Maiestati Suae per idem decretum minuere, labefactare vel evertere libertatem Reipublicae Genuensis, verum aequum et iustum est Rempublicam Genuensem in tuenda et conservanda libertate sua talem adhibere modum, ne id agere videatur, ut praetextu assertae suae libertatis, nomen, dignitatem et auctoritatem Maiestatis Suae Caesareae et Sacri Imperii laedat atque oppugnet, Maiestati Suae Caesareae legem atque modum praescribendo, iuxta quem eidem oratori respondeat'). Decree of Ferdinand I, Vienna 1564 V 16, ASG, AS 256. See also the 'Formula declaratoria' which had been exhibited to Lomellino, ASG, AS 2521, and that of Ferdinand I to his ambassador in Spain Adam von Dietrichstein, Vienna 1564 V 19, in Strohmeyer and Edelmayer, *Die Korrespondenz der Kaiser*, pp. 208–10. With this letter, the Emperor not only informed Dietrichstein of the efforts of the Genoese envoy, but at the same time instructed him to defend the Imperial position towards the Republic in Spain.

34 Decree of Ferdinand I, Vienna 1564 VII 9, ASG, AS 256. The decree explicitly mentions the mediation of the King of the Romans Maximilian (II). Schnettger, 'Principe sovrano', p. 255. Lucchini, *Dominio e Sopravvivenza*, p. 65, does not place the decree precisely in its context.

35 Pugliese, *Le prime strette dell'Austria in Italia*, p. 67.

36 The new Emperor Maximilian II informed his envoy in Spain with satisfaction that the conflict had been settled 'cum autoritate' just before the death of his father. Maximilian II to Adam von Dietrichstein, Vienna 1564 VIII 2, in Strohmeyer and Edelmayer, *Die Korrespondenz der Kaiser*, pp. 266–269. But the submission of the Republic to Imperial sovereignty was not quite as unequivocal as Laubach, *Ferdinand I. als Kaiser*, p. 660, states in reference to Pugliese.

37 'The Freedom of Genoa recognised as independent by the Emperor himself stands out, while the Republic understood Ferdinand's sentence about Finale to be badly received by a Herald, and serious uprisings of war in Italy being about to be born, the controversy was brought to an end by the interposition of the Catholic King with an amicable settlement between the Emperor and the Republic itself' ('Fa spicco la Libertà di Genova riconosciuta indipendente dallo stesso Imperatore, mentre intesa dalla Repubblica per un Araldo malamente accolto la Sentenza di Ferdinando circa il Finale, essendo per nascere gravi moti di Guerra in Italia, fu ad interposizione del Re Cattolico la controversia terminata con amichevole transazione fra lo stesso Imperatore, e la stessa Repubblica'). Accinelli, *Compendio*, I, p. 159.

38 Andrea De Andreis [Gerolamo Maria Del Carretto], Enucleatio iuris immediati S.R.I. super urbe Genua eiusque statibus (1729), in [Senckenberg], *Imperii Germanici Ius*, pp. 817–70.

39 Costantini, *La Repubblica di Genova*, pp. 101–52; Savelli, *La Repubblica oligarchica*; for the Imperial perspective Schnettger, 'Principe sovrano', pp. 264–80.

40 Only later did the Republic have her elevation in rank confirmed by an Imperial privilege of Rudolph II. Schnettger, 'Principe sovrano', pp. 170–83.

41 Bitossi, *Il governo dei magnifici*, pp. 193–98, 207–10, 217–33; Bitossi, 'Un lungo addio'; Costantini, *La Repubblica di Genova*, pp. 239–44, 267–71; Costantini, 'Politica e storiografia: l'età dei grandi repubblichisti'; Costantini and others, *Dibattito politico e problemi di governo a Genova nella prima metà del Seicento*, pp. 9–74.

42 The first Italian translation of Bodin's *Six livres de la République* appeared, in Genoa, as early as 1588. Visceglia, 'Il cerimoniale come linguaggio politico', pp. 165–66. For the reception of Bodin in Genoa, Savelli, 'Tra Machiavelli e S. Giorgio'.

43 Oresko, 'The House of Savoy in search for a royal crown in the seventeenth century'; Stollberg-Rilinger, 'Honores regii'.

44 For the adoption of royal rank by the Republic of Genoa, Ciasca, 'Affermazioni di sovranità della Repubblica di Genova nel secolo XVII'; Ciasca, 'La Repubblica di Genova "testa coronata"'; Vitale, *Breviario della storia di Genova*, I, pp. 249–60; Bottaro Palumbo, '"Et rege eos"'; Oresko, 'The House of Savoy in search for a royal crown in the seventeenth century', pp. 294–301; Schnettger, 'Die Republik als König'; Schnettger, 'Principe sovrano', pp. 183–92; Zunckel, 'Tra Bodin e la Madonna'.

45 Schnettger, 'Principe sovrano', pp. 192–200.

46 Schnettger, 'Principe sovrano', pp. 84–87.

47 Schnettger, 'Principe sovrano', pp. 194–200. A valuable precedent for Genoa was that Ferdinand III had referred to the Republic – apparently by mistake – as 'Serenissima' at an audience for Rodino. Schnettger, 'Principe sovrano', p. 195.

48 Legal opinion of the Imperial Aulic Council, conclusum 1638 IV 18, lectum et approbatum 1638 IV 20, with undated Imperial resolution, ASG, AS 2546. Apparently, at least one member of the Imperial Aulic Council or another Imperial minister or secretary was susceptible to Genoese bribes, because there is a complete copy of the expert opinion in the Genoese Archivio segreto. In contrast, I have not found a copy in OSW, HHS. See also the short protocol of the Imperial Aulic Council, 1638 IV 19, OSW, HHS, Feula 22; and Gerolamo

Rodino to the *Collegi*, Vienna 1638 IV 29, ASG, AS 2545. Alongside the Imperial Chamber Court, the Imperial Aulic Council functioned as the highest court of the Empire. It had sole jurisdiction over all matters of feudal law and thus also over Imperial Italy. In addition to its function as the highest court, it acted as an advisory body to the Emperor in all Imperial matters. For an overview, Auer, 'The Role of the Imperial Aulic Council'; Oestmann, 'The highest courts of the Holy Roman Empire'.

49 Schnettger, 'Principe sovrano', pp. 201–03.

50 Schnettger, 'Principe sovrano', pp. 203–06.

51 Thus with the request for the renewal of all four privileges. Gerolamo Rodino to the Collegi, Vienna 1638 VI 26, ASG, AS 2545. Schnettger, 'Principe sovrano', pp. 87–89.

52 Schnettger, 'Principe sovrano', pp. 89, 208–09.

53 The members of the deputation: the president of the Imperial Aulic Council Johann von der Recke, the Vice-Chancellor of the Empire Ferdinand Sigismund Kurz von Senftenau, the member of the Imperial Aulic Council Konrad Hildbrandt and the secretary of the latin expedition of the Imperial Court Chancery Johann Walderode von Eckhausen. Schnettger, 'Principe sovrano', pp. 209–10.

54 Legal opinion of the deputation on the question of the Genoese title, 1640 III 26, OSW, HHS, RHR, Voten 18.

55 Thus the new address is another example for early modern ambiguity.

56 Schnettger, 'Principe sovrano', pp. 211–13.

57 Imperial decree, 1641 IX 2, ASG, AS 483A. Transcripts among others in the Genoese Ceremoniale for the years 1639–1658, ASG, AS 476, fol. 64', and in ASG, AS 2778. Admittedly, the Imperial chancellery does not always seem to have proceeded carefully on this point: for the time after 1641 there are several letters with 'nobis' instead of 'nostro'/'nostris'. The Genoese letter of thanks is dated 24 October 1641. The Signoria to Ferdinand III, Genoa 1641 X 24, ASG, AS 1902, n. 364, fol. 182', also in ASG, AS 2757a. There was a further quarrel over the sum to be paid by Genoa. In August 1641, Rodino had offered the leading Imperial minister Trauttmansdorff, out of his own authority, to obtain permission from the Signoria to pay a further 50,000 fl. over and above the 100,000 fl. granted, whereupon the Imperial decree was issued in the form described. Since the Signoria refused to increase the sum, the 100,000 fl. remained, however, without the Imperial claims to the additional 50,000 fl. being forgotten. Schnettger, 'Principe sovrano', p. 213.

58 Schnettger, 'Principe sovrano', p. 89.

59 When Ferdinand III's son Leopold I succeeded to the Imperial throne (1658), the Genoese Signoria completely renounced the request for confirmation of the Imperial privileges, with the result that the Imperial Aulic Council was anxious to impose the confirmation of privileges on her. When this failed, the renewal of the investitures with the Genoese Imperial fiefs was also denied. Until the end of the Old Empire, this topic was raised with varying intensity every time a new Emperor took office. Schnettger, 'Principe sovrano', pp. 89–168. During the Nine Years' War (1688–1697) and especially during the War of the Spanish Succession (1701–1713/14), the Imperial demands for contributions were added as a new area of conflict. Schnettger, 'Principe sovrano', pp. 577–99. Even more spectacular were the conflicts over Campo freddo and especially San Remo in the second half of the eighteenth century, which raised the question of the Imperial jurisdiction over Genoa again and in a more acute form. Schnettger, 'Principe sovrano', pp. 334–412.

II THE AGE OF LIBERTY
1528–1620

4

Laura Stagno

THE GIFT OF CONCORD AND FREEDOM

Images of Andrea Doria
in Late Sixteenth-Century Art

This essay investigates the iconographies centred on the representation of Andrea Doria procuring and preserving Genoa's internal peace and freedom, as a gift born of his love for the Republic. They can be found mostly in late sixteenth-century art, largely – but not exclusively – in connection with Giovanni Andrea Doria's patronage. The construction of Doria's myth as saviour and a new founder of the Genoese state – of which Pacini, among others, has illustrated the genesis and the characters, identifying its founding act in the preamble to the corpus of laws issued in the first days of October 1528, after Doria had entered Charles V's service and liberated Genoa from the French[1] – is the antefact and the basis of this specific strand of the multi-faceted fortune of Doria's image in the arts.

This narrative celebrated Andrea Doria as 'the most illustrious leader and the best citizen' ('ducem clarissimum et civem optimum'), who brought about a 'golden age of freedom' ('aureum libertatis saeculum'), the founder of the new Republic who gifted concord and freedom to Genoa after centuries of internecine conflicts and intermittent foreign dominations.[2] These two concepts – Concordia or Unione, and Libertà – were key elements both in the political project which culminated in the Reformationes Novae and in the subsequent interpretation of the 1528 events, prevailing in the late sixteenth and seventeenth centuries. The ideal of unione dominated the Genoese political discourse before being related to Doria's action (at least since the beginning of the wars of Italy, in fact): Pacini cites as relevant proof the 1506 Libro di pace e concordia de lo populo de Genoa ('Book of Peace and Concord of the People of Genoa'), with its condemnation of the 'discordia, divisione e parcialità abominanda',[3] which reigned in Genoa and led to its ruin,[4] and the preamble to the first, incomplete version of the 1528 laws produced in April. In the latter, 'concordia' was heralded as the only remedy to the grave evils caused 'by dissensions and factions' ('dissidiis et factionibus'),

which for too long had plagued the city.[5] According to Grendi, Andrea Doria seized the old myth of the unione – a sequestro, he calls it.[6] The novelty of the October version of the laws was the addition of the previously absent theme of freedom, associated with the introduction of the figure of Doria as the God-sent saviour of the state.[7] The motif of freedom had already been introduced in August, in the asiento between Doria and the Emperor which guaranteed that Genoa would have been 'posta in libertà soa',[8] and on 12 September, by Doria's men taking possession of Genoa to the cry of libertà. More significantly, it featured prominently in Doria's own speech in Piazza Doria, given after chasing out the French, in which the opposing poles of freedom and tyranny stood central, as a number of sources attest[9] (it is worth noting that this latter episode was not represented, as far as is known, in Doria's lifetime, while it was chosen as a subject of artworks in the last decades of the century, as will be discussed further on). Along the same lines, the decree of 7 October that established how to honour Doria (including the commission of an enea statua, a bronze statue)[10] declared him 'father and rescuer of his homeland' ('patrie ipsius et pater et liberator').[11] Doria's disinterested love for republican freedom and his rejection of personal advantages or supreme power were recurrent tropes,[12] which found vast literary echo outside Genoa, too.

The celebrated Italian poet Lodovico Ariosto, in the 1532 edition of his Orlando furioso, published in Ferrara, after the acknowledgement of Doria's role in support of Charles V's achievements, wrote: 'But on his country, not himself, that fee / Shall he bestow, which is his labours' pay; / And beg her freedom, where himself perchance / Another would to

Detail of 4.3
Enea Vico, *Engraved portrait of Andrea Doria.*

4.1

Niccolò della Corte (attributed) after Perino del Vaga's design, *Peace burning arms*. Genoa, Palazzo del Principe, Hall of the Giants' monumental fireplace. Photo: Author. Reproduced with permission of Amministrazione Doria Pamphilj.

sovereign rule advance'.[13] Pietro Aretino, another renowned Italian writer, in a letter written in 1541, argued that posterity would admire Doria's ambition together with his modesty, because, though 'primo nella patria', he preferred 'to show himself as an equal in the assembly of the citizens, rather than to sit as lord of the whole multitude in the civic orders'.[14] These are but a couple of significant examples, among several others.

During Andrea Doria's lifetime

In general terms, the complex topic of the representation of Andrea Doria in the arts – mostly hitherto studied with reference to artworks produced during his lifetime – encompasses a plurality of iconographic models, often classical, among which prevailed the celebratory projection of his image as Neptune, in connection with his position as *generale del mare*, and as victorious ancient Roman *dux*.[15]

During Doria's time, the political events of 1528 were explicitly represented only in the context of the two ephemeral triumphal arches erected the following year to celebrate emperor Charles V's arrival and stay in Genoa; in fact, on that occasion they took centre stage. The arches were designed by Perino del Vaga, and the whole event of the imperial *hospitaggio* was staged following Doria's detailed orders.[16] The scenes are not legible in the surviving drawings, but contemporary sources give an idea of their contents. The chronicle offered by the *Reporto di una persona degna di fede, venuta da Zenoa* ('Report of a Trustworthy Person, who came from Genoa'), inserted in Sanudo's diary, suggests that the arches bore 'several painted scenes and writings, among others one showed how Genoa returned to freedom at the hands of Andrea Doria'.[17] Their decoration therefore included a scene showing how Genoa had regained freedom (*libertas*), and also how Doria had chased all the 'capelazi' – the heads of the old factions – out of the city, a message which illustrated the two capital concepts of freedom and union, crediting the retrieval of both to Andrea. According to Benedetto Varchi, who described it in his *Istoria fiorentina*, the arch installed in the port area 'was full of various and beautiful stories mostly demonstrating the good will of the Genoese'[18], even if Varchi was baffled by this attitude ('as if they had forgotten the 1522 sack of the city, at the hands of the Spaniards').[19] In one of the scenes 'Andrea Doria was depicted, helding in his left hand the city of Genoa, and in his right a naked sword, and the emperor with both hands was

4.2

Christopher Weiditz, *Neptune flanked by the kneeling personifications of Libertas and Pax*, silver medal's reverse (the obverse bears Andrea Doria's bust), Hamburger Kunsthalle. Photo: Scala, Florence.

crowning Genoa'[20], an image which was a veritable visual manifesto of the political situation of the time as seen in a Dorian perspective. No doubt, in this case, the message was loud and clear, with Andrea Doria cast in the role of defender of the city and the new imperial connection celebrated; while in permanent artworks like frescoes and paintings, references to Doria's political role, when existing, were subtle and indirect.

A quite cryptic reference to the two poles of republican *Libertas* and allegiance to the Habsburg empire might be conveyed by the oil portrait of Andrea Doria as an old man with a cat (sometimes associated with the idea of freedom) and a golden clock (frequently used as symbol of the intricate harmony of the imperial system), according to Ines Aliverti's interpretation. However, other readings have also been proposed for this picture, whose early material history is unknown, though it is very unlikely that it was commissioned by Andrea Doria.[21]

In the most important of Doria's own artistic commissions, the vast fresco and stucco cycle executed between 1529 and 1533 by Perino del Vaga in the Palazzo del Principe, Doria's palace in the suburb of Fassolo – an outstanding masterwork and a crucial milestone of Genoese Cinquecento art –, there is no direct reference to contemporary events of any kind. Classical subjects, both mythological and taken from Roman history, mediate celebratory allusions to the patron, which are mostly connected to the generic idea of his heroic virtue and to his dominion of the sea (as attested by the depiction of Neptune in the illustration of the Virgilian *Quos Ego* in the east hall).[22] As I have argued elsewhere,[23] Doria's role as rescuer of the Genoese state may have been indirectly evoked by the iconographic programme of the atrium's frescoed lunettes and – more specifically – by the planned decoration for the north façade, never carried out but attested to by Perino's preparatory drawings, with inscriptions. While Romulus and the foundation of Rome are represented in detail in the lunettes (circa 1530), Furius Camillus – in Livy's words, a new Romulus, a second founder of Rome, 'Romulus ac parens patriae conditorque alter Urbis'[24]

– is the protagonist of the façade design. This is the first known project for a biographical cycle dedicated to this hero and the only one in Renaissance art in which *rifondar Roma per Chamillo* and *rifondare Roma la seconda volta* (the subject described in the captions to the last scene) play such an essential part, recalling the rebuilding and refounding of the city described by Livy, who at the beginning of the second pentad of his *Ab urbe condita* describes Rome, after Camillus saved it, as a city reborn, preparing to recount its history 'from its second origin' ('ab secunda origine').[25]

It is significant that the façade programme focused on two main themes: Camillus's confrontation with the Gauls, including the weighing of the gold interrupted by the hero and his subsequent triumph, and the saving and second foundation of Rome, both clearly resonating with the events of 1528, when Andrea Doria, according to the accepted narrative, set Genoa free from the French yoke and commenced the *renovatio* of the Genoese state.[26] This visual narrative is reinforced by the positioning of a bust of Augustus – also celebrated as founder of a new Rome and initiator of a golden age – in the palace above the Hall of the Giants' entrance, which has been convincingly considered as part of a wider Augustan inspiration in Doria's strategy of images.[27] The monumental fireplace in this same hall is also significant: it bears a tondo with marble bas-reliefs illustrating the foundation of civilization thanks to Prometheus' mythical gift of fire to mankind, while the two statues flanking its overmantel evoke Concord by presenting the iconography of Peace burnings arms (fig. 4.1: an allegory also depicted in the Loggia degli Eroi's stuccoes), symbolically referencing the union brought to Genoa by Andrea[28]. Medals also offer references to freedom and concord/peace as key components of Andrea's public image. A 1533 silver medal depicting the admiral has been recognised as the work of Christopher Weiditz (fig. 4.2), a German artist who spent time in Charles V's entourage between

4.3

Enea Vico, *Engraved portraits of Andrea Doria*. From Lorenzo Capelloni, *Vita del prencipe Andrea Doria discritta da m. Lorenzo Capelloni con un compendio della medesima vita, e con due tauole; l'una delle cose più generali, & l'altra delle cose più notabili. Vinegia, Appresso Gabriel Giolito de' Ferrari, 1565.* LWL-Museum für Kunst und Kultur, Westfälisches Landesmuseum, Münster. Reproduced with permission.

1529 and 1532 (possibly accompanying him on his 1529 journey from Barcelona to Genoa on Doria's galleys) and produced medals for the emperor as well as other high-ranking patrons of his circle.[29] The obverse bears a bust of Doria based on a Nuremberg engraving, while the reverse presents an effigy of Neptune as mythic projection of the admiral, flanked by the kneeling personifications of Libertas, offering him a Frygian cap, and Pax presenting an olive branch, with the inscription 'PATRIAE LIBERATORI'. One of the medals produced by Leone Leoni at the beginning of 1541 in gratitude to Doria – who had freed him from serving his sentence on a galley and whose bust is displayed on the obverse – bears on the reverse a personification of Libertas publica: in the words of the nineteenth century scholar that published it, this image celebrated 'the most illustrious of all his deeds,' – even compared to his glorious naval feats – 'the gift of freedom to his homeland'.[30]

In the second half of the sixteenth century

After the instant manifesto provided by the 1529 ephemeral arches, a direct representation of the 1528 seminal events seems to be found only after Andrea Doria's death (1560), in the frame of an intensely political use of his myth. Testimonies include a lost silver relief, a preparatory drawing and a fresco – centred on the representation of Andrea's speech after he liberated Genoa, and his rejection of supreme personal power – dated to the last decades of the sixteenth century, as well as a much later reprise of the theme in allegorical form in the 1760s. These artworks pose a series of challenging questions. It is often not clear by whom and exactly when they were commissioned, and how they might be interconnected. Giovanni Andrea Doria, the admiral's heir, certainly played an important part in the fortune of this and other related themes. His first relevant initiatives were linked to the publication of Andrea Doria's biography, after his death on 25 November, 1560. While he lived, the admiral – allegedly out of contempt for earthly fame – 'never gave anything to the poets, for them to sing his praises; neither did he consent to give historians – by many of whom he was asked – the commentaries to his feats'.[31] Andrea Doria's first *Vita*, written by Lorenzo Capelloni and published in 1562 by Giolito in Venice, was dedicated to Giovanni Andrea, whom the author described as heir not only of the deceased's material possessions, but also of his 'pensieri dell'animo', as well as a future 'imitatore delle vestigia sue', thus celebrating him as continuing the admiral's moral and political legacy.[32] Giovanni Andrea presumably sponsored this work (which enjoyed significant success, and was republished with a partly different title in 1565 and later on), as well as being its dedicatee.[33] Almost a quarter century later, he commissioned the Latin biography by Carlo Sigonio, *De vita et rebus gestis Andreae Auriae*, published posthumously in Genoa in 1586 by Giuseppe Bartoli, and also, after another twelve years, the Italian translation of this work by Pompeo Arnolfini, published in Genoa as well, in this case by Pavoni, in 1598.[34] Capelloni's biography is opened by two engraved bust portraits of Andrea Doria, facing each other (an infrequent occurrence, due to the complications and costs implied)[35] (fig. 4.3). The two effigies – designed by renowned engraver Enea Vico[36] and indebted to well-attested, separate iconographic typologies – are set in oval frames bearing an explanatory caption, inside an identical decorative structure containing different coats of arms, emblems and allegorical personifications.[37] The first portrait shows Andrea Doria in contemporary clothes, as citizen, father of his homeland and restorer of its freedom ('UT CIVIS PATER PATRIAE ET LIBERTATIS RESTITVTOR', the caption reads); the second shows him in classical attire, loricate and laureate, as general and prince victorious in battle ('VT DVX ET PRINCEPS PRELIORVM VICTOR'). This double image is consistent with the *Vita*'s insistence on the dual character of Andrea's public persona. It is in fact the first aspect – that of loyal citizen of a Republic – which is given the task of distinguishing Doria from all the other *condottieri*. To the usual heroic virtues, to the description of military feats which constitutes a large part of the narrative fabric of his work, Capelloni, in the context of the 'Suetonian-Plutarchan model' he adopted as a paradigm, adds as a characterising element – as Cochrane observes – the quality of 'moderation in the face of opportunities for self-aggrandisement'.[38] The *topos* of Andrea Doria rejecting the *signoria* of Genoa because he is a good citizen and considers the Republic's freedom more important than personal power is central in this text. Capelloni had already presented this tenet of the myth in his oration in praise of Doria in 1550.[39] In a more

4.4
Anonymous, *Andrea Doria handing over power to Giovanni Andrea Doria (Triumph of Andrea Doria)*. Genoa, Palazzo del Principe, late 16th century. Reproduced with permission of Amministrazione Doria Pamphilj.

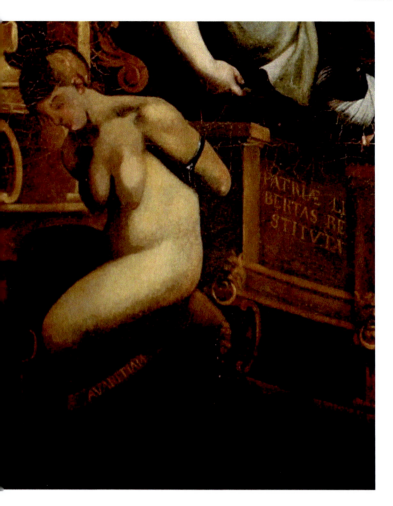

4.5
Detail of 4.4.

Giovanni Andrea (fig. 4.4) – probably commissioned by the latter many years after the admiral's death, in the last two decades of the sixteenth century, and destined to hang in the Doria palace in the fiefdom of Melfi, where it is registered in the earliest known inventory mentioning it[43] – the highlights of the great admiral's career are illustrated in both inscriptions and images, interwoven in a way reminiscent of the features of celebratory ephemeral art. *Libertas*, together with the ongoing fight against the Turks, is one of the main themes. The introductory inscription at the top of the picture defines Andrea Doria as 'the great Andrea Doria, a second Neptune, archenemy of pirates, father and liberator of his homeland'.[44] The flank of the allegorical ship where the scene takes place bears the words 'freedom restored to the homeland',[45] and the long *Explicatio Triumphi* in the cartouche in the bottom-left corner asserts that the admiral 'leads Avarice and Greed – by which he could never be led astray, so that he would subjugate his homeland – shackled in chains',[46] referencing the personification of chained *Avaritia* depicted close to the inscription devoted to the restoration of freedom (fig. 4.5).

For his main residence, the Palazzo del Principe which he had inherited from Andrea and greatly extended, Giovanni Andrea Doria commissioned a series of works depicting his illustrious ancestors, most notably his great predecessor. The principal stage for this celebratory representation was the new Galleria Aurea, which, starting around 1597, was ornamented with a rich decoration comprising Marcello Sparzo's *all'antica* stucco statues of the most glorious members of the Doria house since its origin (with Andrea trampling a Turk's head under his foot), while the central *quadri* should have been frescoed with images of their feats, especially those of Andrea ('The feats of the illustrious men of his house, and particularly those of his predecessor').[47] But, in his quest for the highest artistic quality, Giovanni Andrea was not able to allocate the work before his death, and the iconographic programme was later changed.[48] No further details are available about which episodes were meant to be illustrated. Previously, Giovanni Andrea had chosen precious silver objects, of which he had an exceptional collection – on a par with those of contemporary sovereigns – as means to convey the same kind of message. Specifically, a much admired *buffetto* – a small table – covered by silver plaquettes with bas-reliefs designed by renowned painter Bernardo Castello and executed by silversmith Arrigo Fiammingo, was 'historiated

articulated way he insists on this concept in his biography, in which he recounts that, once Doria had received the proposal from the Emperor 'to make him Lord of Genoa, under imperial protection', he refused this role 'because he never wanted to be Lord of his homeland, on the contrary, setting it free was close to his heart above all other things'.[40] The narrative also focuses on Andrea Doria's speech in Piazza Doria after liberating Genoa, during which, according to Capelloni, he asked only that the Genoese, in return for the liberty they had received from him, undertake to act so as to preserve it in the future.[41]

In Sigonio's Latin biography (1586), later translated into Italian by Pompeo Arnolfini, similar points are made. The author celebrates Andrea Doria's decision to live as a private citizen, but a significant shift in the narrative concerns the nature of the offer Doria virtuously rejects: not the role of 'signore' or prince offered by the Emperor, as in Capelloni's biography, but that of doge for life – *Dux perpetuus, Duce perpetuo* in Arnolfini's translation – proposed by the Genoese people ('as many proposed that he were doge in perpetuity').[42]

These are the motifs that recur in works produced under Giovanni Andrea Doria's artistic patronage. In a painting depicting the passage of power from an old Andrea to a young

4.6
Bernardo Castello, *Andrea Doria's speech on September 12th, 1528*.
Florence, Gallerie degli Uffizi, c. 1590s. Gabinetto Disegni e Stampe,
Inv. GDSU n. 2592 s. Reproduced with permission from the Italian
Ministry of Culture – Le Gallerie degli Uffizi.

with the feats of His Excellency Andrea Doria, of good memory' (while a twin one, by the same artists, bore scenes illustrating the Labours of Hercules).[49] It was to be delivered in October 1592, according to the contract, presumably as one of the new prestigious objects and pieces of furniture acquired on the occasion of the nuptial union of Giovanni Andrea's first son with Giovanna Colonna.[50] Both tables are recorded in the inventory of Giovanni Andrea's possessions, drawn up after his death;[51] they were part of the array of exceptionally expensive furnishings that characterised the residence and greatly impressed Joseph Fürttenbach, John Evelyn and other seventeenth-century visitors to the palace, who admiringly mentioned silver tables and beds.[52] Two drawings of a narrow rectangular format by Bernardo Castello in the Uffizi's Gabinetto Disegni e Stampe, representing Hercules's seventh and eighth labours, have been related by Mary Newcome to the silver reliefs on the Palazzo del Principe's *buffetto* cited above.[53] Another drawing in the Gabinetto (fig. 4.6), also attributed to Castello and dated to the 1590s by Newcome, has been considered by the author as possibly being a preparatory drawing for the decoration of a silver parade plate (it has an oval format, with the contour lines perforated for transfer), and the scene depicted has been interpreted as the proclamation of the 1548 *Leggi del Garibetto*.[54] In fact, it certainly represents Andrea Doria's speech to the Genoese in September 1528 and his rejection of the *signoria*. I argue that it could be a preparatory drawing for one of the silver plaquettes ornamenting the second *buffetto* commissioned by Giovanni Andrea, decorated with the depiction of his predecessor's feats, as the format and the measures of the scene, as well as the subject, are consistent with such a function.[55] The table is lost, and so are its plaquettes, therefore a direct comparison is impossible. In the 1760s the *buffetto* was probably brought to Rome, together with other important silver pieces, when the princes of Melfi came to be recognised as heirs to the Pamphilj fortune and established

4.7
Lazzaro Tavarone, *Andrea Doria's speech on September 12th, 1528*. Genoa, Museo di Sant'Agostino. Photo: Comune di Genova, DocSAI – Archivio Fotografico. Reproduced with permission.

Palazzo Doria Pamphilj in via del Corso as their main residence.[56] It is worth noting that in the Roman palace's private apartments the Marquis De Sade saw a couple of silver tables (which some years later, in 1790, Pietro De Lama would describe as representing 'Andrea Doria's feats'),[57] in relation to which he mentioned the theme of Doria's rejection of sovereign power over his homeland: 'there are two silver tables supported by two eagles and decorated with bas-reliefs. This present was given to the family by the Republic of Genoa. We know the story of Andrea Doria who refused to be the sovereign of his homeland'.[58]

If the drawing's connection to Giovanni Andrea's *buffetto* remains likely but unproven, the iconography of the scene depicted is certain and very clear. Andrea, depicted as an ancient Roman *dux* – following the model of the influential celebratory statue by Montorsoli – and with his arm raised in the *adlocutio* gesture, is portrayed while haranguing a crowd of Genoese citizens in the Piazza Doria, as he did on 12 September 1528. The lower part of the thirteenth-century façade of the Doria church facing the square, San Matteo, is recognisably represented as the scene's backdrop, with its striped façade, the lunette bearing the figure of the titular saint, and the coats of arms of both the Doria family and the Republic on the portal jambs. The citizens surround the admiral. They are engaged in lively conversations, favourably commenting on his speech. As previously indicated, contemporary sources report that the speech was constructed on the two crucial concepts of union and freedom ('unione d'animi' and 'intiera e amplissima libertà', in Jacopo Bonfadio's words).[59] Agostino Giustiniani, quoting the same two central tenets, observed that the ideas of freedom and of living in a free Republic proposed by Andrea Doria in his oration were favourably received ('piacque a molti').[60] The words written on the drawing (PATRIAE DOMINIUM A CIVIB[US] OBLATUM / RESPUIT EAMQ[UE] LIBERTATE DONAT)– previously mistakenly interpreted as one of the inscriptions engraved on the church's medieval façade, celebrating the family's military victories[61] – provide a sort of caption clarifying how the episode is to be read. Beyond the generic theme of freedom, it is, more precisely, the rejection of a supreme power offered by the citizens themselves, as suggested in the *Vita* written by Sigonio and translated by Arnolfini, that is here proposed as the key element associated with the scene: 'he rejects dominion over his homeland, offered by the citizens, and presents the homeland with freedom'. Compared with the biography's text, which attributes the proposal to 'many people', the inscription is more precise in indicating that the *dominium* over the Republic was offered to Doria by Genoa's citizens, directly connecting the offer and its rejection to the admiral's speech in the Piazza Doria. Moreover, Pompeo Arnolfini – a renowned man of letters, native of Lucca, who was secretary to Giovanni Andrea Doria from at least 1578 to 1598, when he died – played a crucial role in curating the posthumous publication of Sigonio's biography of Andrea and then provided its Italian translation. Enjoying a close association to Doria and a reputation as an *intendente* of the fine arts, he is the obvious candidate for the role of iconographer for the cycles of frescoes and tapestries that Giovanni Andrea commissioned.[62] If this drawing is related to the latter's patronage, Pompeo Arnolfini may well have played a part in the definition of its iconography and in the choice of the inscription, too.

The same scene represented in the drawing also appears, with some variations (Andrea's gesture, the addition of a boy bearing his helm, differences in the figures of the citizens listening to the admiral's speech), in a fresco attributed to Lazzaro Tavarone (fig. 4.7), which has always been recognised as a depiction of the September 1528 speech.[63] The more defined image of the church in the background allows a glimpse of the interior through the open door, revealing the high altar with Montorsoli's statues of kneeling angels, later transferred to

4.8
Castellino Castello (attributed), *Andrea Doria*. From *Genealogy of the Doria family*, Rome, Archivio Doria Pamphilj, Banc. 79.39. Photo: Archivio Doria Pamphilj. Reproduced with permission.

4.9
Castellino Castello (attributed), *Giovanni Andrea Doria*. From *Genealogy of the Doria family*, Rome, Archivio Doria Pamphilj, Banc. 79.39. Photo: Archivio Doria Pamphilj. Reproduced with permission.

a different location.[64] This is the most monumental work of art illustrating the theme.[65] On stylistic grounds, it has been dated to circa 1575[66] or to the 1590s,[67] a period that is persuasively closer to the date proposed for the drawing (the similarities point to the likely dependence of one work's composition on the other's, though they are by different artists). Unfortunately, the first phases of the fresco's material history are unknown. It decorated a ceiling in a Strixioli residence in the Carignano area, close to the Mura di Santa Chiara, belonging to the Fidecommissaria established by Giacomo Filippo Strixioli and involved in the urbanistic changes connected to the opening of the street later called Via Alessi, deliberated in 1850.[68] In the context of the efforts made by the Accademia Ligustica to safeguard frescoes from churches and palaces destined to be demolished, Matteo della Rocca wrote about the fresco to the Accademia's president, Nicolò Crosa di Vergagni, in 1850.[69] Before the *casa* Strixioli was destroyed, the fresco was 'accurately detached' and transferred to Palazzo Tursi in Strada Nuova, where it was displayed along the grand staircase, together with frescoes salvaged from other monuments.[70] It was then moved to the town hall of the formerly independent neighbourhood of San Fruttuoso, and then, in 1940, to Palazzo Ducale, from which it was transferred to the storage rooms of Museo di Sant'Agostino, where it is still kept.[71] The palace where the fresco was originally located was not connected to the properties of Giovanni Andrea Doria,[72] which implies that a different patron commissioned the fresco. There were several other branches of the Doria family, and it has been suggested – though no archival evidence has been cited – that the Strixioli palace in Carignano might have formerly belonged to a Doria.[73] In any case, the fresco attests that the theme of Andrea's speech, with its focus on concord and freedom, was considered important beyond the limits of his successor's image strategy.

The pattern that led Giovanni Andrea Doria to emphasise the image of Andrea guaranteeing Genoa's *unione* and *libertà*, acting as an exemplary citizen of his Republic and forsaking the offer of *dominium* offered to him, can be linked to Giovanni Andrea's long-lasting efforts to build and sustain his own public role in the city. The transmission of the 'immaterial inheritance' from Andrea to his designated successor – the reconstruction of a political prominence rooted in the role of 'interface' between the Hispanic-Hapsburg system and the Genoese oligarchy – was slow, difficult, and encountered opposition.[74] In pursuing this goal, only partially achieved, the myth of the great admiral was frequently evoked, and Giovanni Andrea was celebrated as the one who preserved the concord and freedom procured by his predecessor. In 1601, at the end of his career as *Generalissimo* of the sea, a decree[75] was issued to honour him by granting him the official appellation of 'Patriae libertatis conservator'.[76] (in the same way – it is explicitly stated in the document – his predecessor, 'the old Prince', had rightly been called 'Patriae pater'), for having worked incessantly 'for the good of the Republic and for the conservation of our Freedom',[77] and by erecting a celebratory marble statue (next to the one depicting Andrea). The same concept was expressed in the inscription associated with Giovanni Andrea's frescoed portrait in the Palazzo Doria Spinola De Fornari in San Domenico, in which it was stated

4.10

Domenico Corvi, *Andra Doria refusing the signoria of Genoa*, modello for a ceiling painting in Palazzo Doria Pamphilj in Rome. Minneapolis, Minneapolis Institute of Art, after 1768. Photo: Public Domain.

that 'Little would the homeland have profited from the freedom restored by Andrea, had he not been succeeded by him (Giovanni Andrea), through whose virtue the Republic flourishes more and more every day'.[78]

A genealogical manuscript in the Archivio Doria Pamphilj in Rome offers further testimony of how the construction of Giovanni Andrea's persona was largely grounded on this aspect of Andrea's myth.[79] In the short synopsis of Andrea's *vita* – titled *De magno Andrea de Oria Patriae Liberatore* – the harmony and 'union of souls' of all citizens he propitiated are emphatically mentioned, as well as the fact that 'while he could have claimed sovereign power and the sceptre of his homeland, he disdained royal pomp and the name of tyrant'.[80] Giovanni Andrea Doria, who is presented as heir to Andrea's titles and virtues, is rhetorically compared to the gods that have power on the sea, and then defined 'tamer of tempests on the sea, queller of seditions on the land, restorer of the vacillating freedom of the homeland'.[81] In the series of ink drawings portraying the most illustrious members of the Doria family that decorate the manuscript (fig. 4.8–4.9: tentatively attributed to Castellino Castello, particularly active for the Doria family in the second decade of the seventeenth century),[82] Giovanni Andrea is represented as peacekeeper. His image is accompanied by a cartouche with inscribed the words 'SEDITIONUM SEDATOR', 'sedator of seditions' (while Andrea's effigy bears the caption 'ANDREAS PATRIAE LIBERATOR ET PATER'): a definition that chooses to underline Giovanni Andrea's role in Genoese politics, presenting him as a new Andrea, still a defender of the state from internal threats and uprisings, especially for what he did in the 1575–1576 conflict between 'old' and 'new' nobles,[83] the 'last civil war' in Genoa[84]. It is therefore clear why Giovanni Andrea was involved in a series of commissions that explicitly celebrated those aspects of Andrea's political myth that the admiral himself, as far as is known, never had directly illustrated by the visual arts during his lifetime, except in the ephemeral 1529 arches for Charles V's entrée into Genoa.

In absence of more precise information on the commission of the Carignano fresco depicting Andrea Doria's speech, it is hard to contextualise it correctly and fully appreciate the message it conveyed. But the choice of the subject makes clear that the concepts associated with Doria's September 1528 speech – concord and freedom – and the myth of Andrea Doria as exemplary citizen and defender of the Republic had

4.11

Paolo Gerolamo Brusco, *The landing of Andrea Doria*. Genoa, Palazzo Doria De Ferrari, c. 1780. Photo: Genoa, Banco BPM. Reproduced with the permission of Explora S.p.A.

4.12

Paolo Gerolamo Brusco, *Andrea Doria's speech on September 12th, 1528*. Genoa, Palazzo Doria De Ferrari, c. 1780. Photo: Genoa, Banco BPM. Reproduced with the permission of Explora S.p.A.

relevance, in the last decades of the sixteenth century, also beyond the personal and dynastic projections of Giovanni Andrea, appropriating this narrative to strengthen his own image. The political discourse that formed the basis of the 1528 reforms (as well as the root of the Dorian myth's construction) and the related interpretation of that year's events remained a tool in the arena of political confrontation throughout the sixteenth century, and beyond.[85] Though it is not certain that the palace where the fresco was originally located belonged to a branch of the Doria family, the choice of this subject would arguably be linked to members of the old nobility, the *nobili vecchi*, in the context of the tensions still persisting after the resolution of the civil conflict through the 1576 *Leggi di Casale*. This conflict largely turned into a social one, with art and especially fresco decoration seen as a powerful means to stake competing family claims and exhibit political allegiances.[86]

The persistence of the theme

The theme of Andrea Doria refusing the *signoria* of Genoa offered to him would enjoy a long run in Doria patronage, being singled out as the most significant image, the epitome of his greatness by his descendants, who perceived this as the acme of their family's glory. Significantly, after the Doria di Melfi moved to Rome, having inherited the Pamphiljs' palaces and possessions (1763),[87] Prince Andrea IV chose to impress his own seal on the Pamphilian palace in Via del Corso by commissioning for a hall's ceiling a scene described in a document as 'the entrance of Andrea Doria in Genoa, when the Most Serene Republic presents crown and sceptre to him, and he, refusing them, gives her back her freedom'.[88] In fact, the large sketch by Domenico Corvi for the lost painting (fig. 4.10) shows a different illustration of the same concept: an allegory staged on a ship, in which a Roman general (probably Pompey, to whom Andrea Doria had often been compared)[89] offers Doria a sceptre, which he rejects with a gesture of his left hand. At the same time Doria, with his right hand, places a golden crown on the head of a kneeling female figure with a turreted crown, the personification of the Republic to which he thus restores sovereign power and freedom.[90] Under the sceptre it is possible to glimpse the end of the huge keys to the city, a further symbol of the signoria offered to Doria.

The use of an allegorical language and the depiction of crown, sceptre and city keys was unprecedented for the representation of this theme; at least partially, the choice must have been determined by the work's collocation in a Roman context which was necessarily less familiar with Andrea's biography and the significance of his 1528 speech, thus needing more universally understandable symbols. In Genoa, some years later (circa 1780) another Doria, Ambrogio 'fu Carlo', belonging to a different branch of the family (who descended from Lamba, defeater of the Venetians in 1298), chose to celebrate the feats of some of the most illustrious members of his noble lineage in a room of the palace 'in contrada San Domenico', close to the church of San Matteo, that he had inherited and enlarged.[91] He commissioned to Antonio Giolfi the depiction of the most significant deeds of Ansaldo and Pagano Doria, leading figures of the twelfth and fourteenth centuries, in the vault fresco. Two episodes of Andrea's life were represented in large canvases, convincingly attributed to Paolo Gerolamo Brusco,[92] both focusing on the 1528 events. One of them illustrates the rare subject of Andrea and his soldiers landing in the Malapaga area (here anachronistically alluded to through the depiction of the majestic Porta del Molo, designed almost a quarter century later by Galeazzo Alessi), to liberate Genoa (fig. 4.11). Contrariwise to the descriptions in sixteenth-century sources, the detail of the city keys offered to Andrea is added on the left side of the scene. The other painting shows Andrea's speech in front of the church of San Matteo after the city's liberation (fig. 4.12). In line with Brusco's approach, this composition echoes sixteenth-century models, often paying an evident stylistic homage to the earlier Genoese painting, by displaying a mimetic virtuosity.[93] It eschews the allegorization of events selected for the Doria Pamphilj's Roman palace's decoration, reverting to the iconography of the admiral's oration familiar to the Genoese, as shown in Tavarone's fresco. The centrality of the concept of freedom is here underlined by the presence of the flag bearing the motto 'LIBERTAS' (which had also been inscribed in the Republic's coat of arms). This painting clearly belongs in the tradition of artistic patronage through which the Doria family's branches continued to celebrate the unique role of their house's most illustrious member.

1 Pacini, 'Ideali repubblicani', pp. 189–236 (p. 222 for the reference to the 1528 laws as the first act in the building of Doria's political myth). See also Pacini, *I presupposti politici*.

2 Preamble of the October 1528 laws, ASG, *Manoscritti tornati da Parigi*, ms 8, cc. 1–3, quoted in Pacini, 'Ideali repubblicani', p. 222.

3 'Discord, division and abominable factiosity'.

4 BCBG, m.r. I.4.9. In the *Libro 1641* citizens of the popular part subscribe an oath to support the overcoming of factions and internal divisions (Pacini, *I presupposti politici*, pp. 151–52; Pacini, 'Ideali repubblicani', pp. 216–18). Not all historians agree on Pacini's interpretation of the text as a key passage in the process leading to the 1528 reforms (see Grendi, 'Le Società dei Giovani a Genova', pp. 518 and 527, note 27.

5 Pacini, 'Ideali repubblicani', pp. 216–19.

6 Grendi, 'Doria, Andrea'.

7 Pacini, 'Ideali repubblicani', pp. 222–23.

8 'Set free'. Pacini, *La Genova di Andrea Doria*, p. 21.

9 Pacini, 'Ideali repubblicani', pp. 220–21.

10 On the commission of a marble – not bronze – statue to Baccio Bandinelli, the related drawings and the subsequent vicissitudes (at the end of which the commission was transferred to Montorsoli, who in 1539 executed a colossal statue representing Andrea Doria as an ancient Roman general) see Boccardo, *Andrea Doria e le arti*, pp. 111–15; Gorse, 'Body Politics and Mythic Figures', pp. 15–19; Boccardo, 'Michelangelo e Genova', pp. 108–17.

11 Alizeri, *Notizie dei professori*, V, pp. 312–13 (recently republished in Waldman, *Baccio Bandinelli*, p. 99, doc. 182).

12 Pacini, 'Ideali repubblicani', p. 223.

13 Ariosto, *Orlando furioso*, XV, 30–33 ('Veggio che il premio che di ciò riporta / Non tien per sé, ma fa a la patria darlo; / con prieghi ottien ch'in libertà la metta, / dove altri a sé l'avria forse suggetta', in the translation by Rose, *The Orlando Furioso*, I, p. 263).

14 Aretino, *Al Sacratissimo Re d'Inghilterra*, p. 390 ('mostrarsi uguale nel collegio de i suoi cittadini, che seder duce di tutta la moltitudine ne gli ordini civili').

15 The iconographies of works of art related to Andrea Doria have been the object of several studies, including works by Parma (Parma, 'Il palazzo del Principe'; Parma, *Perin del Vaga*); Boccardo (Boccardo, *Andrea Doria e le arti*); Gorse (Gorse, 'Entrate e trionfi'; Gorse, 'La "corte" di Andrea Doria a Genova'; Gorse, 'Body Politics and Mythic Figures'); Stagno (Stagno,

'Triumphing over the Enemy'; Stagno, 'Roman History Themes'). On the interpretation of the images conveyed by Andrea Doria's portraits by Sebastiano del Piombo and Bronzino, see Boccardo, *Andrea Doria e le arti*, pp. 108–09; Leoncini, 'Deduzioni iconografiche'; Costamagna, 'Entre Raphaël, Titien et Michel-Ange'; Brock, 'Le portrait d'Andrea Doria'; Cieri Via, 'L'immagine del potere'; Gorse, 'Augustan Mediterranean'; Gorse, 'Body Politics and Mythic Figures'; Caruso, 'History in a Painting'; Eliav, 'Trident and Oar'.

16 Stagno, 'Sovrani spagnoli a Genova'. See also Valentina Borniotto's essay in this volume, with extensive bibliography.

17 'Varie storie depente e scritture, tra le altre una dimostrava come Zenoa ritornava in libertà per mano di messer Andrea Doria'. Sanuto, I Diarii, col. 399.

18 'Era pieno di varie e vaghe storie dimostranti per lo più il buon animo de' Genovesi'. Varchi, *Istoria fiorentina*, p. 17.

19 'Quasi avessono posto in oblio l'ultima presura di Genova, e il sacco datole dagli Spagnoli'. Varchi, *Istoria fiorentina*, p. 17.

20 'Era figurato Andrea d'Oria, il quale colla sinistra mano reggeva la città di Genova, e nella destra teneva una spada ignuda arrancata, e l'imperadore con ambe le mani incoronava Genova'. Varchi, *Istoria fiorentina*, p. 17.

21 See Aliverti. Other readings include the interpretation of the cat as symbol of the Fieschi, who had instigated a failed *coup* in 1547 against the Dorian system of power, and whose coat of arms included a cat with the motto *Sedens ago* (Federici, *Della famiglia Fiesca*, p. 20).

22 On the palace and its frescoes, see: Merli and Belgrano, 'Il palazzo del Principe d'Oria' (based on archival documents which are now partly lost); Askew, 'Perino del Vaga's Decorations'; Davidson, 'Drawings by Perino del Vaga'; Parma, 'Il palazzo del Principe'; Gorse, *The villa Doria*; Parma, *Perin del Vaga*; Magnani, *Il tempio di Venere*, pp. 27–46, 115–24; Boccardo, *Andrea Doria e le arti*; Gorse, 'Entrate e trionfi'; Stagno, *Il Palazzo del Principe*; Parma, ed., *Perino del Vaga* (2001); Parma, ed., *Perino del Vaga* (2004); Stagno and Di Marco Baffi, eds, *Il Palazzo del Principe*; Pierguidi, 'Perin del Vaga versus Pordenone'; Altavista, *La residenza di Andrea Doria a Fassolo*; Ginzburg, 'Perino del Vaga e la generazione di Salviati'; Stagno, 'Roman History Themes'.

23 Stagno, 'Roman History Themes'.

24 Livy, *Ab urbe condita*, V, 49; Plutarch, *Camillus*, 31–32.

25 Livy, *Ab urbe condita*, VI, 1.

26 Stagno, 'Roman History Themes', p. 237.

27 For the relevance of Augustus's image in Doria's celebratory programmes, see Gorse, 'La "corte" di Andrea Doria'.

28 On this, see Stagno, 'Prometheus in Palazzo del Principe'.

29 Grotemeyer, 'Eine Medaille des Andrea Doria'; Boccardo, *Andrea Doria e le arti*, p. 110.

30 Olivieri, *Monete, medaglie e sigilli dei principi Doria*, p. 28.

31 'Non diede mai cosa alcuna a i Poeti, acciò fossero celebrate da loro le sue lodi, nemmeno volse dare a gli Historici (da quali fu ricercato molte volte) i commentarij delle sue attioni'. Sigonio, Arnolfini, *Della vita et fatti di Andrea Doria*, p. 340.

32 'The thoughts of his soul', 'imitator of his traces'. Capelloni, *La vita, e gesti di Andrea D'Oria*, dedication to l'*Illustrissimo Signore, il Signor Gio. Andrea Doria*.

33 Capelloni's biography of Andrea was republished in 1565 by Giolito with the title *Vita del prencipe Andrea Doria*.

34 Sigonio, Arnolfini, *De vita et rebus gestis Andreae Auriae*; Sigonio, *Della vita et fatti di Andrea Doria*.

35 Zappella, *Il ritratto librario nel libro italiano del Cinquecento*, p. 130.

36 Bongi, *Annali di Gabriel Giolito de' Ferrari*, p. L, note 2; Andreoli, 'Andrea Doria fra le righe'.

37 For a more detailed description, see Stagno, 'Lorenzo Capelloni'.

38 Cochrane, *Historians and Historiography in the Italian Renaissance*, p. 407.

39 Capelloni praises Doria's rare and virtuous behaviour, 'non sapendosi che, se non di pochissimi, alcuno liberasse la Patria sua, che havesse commodità di poterne usurpar il Principato, come voi havevate di Genova' ('as it is not known, except for a very few, that anyone would free his homeland, who had the opportunity to usurp the role of prince, as you had in Genoa'). Capelloni, *Al vittorioso principe D'Oria*, reprinted in Sansovino, *Delle orationi*, pp. 224–27.

40 Capelloni, *La vita, e gesti di Andrea D'Oria*, p. 39. After receiving from the Emperor the offer 'di farlo Signore di Genova, sotto la Cesarea protettione', he refused this role 'perché mai

40 volle sentire di voler essere Signore della Patria sua, anzi il porla in libertà sopra tutte le altre cose gli era a cuore'.

41 Capelloni, *La vita, e gesti di Andrea D'Oria*, p. 41. It is worth noting that the rejection of the *signoria* is not directly associated with Andrea Doria's speech in Capelloni's biography.

42 'Proponendo molti che fosse creato duce perpetuo'. Sigonio, *De vita et rebus gestis Andreae Auriae*, c. 41v; Sigonio, Arnolfini, *Della vita et fatti di Andrea Doria*, p. 123.

43 Stagno, 'Triumphing over the enemy', pp. 158–60.

44 'MAGNVS ANDREAS DORIA ALTER NEPTVNVS PIRATARVM ACERRIMVS HOSTIS PATER ET LIBERATOR PATRIAE'.

45 'PATRIAE LIBERTAS RESTITUTA'.

46 'AVARITIAM ATQVE CVPIDITATEM CATENIS VINCTAS DVCIT A QVIBVS ABDVCI VNQVAM POTVIT, VT SVAM PATRIAM SVBIUGARET'.

47 'Le gesta degli uomini illustri del proprio casato, e quelle in ispecie del suo predecessore'. Stagno, *Giovanni Andrea Doria*, p. 227.

48 Stagno, *Giovanni Andrea Doria*, pp. 242–60.

49 'Istoriato con li fatti dell'Eccell. Signor Andrea Doria di felice memoria'. Alizeri, *Notizie dei professori*, VI, pp. 371–72; Boggero and Simonetti, *L'argenteria Genovese del Settecento*, pp. 70–71.

50 Stagno, *Giovanni Andrea Doria*, p. 268.

51 Stagno, *Giovanni Andrea Doria*, p. 334.

52 Fürttenbach, *Newes Itinerarium Italiae*, p. 215; Du Val, *Le voyage et la description d'Italie*; Evelyn, *The Diary of John Evelyn*, p. 131.

53 Newcome, *Disegni genovesi*, nn. 13695 F, 13696 F, catalogue entry 12, pp. 38–39; Boggero and Simonetti, *L'argenteria Genovese del Settecento*, fig. 29.

54 Newcome, *Disegni genovesi*, n. 2592S6 S, catalogue entry 14, pp. 41–42. The author suggests that the drawing may be preparatory either for a silver plate or a book illustration.

55 For a first suggestion of this possible connection, see Stagno, 'Da Genova a Roma', pp. 199–200. Of the five silver plaquettes for the 1629 Spinola *buffetto*, the closest surviving example of this kind of artefact, two have comparable measures; four are rectangular and one is oval (on the Spinola plaquettes, now in Amsterdam's Rijksmuseum, see Boggero and Simonetti, *L'argenteria Genovese del Settecento*, pp. 117–8, 236–7; Boggero, 'La produzione della grande argenteria',

pp. 341–61; Boggero in Gavazza and Rotondi Terminiello, eds, *Genova nell'età barocca*, catalogue entry 226, p. 344; Boggero, 'Gli argenti', p. 332.) The drawings in the Gabinetto with two of Hercules's labours, while similar to each other in width, are much narrower.

56 Stagno, 'Lorenzo Capelloni', pp. 199–200.

57 'Le gesta di Andrea Doria'. Riccomini, *Il viaggio in Italia di Pietro De Lama*, pp. 152–53. Both tables are described as depicting Andrea Doria's deeds.

58 'On y voit deux tables d'argent soutenues par deux aigles et ornées de bas-reliefs. Ce présent fut donné à la famille par la République de Gênes. On sait le trait d'histoire d'André Doria qui refusa d'être le souverain de sa patrie'. De Sade, *Voyage d'Italie*, p. 152. De Sade had arrived in Rome on 27 October 1775.

59 Bonfadio, *Gli annali di Genova dell'anno 1528*, pp. 9–10.

60 Giustiniani, *Castigatissimi annali*, col. CCLXXXIV.

61 Newcome, *Disegni genovesi*, n. 2592S6 S, catalogue entry 14, pp. 41–42.

62 Stagno, *Giovanni Andrea Doria*, pp. 27–28, 71.

63 See the bibliography cited in the following notes, especially notes 66 and 67.

64 Parma, 'Due Angeli di Giovannangelo Montorsoli', pp. 61–69.

65 The frescoed scene measures 2.79 per 3.86 cm.

66 Parma, 'Il palazzo del Principe', p. 42.

67 Newcome, *Disegni genovesi*, n. 2592S6 S, catalogue entry 14, pp. 41–42.

68 Alizeri, *Guida illustrativa*, p. 174; Torriti, *Tesori di Strada Nuova*, p. 228; Newcome, *Disegni genovesi*, n. 2592S6 S, catalogue entry 14, pp. 41–42. On the opening of Via Alessi, see Luccardini, *Carignano*, pp. 36–41.

69 Tagliaferro, '1882–1892', p. 79, note 24.

70 Chiozza, *Guida commerciale descrittiva di Genova*, p. 72; Alizeri, *Guida illustrativa*, p. 174 ('Vi ritorni in esempio quel picciol soffitto del Tavarone ov'è Andrea Doria nell'atto d'arringare il popolo presso la gentilizia di s. Matteo, distratto a gran cura dalle case Strixioli lunghesso le mura di s. Chiara'); *Annuario Genovese*, p. 66 (Guida artistica, riproduzione di *Genova bella*).

71 Unfortunately, the fresco needs restoration and is not currently visible.

72 Giovanni Andrea Doria's properties are listed in his will, and none was in the Carignano area. Stagno, *Giovanni Andrea Doria*, pp. 320–21.

73 Newcome, *Disegni genovesi*, n. 2592S6 S, catalogue entry 14, pp. 41–42, quoting a note by the hand of Mario Bonzi on the back of a photo in the Centro Doc SAI - Archivio Fotografico in Genoa, reading 'Proveniente da una delle case Strixioli (già Doria) sulle Mura di Santa Chiara'; Parma, 'Tavarone, Lazzaro', p. 413.

74 On Giovanni Andrea Doria: Savelli, 'Honore e robba'; Savelli 'Doria, Giovanni Andrea'; Borghesi, ed., *Vita del Principe Giovanni Andrea Doria*; Pacini, 'Pignatte di vetro'; Borghesi, 'Doria, Giovanni Andrea'; Carpentier and Priotti, 'La forge instable d'une domination', pp. 75–96; Beri; Hanss, '"Event and Narration"'. On his artistic patronage: Magnani, 'Committenti e architetture'; Magnani, 'I Doria e il Carmelo'; Boggero, 'Il cantiere di S. Agostino'; Leonardi, 'La committenza doria'; Spiriti, 'Loano città imperiale e ideale'; Stagno, 'Villa Centurione'; Stagno, 'Caravaggio a Genova'; Stagno, 'A honor e servicio di Dio'; Magnani and Stagno, 'Il Carmelo di Loano'; Stagno, *Giovanni Andrea Doria*; Stagno, 'Celebrating Lepanto'.

75 ADP, Scaff. 77.25.3: 1601: 10: Dicembre Decreto della Repubblica di Genova per l'erezzione [sic] della statua del Principe Gio: Andrea Primo alla parte sinistra di quella del Principe Andrea Primo su la Piazza del Palazzo, e di che esso Principe Gio. Andrea fosse trattato come se avesse continuato ad essere Generalissimo del mare – Autentico in carta pergamena. The decree is published in Doria, *La Chiesa di San Matteo*, p. 317, and Bracco, *Il principe Giannandrea Doria*, pp. 169–70.

76 'Conservator of his homeland's freedom'.

77 'Pro Reipublicae salute ac Libertatis nostrae conservatione'.

78 'PARUM PATRIAE PRODESSE POTUISSET LIBERTAS AB ANDREA RESTITUTA, NISI HIC ILLI SUCCESSISSET, CUIUS VIRTUTE RESPUBLICA IN DIES MAGIS FLORESCIT'.

79 ADP, Banc. 79.39.

80 'Dum patriae regno posset sceptroque petiri, contempsit regum fastus nomenque Tyranni'.

81 'Tempestatum in salo domitor, seditionum in solo sedator, libertatis patriae vacilantis firmator'.

82 Parma, 'Genealogie Doria'.

83 Savelli, 'Honore e robba' and Borghesi, 'Doria, Giovanni Andrea', pp. 112–13.

84 Bitossi, 'L'età di Andrea Doria', pp. 76–78.

85 Pacini, 'Ideali repubblicani', p. 216.

86 Kliemann, 'Gesta dipinte', p. 132.

87 Stagno, 'Lorenzo Capelloni', p. 193.

88 'L'ingresso nella città di Genova di Andrea I Doria allorquando la Serenissima Repubblica le presenta la Corona, e lo Scettro, ed Egli ricusandolo, le ridona la Libertà'. Archivio Doria Pamphilj, Rome, *Pitture del appartamento nobile*, 1760s manuscript, published in Stagno, 'Lorenzo Capelloni', pp. 214–25 (quotation at p. 214).

89 The parallel between Andrea Doria and Pompey is analysed in Gorse, 'La "corte" di Andrea Doria', pp. 259–260 and Gorse, 'Body Politics and Mythic Figures', pp. 14–15.

90 Stagno, 'Lorenzo Capelloni', pp. 197–99. Immediately below the sceptre, the end of the huge keys to the city can be glimpsed, a further symbol of the *signoria* offered to Doria.

91 Boccardo, Boggero, 'Palazzi storici', p. 21.

92 Boccardo, Boggero, 'Palazzi storici', p. 21.

93 Pesenti, 'L'Illuminismo e l'età neoclassica', pp. 363–366, 375; Bartoletti, 'Brusco, Paolo Gerolamo'.

5

Wouter Kreuze

PERSPECTIVES ON A REPUBLIC

*The Genoese crisis of 1575
in Italian avvisi*

The avvisi, or manuscript newspapers, brought dramatic news from Genoa in the early months of 1575. Tensions between the two elite groups in the city, the old and new nobles (*vecchi* and *nuovi*), escalated significantly and showed no signs of easing. Dramatic scenes ensued when the *vecchi* packed their belongings and left the city in the hands of the lower classes and their *nuovi* rivals. For the avvisi of that time, this confrontation was possibly the single most important event of the year. This attention offers historians a unique outsider's perspective on the political climate in the Ligurian city.

This paper studies avvisi from the collection of the Florence State Archives (fig. 5.1).[1] They have been drawn from three volumes in particular: those from Milan, Venice, and Rome.[2] The latter two cities are traditionally the most important Italian news hubs and also the former was a prolific center of news production in those years.[3] All of them were rather well connected to Liguria.[4] In this study, I have aimed to maintain the difference between the origin indicated in the volumes, which is the location from which diplomatic personnel dispatched the documents to Florence and of the so-called headers, in other words the location indicated within the documents. This was supposedly the place where the text following the header had originally been created.

The most striking difference in this respect, is that whereas the volumes from Milan and Rome contain many headers directly from those cities, the volume from Venice bears little news from its home base. What we see instead is that also here Rome features prominently. As a matter of fact, the two separate series of Roman newsletters share many similarities,[5] probably because they used the same sources. These headers would be followed by one or more individual news items. The total number of news items from this period follow here below.

Table 1

Most common news locations from March 1575 to March 1576[6]

#		Total	Venice	Rome	Milan
1	**Rome**	554 (26%)	284 (26%)	270 (48%)	0 (0%)
2	**Milan**	235 (11%)	28 (2.6%)	6 (1.1%)	201 (45%)
3	**Genoa**	165 (7.8%)	98 (9%)	27 (4.8%)	40 (8.9%)
4	**Naples**	141 (6.7%)	92 (8.4%)	40 (7.1)	9 (2%)
5	**Paris**	117 (5.6%)	63 (5.8%)	33 (5.9%)	21 (2%)
	[...]				
14	**Venice**	36 (1.7%)	19 (1.7%)	17 (3%)	0 (0%)
	[...]				
16	**Casale Monferrato**	35 (1.7%)	12 (1.1%)	7 (1.3%)	16 (3.5%)
26	**La Spezia**	18 (0.9%)	6 (0.5%)	0 (0%)	12 (2.7%)
36	**Finale Ligure**	12 (0.6%)	7 (0.6%)	0 (0%)	5 (1.1%)

5.1

Avviso from Genova. Florence, Archivio di Stato, Mediceo del Principato, f. 3082, cc. 399v–400r. Reproduced with permission from the Italian Ministry of Culture – Archivio di Stato di Firenze.

DOI 10.1484/M.DUNAMIS-EB.5.142034

Di Genova Il primo di Ap.le 1575.

... se fosse poi tutta quieta, et se quelli nobili che si sono partiti dalla città et con...
... se si volessero osservar le leggi fatte l'anno del 76. si poteria scriver
... lasciando che la città doverà per l'avvenire godere più d'ella libertà de non ha
... però si è a les, l'esser assai dal gran parte de cittadini de una delle
... gli si farà di deboletà a coloro che hanno più desiderio di quella libertà invitati
... se si può pensar de cosa, l'altra nessuno à partire, molto dicono de Saona
... sono poi a esser saude ggiali, et viene, poi suano potere condisore
... de mercantie, perde ne in fatti, ne in parole son stati visti, molto a tutti do...
... per le sue parte oro, però la maggi parte concorde de non possia
... fatte sia stata levata la legge del anno 70. del galiberti, la quale fu
... fatta senza saputa del popolo, il quale à venir nissuno ne vuole al con...
... di quella senza giudica l'anno del 76. et essi gli mosse quasi al
... giudica di esse senza ragione, de volendo il popolo, ch'à osservate
... le leggi de hanno giudicato, li nobili vecchi senza rivelar ne content...
... et alla fine bisogna a de bisacin per se il popolo et li veri
cittadini amatori della Rep.ca et quelli non vogliono altre guerre
... de gli sta speso et sempre desidera ce fede alla serenità della
... cat.co et è pur cosa di gran maraviglia de in tutti questi
tumulti della città non sia stato più un se che in parole ne in fatti

5.2

Most common news locations from March 1575 to March 1576. Map designed by the author, https://www.datawrapper.de/. Public Domain.

Table 2

Word frequency for the period March 1575–March 1576 with relative frequency per 1000 meaningful words between brackets

# (total)	Word	Total	Venice	Milan	Rome
1	signor	699 (10.8)	188 (6.2)	286 (15.9)	235 (13.4)
2	duca	506 (7.78)	208 (8.86)	137 (7.62)	161 (9.61)
3	re	461 (7.09)	272 (8.97)	82 (4.56)	107 (6.39)
[...]					
10	città	272 (4.18)	96 (3.17)	112 (6.23)	64 (3.82)
17	genova	236 (3.63)	133 (4.39)	61 (3.39)	42 (2.51)

Although unknown to many today, the Genoese troubles of 1575–76 were among the main conflicts of the time and featured prominently in the *avvisi*. One of the documents explicitly commented on the perceived significance of the event, stating that at Rome, 'one does at the moment not speak of anything else than of the matters of Genoa'.[7] We do not have to rely on anecdotal evidence alone, however, as the importance of the occasion is also backed up by statistical data. As we can see, the Ligurian capital features prominently among the most common news locations during this timeframe. Moreover, considering that Milan and Rome appear so predominantly because they were centers of news production, Genoa emerges as the single most important news location for that time.[8]

Naturally, the conflict did not unfold in Genoa alone; it also affected nearby cities and towns, such as La Spezia and Finale Ligure.[9] Towards the end of the conflict, Casale Monferrato gained more prominence thanks to the negotiations for a new constitutional draft that were organised there. Additionally, news sources from outside the conflict zone reported on the incident, as evidenced by a report from the papal consistories. Consequently, it is noteworthy that the word 'Genoa' is among the most common terms found in this collection of *avvisi*, appearing almost as frequently as the word for 'city.' In the table, we can also see that Genoa received relatively less attention in the volume from Rome.[10]

Even though the conflict came to a head in 1575, it had troubled the city for a long time. It stemmed from a number of underlying oppositions within the social fabric of Genoa, which did not stand alone but reinforced each other. In particular, I will argue that the avvisi generally relate the conflict within the city to the greater struggle for power in Italy and Europe. By doing so, they often depict a strict delineation between French and Spanish powers, as known from the historiography.[11] However, as we will see, some individual *avvisi* do not fit this pattern and introduce nuance to the hard divide between pro-Spanish and pro-French forces.[12]

Between 1528 and 1547

Ever since the city had changed its loyalties from France to the Spanish Habsburgs in 1528, it had strongly nested itself under the wings of Spanish dominance under instigation of Andrea Doria.[13] But also before that date, the Genoese had frequently changed their relations with foreign states, often entering into different positions of nominal subservience.[14] The constitutional changes of 1528 did not succeed in eliminating the political tensions that had plagued the city for so long. In the 1548 conspiracy that bears his name, Gian Luigi Fieschi attempted to overthrow the current regime. He did not succeed in changing the turn of events, however, nor in killing Andrea Doria. The brother of the latter, Giannetto, however, was not as fortunate. He would leave behind his young son Giovanni Andrea, who would eventually succeed his uncle as the leader of the old nobility and as such play an important role in the events of 1575–1576.

While the old and new nobility together formed the city's ruling class, they also constituted the main fault line along which the principal political battles were fought. The so-called old nobility boasted about their older pedigree and as such they claimed to constitute the only real nobility of the city, whereas the new nobility was often said to descend from merchants incorporated into the ruling class at a later stage.[15]

In general, the *avvisi* referred to both the *vecchi* and *nuovi* as representing Genoa's nobility. There are, however, also instances in which they seem to hint at a privileged position of the *vecchi* as the only genuine group of nobles in the city. A Roman *avviso* from 18 March – dating in other words shortly after the beginning of the conflict – informs us that Giovanni Andrea Doria had been made head of the nobility, without specification.[16] In addition we also found references to the old nobility as the *primati*, meant to indicate that they were the prime of Genoa's nobility. This term, furthermore, is exclusively found in one *filza* only, that from Venice.[17] Behind this terminology, too, there seems to lurk the interpretation of the *nobili vecchi* as the foremost and above all only genuine members of Genoa's nobility. In addition to the nobles, the *avvisi* also identify the *popolo*, for which the term *plebe* is used indiscriminately.[18]

After the failed Fieschi conspiracy of 1547, Andrea Doria and the *vecchi* took the opportunity to revise the organisation of the Genoese republic. They termed this intervention the *garibetto*, which meant something like 'adaptation', intended to create the illusion that the revisions in question amounted to some minor changes to the constitution of 1528. In reality, the intervention was meant to put power more firmly in the hands of the *vecchi* and prevent any new attempts to overthrow Doria's regime.[19] The *garibetto* strongly cut back on the old usage of random extraction for selecting the members of the governing councils, whereas it had still featured prominently in the arrangements dating from 1528. This was a severe blow to the *nuovi*'s participation in government. In general, their coffers were not as well-furnished as those of their adversaries, which made it harder for them to provide potential supporters with the necessary financial incentives.[20] In addition, the sortition had been relatively advantageous to them, as they represented a numerical majority.[21]

The *nuovi* were well aware that the very essence of the *garibetto* of '47 was to curb their influence. As a consequence,

its abolition became one of their main goals during the turmoil of 1575. Direct references to the laws of 1528 and 1547 in *avvisi* were far from uncommon. They frequently communicate the unwillingness of either side to depart in any way from their preferred constitutional mode. In some specific cases, the *garibetto* is explicitly singled out: 'the representatives favoured by the *plebe* wanted to have it their way and have the *garibetto*, implemented in the year of 1547, abolished and observe the law of 1528 instead'.[22]

There follows a further list of demands, comprising for instance a description of how the offices ought to be selected and a suggestion to stimulate the production of velvet, objectives that seemed to belong to the *nuovi* rather than their *popolo* allies. But there also appear demands that seem to pertain more specifically to interests of the lower classes, for instance changes in the tax levied on wine, oil, grain and similar products. These burdens were often exclusively carried by the poor, as they applied to purchases in small quantities, which the rich could circumvent by buying these products in bulk.[23]

At the beginning of the conflict, the *nuovi* formed a common front with the *popolo* against the *vecchi*. It is also repeatedly made clear that the people, too, opposed the laws of 1547, as seen above. In the Roman *filza* we find one particularly outspoken news item directly under a header from Genoa. In general, the *avvisi* tried to maintain an objective tone, but this particular specimen shows a clear preference for 'those on the inside'. Referring to the *garibetto* implemented three decades earlier, it claims that it was made 'without the knowledge of the *popolo*'.[24] In another *avviso* we find confirmation that once control over the city had been established, they had sworn allegiance to the laws of 1528. The alliance between the *nuovi* and the *popolo* was not to last. Since their interests had diverged from the beginning of the conflict, so did their political paths in later stages.[25]

Caught between France and Spain

The fate of *la Superba*, however, was decided by more than the ups and downs of its various factions. Events inside Liguria were strongly connected to those beyond its borders, as had long been the case. In fact, the *garibetto* is said to have been conceived to assure Spain of Genoese loyalty.[26] In the *avvisi*, this interconnectedness between Genoa's conflict and those of the rest of the world was strongly felt. Already in the very first days after the *vecchi* had left the city, we find incoming reports about adjacent states, such as Savoy and Florence, moving troops to the Genoese borders.[27] But these constituted only two minor players that could never autonomously shift the course of European politics. The two real antipodes that dominated the theatre of continental politics and pulled all the other forces within their gravitational field were – of course – France and Spain. The *avvisi* generally acknowledge their key position in European politics.[28]

Despite any imperialistic ambitions that he might have cherished in those days, the King of France already had his hands full with domestic problems.[29] The kingdom of Henri III in those years was devastated by religious turmoil and dynastic tensions. The *avvisi* from this time give ample space to the military conflicts between Catholics and Huguenots. On various occasions, the reports suggest that the King of France might look more favourably upon the possibility of peace at home, as that would give him free rein to defend his interests in Genoa. In the following excerpt, this alternation of the monarch's ambitions on different levels is particularly well expressed:

> Many say that these rumours have accelerated the peace in France, as that crown also wishes to act upon this golden opportunity. Moreover, it is considered certain that if there will not follow an agreement [in Genoa], His Most Christian Majesty will send an army of Huguenots and Catholics combined, as the *nuovi* call for the aid of France, and the *vecchi* of Spain. It is clear that *Il Christianissimo* aspires to do so, as he has sent Galeazzo Fregoso and Scipione Fieschi with 600 men cavalry and 2000 infantry to the Marquisate of Saluzzo because of its proximity to the occasion that could present itself because of the earlier mentioned discord in Genoa.[30]

As one can see, France had its own Genoese exiles at its disposal that could strategically be employed in the conflict. The same Scipione Fieschi was exiled and had all his goods confiscated after the conspiracy of 1547, and in 1569 was once more involved in an attempt to overthrow the ruling class.[31] The remark about the possibility of creating an army of combined Huguenot and Catholic forces could easily be read as an admonition to *Il Christianissimo*, who in the *avvisi* is frequently criticised for his alleged lack of Christian zeal.

The Spanish, on the other hand, had always enjoyed fervid support from Doria and the *vecchi*. Furthermore, Philip II himself controlled large swathes of land in the Italian peninsula directly as their legitimate prince. As such, he was represented in the neighbouring Duchy of Milan by the Duke of Ayamonte, who had been appointed gouvernor there and monitored the situation closely. Before their eventual exodus from the city, the *vecchi* had requested support from Ayamonte, who acted accordingly and had sent Pietro Antonio Lonati to Genoa.[32]

Seemingly, this military assistance was meant to placate the situation in the city by sheer presence rather than actual intervention. A later *avviso* reports that Lonati brought his men back to Milan because they were no longer needed. The reason was that the *popolo* had calmed down after the departure of the *vecchi*, who had ceded control over the city to the *nuovi* and the *plebe*.[33] Many of the *vecchi* found refuge in Milan after leaving their native city.[34]

That is not to say that the relations between the Spanish representatives in Milan and the *nobili vecchi* were always without problems. The *vecchi* were involved in a conflict that at times became armed and in that sense devolved into a full-fledged civil war. In fact, one of the *avvisi* claimed that it was the desire of the *vecchi* to resolve the issue by force.[35] They had every reason to, as they usually possessed stronger forces than their *nuovi* adversaries. The Genoese Republic itself had no strong tradition of public armament. The lion's share of the forces that the Genoese could count on in times of war were in private hands. In addition, the old nobles more often possessed fiefdoms in the *riviere*,[36] to which they could not only comfortably retreat for the duration of the troubles, but where they could also gather and command their military forces. On various occasions, the *avvisi* make mention of how *signori vecchi*, such as Alberto Cybo Malaspina, Prince of Massa, were organising themselves while hiding in their domains.[37]

Moreover, also the forces at sea were overwhelmingly in the hands of the *vecchi*. Their members included *asentistas*, who offered the services of the galleys under their command to the Spanish crown as well as bridge loans to keep these afloat. The most important *asentista* of all was Giovanni Andrea Doria himself, who alone already had more than ten galleys.[38] In comparison, the public galleys under direct control of the *Signoria* constituted a meagre force; at the time of the rumours there were merely two.[39] It may therefore be no surprise that most of the time the *nuovi* tried to evade confrontation. When Giovanni Andrea caught sight of the *Signoria*'s two galleys near Chiavari under command of Tomaso Spinola,[40] the forces of the *Signoria* had reportedly sought shelter rapidly under the island of Sestri until reinforcements could back them up.[41]

Some friction arose between the *vecchi* and their Spanish beneficiaries as the former expected financial and military support from their allies whose interests they claimed to defend. This was the world turned upside-down. Over the last decades, there had been a shift in the economic activities of the *vecchi*, who increasingly opted out of the city's traditional mercantile enterprises and invested their assets in banking instead. These financial services were first and foremost delivered to the Spanish crown, to whom the old nobles also delivered military assistance in the form of the earlier mentioned *asientos*. It was also in this respect that the interests of the two factions diverged. As a consequence, the *nuovi* were also less successful in accumulating wealth. For the new nobles, however, it was not that easy to allocate their revenues in the same assets. The only way in which they too could invest in the debt of the Spanish crown was by accepting the *vecchi's* role of intermediaries in the transaction, who as middleman would claim part of the revenue.[42] In that sense, the *vecchi* monopolised the philo-Spanish viewpoint in the city with such a tenacity that the confrontation with their *nuovi* counterparts was practically inevitable. But this also means that the appeal the *vecchi* made to their Spanish protectors for money and troops was an inversion of their traditional relationship as it had developed over the last five decades.

The most violent aspects of the conflict did not occur directly after the sedition but took until the summer of 1575 to arrive. As tensions were rising, in mid-July, there was word that all women had been evacuated from Savona, anticipating an attack on the city.[43] Around the same time, there also appeared news reports on the attempts made by the *vecchi* to recruit troops from Lombardy, where the Spanish representatives appeared to be reluctant:

> The Genovese *vecchi* are looking for men who want to accept the function of colonel, making many promises, but many laugh this away, as they do not want to pay out money, nor to show the consent of the gouvernor or the Catholic Majesty.[44]

Contesting the king

Even though the *avvisi* often prefer to draw a clear-cut distinction between the pro-Spanish *vecchi* and the philogallic *nuovi*, in reality matters were much more complicated. The matter of Genoa were also a hotly debated issue among the contending parties within the Catholic court. Everyone in Madrid agreed that Genoa should remain within the Spanish sphere of influence. Whereas the party around the Duke of Alba, however, preferred to support the *vecchi* unconditionally, others, including the General Inquisitor de Quiroga, who saw the uprising as a punishment from God, argued for a more cautious approach.[45] It was through these tides that both Genoese sides had to steer in order to defend their interests. These particularities concerning Spanish politics can be understood from the secondary literature, but they are hardly ever explicitly outlined within the news.

Despite this lack of stable support from the Catholic court, the *vecchi* actually did push their offensive forward.[46] From about September, news reports started coming in about their victories in Liguria's smaller settlements as Giovanni Andrea

Doria succeeded in taking the cities of Chiavari, Rapallo and La Spezia.[47] The *nuovi*, who still were in control of the city of Genoa, could do next to nothing in return as they did not dispose of the necessary forces to have any hope of a positive outcome of a direct confrontation.

Therefore, they had to come up with a different plan. We have already seen that from a fairly early point, the French had attempted to get a foot in the door. Already in May, Swiss representatives had arrived at the *signoria* offering their assistance in return for a military alliance. The *avviso* from Milan outright suggested that in reality it would have been a ploy designed by the King of France.[48] Yet another *avviso* pointed out that we are dealing here with Lutheran Swiss, hence highly suspected of heterodoxy.[49]

Furthermore, there is also a number of news items about the shipment of grain, including from France to Genoa. At first glance this might seem insignificant, but in reality, these acts were far from apolitical.[50] It is well-known that in order to feed all its inhabitants, Genoa depended on the import of grain from beyond its own territories. What is more, it was claimed that France had put its warm connections with the Islamic East to use for the shipment of grain in their negotiations with the Ligurian city.[51] For the Spanish, on the other hand, the city's need for grain could be used as leverage. Traditionally, Genoa's shortage of internal grain production had been supplemented by shipments from Spanish-controlled Sicily. One of the *avvisi* reported on Henri III's decision to grant Genoa significant quantities of grain free of charge after he had heard about the arrest on this island of several grain-filled vessels destined for Liguria.[52] As far as direct military assistance was concerned, the *signoria* of the *nuovi* seems to have treated the French with the utmost courtesy but decided not to take their offer.

Italy and christendom

That left them to arrange something with the other powers of the time. In the *avvisi*, the confrontation was presented as tightly connected to other conflicts on the continent. First, there remained a sense of preserving the status quo among 'Italian princes' on the peninsula, a collection of rulers that is explicitly referred to on several occasions. Let me cite here a particularly clear example in order to convey the general idea of the concept: 'they say that many princes in Italy have offered money and men to the *signoria* of Genoa, so that this city will not fall in the hands of strangers (*estranei*)'.[53]

The tone is reminiscent of the discussion about Italy in the years 1494–95, and sometimes we see recurrent phrases similar to those found at that time, such as the 'quiet of Italy'.[54] The curious thing is that these cases of the words

Italia and *quiete* are most frequently found among the *avvisi* from Venice and Rome and much less often among those of Milan. Does this suggest that the documents originating in Lombardy express less of an Italian sentiment in order to condone its Spanish-led government? It cannot be that easily established, but it constitutes undoubtedly a remarkable pattern.

Table 3
Word frequency for the period March 1575–March 1576 with relative frequency per 1000 meaningful words between brackets

Volume (*filza*)	Total	Venice	Milan	Rome
Quiete	19 (0.28)	9 (0.3)	0 (0)	8 (0.48)
Italia	65 (0.97)	33 (1.09)	8 (0.45)	24 (1.43)

In that respect, it seems that the idea of a balance of power among Italian princes, which is often said to have emerged after the peace of Lodi around the middle of the fifteenth century,[55] was transformed rather than terminated by the Italian Wars. Then, the question remains whether this collectivity of rulers has to be interpreted as Italian princes being culturally rooted within the peninsula or rather taken literally as princes of Italy, whatever their origins might be. If one takes the quotation above as well as the aforementioned pattern into consideration, it becomes clear that the former interpretation should be preferred.

Because of their dependency on aid from outside, the *nuovi* sent embassies to the most important centres of power on the peninsula and beyond. In one *avviso* we find the mirror image of the one seen above.

> As one has come to understand, *la fattion nova* ('the new faction') has sent ambassadors to all Italian princes, in order to bring to their attention that without any reason these *vecchi* are waging a war on them, and they are asking for aid and for being favoured.[56]

They also sent a representative to make their case regarding another important factor that we have not touched upon yet: the papacy. From the earliest stages, the Pope had expressed his concern about the situation and also sent a papal legate in the person of cardinal Morone.[57] He was supposed to function as an intermediary between the parties, but by many on the Spanish side he was suspected of *nuovi* sympathies.[58] In general, the *avvisi* often speculate about what 'enterprise'[59] the Spanish troops were going to as they monitored their movements closely. One of the Roman *avvisi* tells us that Gregory XIII made known to the cardinals the contents of a letter that he had sent to Don Juan, Philip's half-brother. Besides giving a succinct overview of the panorama I have sketched out before, it also gives voice to the distrust with which the papacy followed the Spanish undertakings.[60]

> That supposing that His Highness [Don Juan] might have the intention to leave for Genoa with all his forces in order to enter that city and take possession of it, he makes him known that if he would get to that enterprise, it would incite the King of France, who might also have a claim upon that same city, in such a way that all Italian princes would oppose it, and that therefore he might consider directing his forces to another enterprise.[61]

In that respect, the turmoil in Genoa belongs not only within the context of Italian politics, but also takes on a continental significance, where it relates to the ordeal of Catholicism. In the *avvisi*, which in general are characterised by a strain of religious undertones, the Pope appears as the main spokesman for this cause. He regularly makes his appearance in the *avvisi* to admonish soldiers to take up arms against the 'infidel' instead of the Republic of Genoa.[62] In a letter that Cardinal Morone allegedly wrote to Gregory, he links the two levels directly together: 'the Cardinal writes that he is hopeful that this Republic that threatened to endanger Italy and Christendom will quiet down in two months' time'.[63]

It also has to be said that in the *avvisi*, the *nuovi* often make their appearance clouded with an odour of heterodoxy. This also becomes visible in the following example which is reminiscent of the opposition against the Spanish influence in other parts of Europe: 'That the Genoese *nuovi* would go as far as calling in the aid of the Turk rather than to give themselves to the Spanish and make peace with the *primati*'.[64]

Towards a new status quo

That is not to say that the foreign actors in the conflict were vocal about any desire they might have had to dismantle or curtail Genoa's republican constitution. Quite the contrary, all parties were very outspoken about their wish to maintain Genoa's liberty (*libertà*). For example, the aid the French offered to the *nuovi* is presented as being driven by the desire to maintain Genoa's independent status: 'they offered all the forces of His Majesty in defense of Genoa's liberty and tranquillity'.[65]

But also their Spanish adversaries make their appearance in the *avvisi* as the Republic's benefactor, exactly as it has been said that Philip liked to fashion himself.[66] According to one document, Don Juan sent a messenger to Giovanni Andrea Doria in order: 'to make known that he had orders from His King to aid the liberty of that city with all his forces'.[67]

In the rapprochement between the parties, the preservation of the republic's autonomous character was once more underlined in the mandate of the so-called *compromissari* that had to redraw the city's constitution at Casale Monferrato which purportedly included the authority to 'review all the laws, decrees, statutes and uses of the government of the Republic, excepting only its liberty'.[68]

There has been discerned a shift in the meaning of 'liberty' in the history of Genoa during the sixteenth century.[69] It has been said that before that time, the Genoese had another understanding of what this term implied as it took the form of freedom to do business rather than being free from foreign intervention.[70] In the early modern news production, however, *libertà* features predominantly in that latter sense, as political autonomy. The term itself is also found in all three volumes. Even though it appears slightly underrepresented in the *avvisi* from Rome, this might be explained by the lesser attention this series pays to the conflict in general.[71]

No sooner had the offensive of the *vecchi* gotten underway than they suffered an enormous setback from a direction they had expected support. In September 1575, the Spanish announced the suspension of payments, which hit the *vecchi* particularly hard as it was their side that had invested huge sums in the Spanish state debt. Even though the immediate cause of this bankruptcy was the precarious financial state of Philip's realm, and had already been long underway,[72] even within Spanish circles, it was said to have been partly motivated by the desire to discourage the aggressors from continuing their campaign. The same thing is being suggested in the *avvisi*.[73] In that respect, Alva *cum suis* failed to back his *vecchi* protégés with sufficient support. The *avvisi* also acknowledges this:

> One has come to understand that His Majesty suspended all payments to the Genoese, which will be of great damage to them, especially to the *vecchi*, who they say have invested more than the others.[74]

Much later, in December, the newsletters also brought news on the specific conditions of the bankruptcy, in which the victims of this action are recognised as Genoese, but not specified as *vecchi*.[75] The incident in general, however, resonated strongly in the *avvisi*.[76]

The peculiar thing is that, as we have seen, many of this continuous series of *avvisi* under headers from Rome and Milan make a strong distinction between the *nuovi* who were strongly opposed to the Spanish influence, and the *vecchi* who would not only have embraced it but were dependent upon it. However, a closer look at some *avvisi* nearer to the place of conflict reveals a more nuanced picture. Additionally, reading carefully, one can find traces under the other headers where the *vecchi* were portrayed as giving their adversaries a bad reputation: 'the said *Signoria* sends *maestro* Francesco Tagliacarne as ambassador to the Catholic King to open his eyes about the sinister information given to His Majesty by the *vecchi*'.[77]

Among the documents directly under a Genoan header, some appear to be very sympathetic towards the *nuovi*. The narrative they present starkly contrasts with the general outline of the regular series: 'The *popolo* and the citizens who feel true affection for the Republic and for tranquillity do not want any other government than this *signoria illustrissima*, and will always be loyal and ready to serve the Catholic Majesty'.[78] Ultimately, the representatives from the European powers, in whose hands both *nuovi* and *vecchi* had placed their fate, managed to craft a plan for reconciliation. At the year's end, news arrived of the *vecchi* disbanding their troops. The conclusions, extensively detailed in the *avvisi*, were published only in March 1576.[79]

According to one *avviso*, the *nuovi* were not pleased with the final arrangements but feigned satisfaction.[80] Elsewhere, doubts were raised about the sustainability of the recently concluded settlement.[81] Later historians, however, have interpreted the changes of this year – also known as the *Leges Novae* – as a new watershed in the history of the Genoese republic. It became a point of reference, much like 1528 and 1547 had been during 1575–1576, and it was regarded as the moment when the *nuovi*, or at least some among their ranks, began to gain momentum.[82]

Not all news hubs shared the same focus. Those mainly drawing on information from Rome (i.e. the *filze* from Venice and Rome) appear more interested in the idea of an Italian status quo and in the stability of Christendom. Between these two, again, the one directly from Rome is more introspective. The peculiar thing about the series from Milan, on the other hand, is that, as a consequence of its geographical origin, it seems to have been written from a relatively pro-Spanish viewpoint. In all three main Italian news hubs of the time the rumours of Genoa of 1575–1576 appear as a conflict built on a sharp distinction between pro-French and pro-Spanish forces. While this cannot be ruled out as completely unfounded, there are also other documents that paint a more nuanced picture. In these, the *nuovi* do not seem very anti-Spanish after all. The coverage of the conflict in general therefore seems to play into the hands of the *vecchi*. After all, it was they who endeavoured to be the sole defenders of the Spanish cause in the Ligurian city and to monopolise all the resulting favours.

1 The documents discussed in this article have been collected, transcribed and encoded in preparation for my PhD thesis. All the data presented in this article were processed using Python scripts developed by me, following the XML encoding guidelines established within the Euronews project. For each *avviso* cited in the notes, I have endeavored to provide the header, geographical indication of the file (in brackets), and the date of the header. For more details, refer to the Euronews guidelines: [https://github.com/lallori/euronews-xml-corpus/wiki/transcription-xml-encoding-guidelines]. [2021/8/18] This research reflects the stage of my research conducted during the COVID-19 lockdowns in 2021; therefore, the historiography may not be fully up-to-date.

2 To be even more specific: for Rome we are talking here about the ASF MdP 4026, for Venice about ASF MdP 3082. These are both *filze* that have been archived as collections of *avvisi*. The documents of Milan, on the other hand, have been found in two separate *filze*. The greater part is preserved in a volume of *avvisi*, ASF MdP 3254. However, for the year 1575 there have also been found many *avvisi* dispersed among the volume of letters from the diplomatic agents of the Medici in Milan, which is ASF MdP 3114.

3 For a general introduction to early modern news and *avvisi*, Infelise, *Prima dei giornali* and Pettegree, *The Invention of News*.

4 Schobesberger and others, 'European Postal Networks', p. 28.

5 Keller and Molino, *Die Fuggerzeitungen im Kontext*, pp. 120, 157.

6 Locations that have been attested fewer than 10 times have not been listed. Percentages are of the total of the whole volume (or of all volume for the total number).

7 'Et per hora in questa corte non si regiona d'altro, che delle cose di Genova'. *Avviso* from Rome (Venice), 15 October 1575, ASF MIA DocId 27253 MdP 3082 f. 333v.

8 Genoa has itself been identified as an important news hub. For instance, Keller and Molino, *Die Fuggerzeitungen im Kontext*, pp. 144–45.

9 As well as other smaller localities that have not been included in this overview when they appeared fewer than 10 times.

10 In other years Genoa has actually also been found to be a relatively important centre of news production, such as in the Fuggerzeitungen. Keller and Molino, *Die Fuggerzeitungen im Kontext*, p. 143. Also within the Euronews program, Genoa has been found to be one of the most important locations of news production for the year 1600. But this could also be caused by the particularity of that specific year as Venice and Rome, usually the most important, are almost completely missing. Brendan Maurice Dooley and others, '1600 Experiment': https://www.euronewsproject.org/1600–experiment/ [2021/7/20].

11 There has been an ongoing discussion about the nature and extent of the Spanish control over the Italian peninsula. Dandelet, *Spanish Rome*; Levin, *Agents of Empire*.

12 A few years ago there appeared a collection of papers nuancing the extent and nature of Spanish control. Baker-Bates and Pattenden, eds, *The Spanish Presence in Sixteenth-Century Italy*.

13 For relations to France: Lazzarini, *Communication and Conflict*, p. 19. Galasso sees Genoa as practically part of Spanish territory: Galasso, *Alla Periferia Dell'impero*, p. 6. For the strategic importance of Genoa: Pacini, '"Poiché gli stati non sono portatili"', p. 414.

14 Gorse, 'A Question of Sovereignty', p. 203.

15 Kirk, *Genoa and the Sea*, pp. 22–28.

16 *Avviso* from Rome (Venice), 18 March 1575, ASF MAP DocId 27103 MdP 3082 f. 221v.

17 In a limited number of cases, however, it also refers to the most important nobles in Poland.

18 For example, I found an instance where it is specified as 'il popolo, cioè la plebe': *Avviso* from Genova (Rome), 1 April 1575, ASF MAP DocId 52620 MdP 4026 f. 407r.

19 Costantini, *La Repubblica di Genova*, p. 47.

20 Since they were generally poorer, Bitossi, *Il governo dei magnifici*, p. 121.

21 'Il popolo cioè la plebe', says one of the documents. *Avviso* from Genova (Rome), 1 April 1575, ASF MAP DocId 52620 MdP 4026 f. 407v.

22 'Gli aggregati favoriti dalla plebe l'hano voluta a modo loro havendo fatto levare il garibetta eretta l'anno del 47, et vogliono che s'osservi la legge fatta l'anno del 28'. *Avviso* from Rome (Venice), 26 March 1575, ASF MIA DocId 51643 MdP 3082 f. 225r.

23 Kirk, *Genoa and the Sea*, p. 67.

24 'La quale fu fatta senza saputa del popolo'. *Avviso* from Genoa (Rome), 1 April 1575, ASF MAP DocId 52620 MdP 4026 f. 407r.

25 Costantini, *La Repubblica di Genova*, pp. 111–15, 127–29.

26 Kirk, *Genoa and the Sea*, p. 57.

27 The Duke of Savoy was said to have done so, and Aurelio Fregoso was said to lead ten thousand troops for the Grand Duke of Florence to Pietrasanta. *Avviso* from Milan (Milan), 16 March 1575, ASF MAP DocId 9922 MdP 3254, f. 142v; *Avviso* from Milan (Milan), 16 March 1575, ASF MAP DocId 51395 MdP 3254, f. 144r; *Avviso* from Rome (Venice), 26 March 1575, ASF MAP DocId 51643 MdP 3082 f. 225r-v.

28 For the importance of Genoa for the Spanish Empire: Pacini, '"Poiché gli stati non sono portatili"', p. 417.

29 For Dauverd, France's relation with Genoa had always been problematic: Dauverd, *Imperial Ambition in the Early Modern Mediterranean*, p. 38.

30 'Dicendo molti che questi rumori habbino accelerata la pace in Francia havendo quella corona anco disegno in sì buon boccone, anzi si tien per certo che se loro non s'accordano, Sua Maestà Christianissima manderà essercito d'ugonoti, et cattolici insieme perché li nuovi chiamano Francia et li Vecchi Spagna et è chiaro che il Christianissimo aspiri poi che s'intende haver mandato li signori Galeazzo Fregoso et Scipione Fiesco [Scipione Fieschi] con 600 cavalli et 2 mila fanti nel marchesato di Saluzzo per esser più vicini all'occasione che si potesse loro presentare per causa delle sudette discordie di Genova'. *Avviso* from Rome (Venice), 14 May 1575, ASF MAP DocId 27154 MdP 3082 f. 251r.

31 Costantini, *La Repubblica di Genova*, p. 42–51, 89–90.

32 *Avviso* from Milan (Milan), 23 March 1575, ASF MAP DocId 51451 MdP 3254 f. 147r.

33 Especially Franco Lercaro was said to have no intention of returning any time soon, as he had rented a big *palazzo* where he could settle down with his family. *Avviso from Rome (Venice), 4 June 1575, ASF MAP DocId 27166 MdP 3082 f. 259v.*

35 *Avviso from Rome (Venice), 4 June 1575, ASF MAP DocId 27166 MdP 3082 f. 259r.*

36 Bitossi, *Il governo dei magnifici*, p. 83.

37 For Malaspina: *Avviso from Rome (Rome), 3 September 1575, ASF MAP DocId 26273 MdP 4026 f. 450r; Avviso from Genova (Rome), 9 September 1575, ASF MAP DocId 52844 MdP 4026 f. 453r.*

38 Kirk, *Genoa and the Sea*, p. 42.

39 Kirk, *Genoa and the Sea*, p. 60.

40 Tomasi Spinola remained loyal to the *Signoria* within the city even though he himself was actually considered a *vecchio*, Costantini, *La Repubblica di Genova*.

41 On the other hand, the *avviso* also mentions that by his return, Spinola had managed to confiscate two vessels carrying Doria's provisions. *Avviso from Rome (Venice), 24 September 1575, ASF MAP DocId 51827 MdP 3082, f. 322r.*

42 Kirk, *Genoa and the Sea*, p. 31.

43 *Avviso from Milan (Milan), 13 July 1575, ASF MAP DocId 51583 MdP 3082 f. 183v.*

44 'Li Genovesi vecchi vano cercando gente che vogliono acettare carico de colonelli facendoli molte promesse ma molti se ne burlano, poiché non vogliono né sborsare danari né mostrare il contento di questo governatore [Antonio de Guzman y Zuniga] o della Maestà Cattolica [Felipe II de Austria]'. *Avviso from Milan (Milan), 20 July 1575, ASF MAP DocId 51610 MdP 3254 f. 190r.*

45 Pacini, 'El "Padre" y La "República Perfecta"', p. 127.

46 Pacini, 'El "Padre" y La "República Perfecta"', p. 125.

47 For Chiavari and Rapallo: *Avviso from Milan (Milan), 28 September 1575, ASF MAP DocId 51714 MdP 3254 f. 218v; For La Spezia: Avviso from Milan (Milan), 21 September 1575, ASF MAP DocId 52450 MdP 3254 f. 217r.*

48 *Avviso from Milan (Milan), 18 May 1575, ASF MAP DocId 9941 MdP 3254 f. 164r; Avviso from Milan (Milan), 19 May 1575, ASF MAP DocId 51494 MdP 3254 f. 167r.*

49 *Avviso from Venice (Rome), 11 June 1575, ASF MAP DocId 52635 MdP 4026 f. 429v; See also: Avviso from Piacenza (Milan), 13 June 1575, ASF MAP DocId 23868 MdP 3254 f. 176r.*

50 Some of these news items announce nothing more than the arrival of a certain quantity of grain in the port of Genoa. *Avviso from Rome (Venice), 6 August 1575, ASF MAP DocId 27224 MdP 3082 f. 294v; Avviso from Genova (Venice), 5 August 1575, ASF MAP DocId 27225 MdP 3082 f. 296v; Avviso from Rome (Venice), 20 August 1575, ASF MAP DocId 27227 MdP 3082 f. 298r.*

51 Grendi, *La Repubblica aristocratica*, p. 213.

52 *Avviso from Genova (Venice), 5 August 1575, ASF MAP DocId 27225 MdP 3082 f. 296r.*

53 'Dicono molti principe d'Italia hanno fatto offerta di danari et gente alla signora di Genova, acciò quella città non caschi in poter d'estranei'. *Avviso from Rome (Rome), 21 May 1575, ASF MAP DocId 26264 MdP 4026 f. 424r.*

54 'Quiete d'Italia'. For example, *Avviso from Rome (Venice), 16 July 1575, ASF MAP DocId 51771 MdP 3082 f. 281r.*

55 See for example Fubini, 'The Italian League', p. 166.

56 'La fattion nova per quanto s'intende ha mandato ambasciatori da tutti li principi d'Italia, a farli intendere che senza alcun cagione gli vien fatto guerra da questi vecchi pregandoli tutti a volergli porgere aiuto, et favore di gente come di quanto gli sarà bisogno'. *Avviso from Milan (Milan), 28 September 1575, ASF MAP DocId 51714 MdP 3254 f. 218v.*

57 In the *avvisi* he is portrayed as being quite pro *nuovi*. But originally he had risen through the ranks with the help of Charles V. Pattenden, 'Rome as a "Spanish Avignon"?', p. 68.

58 Pacini, 'El "Padre" y La "República Perfecta"', p. 129.

59 'Impresa'.

60 This tension has also been found by later historians, for example Galasso, *Alla Periferia Dell'impero*, p. 34.

61 'Che presentendosi che Sua Altezza havea forse intentione d'andar alla volta di Genova con tutte le sue forze per entrarvi et impatronirsi le faceva sapere che quando venisse a tal impresa saria un'incitar il Re Cristianessimo [Henri III de Valois] che forse ha qualche pretensione sopra la medesima città, et in altra che tutti li principe de Italia

s'opponeriano, e che perciò l'essortava a voltar sue forze ad altra impresa'. *Avviso from Rome (Venice), 9 July 1575, ASF MAP DocId 51699 MdP 3082 f. 279r.*

62 For example: *Avviso from Rome (Rome), 8 July 1575, ASF MAP DocId 26270 MdP 4026 f. 444v.*

63 'Il Cardinale scrive haver speranza in dui mesi quietar quella Republica che minacciava tanto foco in Italia et nella christianità'. *Avviso from Rome (Venice), 17 September, ASF DocId 27260 MdP 3082 f. 317r.*

64 *Avviso from Rome (Venice), 1 November 1575, ASF MAP DocId 27249 MdP 3082 f. 324v.*

65 'Hanno offerto tutte le forze de Sua Maestà in defension della libertà et quiete di Genova', *Avviso from Venice (Rome), 16 July 1575, ASF MAP DocId 51771 MdP 3082 f. 281r.*

66 Pacini, 'El "Padre" y La "República Perfecta"'.

67 'Per farlo intendere che havea ordine dal suo Re [Felipe II] di agiutar con tutte le sue forze la libertà di quella città'. *Avviso from Venice (Rome), 11 June 1575, ASF MAP DocId 51648 MdP 3082 f. 268r.*

68 'Di riveder tutte le leggi decreti, statuti et consuetudini del governatore della Repubblica riservando solo la libertà'. *Avviso from Venice (Rome), 1 October 1575, ASF MAP DocId 27249 MdP 3082 f. 324r. Also found elsewhere, Avviso from Rome (Venice), 10 September 1575, ASF MAP DocId 51825 MpD 3082 f. 314r.*

69 Shaw, 'Concepts of Libertà in Renaissance Genoa'.

70 Salonia, *Genoa's Freedom*, p. xix.

71 Of course, it cannot be excluded that *libertà* is also used in cases that have nothing to do with Genoa.

72 Parker, *Imprudent King*, p. 225.

73 *Avviso from Rome (Rome), 18 November 1575, ASF MAP DocId 52879 MdP 4026 f. 478v–479r.*

74 'S'intende che Sua Maestà [Felipe II de Austria] havea fatto soprasedere tutti pagamente de Genovesi, il che a loro sará di grandissimo danno, tanto piú alli vecchi, che dicono essergli piú interessati de gl'altri'. *Avviso from Rome (Rome), 16 December 1575, ASF MAP DocId 51714, MdP 3254 f. 219r–226r.*

75 *Avviso from Madrid (Rome), 12 December 1575, ASF MAP DocId 26290 MdP 4026 f. 515r–516v; Avviso from Milan (Milan), 19 January 1576, ASF MAP DocId 53178 MdP 3254 f. 252r–253v.*

76 For example, Niccolò Grimaldi was individually discussed as being particularly strongly affected: *Avviso from Rome (Rome), 25 June 1575, ASF MAP*

DocId 51650 MdP 3082 f. 271v; *Avviso* from Rome (Rome), 18 November 1575, ASF MAP DocId 52879 MdP 4026 f. 478v–479r. Even though another *avviso* claims that the rumours are false: *Avviso* from Rome (Venice), 15 October 1575, ASF MAP DocId 27253 MdP 2082, f. 334v.

77 'La detta signoria manda messer Francesco Tagliacarne Ambasciatore al Re cattolico per desinganarlo delle sinistre informationi date a Sua Maestà dalli nobili vecchi'. *Avviso* from Venice (Rome), 16 July 1575, ASF MAP DocId 51771 MdP 3082 f. 281v. As said, something similar is also found under the header of Milan: *Avviso* from Milan (Milan), 21 December 1575, ASF MAP DocId 52450 MdP 4254 f. 217r; According to another *avviso*, Tagliacarne's mission proved eventually successful and he also acquired permission to ship a certain quantity of grain from Sicily. *Avviso* from Milan (Milan), 19 January 1576, ASF MAP DocId 53178 f. 251r.

78 'Il popolo et li veri cittadini amatori della Repubblica et quieta non vogliono altro governo che questa signoria illustrissima, et sempre dovuto et fedele, alla servitù della Maestà Cattolica'. *Avviso* from Rome (Genoa), 1 April 1575, ASF DocId 52620 MdP 4026 f. 407r.

79 For example: *Avviso* from Rome (Rome), 11 November 1575, ASF MIA DocId 26277 MdP 4026 f. 475r-v; *Avviso* from Milan (Milan), 9 November 1575, ASF MIA DocId 51926 MdP 3254 f. 232r; *Avviso* from Milan (Milan), 19 January 1575, ASF MIA DocId 53178 MdP 3254, f. 251r.

80 *Avviso* from Rome (Venice), 31 March 1576, ASF MIA docId 27550 MdP 3082 f. 421r.

81 *Avviso* from Milan (Milan), 23 February 1576, ASF MAP DocId 9995 MdP 3254 f. 264v.

82 For Bitossi, *Il governo dei magnifici*, for example, the so-called quattro case were the real winners of the conflict. Bitossi, *Il governo dei magnifici*, pp. 33–36, 79; Kirk, 'The Apogee of the Hispano-Genoese Bond, 1576–1627', p. 47.

6

Benoît Maréchaux

CONTENDING REPUBLICANISMS

Pamphlets, Liberty, and Political Uses of the Past in Genoa, Venice, and Rome at the Time of the Interdict (1606–07)

As the publication of the book that includes this article shows, a renewed approach to the republics and republicanism in early modern Europe aims at analysing the republican phenomenon beyond certain historiographical traditions that have been prone to isolate republican discourses from their context and surrounding environment. While works on Italian and European republics have, on the one hand, often been the subject of studies at a local, regional, or national level, the Cambridge School of Intellectual History ideas has, on the other hand, adopted a genealogical view of republicanism mostly based on republics that appeared to be (at least on the paper) independent from monarchies.[1] Despite their important contribution to our understanding of republicanism, these research lines have often tended to dissociate the words and the thing from the surrounding historical realities, which has led to an exceptionalist view of certain republics, as well as to a certain essentialisation of the republican phenomenon. In particular, the binary opposition to the monarchies has often been described in a way which is largely disconnected from the political practices of early modern republics. In this context, several studies have recently attempted to better situate the analysis of republics in relation to the value systems and political models that surrounded them and with which they often interacted to a greater extent than scholarship has traditionally considered. Building upon relevant contributions on single republics (e.g., on Genoa), this approach has helped to obtain a better idea of the multifaceted nature of republican uses and representations and to focus on the complex interactions that were often at work between different political regimes. In the same manner, research is also currently analysing, from a perspective of connected and comparative analysis, how republics represented themselves and were represented on the 'stage of the kings', with reference to the political regime that was dominant at the time.[2]

This contribution seeks to enrich our understanding of the latter question by analysing three short opuscules produced at the beginning of the seventeenth century, specifically during the 'war of writings' of 1606–1607 that involved the Republic of Venice, the Papacy and, by proxy, as we shall see, the Republic of Genoa. By analysing pamphlets whose main object was the attack or defence of Venetian policy and ideas during the Interdict, by means of a continuous and purposeful comparison with its Genoese counterpart, we aim to contribute to this cross-history of republican states whose representations tended to enter into conflict more frequently than the literature on republicanism usually assumes. As we shall see, these opuscules were not produced in a vacuum, nor did they concentrate on classical republican values. On the contrary, they were forged in contact with other contemporary states with which the republics of Venice and Genoa were interdependent.[3] Although it opposed the two republics, the first pamphlet was likely produced by a Roman theologian, which points out how republican representations were also shaped by external thinkers. In this context, the question of the differing relationship that the two republics maintained with some of the major European powers was central to the three pamphlets. The problem was not so much that of republican liberty per se (as opposed to the tyranny of dynastic regimes), but rather the instrumental comparison between the past and present policies pursued by each republic in relation to these monarchical powers.

As it could hardly be otherwise, the strong multi-secular rivalry between the two republics was at the heart of the

6.1

Ludovico Leoni (Padovanino, attributed),
Portrait of Paul V Borghese. Rome, Galleria Borghese, 1633 ca.
Photo: © Galleria Borghese,
Mauro Coen. Reproduced with permission.

DOI 10.1484/M.DUNAMIS-EB.5.142035

multi-media discourses under scrutiny. As is well known, the two republican states had shared a common history since the Middle Ages, which had stimulated cross-views where rivalry, admiration and emulation coexisted. This was still true in the early modern period, and not only in the time of Machiavelli, Botero or Campanella. In the first half of the seventeenth century, many Genoese reformist thinkers took Venice as a model for reforming their institutions and forging collaborative links with its patriciate.[4] As we shall see, the Republic of San Marco claimed to enjoy liberty (e.g. independence from other states), which made 'comparison' between the two republics both a source of influence for Genoese reformers and a form of political distinction for Venetian patricians. Yet, the same comparison could also become a rhetorical instrument to be used against the jurisdictional policy pursued by Venice. The discourses here analysed discussed these questions in the context of the Interdict when the question of the relation between the two republics and the Papacy became a subject of controversy. By looking at how the comparison between the republican states was used for purposes that had little to do with republicanism and was instead very connected to jurisdictional disputes, we will examine how conflicts shaped the representations of republics, their real or alleged view of freedom, and their interdependent nexus with monarchical powers. We shall deal with the Ottoman Empire, the Spanish Monarchy, and the Papacy.

The Genoese letter: an anti-Venetian Roman Pamphlet

In seventeenth-century Italy, the boundaries between governmental, private and public spheres were sometimes blurred when dealing with political communication. Letters were inclined to escape their authors and their recipients. Not only were the private letters of rulers and intellectuals read within their circles of sociability; those sent or received by the chancelleries might also be leaked.[5] Another sort of letter was also circulated, however, always for political purposes: the fake ones, which made institutions or real people communicate ideas whose offbeat use aroused the reader's curiosity and produced rhetorical effects for political purposes that were very real.

The starting point of this article belongs to the latter sort of letters. In 1606, an anonymous author produced a letter that the Republic of Genoa had allegedly written in response to another that the Republic of Venice had sent to it to complain about political concessions made to the Papacy. Known as *Copia della lettera scritta dalla Serenissima Repubblica di Genova in risposta d'una scrittale dal Doge et Repubblica di Venetia* ('Copy of the Letter Written by the Most Serene Republic of Genoa in Reply to the One Written by the Doge and Republic of Venice'), it circulated as a manuscript.[6] As was often the case, the fiction started from a real pretext. After having enacted, in August 1605, measures to dissolve ecclesiastical confraternities, the Republic of Genoa had withdrawn the decree a few weeks later under pressure from the newly elected Pope, Paul V (fig. 6.1).[7] As a Genoese patrician noted in a diary entry dated 25 October 1605:

> They told that the Most Serene Senate, with the necessary votes, had retracted and annulled the decree made to dissolve the confraternities and the companies, and left everything as it was before, so as not to bring upon themselves the wrath of the Pope, who felt it was wrong.[8]

Far from being satisfied, the Pope had then taken offence that the Republic had not asked for the absolution of the ecclesiastical censure, leading the Genoese Senate to use Cardinal Antonio Maria Sauli to avoid excommunication.[9] The *Lettera scritta dalla Serenissima Repubblica di Genova* written a few months later starts from this Genoese concession to the Papacy by imagining that the Genoese Republic had to justify itself after receiving complaints from Venice. The production of the letter is obviously to be understood in the context of the critical political crisis following the Pontifical Interdict to the Venetian Republic issued in April 1606. It is well known that Paul V excommunicated Venice following its refusal to abrogate several laws that required the authorisation of the Senate for the construction of places of worship, as well as for the alienation of ecclesiastical real estate. The arrest and detention of two clergymen by the Venetian justice system had also been critical. From this point on, a famous *guerra di scritture* ('war of writings') took place that opposed the two powers and their visions of the Papacy's temporal power and republican liberty. More broadly, the conflict involved a vast Venetian, Roman, and European public.[10]

Although the handwritten versions of the *Copia della lettera* in our possession are undated, their production and distribution took place in the midst of the 'war of writings'. A copy published in a Venetian collection of the eighteenth century indicates that the first copy would have been received by the College of Venice in May 1606, being attributed to the Jesuit Possevino.[11] This dating is doubtful, however, since the manuscript copy kept at the Biblioteca Apostolica Vaticana was very likely sent from Rome with the *avvisi* of 26 July 1606, that is, during the summer period in which a large series of writings of Roman origin circulated in Italy to discredit the Venetian cause.[12] The *avvisi* of Rome of 29 July (which were attached to those of the 26), indeed referred to the publication of the letter considered by the Lordship of Genoa a fake meant to reply to the Doge of Venice. According to the same *avvisi*, the contents of this letter were 'completely innocent, but not entirely praiseworthy, since they showed too much resentment towards Venice.[13] A *Copia della lettera* published in 1868 is dated 28 July 1606, which seems to confirm this approximate dating.[14]

The pamphlet was therefore distributed when an explosion of writings was taking place. The already mentioned *avvisi* of 29 July informed that a second fake letter written by the city of Verona to that of Brescia was actually circulating. It targeted Venice, too, since both cities were presented as dominated by the latter after having lost their liberty.[15] The pamphlet was clearly one among several opuscules produced – likely by the same author – in July 1606. Depending on the place where it circulated, the pamphlet could be purposely complemented by documents related to the news, whose analysis is both indicative of the context of its circulation and its connection with the city of Genoa. Hence, the copy kept in Vicenza was supplemented by *avvisi* from Genoa dated, here again, 28 July 1606.[16]

Interestingly, the *avvisi* stated that the Spanish ambassador in Genoa had visited the Senate to ascertain the position of the Republic, which had expressed its willingness to support 'con tutte le forze' the resolution of the King of Spain, i.e., to back the Papacy in the event of an armed conflict.[17] In the same way that, 'as good Catholics' ('come buoni catholici'), they had already granted 500 Corsican mercenaries to the Papacy, the Genoese patricians showed interest in continuing the collaboration. The purpose of attaching this news to the pamphlet was undoubtedly to make the false letter more polemical by linking it to real events that showed the hostile attitude of the Genoese Republic towards Venice. Three days earlier, the Spanish ambassador in charge in Genoa, Juan de Vivas, had indeed written to Philip III to inform him that he had visited the Republic's councils and received such favourable support for the King of Spain and the Pope that Genoa deserved to be praised.[18]

The texts produced during the Interdict were published through various interdependent media (manuscripts, printed, and oral) and took multiple forms (*avvisi*, pamphlets, letters, official statements, etc.). The transfers between media, contents and formats were frequent since their combination served both specific political and economic purposes.[19] From this point of view, it was no accident that the pamphlet studied here took the form of a letter from the Republic of Genoa. In order to attack the government of Venice, the author used this procedure to put into the mouth of another republic – Genoa – the argument according to which obeying the Papacy was not a form of servitude detrimental to the interests of the Republic and its patriciate, but was on the contrary a source of honour and dignity:

> Most Serene Prince, we have received Your Serenity's letter, which has caused us a different effect from what you thought. Since we have yielded to the will of the Supreme Pontiff in revoking the decrees we have made against the orators, not only does it not harm us, but it is more likely to increase the dignity of our Republic, and to shame those who, on such an occasion, would be in defiance of the pious mind of His Holiness.[20]

Rather than merely stating this argument from the perspective of the Papacy, the author thus instrumentalised the Roman-Genoese dispute of 1605 in order to adopt the point of view of the Genoese Republic which had reacted in a very different way to Paul V's injunctions than had Venice, even though it shared the same republican form of government. In its answer to the alleged critiques made by Venice, the Republic of Genoa justified its decisions by criticising the Venetian policy, especially in relation with the Papacy and the Ottoman Empire. Throughout the text, the author thus confronted the two states, constantly playing on the opposition between 'la nostra Republica' (Genoa) and 'la vostra Republica' (Venice). Quoted 16 times in the text, the term 'republic' was always present in this form (and thus as a synonym of the one or the other state), without any association with liberty being found here.

As already argued, Venice and Genoa were not just two republics. They shared a long history of military, maritime and commercial rivalry that was continually reactivated by historians and political observers who were fond of a comparative reading that had become, over the centuries, a common practice.[21] From this point of view, using the counterpoint of the Genoese Republic was a very clever way of demonstrating the mistakenness of the Venetian position during the Interdict, since it gave voice to a similar political entity that instead affirmed that obeying the temporal power of the Pope was a duty that brought benefits, and refusing to do so was a threat to the Catholic faith in Italy. This comparison with Genoa actually echoed the *Risposta del Sig. Paolo Anafesto*, another pamphlet attributed to Possevino and published in 1607. In this opuscule, the author praised in the same way the fact that, unlike Venice, the Republic of Genoa had withdrawn some of the controversial decrees, for which the Genoese deserved 'to be praised, and magnified as true Catholics, and most faithful Christians; nor therefore have they lost their freedom: nay, by such an action they have added to themselves an inestimable joy'.[22] The truth was obviously less simplistic, since the Genoese Republic had during those years defended with some vigour some of its jurisdictional prerogatives through the social and political connections – much more discreet though – woven by its patriciate within the Roman Curia.[23] This question of historical truth was not, however, the concern of the pamphlet under consideration. By portraying a republic that was not ashamed but honoured to defend the cause of the Papacy, even at the expense of its own political prerogatives, the author presented an alternative path that helped to portray Venetian politics as radical. Behind this, the text defended a definition of liberty that was compatible with obedience to papal authority since – it was argued – the Genoese had not lost their liberty despite the fact that they had withdrawn some of the decrees under papal pressure. By doing so, it was a different view of liberty – the one promoted by the Venetians – that was criticised and questioned. Although the text was not signed, it has been repeatedly attributed to the Jesuit Possevino, a theologian who was very active during the Interdict and known for many of his writings against the Venetian cause.[24] The confrontation with the Republic of Genoa, from this point of view, was an excellent pretext to defend the papal jurisdiction, as well as a way of attracting the attention of the public, and therefore the publishers' investments. The manuscript letter was printed in 1606, and we shall see that it would not be the only edition.[25] The text was short (one double-sided folio in its printed version), which favoured its distribution due to limited production and purchase costs.

Despite this short format, the pamphlet attempted to develop a comparison in which religion played a key role. By opposing the very Catholic Genoese to the Venetians who were not, the text sought to associate the Venetian position with an anti-Catholic policy. In the fake letter, the Genoese proudly boasted of having defended the Catholic faith in the East and West against the 'Turchi, Mori, and Saraceni', in reference to the naval (and colonial) power they had developed in the Mediterranean since the Crusades. Moreover, the text argued that the Genoese had always been faithful supporters of the Papacy; unlike their Venetian counterparts, they had never suffered the disgrace of being excommunicated by the Pope.

More importantly, the text criticised what would later be known as *giurisdizionalismo*. In contrast to the reason of state that led the Venetian republic to 'not yielding in nothing to the Pope' ('non cedere un punto al Papa') in terms of temporal power, the Genoese defended – always allegedly – a Roman vision of the controversy, assuming that no Prince could exercise a form of superiority over the heir of St Peter and the members of the ecclesiastic hierarchy. Using language accessible to a wide public, the text did not dwell so much on the deep theological reasons for the controversy as on the alleged consequences for the preservation of the Catholic faith in Italy.[26] To justify non-obedience to the Pope, Venice actually employed theologians defined as 'sad and lurking', 'of false religion, and of bad conscience' ('tristi et appostati', 'di falsa religione, et di mala conscienza'). The reference to Paolo Sarpi, who was one of the direct targets of the text, was obvious. The Republic of Genoa, on the contrary, employed theologians 'very wise and incorruptible' ('di molta dottrina, et de integrità de vita'), who did not divide the Catholic world.

Moreover, the text discussed religious matters in order to overturn the central argument of Venetian republicanism, that is, the original liberty of Venice born as a territory free of any foreign *dominio* and able, over the centuries, to remain independent thanks to divine favour (since the *predestinatio* of St Mark) and to the armed defence of its sovereignty in the Adriatic.[27] If the 'Genoese letter' recognised that the Republic of Venice had never been dominated by foreign lords in terms of temporal power ('vergine quanto al Dominio temporale di forastieri'), it argued, on the other hand, that Genoa had always maintained itself 'virgin in the Catholic faith to this day, persecuting with assiduous study the heretics, and the enemies of the Holy Church' ('vergine nella fede Cattolica fin'a questo giorno, perseguitando con assiduo studio gli heretici, & nemici della Chiesa Santa'). Such success had not been seen in Venice, which had become a 'recitals of various sects, and religions' ('recettacolo di varie sette, et religioni'). Using the same metaphor of virginity (in the sense of absence of heretics and of foreign soldiers), the author thus took advantage of the presence of Protestants, as well as people of Jewish and Muslim faith, to put Venice on the same level as Genoa and to challenge the argument of original liberty ('libertà originaria').[28] Here again, it is possible to read how the letter mirrored the Roman vision of Venetian politics and perhaps, that of Possevino. The Jesuit thinker continuously confronted the myth of Venetian original liberty in his writings, and it is well known that the Roman authorities opposed Venetian policy of welcoming religious minorities.[29]

Religion was furthermore brought into play in order to discuss the central issue of liberty, understood here as the degree of autonomy that the two republics had in their relationship with the surrounding dynastic and elective monarchies. Not surprisingly, the strong ties maintained between Venice and the Ottoman Empire played a central role. Hence, the *Lettera* emphasised that the Republic of Genoa sought to maintain friendly ties with the Vicar of Christ, while the Venetian Republic 'cherishes the peace and friendship of the Turk' ('tiene gran conto della pace, et amicitia del Turco'), another classic way of attacking Venice for the collaborative relationship it maintained with the Ottoman Empire. Interestingly, the text did not stop there, however. It attacked Venice's liberty, arguing that although the Republic of Genoa was protected by the King of Spain, it did not pay any kind of secret or manifest tribute ('tributo, o donativo secreto, o manifesto'). The pamphlet thus questioned the Venetian liberty, arguing that far from being independent, 'it depends on a Barbarian king, for whom we know, that under the name of donations to his ministers, he continually disburses tribute of large amounts of gold'.[30]

The author thus pointed out a true, but highly problematic, aspect of the Venetian republican narrative as it had been built over the centuries. In the same way that in its origins, the Republic was subject to Byzantium, which it had left out of its first chronicles, such as that of Giovanni Diacono, it now paid a tribute, albeit symbolic, for the occupation of the island of Zante.[31] Furthermore, at the beginning of the seventeenth century, it had become a frequent practice to make donations and payments to the Ottoman authorities, both in money and in kind (cloth, clocks, glass objects, etc.), for very large amounts. It is important to note that these payments were part of a much more complex system of donations with which other Christian nations had to deal in Istanbul. Yet they materialised the asymmetrical relationship, not to say of dependence, between the Venetian Republic and the Ottoman monarchy. The estimation of the monetary flows involved goes far beyond the objectives of these few pages, but the payments made when the new sultan ascended the throne, for the renewal of peace agreements, or in the course of diplomatic conflicts (which resulted in the payment of tens or even hundreds of thousands of ducats), do not cast any doubt on the scale and significance of the phenomenon.[32] In Istanbul, as in other cities of the empire, it was not uncommon for certain Ottoman elites to consider Venice as a dependent state of the empire (such as Ragusa), and the Ottoman administration's own records were sometimes quite explicit about it.[33] Although it always defended its own political and jurisdictional prerogatives, the Venetian Republic could not be inflexible on these matters in view of the very close economic and diplomatic interdependence that linked the two empires (i.e.: grain supply, trade, shared frontier, merchant communities, soldiers' recruitment, etc.). Like the Ottoman Empire, the Venetian Republic had to compromise some of its principles and mobilise intermediaries (essentially, through the activity of the drogmans) to find common ground at the margins of the respective legal systems.[34]

In the context of the Interdict, this argument led to questions about the rationality of the Venetian policy towards the Papacy: what sense did it make to claim full sovereignty in relation to the Holy See, while at the same time Venice continuously accepted clear infringements of its sovereignty when dealing with the Ottoman Empire? The pamphlet therefore shows that the representation of Venetian republicanism escaped its official narratives and histories. Beyond the 'Venetian myth', in early seventeenth-century Italy not everyone took at face value the narrative of Venetian liberty.[35] On the contrary, there were those in Rome who conveyed the image of a republic dependent on the Ottoman Empire and thus implicitly maintained that the Republic of Genoa was

freer, because it was less subordinate to the Spanish Monarchy, than the Republic of Venice was to the Ottomans.

In what was ultimately a critique of the Venetian jurisdictional ambitions, the text also came to deal with the economic implications of such a difference with the Republic of Genoa. 'Our people go all over the world negotiating, and this world is not only confined to your domain, so that when they lack your lands, they are not lost' ('Gli nostri huomeni vanno per tutto il mondo negotiando, il qual mondo non si vi stringe solamente nel vostro dominio, onde quando manchassero ad essi le vostre terre, non sono pero perdute'), argued the pamphlet, in clear reference to the extension of the Genoese diaspora and its ability to develop commercial and financial activities without having territorial control over large possessions. Again, the contrast with Venice, which had based its wealth on control of the *Terraferma* ('Mainland'), the Adriatic, its colonies, and major maritime routes, was striking. By concluding that the world was not limited to the Venetian *dominio*, the author of the text, again, questioned (and mocked) the benefits of Venetian jurisdictional and territorial ambitions.

A diplomatic Venetian answer

The controversy did not end there, however, since a reply to this letter was produced in 1606, probably in Venice. It circulated as a manuscript copy, as evidenced by the one kept in the Correr Museum.[36] Its title, 'Risposta per l'auttore della lettera scritta dalla Serenissima Republica di Genova al Serenissimo Doge di Venetia [di G.B.L.] scritta da un nobile, à cui fu mandata, come opera novamente stampata', indicates that the reply was conceived as a response to the printed version of the first letter. By indicating that the text had been written by a nobleman, the title also shows that the author(s) sought to avoid a confrontation with the Republic of Genoa. Although everything was a fiction, but precisely because fiction could have an impact on political and diplomatic reality, the letter was not formalised as a response from the Republic of Venice to the Republic of Genoa, but as the response of an anonymous patrician to an anonymous writer. By removing any assignment of authorship to the Republic of Genoa, the intention was to target the anonymous author, and by proxy, the Papacy.

Once again, a transfer between media took place: the answer was printed twice, probably because of market opportunities, and perhaps also because the Venetian government viewed it positively. As explained above, both because of the similarities and differences between the two republics, it was obvious that the production of pamphlets featuring a dispute between them could attract the curiosity of potential readers. The possible outlets of the letter were optimised by the form given to the publication. As with other Venetian pamphlets that addressed the papal policy (e.g., Marc'Antonio Capello's *Risposta* to the aforementioned Antonio Possevino), the reply was not printed on its own, but in conjunction with the first letter.[37] The editors thus created a booklet of eight pages that included both letters and had as title *Due lettere una publicata sotto nome della Republica di Genova alla Republica di Venetia. L'altra che contiene il parere sopra la medesima Lettera*. A first edition was published in Venice in 1606.[38] As a sign of its circulation, many copies of this edition are preserved in Italy (in Venice, Padua, Florence, Bergamo, Genoa, and Ravenna), but also in Paris, London and Madrid.[39] A second edition was released the following year, in Vicenza according to the frontispiece.[40]

The document was obviously not signed by the Venetian government, nor did it have an official licence. We do not know if the Republic intervened directly in its publication. However, it is now well known that, aware of the magnitude and implications of the flood of writings that were being published against them, the Venetian authorities reacted in the late summer of 1606 by promoting the publication of works favourable to their cause. Following Sarpi's precepts and adopting the concept of tacit licence ('permesso tacito'), the Republic did not necessarily grant licences but encouraged or turned a blind eye to publications critical of the Papacy's policies.[41] From this point of view, it is important to observe that the 1606 edition of the *Due Lettere* is dated 2 September 1606. The pamphlet, whether on the initiative of the publishers and/or the government, thus participated in the communication campaign of the autumn 1606.

On the other hand, there is no doubt that the Republic, through its representatives, did its best to spread the pamphlet. The two editions mentioned were indeed included in the compilation *Pro libertate status et reipublicae Venetorum Gallofranci ad Philenetum epistola* published in Paris in 1607.[42] Edited by Louis Servin, an influential Gallican jurist and parliamentarian, the work included 19 writings on the Interdict that had previously been published separately.[43] The work was published following the solicitations made by the Venetian ambassador in Paris Piero Priuli, who, in agreement with the government but also on his own initiative, promoted the Venetian cause beyond the republican territory.[44] The pamphlet would later be included in another collection published in 1607, this time in the Calvinist stronghold of Geneva.[45]

The content of the document was in line with its format. It was tough on the anonymous author, but very diplomatic with regard to Genoa, towards which it was not appropriate to create a diplomatic conflict. After underlining that the two supposed letters were fake, which amounted to denying the existence of a complaint from the Venetian Republic to its Genoese counterpart, the authors of the Venetian text sought to unveil the intentions of the author of the anti-Venetian

pamphlet, in order to better underline how much his objective was to add fuel to the fire by forcing Venice to take a position against both the Republic of Genoa and the Ottoman monarchy. Rather than not answering, which was presented as the second alternative pursued by the author of the *Lettera*, the text sought therefore to criticise and to discredit the 'diabolic, and scelerate considerations' ('diaboliche, e scelerate considerationi') of the 'false, malicious, petulant, and scandalous' ('falsario, maligno, petulante, e scandaloso') author, also qualified as a 'lying historian' ('historico fraudolente') for his erroneous reading of the past of the two republics. Interestingly, the text also provided a positive judgement towards Genoa by highlighting the common points that the two republics shared. In this way, the text argued not only that they shared the same political regime, but also that they professed esteem for the Holy See and looked after the liberty of Italy. Both republics were governed by prudent senators and did not submit their deliberations to the judgement of 'consultori', in reference to Paolo Sarpi:

> Just as Genoa and Venice, two republics, which are the ornament and glory of Italy, esteem the Apostolic seat in the same way as their elders did, so they are both attentive to the preservation of the liberty of Italy and the greatness of the Christian name, they regulate and conduct their affairs according to the opportunities with circumspection and vigilance of prudent senators and ministers, and do not submit their deliberations to the foolish and angry petulance of contagious and insolent consultants. […] This very indiscreet slanderer has to understand that just as Genoa, with great maturity and prudence, is united with that great King, so Venetia on her own, and with arms and negotiation for so many years has made and continues to make glorious [resistance] to the forces of the Turks, who have absorbed so many vast kingdoms, and all this no less for the defence of her own liberty, than for the rest of Italy, and in particular of the Apostolic seat.[46]

As much as highlighting commonalities was necessary in order not to arouse tensions with the Republic of Genoa, it was dangerous since it risked placing the two republics on the same level, which was inconceivable for at least a large part of the Venetian patriciate. In the second part of the quoted extract, the authors thus acknowledged that Genoa was under the protection of the Spanish Monarchy, while distinguishing very clearly the Venetian case. Rather than depending on another state, the Venetian Republic acted independently by mobilising its own armies and trading with the Ottoman Empire, which was beneficial to the whole of Christendom, including the Papacy. This was a very diplomatic way of recalling some of the essential principles of Venetian republican thought, namely that it was not dependent on other powers and was therefore free.

The unpublishable Venetian answer?
A handwritten anti-Genoese pamphlet

However, this answer was not welcomed by everyone in Venice. In the archive of the Correr Museum, a manuscript is preserved that has remained unnoticed so far. Entitled *Un'altra nova. Risposta alla lettera da Genova*, the document attests the writing of another answer, which probably remained handwritten, to the first letter allegedly produced by Genoa.[47] The fact that this document remained handwritten does not mean that it was not distributed.[48] Before joining the Correr collection, it was actually part of the library of the Congregazione dei Chierici Regolari Somaschi in Venice.[49] Although its author is unknown, it is quite possible that it was written by a patrician or a group of Venetian patricians who were not satisfied with the first *Risposta*. Although diplomatic, and effective, the letter had left the harsh attacks on Venice without a real response. It is well known that the production of writings following the Interdict went far beyond governmental control, and from this point of view, it is likely that some members of the patriciate, with or without the support of the Republic, took the initiative to produce another response. It is difficult to know at this point whether the two versions represented different pressure groups; in any case, the Republic could never have given its authorisation to a text of such violence towards its Genoese counterpart.

As a matter of fact, the response used a tone and an argumentation that were completely different from those previously chosen. Focusing on the dialectic relation liberty/servitude, the incipit of the text revealed the harsh tone and the general aim of the whole text:

> It is no wonder that you, who are accustomed to the Spanish servitude, are happy to receive the Church's yoke, for once you have lost your freedom, you appreciate little more the one than the other kind of servitude, and it may even be that you have done it in revenge for the violence that you feel in their oppression and from the envy of seeing us others free, hoping by this example to make us capable of your misery and unhappiness. But you deceive yourselves, if you believe that you can live in servitude, from those who are nourished in freedom. You, servants by the election of your elders and by your birth and nature, also wait to celebrate this false freedom, which you think you have, because as in other times your own discord caused you to lose the name of the Republic and submit to the Dukes of Milan and foreigners, so, since at present the interests and ambitions of your citizens have made you accept the laws of the will of others, contrary to the custom of free principalities. They make you little less than worthy of the name of slaves, whose only right is to obey their patron without distinction of reason or time. And you enjoy this

great dignity and such a great privilege, which you seem to have acquired, by registering it in the memory of your posterity, so that they may detest your name in every age.[50]

The opuscule differed from the previous one in that it responded directly to the Genoese Republic, as if the latter had been the real producer of the first letter. Although the authors were not fooled, it probably seemed to them that the defence and the honour of the Republic required a strong and sharp answer to the Genoese Republic, which, in any way, could not be placed on the same level as the Venetian one (or serve as pretext to jeopardise some foundations of the republican edifice). The political thoughts linked to republics here appear closely interdependent on each other in the sense that one of them – Venice – distinguished itself from the other to define its own identity, status and prestige. For this reason, the author(s) of the text rejected any kind of republican relativism, and, adopting a conception of full sovereignty, represented the Republic of St George as a slave subordinate to the Spanish Monarchy, as well as a political body dependent on the temporal power of the Catholic Church. From its point of view, this type of dependency was incompatible with the idea of a free republic, which was obviously a way to define and represent Venice as different and unique.

Not surprisingly, the central argument rested on the notion of original liberty (*libertà originaria*) so important to Venetian thinkers because of the continuous *dominio* that Venice had allegedly exercised over its territory. This notion was a source of political distinction, since other states, such as Genoa, could hardly claim the same. In this very Venetian perspective, the fifteenth century occupation of Liguria by the Viscontis of Milan was interpreted as a point of no return. By recalling that the *leggi nuove* of 1576 (which had followed the civil war of 1575) had been signed thanks to the intermediation of a papal representative, the text again described Genoese political practice as contrary to the usages of free princes.[51] On the basis of these historical events, the pamphlet essentialised the supposed Genoese servitude as the very nature of a state that was by definition submissive and therefore inferior to the Venetian Republic. The loss of freedom under Milan's rule was thus not compatible with the possibility that a free republic could later emerge in Genoa.

Moreover, the authors attacked the Genoese republic to better target the Papacy. History books in hand, the Venetian author(s) affirmed that the excommunications against Venice had been essentially due to the ambition of misguided Popes to compete in political and military affairs with the Venetian Republic. To illustrate their point, they chose, not without irony, two Ligurian popes, Sixtus IV and Julius II:

> The fact that some of these Popes argued that we were opposing that Seat, can be ascribed more to the fault of the ambition, or emulation, that they have exercised with the Republic, than the demerit of it. Sixtus and Julius, one the Fourth and the other the Second, by name, dared to do so with so little reason, that in addition to the censure of the people they manifestly incurred the indignation of the Lord God [...] since the one who was Sixtus died of rabies five hours after the notice, which he had of the peace concluded by us with his adherents with so much glory, and useful to our state, and so little dignity of him [...]. And the other, who was Julius, died unexpectedly in a few days, oppressed by the fear that the Council would depose him of that dignity, in which he had given occasion to shed so much blood of Christians and to send so many souls to perdition [...] having made himself known [...] more worthy to handle the sword than the cross.[52]

According to the pamphlet, the two Popes had excommunicated Venice with so little reason that they had outraged God and had been punished. Sixtus IV was a member of the Della Rovere family from Celle Ligure (near Savona), who had actually excommunicated Venice in 1483. According to the pamphlet, he had died of anger five hours after learning that the Venetian Republic had signed the peace with its allies.[53] The reference to his nephew Julius II, who was so much a part of the Venetian collective memory, was even less hazardous. The instigator of the League of Cambrai (1508) which had led the allied troops to the outskirts of Venice, had excommunicated the Republic at the risk of becoming, during the wars of Italy (1494–1559), the archetype of the 'warrior pope'.[54] Julius II had at the time been vilified by Venice, but also by writers such as Erasmus, Guicciardini or Machiavelli, becoming the heart of battles of multimedia communication which had set fire to Italy and a part of the European continent.[55] A century later, during this new (albeit different) confrontation between Venice and the Papacy, he was mobilised in a pamphlet that sought to associate the Roman power with one of its most controversial figures. Julius II was here remembered for having worn more 'the corselet, that the mantle' ('il corsaletto, che il manto') and shed Christian blood. The text finally ironised the fact (not proven) that he died abruptly for fear of being deposed by a hostile council, in reference to the failed one of Pisa. These criticisms echoed the diatribes uttered at the time of the defeat of Agnadello (1509) when illustrious Venetians like Sanudo presented Julius II as both a trouble-maker among Christians, and as being hostile to the Venetians. In May 1509, another famous Venetian patrician, Girolamo Priuli, also blamed 'Julius II Pope of Savona, great enemy of the Venetian name, and always the Venetians will remember him' ('Iulio pontifice secundo de Saona, inimicissimo del nome veneto, et sempre li Signori Venetiani se ricorderanno

de lui').[56] A little less than a century later, there is no doubt that the Venetians still remembered him very well.

As was common practice in writings that linked Venice and Genoa, the political use of the past was thus central to the narratives in place. The great Genoese-Venetian wars of the thirteenth and fourteenth centuries, as well as the interest that the governments had had in each other, had constantly fuelled the historical cross-views.[57] In the Middle Ages, the historians and chroniclers of the two city-states read and discussed writings that composed and recomposed their Mediterranean past.[58] Yet the history of Genoa was not written in the same way as in Venice, where the considerable and constantly renewed effort of the ruling group had led to the construction of a unified – and mythical – narrative about the original liberty of the Republic, the perfection of its institutions, its sovereignty over the Adriatic and its Christian vocation. The asymmetry was such that it was still felt in the early modern period. The Genoese writers of the first half of the seventeenth century, such as Foglietta, Andrea Spinola, or Giovanni Vincenzo Imperiale, were great readers of Venetian classical works. They were inspired by them and also appropriated them to promote a policy less dependent on the Spanish Monarchy.[59]

In this case, it is interesting to observe that it was the Venetians who read and quoted Genoese works, specifically the *Annali* of Agostino Giustiniani (1537), which the author(s) of the pamphlet quoted in order to show that the Genoese had actually been banned by the papacy on several occasions. Examples of the excommunications issued by Pope Gregory X (1272–76) and Innocent VIII (1484–92) were made.[60] Using a Genoese source was obviously a convenient way to learn about these issues; quoting it explicitly in order to deny an alleged Genoese pamphlet brought another ironic touch to the story. In the same way, the author used the *Ristretto delle Historie genovesi* (Lucca, 1551) by Paolo Interiano, a History of Genoa from the year 1000 to 1506 that the Genoese Republic had also approved.[61] The Venetians here used this history of Genoa to trace the excommunication of Genoa by Pope Urban IV (1261–64). By using historical examples found in Genoese literature, the Venetians thus attempted to show that the Genoese had also disobeyed the Papacy because of Roman political ambitions. With the same purpose, they ultimately quoted a (true) excerpt from Interiano's *Historie* concluding that 'in those times the love of the fatherland was esteemed more than the fear of the Pontiffs' ('in quei tempi più l'amor della Patria, che il timor dei Pontefici era stimato') by the Republic of Genoa.[62] Ironically, Genoese Histories now appeared to be instrumental to the Venetian cause.

Moreover, the text addressed the central issue of the relationship with the 'infidels'. Here, the pamphlet accused the Genoese for their role in the eastern Mediterranean, where they had prioritised their merchant interests over religious ones. In particular, the Genoese were accused of infamy for having brought the Turks to Europe on their own ships at one ecu per head, which would have led to nothing less than the loss of Eastern Christianity:

> You have defended our religion against the infidels according to your interests, for which several times you mercenarily sailed to the East, but they cannot exonerate you from the infamy that you earned when, at the price of a shield per head, you ferried the Turkish nation from Asia to Europe with your own ships. And from this fact derived the loss of Christianity in the East, and the dangers of Western Christianity were accelerated[63].

The text referred to the Varna Crusade (1443–1445), when Genoese ships allegedly transported Murad II's army from Anatolia to the Balkans, allowing the Ottomans to defeat the Crusader troops mobilised by Pope Eugene I (who was Venetian), and the Venetian Republic itself. According to some chronicles, such as that of Jean de Wavrin, the Genoese had indeed provided many ships to transport the Turkish troops across the Dardanelles Strait, precisely south of Gallipoli.[64] During the previous decades, and partly because of the rivalry with the Venetians, the Genoese had collaborated on several occasions with the rising force of the eastern Mediterranean, and the Venetians had already been quick to disseminate news of this activity for propaganda purposes. In the same way, they had spread the rumour of Genoese complicity when Constantinople was taken in 1453. By playing on the reputation of the Genoese as mercenaries, the Venetian pamphlet therefore reversed the arguments of the first letter concerning the defence of the Catholic faith.

The text also shows that the Roman initiative led one or more Venetians to feel the necessity of defending the privileged relations they maintained with the Ottoman Empire. Hence, the author of the third pamphlet took care to explain that the commercial interests with the 'infidel' corresponded exactly to those that any prince maintained with the surrounding territories because of the bilateral nature of trade. The text therefore tried to normalise the political relations maintained with the Ottoman Empire: the other Christian princes also paid money to the ministers of the Empire and to the sultan 'when they have to deal with such a barbarous and rapacious nation' ('quando hanno da trattare con natione co[si] tanto barbara e rapace'). The text also formally denied that the Republic was dependent on the Ottoman Empire because of the question of Zante. Rather than truly addressing the issue, however, it shifted it by stating that according to this argument, the King of Spain should be considered tributary to the Papacy because of the census he paid to it. In the same manner, the pamphlet normalised the relationship

with the Ottomans by arguing that the Christian princes also declared war against each other when it was in their interest. On this specific issue, there were therefore no difference between Christians and Muslims ('tra fedeli, che tra infedeli'). The text also denied the accusations of heresy, assuring that 'no Venetian has ever been a heretic' ('non si trovando, che alcun venetiano sia stato giamai heretico').[65]

Ultimately, sharp criticisms were made against the Genoese and about the weakness of their state. It was obviously, here again, a way to support the Venetian political model. The text referred to the allegedly weak protection that the Spanish Monarchy offered to the Republic and introduced several stereotypes about the Genoese financiers who sucked the blood of the Papacy and the rest of Italy due to usury. Lastly, the pamphlet mocked the argument of the first letter according to which the Genoese military forces would support the Pope in case of conflict:

> The offers that you wish to make to the Pope to defend him, the broader they will be in words, the narrower they will be in deeds, since you aim at nothing more than private interest. And what can you give to the Pope, if you have neither public richness, nor forces, nor state, that he will accept, since he is bound to govern himself by his own will alone?[66]

By implicitly comparing Genoa to Venice, the text here referred to the weakness of Genoa's public finances, which were heavily compromised by its dependence on the Bank of San Giorgio, the weakness of the state, and the limited fiscal resources of Liguria.[67] The text thus took up the Botero's parallel that had become classic between Venice and Genoa and the different importance that the two Republics had given to the *res publica* over the centuries.[68]

This distinction was to some extent true, but it also underestimated and disdained the capacity that Genoa had to defend its interests through its privileged links with the Spanish Monarchy. It was the case in the military field, where, at that time, the participation of its elites in the Mediterranean fleet was matched by imperial protection.[69] The price to pay was that of a limited autonomy while Venice, on the other hand, had to assume a role of territorial power with all its implications.

Conclusion

This study has uncovered conflicting discourses exchanged – fictitiously, but with real meanings and implications – between the two main Italian republics of the early modern period. While the School of Cambridge has mostly focused on underlining the similarities between the different components of an alleged European republican heritage, these texts show how, in the concrete context of the early seventeenth century, the two republics were opposed and confronted – both by external and local authors – for political propaganda purposes. The policy of Genoa – indeed more conciliatory towards the Papacy – was instrumentalised by a third party in order to criticise the anti-papal policy of Venice. By portraying a Genoese Republic that considered obeying the Papacy not as a political weakening or even a threat to republican liberty, but as a source of honour, an author – perhaps the Jesuit Possevino – found a very clever way of presenting an alternative path that demonstrated that Venice had opted for a radical position. The apparent similarities between the two merchant republics made the Venetian policy more questionable. Although the letter was not written by the Genoese patriciate, the fiction was closely linked to historical reality.

The republican thinking here portrayed was not far from that assumed by many members of the Genoese *nobiltà vecchia* that had effectively bet on a republicanism compatible with relations of conciliation (and sometimes dependence and obedience) towards the Papacy and the Spanish Monarchy. From this perspective, the text also makes visible certain differences in terms of political culture. Although the imperative of maintaining friendly relations with Genoa prevented Venice from responding vehemently in an official manner, the third pamphlet is nonetheless indicative of the refusal of some Venetians to consider Genoa on the same level as its Venetian counterpart. In this sense, the pamphlets that arose during the Interdict provide another example of the rivalry that often characterised relations between republics.

As shown by the third pamphlet, the representation of Venice was based on its distinction from other republics considered as inferior because they were not originally free. Underlining the dependence of other republics was a way to represent the Venetian one as unique. Hence, the two republican models appeared not only as competing, but also as useful to at least one of the parties. This conclusion is in line with the condescending attitude of the Venetian patriciate when, during the 1640s, Genoese reformers tried to establish collaborative links with it.[70]

However, at the beginning of the seventeenth century it had become complicated to demonstrate that a republic was perfectly free and independent. Even though the texts analysed were short pamphlets, their analysis is significant for how republican representations were shaped by the high degree of political, economic, military, jurisdictional and symbolic dependence of Genoa, but also of Venice, towards the papal authority, the Ottoman Empire, and the Spanish Monarchy. From this point of view, the representations here analysed are different from what emerges from most studies of the School of Cambridge, which have focused on republican liberty in opposition to tyranny and often excluded republican regimes that were not fully sovereign. The limitations of such a selective view of republicanism appear here clearly. Rather than being defined by resistance against the rule and influence of surrounding monarchies, the Genoese Republic was portrayed as a republic that assumed its dependence on the Spanish Monarchy and the Papacy. As for the Venetian Republic, it was forced to defend its close ties with the Ottoman Empire – while recalling past struggles and normalising different ties of interdependence. Behind this, the lack of total autonomy from the Papacy, though heavily fought against, and with great success, was obvious. In the midst of these diatribes, the question of the republican regime became marginal, since the essential issue here was not so much the political model as the degree and the complex forms of liberty and interdependence of both republics with respect to the diverse political regimes directed from Madrid, Istanbul and Rome.

* This article was produced within the frame of the research project 'Res Pública Monárquica. La Monarquía Hispánica, una estructura imperial policéntrica de repúblicas urbanas' (PGC 2018–095224–B-100) directed by Manuel Herrero Sánchez and funded by the Spanish Ministry of Science and Innovation. I am grateful to the École française de Rome, where I completed this article as a visiting scholar.

1 On this important issue, see the contribution of Manuel Herrero Sánchez in this book. About the School of Cambridge: Pocock, *The Machiavellian Moment*; Skinner, *Liberty before Liberalism*; Van Gelderen and Skinner, eds, *Republicanism*; Bouwsma, *Venice and the Defense*.

2 Sánchez, 'Introducción'; Zucchi, 'Repubblicanesimo antico e moderno'.

3 On this topic: Zucchi, 'Repubblicanesimo antico e moderno', pp. 168–69.

4 Maréchaux, 'Cultiver l'alternative'.

5 De Vivo, *Information and Communication*.

6 MCV, MS 1020, fols 246r-247v (henceforth indicated as *Copia della lettera*); BAV, Urb. lat. 1113, fol. 281r-v, 'Copia d'una lettera della Serenissima Repubblica di Genova in risposta di una scritta li dalla Repubblica di Venetia'; BCBV, MS 1202, fols 615r-618r, 'Lettera della Republica di Genova alla Republica di Venetia'. I would like to thank Andrea Savio for providing me with the copy kept at the BCBV.

7 Bitossi, 'L'antico regime genovese', p. 417; Grendi, *In altri termini*, pp. 60–61; ASCG, MBS, ms 109 D4, 'Racconto delle cose successe in Genova dall'anno 1600 sino al 1610', fol. 90ʳ, 18 August 1605.

8 'Fù mandato grida [...] come il Serenissimo Senato haveva con li voti necessari ritrattato, e annulato il decreto fatto circa l'annullare le confrattarie, et le compagnie, et lasciato ogni cosa, com'era prima et questo per non tirarsi adosso l'ira del Pontefice, che fù scritto, che la sentiva male', ASCG, MBS, ms 109 D4, 'Racconto', fol. 93ᵛ, 25 October 1605.

9 ASCG, MBS, ms 109 D4, 'Racconto', fol. 94ʳ, 12 November 1605. On Sauli: Pizzorno, *Genova e Roma tra Cinque e Seicento*; Ben Yessef Garfia, 'Mobilità e cooptazione'.

10 The bibliography on the Interdict is vast. Sarpi, *Opere*; Cozzi, *Paolo Sarpi tra Venezia e l'Europa*; Cozzi, *Paolo Sarpi. Consulti*; De Vivo, *Information and Communication*.

11 Lazzerini, 'Officina Sarpiana', p. 36; Cappelletti, *I Gesuiti e la Repubblica di Venezia*, pp. 169–72.

12 BAV, Urb. lat. 1113, fol. 281r-v, 'Copia d'una lettera della Serenissima Repubblica di Genova in risposta di una scritta li dalla Repubblica di Venetia'. In the upper left corner of the *Copia* there is a reference to the *avvisi* of 26 July 1606.

13 'Assai innosenti', 'ma non in tutto laudate, mostrando tropo risentimento con Venetiani'. AAV, Segretaria di Stato, Avvisi, n. 2, fols 202r-206r, 26 and 29 July 1606.

14 Peirano, *Lettera della Repubblica di Genova*.

15 Cappelletti, *I Gesuiti e la Repubblica di Venezia*, pp. 159–68; Lazzerini, 'Officina Sarpiana', p. 36.

16 BCBV, ms 1202, fols 615r-618r, 'Lettera della Republica di Genova alla Republica di Venetia' with an *avviso* from Genoa, 28 July 1606.

17 Maréchaux, 'Negociar, disuadir y comunicar', pp. 101–04.

18 AGS, Estado, leg. 1433, doc. 176, Juan Vivas to Philipp III, 25 July 1606.

19 De Vivo, *Information and Communication*; Viallon and Dompnier, 'Le traité de la matière bénéficiale'.

20 'Serenissimo Principe [the Republic of Venice], Habbiamo ricevuto la lettera de Vostra Serenità, la quale ha cagionato in noi [the Republic of Genoa] diverso effetto da quello, che ella pensava; poiche l'havere noi ceduto alla volontà del Sommo Pontefice in revocare li decreti da noi fatti contra li oratori, non solo non torna in pregiudicio nostro, ma piu tosto è in augmento della dignità della nostra Republica, et in vergogna di coloro, li quali in simile occasione fossero renitenti alla pia mente di Sua Santità'. *Copia della lettera*.

21 Assereto, 'Lo sguardo di Genova su Venezia'; Maréchaux, 'Cultiver l'alternative'.

22 'D'esser lodati, & magnificati come veri Catholici, & fidelissimi Christiani; né perciò hanno persa la loro libertà: anzi con tale attione si hanno aggiunta una gioia inestimabile', Possevino, *Risposta del Sig. Paolo Anafesto*.

23 Pizzorno, *Genova e Roma tra Cinque e Seicento*, pp. 270–86.

24 Lazzerini, 'Officina Sarpiana', p. 36; De Vivo, *Information and Communication*, p. 222; Mazetti Petersson, *A Culture for the Christian Commonwealth*, p. 191.

25 De Vivo, *Information and Communication*, p. 222.

26 See Sarpi, *Opere*; De Franceschi, *Raison d'État et raison d'Église*.

27 See in particular Gaeta, 'Venezia da "stato misto" ad aristocrazia "esemplare"'; Fasoli, 'I fondamenti della storiografia veneziana'; Crouzet-Pavan, *Venise: une invention de la ville*; De Vivo, 'Historical Justifications of Venetian Power in the Adriatic'. See also Bouwsma, *Venice and the Defense*.

28 Stella, 'La riforma protestante'; Calabi, Camerino, and Concina, *La città degli ebrei*; Pedani, 'Between Diplomacy and Trade'.

29 Gaeta, 'Venezia da "stato misto" ad aristocrazia "esemplare"', pp. 467–68.

30 'Dipende da un Re Barbaro, per il quale sappiamo, che sotto nome di donativo ai suoi ministri sborsate di continuo tributo di gran quantità d'oro'.

31 Crouzet-Pavan, *Venise: une invention de la ville*, p. 241; Maria Pia Pedani, *Dalla frontiera al confine*.

32 Fabris, 'Un caso di pirateria veneziana'; Raby, 'La Sérénissime et la Sublime Porte'; Molà, 'Material Diplomacy'; Maréchaux, '"Non andare mai alla giustizia"'.

33 Pedani, *La dimora della pace*, pp. 34–38; Maréchaux, '"Non andare mai alla giustizia"'.

34 Maréchaux, '"Non andare mai alla giustizia"'.

35 Crouzet-Pavan, *Venise triomphante*.

36 MCV, ms 1020, fols 248r-249v, 'Risposta per l'auttore della lettera scritta dalla Serenissima Republica di Genova al Serenissimo Doge di Venetia [di G.B.L.] scritta da un nobile, à cui fu mandata, come opera novamente stampata'. The added words '[di G.B.L.]' remain unclear.

37 De Vivo, *Information and Communication*, p. 228; Possevino, *Lettera del Padre Antonio Possevino*.

38 *Due lettere una publicata sotto nome della Republica di Genova alla Republica di Venetia. L'altra che contiene il parere sopra la medesima Lettera*, Venice, 1606.

39 Several copies have been retrieved from the catalogues of the Biblioteca Marciana and the Museo Correr, the Biblioteca del Seminario vescovile e della Facoltà teologica del Triveneto (Padova), the Biblioteca Nazionale Centrale (Florence), the Biblioteca Universitaria di Genova, the Biblioteca Civica Angelo Mai (Bergamo), the Bibliothèque Nationale de France, the Bibliothèque Mazarine de Paris, the Biblioteca Nacional de Madrid, the British Library, and the Biblioteca comunale Classense of Ravenna.

40 *Copia di due lettere una publicata sotto nome della Republica di Genova alla Republica di Venetia. L'altra che contiene il parere sopra la medesima Lettera*.

41 De Vivo, *Information and Communication*, pp. 218–19.

42 *Pro libertate status et reipublicae Venetorum Gallofranci ad Philenetum epistola*. Some copies used the edition of 1606 published in Venice, others the one published in Vicenza in 1607.

43 About Servin, see Cozzi, *Paolo Sarpi. Consulti*, pp. 81–82.

44 De Vivo, *Information and Communication*, p. 219; De Vivo, 'Francia e Inghilterra di fronte all'Interdetto di Venezia', pp. 175–76.

45 *Raccolta degli scritti vsciti fvori in istampa, e scritti a mano, nella cavsa del P. Paolo V. co' Signori Venetiani. Secondo le stampe di Venetia, di Roma, & d'altri luoghi*. See De Vivo, *Information and Communication*, p. 167.

46 'Et cio è, che si come Genova, e Venetia due Republiche, che sono l'ornamento, e la gloria d'Italia, stimano egualmente come hanno fatto i loro maggiori la Sede Apostolica, cosi l'una, e l'altra attente alla conservatione della libertà d'Italia, e della grandezza del nome Christiano, regolano e conducono le attioni loro secondo le opportunità delle occasioni con circospettione e vigilanza di prudenti Senatori e ministri, e non hanno da sottopporre le loro deliberationi alla sciocca, & arrabbiata petulanza di consultori contagiosi & insolenti [...] Et insieme intenda questo indiscretissimo calumniatore, che si come Genova con molta maturità, e sicurtà di prudenza stà unita con quel gran Re, cosi Venetia per se sola, e con l'armi, e co'l negotio per tanti anni ha fatto, e fa gloriosa [resistenza]

alle forze de Turchi, che s'hanno assorbito tanti vastissimi Regni, e tutto ciò non meno per difesa, e sostentamento della propria libertà, che del rimanente d'Italia, & in specie della Sede Apostolica'. *Due lettere*, fol. 8.

47 MCV, ms. 1020, fols 250r-255v, 'Un'altra nova. Risposta alla lettera da Genova di [Gier./Gio. Tiep.]'. The indication '[Gier./Gio. Tiep.]' has not allowed us to identify the author of the manuscript so far.

48 Bouza Álvarez, '*Corre manuscrito*'; De Vivo, *Information and Communication*.

49 https://www.nuovabibliotecamanoscritta. it/Generale/ricerca/AnteprimaManoscritto. html?codiceMan=9348&language=EN (catalogue record created by Sabrina Salis).

50 'Non è meraviglia, che voi altri avezzi alla servitù spagnola vi siate contentati di ricevere anco il giogo della Ecclesiastica, poiche perduta una sol volta la libertà, poco si apprezza piu l'una, che l'altra sorte di servitù, potendo essere anco, che voi l'habbiate fatto in vendetta delle violenze, che provate nelle oppressioni loro et dall'invidia di veder noi altri liberi, sperando con questo essempio de farci capaci della miseria et infelicità vostra ; ma ve ingannate al sicuro, se credete, che si possa viver in servitu, da chi è nutrito in libertà. Voi servi per ellettione de vostri maggiori et per nascimento e natura vostra attendete pure à gloriarvi nei cessi di questa falsa libertà, che vi pensate di havere, che come in altri tempi le proprie discordie vi hanno fatto perdere il nome di Republica et sottoporvi ai Duchi di Milano, et à genti straniere, cosi havendovi al presente gli interessi et l'ambitione de vostri cittadini fatto ricevere le leggi dell'altrui volontà, contro al costume de Principati liberi, vi fanno poco meno, che degni del nome de schiavi, de quali non è proprio altro che l'obedire al Patrone senza distintione di ragione, ò di tempo. E godete de questa gran dignità et de cosi gran privilegio, che vi pare, d'haver acquistato, registrandolo à memoria de vostri posteri, à fine, che habbino à detestare il nome vostro in ogni età'. 'Un'altra nova', fol. 250r.

51 On the 1575 crisis, see Savelli, *La repubblica oligarchica*.

52 'Che poi da alcuni di essi Pontefici siamo stati dechiarati contumaci di quella Sede, può forse dirsi con più ragione, colpa dell'ambitione, o emulatione, che hanno essercitato con la Republica, che demerito di lei. De quali due aponto della vostra Patria, o natione, Sisto et Giulio, l'uno Quarto et l'altro Secondo, di nome, ardirono farlo con cosi poca ragione, che oltra il biasimo delli huomeni incorsero manifestamente nell'indignatione del signor Dio […] essendo l'uno che fu Sisto morto di rabbia cinque hore dopo l'aviso, che hebbe della pace conclusa da noi con suoi adherenti con tanta gloria, et utile dello stato nostro, et cosi poca dignità di lui […] Et l'altro, che fu Giulio mancato di vita improvisamente in pochi giorni oppresso dal timore, che il concilio l'havesse à deponere di quella dignità, nella quale haveva dato occasione di spargere tanto sangue de christiani et di mandare in perditione tante anime […] havendosi fatto conoscere […] più degno di maneggiar la spada, che la croce'. 'Un'altra nova', fol. 250r.

53 See Lombardi, 'Sisto IV, Papa', in *Dizionario biografico degli italiani*.

54 Pastore, 'Giulio II, Papa', in *Dizionario biografico degli italiani*.

55 Rospocher, *Il papa guerriero*.

56 Rospocher, *Il papa guerriero*, pp. 242–56.

57 See Lane, *Venice: A Maritime Republic*; Ortalli and Puncuh, eds, *Genova, Venezia, il Levante nei secoli XII-XIV*; Musarra, *Il Grifo e il Leone*.

58 Crouzet-Pavan, *Venise: une invention de la ville*, pp. 235–55.

59 Maréchaux, 'Cultiver l'alternative'.

60 Giustiniani, *Castigatissimi annali*.

61 Interiano, *Ristretto delle historie genovesi*.

62 In the Historie, Interiano argued that 'perciò che piu in quei tempi l'amor della Patria, che il timor dei Pontefici era stimato' (Interiano, *Ristretto delle historie genovesi*, fol. 69ᵛ).

63 'Che habbiate poi diffesa la nostra religione contra infideli, lo possono affirmare i vostri interressi, per i quali vi conduceste piu volte mercenariamente à navigare in oriente, ma non vi possono già escusare dall'infamia, che guadagnaste quando à prezzo d'un scudo per testa traghettaste con le vostre istesse navi d'Asia in Europa la natione Turchesca, dal qual passaggio è nata la perdita del Christianesimo di oriente, et si sono accellerati i pericoli della occidentale christianità'. 'Un'altra nova', fol. 252r.

64 Tuleja, 'Eugenius IV and the Crusade of Varna'; Imber, *The Crusade of Varna, 1443–45*, pp. 5–7, 30, 126–29; Musarra, *Il Grifo e il Leone*, p. 281; Musarra, *Genova e il mare nel Medioevo*, p. 167.

65 'Un'altra nova', fol. 252r-v.

66 'L'offerte, che dite voler fare al Pontefice, per diffenderlo, quanto piu saranno larghe nelle parole, tanto piu ristrette saranno nei fatti, non mirando ciascuno di voi ad'altro, che all'interesse privato. Et che potete voi dare al Papa, se non havete ne publico erario, ne forze, ne stato, che quando haveste consiglio che fosse buono per voi, meno egli lo accettaria, essendo ressoluto di reggersi con la sua sola voluntà'. 'Un'altra nova', fol. 253r.

67 Felloni, 'Stato genovese, finanza pubblica e ricchezza privata'.

68 See, among many other studies, Felloni, 'Ricchezza privata, credito e banche'; Herrero Sánchez, 'Génova y el sistema imperial hispánico'; Maréchaux, 'Cultiver l'alternative'. See also the contribution of Manuel Herrero Sánchez in this volume.

69 Lo Basso, *Uomini da remo*; Maréchaux, 'Business Organisation in the Mediterranean Sea'.

70 Maréchaux, 'Cultiver l'alternative'.

7

Fiorenzo Toso

'VERSCI, MORTE DRO TEMPO'

Civil Commitment and Celebratory Rhetoric
in Genoese Literature in the Sixteenth
and Seventeenth Centuries

The second half of the sixteenth century and the first half of the seventeenth century saw the greatest flourishing of Genoese literature. In that crucial phase for the history of the Republic, the written use of the local language was part of the symbolic enhancement of the cultural specificities of the territory as a reflection of the original political and institutional experience of Genoa. This literary use appears to be characterised by a high level of elaboration. The authors take into account the experiences of international Mannerism and Baroque also in their relationship with the figurative arts and the great Ligurian architecture of the time whose main rhetorical themes they share.[1]

Contrary to what might be suggested by a reading of regional linguistic history focused on the identity needs and nationalistic myths of the Risorgimento, the artistic use of Genoese does not suggest an attitude of nostalgic withdrawal into the past. It is the result of elaboration processes inserted into the European context of the affirmation of vernacular languages, the same impulse that found its main expression in Italy in the *Questione della lingua*. Even the polemic of some local intellectuals against the Tuscan idiom is above all a response to the stigmatisation of Genoese as a 'barbaric' and 'naturally ill' language. This image was a reflection of ancient stereotypes, and can be found in the sixteenth century writings of Tuscan authors such as Benedetto Varchi, but these judgements are overturned to symbolically affirm the originality of the artistic experience of poetry 'in the Genoese style'.

The work of authors such as Paolo Foglietta, Vincenzo Dartonna, Barnaba Cigala Casero, Gian Giacomo Cavalli and Giuliano Rossi represents a significant aspect of Ligurian culture at the time, especially in its political components. For these authors, literary use puts Genoese on the same level as other languages in a context characterised by accentuated multilingualism. Its character of *langue du pays* in fact contributes, more than any other form of expression, to emphasise the rituals and rhetoric of legitimation of republican power in the eyes of the people and the ruling class itself. At the level of elaborated orality, it is almost exclusively used. These aspects must be considered in order to correctly assess the significance of the participation of various Genoese authors in the elaboration of the great multilingual poetic cycle (with texts known, until now, in Italian, Latin, Greek, French, Spanish and, precisely, Genoese) linked to the celebration and praise of the newly elected doges.[2]

The use of Genoese as a language capable of celebrating the ruling class in literature begins with a solid medieval tradition. It starts with some poems by an anonymous thirteenth century poet, and arrives up to the cycle of *cantari* in support of the Doria family in the period leading up to the institutional change of 1528.[3] In spite of the break caused by the reform promoted by Paolo Foglietta with respect to the late fifteenth century multilingual tradition, a continuity of content can be recognised between the various *Opera e lamento de Zena*, *Opera novamente composta* and the celebratory poems by Foglietta himself contained in the first edition of *Rime diverse in lengua zeneise* (1575). This book is the most important document of the new literature in Genoese. It was also promoted outside the territory of the Republic, starting with the second edition in 1583, by the shrewd publisher and cultural operator, Cristoforo Zabata. It can be considered the promotional manifesto of a literary culture that wanted to be a synthesis of local experiences (not only in artistic terms, but also and above all political-institutional) and the 'model' of a new poetics.

From the manifestations of elaborate orality developed in coexistence with the use of Italian and other languages,[4] this presence in written uses, literary and otherwise, will be scaled down from the 1580s onwards, with the emergence of the need for a more extensive extra-local communication code. However, it will leave significant traces in the perception of the Genoese language, until the fall of the Republic, as a constitutive element of official culture and institutional practice.

The importance attributed to political communication in Genoese can also be seen through the history of the removals suffered by some of these texts during the editorial path of the *Rime Diverse*, a book of decisive importance for the construction and clarification of a coherent design of the Genoese republican imagination. It is no coincidence, for example, that the evolution of Paolo Foglietta's political path, up to a critical attitude towards the Dorias (in consonance with the thought of his brother Oberto) corresponds to the removal from the editions of the *Rime*, after 1575, of encomiastic texts such as the one dedicated to Gian Andrea, the sonnet 'Ri doi gren nomi segnò Zane Andria'.[5] This is a resounding repudiation. At the very moment when it reaffirms the far from innocuous character of the anthology, it highlights a harsh criticism of the regime. Paolo, a prestigious figure, 'official' author of the *fróttore* for the annual carnival celebrations,[6] thus expresses his open dissent from the *Leges novae* inspired by Gian Andrea.

Foglietta's celebratory poems are, strictly speaking, still outside the encomiastic 'genre' specifically associated with doges. This type of poetry, as far as we know, appeared in Genoese at the initiative of Barnaba Cigala Casero, in 1593 (fig. 7.1), and continued to develop for over 150 years. A partial survey of the biennial publications for the election of doges and other printed and manuscript collections has so far made it possible to compile the following catalogue, undoubtedly incomplete:

[Cigala Casero], Discorso in lingua genovese, doppo la elettione del Sereniss. Duce di Genova il sig. Antonio Cebà (Genova: per gli heredi di Girolamo Bartoli, [1593]);[7]

[Cigala Casero], Discorso nella elettione del Serenissimo signor Agostino Doria duce, et de l'illustrissimo e reverendissimo signor Oratio Spinola Arcivescovo di Genova (Genova: Pavoni, 1601);

[Anonymous], Encomio nella elettione del Serenissimo signor Bernardo Clavarezza duce de la seneriss[ima] Republica di Genova seguita a XXIII d'aprile MDCXV vigilia / di San Georgio (Genova: Pavoni, [1615]);[8]

Balin ambasciao dri pescuei a ro serenissimo Zorzo Centurion duxe dra Repubrica de Zena canzon, de Gio. Giacomo Cavallo, in Per la coronatione del Serenissimo Giorgio Centurione (Genova: Pavoni, 1622), pp. 149–57;[9]

[Cavalli], Coronna dra Giustitia, mandà da ro Cé a ro Serenissimo Lonardo da ra Torre duxe dra Repubrica de Zena in ra so incoronation, in Ra cittara zeneize. Poexie de Gian Giacomo Cavallo a ro Ser.mo Gian Steva Doria duxe de Zena (Zena: Pavoni, 1636), pp. 177–86;

[Cavalli], Ra muza zeneize nell'incoronation dro Serenissimo Gian Steva Doria duxe dra Repubrica de Zena, in Ra cittara zeneize (Zena: Pavoni, 1635), pp. 161–66;

Pe ra incoronazion dro Serenissimo principe Aostin Paravexin duxe reà dra Serenissima Republica de Zena, dro P. F. Aostin Schiafin, in Applausi della Liguria nella reale incoronazione del Serenissimo Agostino Pallavicino duce della Republica di Genova (Genova: Pavoni, 1638), pp. 124–28 n.n;

A ro Serenissimo Agostin Paravexin duxe de Zena in ra so incoronation. Elogio de Gian Giacomo Cavallo, in Applausi della Liguria nella reale

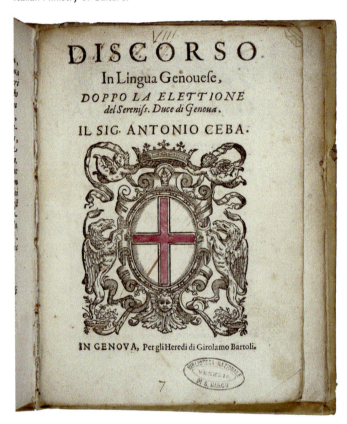

7.1

Title page of Barnaba Cigala Casero, *Discorso in lingua genouese, doppo la elettione del sereniss. duce di Genoua il sig. Antonio Ceba*, in Genoua, per gli heredi di Girolamo Bartoli, after 1593. Photo: Venice, Biblioteca Nazionale Marciana. With permission from the Italian Ministry of Culture.

incoronatione del Serenissimo Agostino Pallavicino (Genova: Pavoni 1638), pp. 177–86 n.n.;

[Cavalli], A ro serenissimo Gian Battista Durasso Duxe de Zena, in ra sò elettion. Panegirico boscareccio (Zena: Pavon, 1640);

Applauzo de Zena e tempomegio dro Parnazo per l'elecion dro Serenissimo Giruœmo de Franchi Duxe. Poemetto de Gian Giacomo Cavallo (Zena: Beneito Guascho, 1653);

Invio e viaggio dre Muze pe ra reale solennitè dro Serenissimo Alessandro Spinnora Duxe de Zena. Poemetto de Gian Giacomo Cavallo (Zena: Gian Maria Farron, 1655);[10]

[Rossi], Sciù re groie dro Ser.mo Allessandro Spinoa Duxe de Ziena;[11]

[De Franchi], Re muze in ra coronaçion dro Serenissimo duxe Agostin Lomellin, in Ro chitarrin ò sæ stroffoggi dra Muza de Steva de Franchi nobile patriçio zeneise dîto tra ri arcadi Micrilbo Termopilatide, dedicao à ri veri e boin Zeneixi amanti dra patria, dra libertæ e dra sò lengua naturale (Zena: Gexiniana, 1772), pp. 128–36;

[De Franchi], Pe ra coronaçion dro Seroniss. Duxe Ridolfo Emilio Maria Brignore, in Ro chitarrin ò sæ stroffoggi dra Muza (Zena: Gexiniana, 1762), pp. 138–41;

[De Franchi], Ro chitarrin zeneize in ra Coronaçion dro Serenissimo Giambatista Negron, in Ro chitarrin ò sæ stroffoggi dra Muza (Zena: Gexiniana, 1769), pp. 142–47;

[De Franchi], Giano bifronte in ra Coronaçion dro Serenissimo Giambatista

Cangiaxo, in Ro chitarrin ò sæ stroffoggi dra Muza (Zena: Gexiniana, 1771), pp. 148–62;

Ro retræto dro Serenissimo Giambattista Airœu, pe ra so coronazion in duxe dra republica de Zena. Canzon (Zena: Scionico, 1783).[12]

In order to formulate some general remarks, we can dwell briefly on the texts of the most significant authors within this literary genre. If this type of poetry can be considered 'minor' as far as the use of Italian is concerned, it is instead of considerable importance for literature in the Genoese language. In fact it confirms, as we have already observed, the full legitimacy of its use and its strong visibility in an institutional context.

What clearly emerges is the far from static nature, in form and content, of encomiastic and celebratory poetry in Genoese. It played an important role, which was recognised by the ruling class and public opinion in Liguria. This celebratory literature was not merely an occasional rhetorical exercise. Following Foglietta's more explicit polemical vein in his sonnets on the decadence of customs and the need for naval rearmament, in his *Discorso* of 1593 Barnaba Cigala Casero combines rhetorical praise with a series of observations on the management of public affairs, and outlines a detailed political programme with references to the economic and social events of the time. He exercises a criticism of the status quo, which in its essential points does not differ much from that of Foglietta. However, the tenor of Casero's proposals differs from Foglietta's in that they are embedded in a fundamentally positive vision of the established order, which may be perfectible but which is suitable for the management of the Republic.[13] In foreign policy, he insisted on the need for an alliance with Spain. Casero thus showed a more pragmatic attitude than Paolo, renouncing the efforts to relaunch the international role of the Ligurian state which, anachronistically, Foglietta had supported in his *Sonetti per armar galee*:

I want to say one more thing of importance
In order to conclude the last stanza
And this is its content:
The best for us is
With the Catholic and Sacred Monarchy
To stay always allied.

Because its friendship is so loyal
And we proceed right and just,
So that we cannot be wrong,

[...]
In Italy every Prince lives in peace
Because the Spanish king allows this,
He is the basis and heart of
The public rest and security
Of all the Christian people.[14]

The slow and almost prosaic progress of the poem confirms the programmatic function of the text, which is a sort of manual of good government for the doge and senators. Its exemplary character also emerges in the reference to the medieval bestiary and in the comparison with the institutions of other countries. It recalls the didactic instances present in the 'political' poetry of the thirteenth-century Anonimo, even if it updates them to a profoundly different historical situation.[15]

References to the Anonimo recur elsewhere, for example when Casero goes on to develop the theme of unity of purpose as an essential condition of civic life. The State is compared to a galley, where all must row in unison in order not to lose the common course. This is effectively re-proposed to support, as in the medieval poetry, the value (confirmed by the Latin quotation) of unity as a source of law and authority:

Although we are many people
we should be one,
each in his rank, for the common purpose.

[...]
But if a ship full of people
leaves for Messina,
and the other one goes to Sardinia, and another in Barcelona,
we cannot do anything good.

[...]
As experience will show,
every divided kingdom will be desolate
and it will not be preserved.[16]

But these echoes, which place Casero in the wake of an illustrious local tradition, are bent on supporting the experience of the government of the oligarchy. Casero reformulates the 'democratic' image dear to the thirteenth-century poet and uses it to describe the hierarchy and discipline in force on board, thus introducing the concept of obedience and respect due to superiors and optimates.

The success of the 1593 poem led Casero to repeat the experience in 1601 with a composition dedicated to the election of Agostino Doria and the simultaneous archiepiscopal mandate of Orazio Spinola. Resuming the structure of the previous poem, Casero preferred, however, to give more space to the praise of the two characters. In the second part, the poet praises the family of the new doge, with the mention of characters such as Ilario, Paganino and above all Andrea Doria; for the eulogy of Andrea he takes up the arguments inserted by Ariosto in a well-known passage of *Orlando furioso*.

The concomitance between the election of the doge and the installation of the new archbishop allowed Casero to reflect on the theme of the distribution of roles between civil and ecclesiastical power. But Barnaba did not indulge

7.2
Title page of Giovanni Giacomo Cavalli, *Ra cittara zeneize poexie de Gian Giacomo Cauallo a ro ser.mo Gian Steua Doria duxe de Zena*, Genoua, Giuseppe Pauoni, 1636. Photo: GAP s.r.l., Biblioteca Nazionale Centrale, Florence. Reproduced with permission.

in polemical declarations, preferring to predict a rosy destiny for the Republic, guaranteed by the renewal of the urban road system that would lead to the transformation of the streets of Pre, Sottoripa and Balbi into modern commercial arteries surrounded by palaces worthy of the opulence of the exponents of the financial aristocracy. The reference to public works recalls considerations of a 'political' nature relating to the symbolic redefinition of urban spaces by the Genoese ruling class and softens the tone of the political proposal compared to the text of 1593. The celebration of the house of Doria takes the place of the commemoration of the glories of the homeland, and marks a further disengagement from active politics. In this way the text of 1601, not only for chronological reasons, comes close to Cavalli's later encomiums, and marks a stage in the transition towards the Baroque encomium and its renewed artistic and ideological demands.

Gian Giacomo Cavalli[17] embodies better than any other poet of his time, and not only in Genoese, the close relationship between literary production and power. Celebrated by Gabriello Chiabrera as a 'troubadour of things not imagined and hardly believed'[18] this member of the notary class[19] conceived encomiastic poetry as a space for poetic experimentation at the service of republican ideology (fig. 7.2). The adherence to the evolution of the political debate within the Republic is very evident in the passage from the first to the second (in chronological order)[20] of the encomiastic poems published by Cavalli in his 1636 collection, *Ballin ambasciou dri pescuei a ro Serenissimo Zorzo Centurion duxe dra Repubrica de Zena* (1621)[21] and *Coronna dra Giustitia, mandà da ro Cé a ro Serenissimo Lonardo da ra Torre duxe dra Repubrica de Zena in ra so incoronation* (1631).[22]

In the 1621 ode, the theme of the delegation of popular sovereignty to the authority of the doge exploits to the extreme the piscatorial decorum he had already used with great skill in the *Amori*,[23] inserting the praise of the new doge in a festive underwater vision. In 1631, with the election of a representative of the absolutist wing of the Genoese oligarchy, Cavalli instead ascends to that paradise in which, according to Counter-Reformation principles, the 'veri imperii e monarchie' ('true empires and monarchies') 'han reixe, e fondamento' ('have roots and foundations').[24] Here he simultaneously celebrates the rhetorical theme of the divine origin of power, the definitive triumph of artifice over nature[25] and his own transfiguration into an 'eagle'[26] dedicated to the highest flights. It is the metamorphosis of a poet who had not disdained, 'per gusto oura dro senso, oura dri tersi' ('indulging the audience and the verse') to transform himself 'oura in hommo de villa, oura in pescou' ('in a farmer or a fisherman').[27]

The succession of two texts celebrating, a decade apart, figures belonging to opposing ideological currents such as Centurione and della Torre, underlines in Cavalli, rather than a change in his 'political' orientation, an evolution of his poetic ambitions. Nevertheless, one cannot help but notice that it is precisely the attention to the political-institutional context that determines the choice of the moment in which to carry out his artistic reconversion. This circumstance confirms the poet's attention to the evolution of the political debate. This sensitivity is also clearly revealed by the symbolic choices made to capture in the collective imagination of the ruling class and public opinion the elements that best fit a coherent celebratory programme.

In 1621, the fisherman Ballin, who in the love poems is the symbol of humanity tormented by passion, brought the doge the homage of the inhabitants of the 'scuœggi e care chiù vexinne' ('from these cliffs and closer coves'),[28] which were the mythical and founding places of Genoese republican life.[29] The ode thus opens with a reference to the rock, a theme linked to a founding myth present in all the celebratory rhetoric of Genoa. Ultimately, it refers to a passage from Cicero (*De leg. agr.*, II, 35, 95), to the well-known Gospel passage on building on stone and finally to the erudite legend of Janus, who according to Iacopo da Varagine founded the primitive Genoa on the rock of Carignano (*Chronica civitatis Ianuensis*, 1,3). This image was widely used, particularly by *repubblichisti* publicists, to advocate a return to a Genoa tied to the mercantile traditions imposed by the natural ruggedness of the territory. Cavalli would return to this image, as we have seen, also in the ode to Agostino Pallavicini (vv. 115–18), grasping all its rhetorical and metaphorical value. Similar references, often reversed in a negative sense, are present in the foreign propaganda of the seventeenth century, and in particular in Spanish propaganda, when the poverty of the territory was used to justify the propensity of the Genoese to commercial and financial activities.[30]

In short, fishermen are the category that best recognises in the figure of the doge the representative of the will of all men. It is illuminated by the sun of reason which, 'indeferentemente compartio' ('indiscriminately shared'),[31] pushes them to choose the most worthy to represent them and manage public affairs. Aside from the ideological cue, Cavalli's Ballin is not so much 'l'interprete politico del consenso popolare al governo della Repubblica' ('the political voice of popular consensus in the government of the Republic') as 'un ingegnoso travestimento del poeta secentista' ('an ingenious disguise of the seventeenth-century poet').[32] This is confirmed, in the continuation of the text, by the riot of marine animals, with which Cavalli precludes any possibility of communicating a real political message, and instead takes care to express the extreme manifestations of his own sense of *maraveggia*, astonishment and surprise.[33]

And yet, even taking into account this prevalence of aesthetic needs over the 'political' tendencies of the composition, one cannot overlook the attention paid by the poet to the echoes of the ode in a public that was attentive to institutional debate, and ready to pick up on the slightest allusions of an ideological nature.[34] The variations between the first edition of 1622 and the text fixed in 1636 show how some aspects of the political message of the ode were bent to new requirements, proving to be much more important in the overall economy of the composition than appears at first sight.[35] In turn, the reference in the first stanza of the 1631 poem to the 'concerto idiotto / d'ambasciou sciabegotto' ('the singular concert / by a marine ambassador')[36] of 1621,

marking a direct relationship between the two texts, clearly indicates how the new composition intends to go beyond the praise of the Centurione.

Aware also of the role he had assumed as a national poet with his patriotic poetry for the war of 1625 (Toso, *Poesia patriottica*, forthcoming),[37] Cavalli conceived for himself an artistic programme that 'passe ogni meta / de venna e canto' ('so that I surpass every goal / of vein and singing').[38] In a riot of *maravegge* and conceptual devices, this placed him at the centre of the Genoese Baroque ideology on a level of originality and expressive power to which no other poet could aspire. Here, his *culteranismo* manifests itself in 'verses all aimed at astonishing through hyperbolic images, sophisticated rhetorical figures, unheard-of combinations, sonorous vocabulary', generating 'sumptuous exercises in style, poetry of the senses rather than of the spirit, as Dámaso Alonso said of Góngora'.[39]

The poem depicts the heavenly investiture of the doge, who receives a crown woven by Divine Justice in a decorative context reminiscent of the great Genoese celebratory frescoes of the time.[40] In this rarefied atmosphere, in which the figure of the doge is submerged by the profusion of scenic effects and crushed by that of the poet, it is not surprising that there are no references to the political and institutional reality of the moment, except for a fleeting reference to the great work in progress, no less propagandistic and symbolic than of concrete strategic utility, the construction of the *Mura Nuove*:

> So after reigning storms
> Thanks to his prayers it was built
> To stop the wars that put the world to fire and sword
> And famine and plague
> [...]
> While all Italy is between the pincers
> A crown of walls
> New to its fortunes
> Erected as a trophy
> Around mountains and plains
> Able to amaze the whole world with one voice.[41]

But here we are also in a phase of political uncertainty which, with the occasion of the rhetorical celebration of a power descended from heaven, does not seem to suggest to the poet anything other than an opportunity to let his own extraordinary poetic virtuosity shine. A further development of Cavalli's 'civil' commitment occurred in 1637, on the occasion of the election of Agostino Pallavicino, proclaimed doge after the symbolic initiative with which the Virgin Mary was acclaimed Queen of Genoa. This was an artifice intended to reaffirm the sovereignty of the Republic before the other European crowned heads.[42]

The exceptional nature of the moment is also underlined by the particular symbolic importance of the linguistic choices made in the corresponding celebratory collection.[43] It also includes compositions in French and Spanish,[44] intended to support the idea of homage to the new royal title on the part of the major European powers. At the same time, the inclusion of three compositions in Genoese conveys, once again in the language most accredited in this sense, some programmatic proposals to be submitted to the attention of a doge called on, certainly too optimistically, to launch a sort of political 'new course'.[45] Thus Cavalli, this time, does not limit himself, as in the ode to Della Torre, to a generic reference to the justice that must characterise the actions of the new doge; instead, it calls for concrete action on two points that are essential to the economic recovery of the Republic, the renovation of the port and the exploitation of Corsica's economic potential:

> Corsica's realm of gold
> So apt to illustrate Genoa,
> Which has no arable land
> As a domestic and fertile country,
> In the light of the world
> Pulling along its retinue
>
> Will make good proof
> Of the government of Genoa and its state.[46]

On the same occasion Agostino Schiaffino,[47] openly supporting the positions of the advocates of naval rearmament, developed the image of the Riviera beaches awaiting the intervention of a doge destined to bend Virtue to their expectations, 'annima dre Repubriche ben fete / perché vive ra gente dent'ro lete' ('Soul of well-governed republics, where people live by swimming in milk').[48] In my opinion, the examples proposed here illustrate the concrete political importance and the emblematic importance of the literary use of Genoese in the context of celebratory and encomiastic poetry in the second half of the sixteenth century and the first half of the seventeenth century. This production takes on the myths and rhetoric that are the foundations of Genoese republicanism, drawing on a centuries-old tradition, and updates, fixes and redefines them through the use of a language that is at the same time the main means of communication of the ruling class and a conscious symbol of the originality and collective identity of the country. In this way, together with the painting and architecture of the time, it is proposed as an essential tool for representing the Genoese institutional experience and, today, as a fundamental vehicle for its interpretation.

---

1 For the history of the oligarchic republic it is sufficient here to refer to Costantini, *La Repubblica di Genova*; Grendi, *La Repubblica aristocratica*; Bitossi, *Il governo dei magnifici*. For the history of literature in Genoese, see Toso, *La letteratura ligure in genovese e nei dialetti locali*, in particular vols III and IV for the period of interest here.

2 This vast series of poems, which lasted practically for the entire duration of the Republic, must be studied as a whole in order to highlight its social and symbolic functions and its importance in the panorama of the celebratory apparatus of the ruling class. Its elements of continuity and internal evolution must be analysed. The study by Ruffini, 'Entro serenissimi fogli', on the more strictly bibliographical aspects is very useful. In this context, the use of Genoese seems to have a particularly important representative role, underlining the direct link between the holding of power and the symbols of territorial identity.

3 For the pro-Dorian *cantari* of the second decade of the sixteenth century and other similar texts, see Toso, *La letteratura ligure in genovese e nei dialetti locali*, II, pp. 146–74, with an anthological selection.

4 On the multilingualism characterising Genoese society in the sixteenth-seventeenth centuries, see Toso, 'Un modello di plurilinguismo urbano rinascimentale'.

5 *Rime diverse* (1575, p. 13 a,b). In addition to those in honour of Gian Andrea, in 1575 Foglietta had published verses entitled *A ro Segnò don Zane d'Austria* and *A ro Principe d'Oria*, which were in turn expunged, along with others, from all subsequent editions of the anthology, starting with *Rime diverse* (1583).

6 For several years, probably from the middle of the sixteenth century, Paolo Foglietta was the author of the *Fròttore*, long songs that were the main theme of carnival celebrations. Some of these compositions can be found in the first edition of the *Rime diverse*, but most of them are preserved in manuscript.

7 A modern annotated edition was compiled by T. Hohnerlein-Buchinger (Cigala Casero, *Discorso in lingua genovese*).

8 Some stylistic and textual traces suggest an attribution to Barnaba Cigala Casero in this case as well.

9 Gian Giacomo Cavalli, the most important Genoese poet (circa 1590–1657), is sometimes mentioned with variations in his first and last names.

10 In the editions following the princeps of the *Cittara zeneize*, the encomiums published by Cavalli in the various commemorative collections after 1636 are added. The complete corpus can be read in *Çittara zeneize* (1745).

11 The poem was composed by Giuliano Rossi, an author who has remained largely unpublished. His poetic production is mainly characterised by a parodistic or satirical style. This poem seems to be in competition with the ode dedicated to Alessandro Spinola da Cavalli, an author with whom Rossi had a sort of friendly rivalry. It is a text outside the 'official' celebratory line, probably intended as a personal homage by the poet to the new doge. There are numerous transcriptions of the text in the manuscripts recording Rossi's works. For the sake of brevity, I will limit myself here to quoting it according to the title that appears in the ms. E.V.9 of the Biblioteca Universitaria of Genoa (one of the most complete and reliable) on pp. 102–07.

12 A work by Micrilbo Termopilatide, the Arcadian name of Steva de Franchi himself.

13 See for example Cigala Casero's *Discorso in lingua genovese*, pp. 14–15 n.n.

14 'Vogio dì un'atra cosa d'importantia / E con quella finì l'ultima stantia, / E questa è ra sustantia: / Che a noi sta ben si ne conven assè / Dra Catholica e Sacra Maiestè / Sempre stà confederè. / Perché ra Sò amicitia si è leà / E ro procede ro giusto e reà, / Onde non poemo errà, / In Italia ogni Principe sta in paxe / Perché così a ro gran re piaxe, / L'é fondamento e baxe / Dro pubblico reposo e segurtè / e un dri oggi dra Christianitè'. Cigala Casero, *Discorso in lingua genovese*, p. 19 n.n.

15 These suggestions are confirmed in the rest of the work by the use of metaphors and images dear to the medieval poet. Thus it happens when, in part VI, the invitation to welcome foreigners is introduced by the image of the Genoese 'che più che y atre gente atorno andemo / e quasi in ogni terra nio facemo'. This recalls a famous quatrain by the Anonimo in a way too strong to be accidental: 'E tanti sun li zenoexi, / e per lo mondo così destexi, / che und'eli van o stan, / un'atra Zenoa ge fan'. Anonimo Genovese, *Rime e ritmi latini* (r. 138, vv. 195–98).

16 'Se ben noi semo assè gente in comun / Devereimo a ro scopo esse tutt'un / In ro so grao cascun, / Ma se una nave ch'è de gente pinna / Voresse chi ra ghia pe ra marinna / Andà l'un a Messinna, / L'atro in Sardegna e l'atro a Barcellonna, / No se porreiva moè fà cosa bonna / Ut ab experientia demostrabitur, / Omnem regnum divisum desolabitur / Et non conservabitur'. Cigala Casero, *Discorso in lingua genovese*, pp. 25–26.

17 For the author and the work I refer to my introductory essay in Cavalli, *Ra cittara zeneize*, pp. 7–55.

18 This is Gabriello Chiabrera's definition of Cavalli himself in the presentation of his collection of poems. See Cavalli, *Ra cittara zeneize*, p. 70.

19 Many Ligurian authors of the sixteenth and seventeenth centuries belonged, at least by family tradition, to the notary class, the backbone of the Genoese administration, custodian since the Middle Ages of the historical memories and symbolic apparatus of the Republic.

20 The original edition also includes, as we have seen, the ode in honour of the doge to whom the entire collection is dedicated, Gian Steva (Giovanni Stefano) Doria.

21 'Ballin, fishermen's ambassador, to the Most Serene Giorgio Centurione, Doge of the Republic of Genoa.' The text is presented with a face-to-face translation in Cavalli (*Ra cittara zeneize*, pp. 222–33, with commentary on pp. 383–88) which is reproduced here.

22 'Crown of Justice sent from heaven to the Most Serene Leonardo della Torre, Doge of the Republic of Genoa, on the occasion of his coronation.' See Cavalli, *Ra cittara zeneize*, pp. 234–45, commentary on pp. 388–91.

23 A section of the Cittara is devoted to the 'seafaring' love affairs of Ballin and the beautiful Lichinna, set against a 'naturalistic' backdrop which, although highly stylised, is in keeping with the environmental reality of the Riviera.

24 Cavalli, *Coronna dra Giustitia*, in *Ra cittara zeneise*, vv. 63, 65.

25 According to the formula inspired by Foglietta whereby art 'con girozo contrasto / asbassa à ra natura ogni sò fasto' ('with jealous contrast / deprives Nature of all her pomp'). Cavalli, *Coronna dra Giustitia*, in *Ra cittara zeneise*, vv. 142–43.

26 Cavalli, *Coronna dra Giustitia*, in *Ra cittara zeneise*, v. 41.

27 These verses are taken from two texts that are in various ways representative of Cavalli's arrangement of his poetic production in *Ra cittara zeneize*, respectively the second sonnet of the *Corona Sacra* (v. 11) and the first sonnet of the *Rime Civili* (v. 11).

28 Cavalli, *Ballin ambasciou dri pescuei*, in *Ra cittara zeneise*, v. 1.

29 'Chi me sæ, ve ro dixe per menuo / Quest'habito, esto pescio, esto cestin: / Ro mè nomme è Ballin, / Pescou per quarche famma conossuo; / Ballin matto attretanto / Dra fossina e dre rè come dro canto. / Ro fin, perché à ri pé ve vegne à cazze / È à fave donativo / D'esto pescio ancon vivo / A nomme dri pescuei dre nostre chiazze, / O chiù presto per segno, / Per tributo, e per pegno / Dro nostro bon affetto, appresentave / Con questo don, dri nostri cuœ ra chiave' ('Who I am, this dress, / and the fish, and the basket tell you so: / my name is Ballin, / a fisherman of some renown; / Ballin, he who is fond / of spears and fishing nets and even of singing. / The purpose is that I fall at your feet / to give you this gift / of a fish still alive / in the name of the fishermen of the beaches, / so that this may be a sign, / the tribute and the pledge / of our strong affection, and the handing over to you / the key, together with the gift, of our hearts'). Cavalli, *Ballin ambasciou dri pescuei*, in *Ra cittara zeneise*, vv. 15–28.

30 As has been observed, 'la ristrettezza e la sterilità del territorio era la constatazione d'obbligo da cui prendeva avvio ogni discorso sulla Liguria' (Costantini, *La Repubblica di Genova*, p. 76); See also, in addition to numerous passages by Paolo Foglietta, Andrea Spinola: 'La massima di noi altri Genovesi, nati su' scogli et in tanta sterilità di paese, dev'esser di saper licitamente guadagnar denari con l'industria del negocio e di conservarli con la parsimonia' ('The rule of us Genoese, born on the rocks in such a barren country, must be to simply earn money with industry, and to conserve it with parsimony'). Spinola, *Scritti scelti*, p. 228.

31 Cavalli, *Ballin ambasciou dri pescuei*, in *Ra cittara zeneise*, v. 38.

32 Croce, 'La letteratura dialettale ligure', p. 445.

33 Cavalli, *Ballin ambasciou dri pescuei*, in *Ra cittara zeneise*, vv. 137–68.

34 Concerning the hypertrophy of the ideological debate within the ruling class and the interest it aroused, it seems possible to extend to the first decades of the seventeenth century what has been observed concerning the prerogatives of Genoa as a 'political laboratory' where every aspect of institutional problems was 'attentamente registrato in ogni sua fase da storici e pubblicisti e discusso appassionatamente (per quanto se ne sa) dall'intera cittadinanza'. Costantini, 'Politica e storiografia', p. 99.

35 On this theme I refer to a more detailed discussion in Toso, 'Tra encomio privato e celebrazione pubblica'.

36 Cavalli, *Coronna dra Giustitia*, in *Ra cittara zeneise*, vv. 9–10.

37 In May 1625, on the occasion of the French-Piedmontese invasion of the territory of the Republic, linked to the Savoy claims on the territory of Zuccarello, the poet composed the song *Invia ra Muza à ro bosco per cantà dre arme*. The patriotic text, later included in the *Cittara zeneize*, is analysed in the introductory essay by (Cavalli, *Cittara zeneize*, pp. 51–55), where it is presented and translated on pp. 246–56 (commentary on pp. 391–95).

38 Cavalli, *Coronna dra Giustitia*, in *Ra cittara zeneise*, vv. 38–39.

39 See Brevini, *La poesia in dialetto*, I, p. 937.

40 Cavalli, *Coronna dra Giustitia*, in *Ra cittara zeneise*, vv. 92–156.

41 'Così da re tempeste / In sò preghera uscia / Dre guerre onde ro mondo pà ch'arraggie / E da famme e da peste / Preservà, favoria / Mentre l'Italia tutta è int're tenaggie, / Coronna de muraggie / Nœva à re suœ venture, / Erzendo per trofeo / Com'in campo ò torneo / Per intorno ri monti e re chianure / Farà tutto à unna voxe'. Cavalli, *Coronna dra Giustitia*, in *Ra cittara zeneise*, vv. 183–94.

42 With the proclamation of the Virgin Mary as Queen of the Republic, which took place on 13 May 1637, a complex political-ideological operation was carried out with which the Genoese oligarchy aimed at strengthening its image as a ruling class at international level, while at the same time reaffirming the sovereignty of the Ligurian state and the possession of Corsica itself. On this episode see among others Di Fabio, 'La regina della Repubblica'; Bitossi, 'A Republic in Search of Legitimation'.

43 *Applausi della Liguria*.

44 See Galiñanes Gallén, 'Le poesie in lingua spagnola'.

45 Costantini, *La Repubblica di Genova*, p. 278.

46 'Ra Corsega reamme apuinto d'oro / così atto à illustrase, / che per no coltivase / va, per muœo de parlà, com'in frolloro, / de paeize sarvego / feta terren domestego e fecondo / a ra luxe dro mondo / tirandose a ri dì dro so duxégho / se farà bonna per provei l'appáto / dro governo de Zena e dro sò Stato'. *A ro Serenissimo Agostin Paravexin*, in *Applausi della Liguria*, vv. 161–70. The theme of cleaning and restructuring the port of Genoa is a constant in the internal political debate and interventions of the sixth and seventeenth centuries; that of exploiting the economic potential offered by Corsica is part of the programme of the *repubblichista* party within the oligarchy, and will find partial implementation during the seventeenth century.

47 A Carmelite, author of various works of civil and religious erudition and poetic texts also in Tuscan. Information about him can be found in Soprani, *Li scrittori della Liguria*, pp. 9–10.

48 *Pe ra incoronazion*, in *Applausi della Liguria*, vv. 78–79.

III THE NEGOTIATION OF GENOESE IDENTITY
1620–1660

8

Valentina Borniotto

PERSONIFICATIONS OF THE REPUBLIC IN GENOA

Before and after Cesare Ripa's Iconologia

In the early modern age, the Republic of Genoa made use of many different images, drawing on the vast repertoire of objects and attributes that had come to be associated with the city, in order to represent itself (politically and symbolically), both within and beyond the boundaries of its territories.[1] During the sixteenth century, because of some distinctive, longstanding features of the Genoese political system – such as the weakness of central authority and the alternation of top government positions among the aristocratic families, in whose hands most of the power resided[2] – the visual representation of civic pride focused primarily on selected episodes from the city's history or – more frequently – on the glorification of Genoa's past heroes, such as Guglielmo Embriaco.[3] Those subjects were common both in private and public decorative cycles, while the personifications of the city appeared less often, and the iconography used in them was inconsistent in permanent art works until it found a new codification in Cesare Ripa's Iconologia. By contrast, the representation of Genoa as a female figure – with heterogeneous, non-standardised attributes – enjoyed a more prominent role in ephemeral triumphal arches built for important entries or ceremonies, obviously with a political purpose.

Ephemeral installations

One of the first official uses of a personification to represent the city was for the first entry of Charles V into Genoa (1529). After 1528 Andrea Doria commissioned the Florentine painter Perino del Vaga – a former collaborator of Raphael in Rome – to decorate his magnificent palace.[4] Perino's commission also included three impressive triumphal arches for the entries of the Habsburg Emperor into the city, in 1529 and then again in 1533.[5]

In 1529, when the Palazzo del Principe was not yet completed, Perino drew two distinct arches, a small one to be erected at the docks – where the Emperor would have come

ashore – and another in the Piazza dei Giustiniani, in the city's historic centre. As other scholars have noted,[6] the arches from 1529 and especially the one erected in 1533 used an elaborate iconography, based on Roman history and classical myth, 'to convey the underlying theme of the exaltation of Doria's role, feats, and ancestry'.[7] However, only the arch erected beside the port in 1529 displayed a personification of Genoa, which is unfortunately impossible to make out in Perino's only extant drawing but is described in some literary sources, such as the *Storia Fiorentina* by Benedetto Varchi:

> There was a triumphal arch filled with various and vague stories, mostly demonstrating the good spirits of the Genoese people […]; one of them portrayed Andrea Doria, holding in his left hand the city of Genoa, and in his right a naked sword, and the emperor with both hands was crowning Genoa.[8]

Twenty years later, the prosperous community of *negociatores genuenses* ('Genoese negotiators') in Antwerp asked the Flemish painter Frans Floris to design a large ephemeral arch for the entry of Charles V and his son Philip into the town on 11 September 1549.[9] For this momentous occasion, several ephemeral arches were commissioned by foreign merchants working in Flanders from Spain, Genoa, Florence, England, and Germany. It is possible to reconstruct what Genoa's arch looked like from an illustrated book by Cornelis Grapheus (also known as Scribonius). The city's government had given him the prestigious assignment of organising all

8.1

Pieter Coecke van Aelst, *Triumphal Arch of the Genoese Nation* (1549). Engraving from Cornelis Grapheus, *Spectaculorum in susceptione Philippi Hisp. Princ. divi Caroli V. Caes. F. An. M.D.XLIX. Antverpiae aeditorum mirificus apparatus*, Antverpiae, Disthem, 1550, p. F 4v. Photo: Staatsbibliothek Bamberg, JH.Top.f. 13. Reproduced with permission.

DOI 10.1484/M.DUNAMIS-EB.5.142037

PRIVATVS GENVENSIVM ARCVS,
In via hospitalaria ad triangulum.

Tota alt.
ped. C.
Lat. lxx.
Profund.
ped. xc.

8.2
Adriaen Collaert after Jan Van der Straet, *Florence and Genoa as Flora and Janus*. Engraving from *Americae Retectio* series, late 1580s. Photo: © The Trustees of the British Museum.

the festivities,[10] and a year later he published the book *Spectaculorum in susceptione Philippi Hisp. Prin.* [...] *Mirificus Apparatus*, which contains a detailed description of all the arches erected in Antwerp, accompanied by woodcuts based on drawings by Pieter Coecke van Aelst (fig. 8.1). A second useful source is *Felicissimo Viaje del muy alto y muy Poderoso Principe Don Phelippe*, by Juan Cristóbal Calvete de Estrella (1552), which is a faithful Spanish translation of Grapheus's text, with minimal variations, though it lacks illustrations.[11] Among the several installations erected in Antwerp during the 1549 entry, the Genoese one was positioned 'ad Triangulum'[12] (at the end of the Lange Gasthuisstraat) and – according to the sources – at twenty-eight metres high, it was the second-highest, surpassed only by the arch of Spain.[13]

Evidently, for the Genoese community residing in Flanders, the previous installations designed by Perino in Genoa – in particular, that of 1533 – were used as a model, at least with respect to their architectural structure.[14] Likewise, they share some iconography, especially figures from mythology or episodes in Roman history. Nevertheless, in this case, the classical motifs – which are ubiquitous in ephemeral and ceremonial buildings – are accompanied by elements that allude more specifically to Antwerp's distinctive identity. For the double-sided arch, Frans Floris, together with numerous collaborators, worked under the direction of Stefano Ambrogio Schiappalaria. This merchant and writer was born in Vezzano (near La Spezia, in eastern Liguria) but later he lived in Flanders. As a writer, Schiappalaria is known mainly for

his amorous poetry and biographical works, such as *La vita di C. Iulio Cesare* ('The Life of Julius Caesar'), published in 1578.[15]

Undoubtedly, the Genoese community in Antwerp viewed Schiappalaria as a figure of great prominence, considering that they commissioned him to direct the arch's iconographic programme. His role is explicitly stated in an inscription on the arch, which reads:

> Stephan Ambrosius Schiappalaria, Ligurian, collected and organised these stories with great labour and energy, and transferred them into pictures and statues, remarkably painted and carved, and the inscriptions are only due to his genius.[16]

The inscription – placed 'in fornice Arcus' – contains other important information about how quickly the arch was completed and the large number of workers who were involved – almost two hundred and eighty people between architects, painters and sculptors, which Grapheus faithfully reports.[17]

By comparing the woodcut and the detailed sources mentioned above, we learn that the Genoese arch depicted mostly mythological Gods – Neptune, Hercules, Jupiter, Venus with Cupid, plus Bellerophon – accompanied by a series of celebratory images of the Habsburgs. However, most interesting for this study is a sculpture placed on the pediment: a female personification sitting on a dolphin, holding an anchor and a golden circle, with the inscription 'Qui vitam optas, hanc vitam vivas'. According to the description by Calvete de Estrella, this figure can be interpreted in two ways: as the goddess Amphitrite or as an allegory of Genoa.[18] Interestingly, at this time, no unambiguous and immediately recognisable allegorical personification of Genoa existed. As a result, the city was often represented by several different elements that together referred to Genoa.

One example is the elaborate frontispiece of the well-known *Americae Retectio* series (late 1580s), by Jan Van der Straet (also known as Johannes Stradanus).[19] Here (fig. 8.2) Genoa is symbolised by her native son Christopher Columbus; the city's mythical founder, Janus; Neptune holding the city's coat of arms; and griffins, a symbol of the city going back to medieval times.[20] As will be seen, some of those symbols will be repeatedly used in conjunction with the personified image of Genoa, even after the creation of Ripa's distinctive personification.

In another important ceremony on 14 June 1594, the entire city of Antwerp welcomed Archduke Ernest of Austria

8.3

Peter Van der Borcht, *Triumphal Arch of the Genoese Nation* (1594). Engraving from Johannes Bochius, *Descriptio publicae gratulationis, spectaculorum et ludorum, in adventu sereniss. principis Ernesti archiducis Austriae*, Antverpiae, ex officina Plantiniana, 1595, p. 90. Photo: Staats-und Stadtbibliothek Augsburg, 2 Bio 33. Reproduced with permission.

– Philip II's nephew – as the new governor-general of the Netherlands.[21] For this celebration as well, foreign merchants residing in Antwerp (from Spain, Portugal, Germany, Milan, Florence, Lucca, and Genoa) again commissioned arches to represent their home territories. As in 1549, the government of Antwerp hired a humanist to plan the ceremony, and, on this occasion, they chose the city secretary and poet Johannes Bochius (Jan Boghe), who later published a detailed account of the entry in his *Descriptio Publicae Gratulationis Spectaculorum, et Ludorum, in Adventu Serenissimi Principis Ernesti*, with engravings by Pieter van der Borcht. The *Arcus Triomphalis Genuensium*[22] was placed on the Lange Klaarenstraat[23] and presented a single-arched structure (fig. 8.3). It was about twenty-one metres high (the tallest of the four Italian arches, and the third tallest overall, after the Spanish and Portuguese ones) and the only one to include all three artistic media: architecture, sculpture, and painting.[24] In some ways it was comparable to the previous models, particularly in the reiteration of celebratory images of the Habsburgs, here exemplified by portraits of Charles V, Maximilian I, Maximilian II, Henry V, and – obviously – Archduke Ernest, on the front, and those of Charlemagne, Henry VII, Frederick I, and Conrad II, on the back. However, compared to the examples mentioned above, the mythological figures were here replaced with allegorical virtues representing Faith, Hope, Charity, and Temperance, on the front side,[25] and – on the opposite side – Justice, Fortitude, Prudence, and Fame.[26]

The arch's allegorical dimension also included other personifications, specifically those of Spain, Austria, and Belgium,[27] on the front side's panel, and, above all, the female symbolisation of Liguria (clearly intended to refer to the territories of the Republic of Genoa), located at the top of the arch. The figure is more recognisable than in the 1549 arch, where we may recall, it was interpreted by Calvete de Estrella as possibly Amphitrite, or Genoa. In fact, according to Bochius's text:

> On the spire's rounder periphery was placed a statue of a woman, eleven feet high, with its base erected, holding a sceptre in the right, and a shield in the left, with a golden letter wherein there was written the name of Liberty: from this detail it was clear that the figure stood for Liguria.[28]

Just as the text describes, the engraving shows, atop the structure, a sculpture of a woman holding a sceptre and the Genoese flag, next to a putto holding a shield with the word 'Libertas', which is part of the Republic's motto. The figure is visible from both sides of the arch, but interestingly, while Bochius transcribes the word *Libertas* correctly, the engraving erroneously shows 'Libari'.

At the very end of the century, in February 1599, Archduke Albert and Margaret of Austria stayed a few days in Genoa – hosted by Giovanni Andrea Doria in his Palazzo del Principe – and, for the occasion, an elaborate installation was erected near the Lanterna (the city's lighthouse).[29] As one document attests:

> It was ordered that a large triumphal arch be built in the area of the Polcevera River, later placed at the Lanterna, not far from a small house and loggia, which were destroyed to make room and to provide a better view of the whole city; it was designed by the sculptor Taddeo and by Giacomo Mancini from Montepulciano.[30]

The iconographer was, therefore, Giacomo Mancini from Montepulciano, whereas the artist involved was a sculptor by the name of Taddeo, probably Taddeo Carlone, who had been hired during those same years by none other than Giovanni Andrea Doria for the Fountain of Neptune in the Palazzo del Principe.[31] Unfortunately, no drawings of this arch are known at present, but it is possible to reconstruct the iconographic programme thanks to the *Descrizione dell'arco trionfale fatto a Genova nel passaggio della maestà della Regina Catolica, e del Serenissimo Alberto Arciduca d'Austria*, published in the same year by Giacomo Mancini himself.[32]

In addition to the customary images glorifying the Habsburgs and the allegorical virtues, here – probably for the first time – two distinct personifications, one each for Genoa and Liguria, were created, each making use of some of the iconographic attributes previously discussed. On a panel immediately below the niche in the right pier – containing the sculpted portrait of the Queen – Liguria was depicted sitting on a rock, bearing the mast of a ship, and wearing clothes adorned with the waves of the sea and a crown of vines.[33] On the left side, under the statue of King Philip III, a personification of Genoa, leaning on a dolphin, wore the Doge's crown and held a sceptre and a rudder.[34]

Ripa's invention of a new image. Some examples in published works

As was previously mentioned, the definitive codification of a unique personified image, for both Genoa and Liguria, comes from Cesare Ripa's *Iconologia*. Though the 1593 *editio princeps* of this work contains no reference to this figure, the first illustrated edition, published in Rome in 1603, presents an allegorical depiction of Liguria, the first of the so-called 'provinces' of Italy. From this time on, the different attributes associated with the town of Genoa, its region (Liguria), and the idea of republican government were combined to create a new distinctive image (fig. 8.4).[35] According to Ripa, the female personification of Liguria is

8.4

Liguria. Engraving from Cesare Ripa, *Iconologia, overo Descrittione di diverse imagini cauate dall'antichità,* Roma, appresso Lepido Facij, 1603, p. 249.
Photo: Rome, Biblioteca Nazionale Centrale 'Vittorio Emanuele II' (6. 9.E.8). Reproduced with permission.

a thin woman, virile and ferocious, sitting on a rock, she will have armour, and a helmet on her head. She will hold her right hand open, on which an eye will be painted, and with her left hand, she will hold a palm branch; to her right there will be a rudder and to her left a shield with two or three arrows.[36]

As is well known, Ripa's *Iconologia* went through several illustrated editions and was widely translated between the sixteenth and the eighteenth centuries, becoming – as noted by Emile Mâle, who in 1927 rediscovered the work's function as a 'Dictionary of allegories' – a fundamental tool for artists 'whenever they had to personify an abstract idea' ('toutes les fois qu'ils avaient à personnifier une idée abstraite').[37]

For the woodcut to illustrate Liguria, the attributes chosen by Ripa were taken, as usual, from several literary sources. The most distinctive feature – the *manus oculata* (the hand with an eye inside) – derives directly from Andrea Alciati's *Emblemata*. This symbol is widely used in emblematic literature and has the double meaning of Prudence and Industry, both virtues, according to Ripa, characterising the Ligurian people.[38]

This unprecedented graphic personification of the city (which, significantly, was invented by a non-Genoese author)[39] also included some other items, such as armour and a helmet, a rudder, a shield and arrows, and a palm branch, attributes which – in their complementary totality – became an unambiguous representation of the Genoese Republic. Thus,

8.5
Martial Desbois after Domenico Piola, *Allegory of Genoa*. Frontispiece of Maria Elena Lusignani, *Conclusiones ex universa theologia iuxta subtilium theologorum principis Ioannis Duns Scoti inconcussam doctrinam*, Genuae, Typis Antonij Casamaræ in Platea Cicala, 1695. Photo: Genoa, Biblioteca Civica Berio. Reproduced with permission.

beginning in 1603 and thereafter, there was a new symbolic image of Genoa that could be easily replicated and mobilised and that quickly began to reach audiences both in published works and in monumental art.

A very early example of the use of the new image, dating from the first decade of the seventeenth century, is a drawing ascribed to Giovanni Battista Paggi, depicting the glorification of Christopher Columbus. A female personification of Genoa is visible at the stern of the ship, whose attributes are taken directly from Ripa and who is labelled by means of a cartouche with the word 'Liguria'.[40] In the same way, the title page of a book published in 1618, for the election of the new Doge Giovanni Giacomo Imperiale, shows the personification of

Liguria, probably drawn by the Genoese painter Luciano Borzone.[41] Again, the picture depicts a female figure surrounded by the usual iconographic attributes – with the addition of griffins and the two-faced head of Janus – holding the hand of Corsica (controlled by the Republic of Genoa), likewise derived from Ripa's *Iconologia*.

Sometimes this personification appears as an illustration in political and celebratory books. In these cases, the figure is often seated on a triumphal chariot drawn by griffins. For example, the figure is represented in this way on the title page of the volume *De Dominio Serenissimae Genuensis Reipublicae in mari Ligustico* ('On the Domain of the Most Serene Republic of Genoa over the Ligurian Sea') by Pietro Battista Borgo (1641), with engravings by Cornelis Bloemaert after a drawing by Giovanni Andrea Podestà.[42] Here the figure is very close to Ripa's model, with the addition of the city shield of Genoa, but above it is also an allegory of Fame and a canopy decorated with the Republic's coat of arms.

A fascinating variation appears on the frontispiece of the *Liguria trionfante delle principali nazioni del mondo* ('Triumphant Liguria of the World's Leading Nations') by Epifanio Ferrari (1643), where Liguria – engraved by Pierre I Loisy – holds a trident to underline her dominion over the sea. More significant, however, is the marine chariot – drawn by a horse and a sea monster – that Liguria is driving and that is trampling a Turkish-headed hydra, which symbolises the Ottoman enemy, in – as Laura Stagno argues – 'one of the most visual projections of the idea of the defeat of the Turks as Genoa's mission'.[43]

Although it conforms to Ripa's model, the personification of the city drawn by the painter Domenico Piola and engraved by Martial Desbois, in 1695, on the title page of the *Conclusiones ex universa Theologia* (fig. 8.5) conveys a completely different meaning. In this particular case, the use of the personification is closely connected with the book's author, Maria Elena Lusignani, a young Genoese writer who was probably one of the first women in history to receive a degree in theology, at the end of the seventeenth century.[44] On 28 May 1692, at just nineteen years of age, Maria Elena publicly defended her thesis on philosophy in Genoa, in what was then the church of San Francesco di Castelletto (now destroyed), in the presence of numerous Genoese noblemen and politicians, as well as the Prince of Denmark, who was temporarily residing in the city, hosted by the Jesuits.[45] A degree in philosophy earned

8.6
Jean Audran after Antoine Dieu, *Allegory of Genoa*. Frontispiece of Luis de Mailly, *Histoire de la république de Gênes depuis l'an 464 de la fondation de Rome jusqu'à présent*, Paris: chez Denys du Puis, 1697. Photo: University of Michigan. Public Domain (Google-digitized).

by a woman was rather unusual, though Maria Elena was not the first in this regard, having been preceded by the Venetian Elena Lucrezia Cornaro Piscopia, who had defended her thesis in the Cathedral of Padua only a few years earlier (1678).[46]

However, the Genoese scholar did not limit herself to this prestigious recognition but continued her studies in theology, a subject that automatically provided for teaching qualification and, therefore, was typically reserved for men (in fact, it had been previously explicitly denied to Elena Lucrezia Cornaro). Three years after finishing her philosophical studies, the young Maria Elena completed her thesis in theology, which was publicly defended in July 1695 over the course of three days (the first in the Palazzo Ducale and the other two once again in the church of Castelletto).[47] Although probable,

the conferral of the second doctoral degree is undocumented. However, the publication of the *Conclusiones* is a fact; it came out the same year and was accompanied by the aforementioned illustrated title page. In Domenico Piola's drawing, a preparatory version of which is held at Windsor Castle,[48] Maria Elena Lusignani is shown offering her thesis to Genoa's personification, while Fame hovers above. The tree on which Genoa sits – bedecked with the city's emblems and the griffins – symbolises the Republic itself. This can be assumed from the author's words,[49] and is noted again on the title page, in the inscription written on the open book in her hands.

Genoa and Liguria's allegorical image spread not only throughout the Republic's territory; some illustrations are also documented in foreign sources. An example is the drawing by Antoine Dieu, which was slightly modified by the engraving of Jean Audran for the title page of the *Histoire de la République de Gênes* (fig. 8.6), a historical account of the city written in French by the Chevallier Louis de Mailly in 1696, with a clearly pro-French bias.[50] Once again, the primary source of the personification is still Ripa's model, but some elements have been changed; in particular, the figure's helmet has been replaced by the ducal hat, and a drawn curtain reveals a vista of the city of Genoa, with the Lanterna in view.[51]

In addition to its appearance in published works, the image was also used in cartography, and this, in fact, was a decisive factor in its dissemination beyond the borders of the Republic. In general, maps are crucial tools for the widespread diffusion of allegorical subjects and civic personifications, and, with regard to Genoa and Liguria's maps specifically, we can find many examples presenting images similar to Ripa's woodcut.[52] While the illustration *Liguria o Stato della Repubblica di Genova* in the well-known *Theatrum Orbis Terrarum* (*Atlas Novus*) by Joan Bleau (1640) is very similar to Ripa's prototype, on the other hand – especially in some eighteenth-century examples – the city's personification is often accompanied by additional allegorical images. In those cases, Genoa's (or Liguria's) personification still shows the attributes taken from the *Iconologia* but is flanked by other figures, such as Neptune and Mercury, alluding to the city's maritime and commercial power.

In addition, some remarkable modifications occur: for example, in the maps by Johann Baptist Homann (1715–1730) and the one by Matthaus Seutter (1730–1740), which present

the same iconographic variation vis-à-vis Ripa's image and thus are possibly derived from a common model (fig. 8.7). First of all, both cartographers added Genoa's flag, probably with the goal of making the maps more intelligible to a wider audience; this is an element not included by Ripa. Moreover, the shield of the female personification is decorated with the head of Medusa. Thus, the two maps present an interesting parallel between Genoa and the goddess Minerva. One possible explanation for this is that Genoa's iconography (the female figure with armour, shield, and helmet) was often confused with that of Minerva.[53]

8.7

Matthaus Seutter, *Reipublicae Genuensis Dominium cum inclytæ istius Urbis et Portus insigniorius Prospectibus Geographica et Topographica Synopsi repraesentatum*, c. 1740 (detail). Photo: From the British Library archive, King's Topographical Collection, Maps K.Top.77.59. Public Domain.

8.8
Gregorio De Ferrari, *Liguria Triumphans*.
Genoa, Palazzo Andrea Pitto, c. 1684.
Reproduced with permission.

8.9
Domenico Piola, *Allegory of Genoa*. Sketch for the decoration of Palazzo Ducale. Genoa, Musei di Strada Nuova – Palazzo Bianco, 1702–1704. Reproduced with permission.

8.10
Giovanni Domenico Tiepolo, *The Glorification of the Giustiniani Family*. Sketch for the decoration of Palazzo Ducale. New York, Metropolitan Museum of Art, 1783. Photo: Public Domain.

The personification of Genoa and Liguria in monumental art

Beginning only in the final years of the seventeenth century, Genoa's and Liguria's female personifications started to be represented in monumental art. Until then (as was previously mentioned), the preferred subjects of 'identitarian' frescoes were instead historical themes or the glorification of Genoese heroes. As for the palaces of the nobility, a significant example of the personification can be seen in the decorative cycle of Palazzo Giovanni Battista Centurione (later Cambiaso, now Pitto), one of the Palazzi dei Rolli, Genoa's UNESCO World Heritage site.[54] In a hall on the upper floor, the Genoese painter Gregorio De Ferrari inserted Ripa's Liguria image within a more elaborate iconographic programme, focused on the glorification of the Centurione family (fig. 8.8). The city's personification, wearing the armour and helmet, is mounted on a griffin rising up into the sky. She holds a palm branch in her left hand, and she opens the right one to reveal her *manus oculata*. An iconographic peculiarity of the fresco is the insertion of the putti, flying towards Liguria, to present to her the attributes that she is missing

– namely, the rudder and the arrows. The artist uses a similar expedient to introduce elements absent from the *Iconologia* but essential to the fresco's civic and celebratory subject, such as Genoa's flag and the Centurione coat of arms, both held by flying putti placed at the lower edge of the vault.[55]

Finally, at the beginning of the eighteenth century, the female personification of Genoa was used in the government palace for the very first time, as far as is known. While Venice's Palazzo Ducale, for instance, has been decorated with several civic personifications since at least the sixteenth century, it was only in the eighteenth that the Republic of Genoa decided to include a similar subject in the seat of political power. Until then, the only room of the Palazzo Ducale decorated with frescoes was the chapel, which was painted in the middle of the seventeenth century by Giovanni Battista Carlone. These frescoes present the basic repertoire of the primary sources of civic, historical, and religious pride for the Genoese people. However, they do not include an allegorical image of the city.[56]

In the early eighteenth century, the Republic of Genoa, with the Giustiniani family's financial support, decided to redecorate the Great Council Hall and consulted privately with some painters, who presented them their sketches. Some of the proposed projects were related to the symbolic glorification of the city or specific local historical events.[57] Thus, for example, a canvas by the Genoese painter Domenico Parodi – now conserved in the Museum of Palazzo Reale – focused on an episode from 1383, when the Doge Leonardo Montaldo freed Jacopo Lusignano, who had been held prisoner in Genoa with his family for ten years, and returned him to the kingdom of Cyprus (a theme that, in general, was ubiquitous in the city's art).[58] Other artists concentrated on celebrating the city more generally, using the already widely known and codified personification of the city. In particular, two of the four sketches painted by the abovementioned Domenico Piola (with his son Paolo Gerolamo) present Genoa sitting on a triumphal chariot drawn by griffins, accompanied by several allegorical personifications (fig. 8.9).[59] In the same way, the sketch by Giovanni Battista Gaulli – once considered lost but recently rediscovered by the scholars Duccio Marignoli and Michele Drascek – includes allegorical figures, with the personification of Liguria clearly recognisable at the very centre of the painting.[60]

The Giustinianis also played a central role in selecting the artist. In fact – after a series of negotiations, recorded in numerous archival documents – Luca Giustiniani obtained from the Senate of the Republic the authorisation to commission the decoration to the Bolognese master Marcantonio Franceschini, with the help of the *quadraturista* Tommaso Aldrovandini.[61] The great vault's decoration was finished in 1704, but, unfortunately, the whole fresco was lost to fire in 1777. Although no iconographic documents are preserved, literary texts describe Liguria at the centre of the ceiling, sitting on a chariot – pulled by griffins and the allegory of Freedom – next to Fortune, in chains: 'In its middle he depicted Liguria, holding Fortune at her feet in chains. She stands on a majestic chariot guided by two griffins and driven by Liberty [...]'.[62]

In 1782, the Giustiniani family were again financial backers of the Council's redecoration project to replace the lost frescoes by Franceschini. On this occasion, an announcement was published in the local and international press encouraging every Italian and foreign artist who wanted to participate to send in their sketches (to be evaluated by a commission of experts), for 'a painting to be located on the main vault of the Great Council Hall'.[63] Interestingly, the Giustinianis left the artists free to use either canvases or frescoes. However, this time they asked them to comply with a very specific and detailed iconographic programme, which included the personification of Liguria in a central position, accompanied by several other allegorical and historical figures.[64] Evidently, by this date, the personification of Genoa/Liguria had caught on, to the point of being explicitly requested for the decoration of an institution of great importance. Once again, few sketches are preserved: among them, we should mention the canvas by the Austrian painter Martin Knoller and the watercolour by the Genoese Giovanni David, where the personification of the city – taken directly from Ripa – is unmistakable.[65] On 28 August 1784, the outcome of the competition was announced in the local journal *Avvisi*: the winner was the Venetian Giovanni Domenico Tiepolo, the son of the renowned artist Giovanni Battista Tiepolo.[66] The painter concluded his work only a year later, but Tiepolo's fresco was also lost, through rapid deterioration, and was replaced in 1875 by Giuseppe Isola's decoration; nevertheless, the iconographic programme is known thanks to the sketch, which is now held at the Metropolitan Museum of Art in New York (fig. 8.10).[67] This sketch diverges from the main stipulation in the announcement, in that Liguria is not placed at the centre of the vault but is sitting on the steps, surrounded by several allegorical figures. In any case, she is identified by a crown, a rudder, a palm branch, and her most significant attribute, the *manus oculata*.

Conclusions

The evolution of the female personification of the city of Genoa and its surrounding region started in the sixteenth century. Its earliest use as the predominant way of representing the city was in the context of public celebrations and ephemeral installations. However, until the publication of the illustrated edition of the *Iconologia* (1603), when a personification of the Republic of Genoa was called for, a variety of different attributes were used, which were then partly taken up by Ripa in his book. Finally, Ripa's codification of a unique image, used for both Genoa and Liguria, created an immediately recognisable model, which undoubtedly popularised the subject and facilitated its dissemination, at first only in works published locally, then in works published beyond the Republic's borders, and finally in private and public decorative cycles.

1 On images of the city's identity in Genoa and their political and symbolic use between the sixteenth and the eighteenth centuries: Borniotto, *L'identità di Genova*.

2 For the historical and political context, among many studies: Bitossi, *Il governo dei magnifici*; Bitossi, 'L'antico regime genovese'; Costantini, *La Repubblica di Genova*.

3 The historical bibliography on the hero is obviously vast. On Embriaco's iconography, Martini, 'Il Tasso istoriato', pp. 213–31; Stagno, 'Turks in Genoese Art', pp. 298–302; Borniotto, 'Ancient Relics', pp. 245–56; Borniotto, *L'identità di Genova*, pp. 144–58 and 159–70; Borniotto, 'Gloria civica', pp. 83–94.

4 On the Palazzo del Principe, see the works by Laura Stagno, in particular: Stagno, *Palazzo del Principe*; Stagno, 'Due principi per un palazzo'; Stagno, *Giovanni Andrea Doria*; Stagno, 'Roman History Themes'. Among several studies, see also: Altavista, *La residenza di Andrea Doria a Fassolo*; Parma, 'Il palazzo del Principe'; Gorse, 'The villa Doria in Fassolo'; Magnani, *Il Tempio di Venere*; Boccardo, *Andrea Doria e le arti*.

5 On the ephemeral structures built in Genoa for the Emperor's entries in 1529 and 1533: Eisler, 'Perino del Vaga'; Gavazza, 'Gli apparati per le entrate di Carlo V'; Gorse, 'An Unpublished Description'; Gorse, 'Between Empire and Republic'; Stagno, 'Sovrani spagnoli a Genova', pp. 73–79; Magnani, 'Temporary architecture', pp. 250–60; Stagno, 'La forza dell'effimero', pp. 62–69.

6 Parma, ed., *Perino del Vaga tra Raffaello e Michelangelo*, pp. 201–03.

7 Stagno, 'Roman History Themes', p. 2.

8 Varchi, *Storia fiorentina*, p. 228. 'Un arco trionfale pieno di varie, e vaghe storie dimostranti per lo più il buon animo de' Genovesi […] in una delle quali storie era figurato Andrea d'Oria, il quale colla sinistra mano reggeva la città di Genova, e nella destra teneva una spada ignuda arrancata, e l'imperadore con ambe le mani incoronava Genova'. The work, written between 1527 and 1538, was published only in 1721.

9 On the ephemeral arches of 1549, in particular: Wouk, *Frans Floris*; Bussels, *Spectacle, Rhetoric and Power*; Meadow, 'Ritual and Civic Identity'; Kuyper, *The Triumphant Entry*; Galassi, 'The Permanence of Ephemera'.

10 Wouk, *Frans Floris*, p. 141.

11 Calvete de Estrella, *El Felicissimo Viaje*, IV, pp. 229–35; see also Aliverti, 'Visits to Genoa', pp. 222–35. A canvas by Frans Floris, depicting *The Capture of Heretics*, was recently found and published by Maria Clelia Galassi, recognized as part of the 1549 arch (Galassi, 'The Permanence of Ephemera').

12 Grapheus, *Spectacolorum in susceptione Philippi*, p. F4v; Calvete de Estrella, *El Felicissimo Viaje*, p. 229.

13 Wouk, *Frans Floris*, p. 144. Grapheus and Calvete provide precise measurements for all the arches described.

14 Parma, *Il palazzo del Principe*, p. 48; Wouk, *Frans Floris*, pp. 145–46.

15 On Stefano Ambrogio Schiappalaria: Chiarla, 'Schiappalaria, Stefano Ambrogio'; Wouk, *Frans Floris*, pp. 145–48.

16 Grapheus, *Spectacolorum in susceptione Philippi*, p. H1v. 'Stephanus Ambrosius Schiappalarius, Ligur, huius tam aegregii operis magno sanè labore et industria, congessit ac ordinavit hystorias, easque in picturas et statuas digestatas, et insigniter pictas et affabrè sculptas, inscriptionesque omneis suo solius ingenio excogitates'.

17 Grapheus, *Spectacolorum in susceptione Philippi*, p. H1v.

18 Calvete de Estrella, *El Felicissimo Viaje*, p. 230. '[…] Una estatua de mugger grande encima un delphin dorado, con una ancora dorada enla una mano, y enla otra un circulo tambien dorado: representava la grandiose d'el mar Amphitrite mugger d'el dios Neptuno, ò la muy rica y maritima ciudad de Genova' ('A female statue sitting on a golden dolphin, with a golden anchor in one hand and a golden circle in the other: it represented Amphitrite, wife of the God Neptune, or the very rich maritime city of Genoa').

19 The series was later reproduced by Theodore De Bry in his *Americae Pars Quarta*. On Stradanus's frontispiece, see Markey, 'Stradano's Allegorical Invention', pp. 400–12; Bettini, 'Americae Retectio', pp. 191–201. The role of Columbus in this context was discussed also by Airaldi and Parma, *L'avventura di Colombo*, pp. 72–100.

20 About those symbols, in the Genoese context, see Pavoni, 'I simboli di Genova'.

21 About the ephemeral installations of 1594, with a specific focus on the Genoese one, see Raband, 'Staging Genoa', pp. 46–70, with previous bibliography; Raband, 'Printed Narrative', pp. 17–32. See also Davidson and Van der Weel, 'Introduction', pp. 492–96.

22 Bochius, *Descriptio*, p. 88.

23 The Street of Antwerp dedicated to St Clare ('Insignem arcus machinam propè vicum, cui a diva Clara nomen est': Bochius, *Descriptio*, p. 88).

24 Raband, 'Staging Genoa', pp. 46 and 57.

25 Bochius, *Descriptio*, p. 89.

26 Bochius, *Descriptio*, p. 91.

27 Bochius, *Descriptio*, p. 88.

28 Bochius, *Descriptio*, p. 89. 'Super fastigij rotundiori peripheria, statua muliebris undecem pedes alta cum sua basi erecta locabatur, sceptrum dextra, laeva scutum complexa, cui literis aureis Libertatis nomen inscriptum erat: ex quo signo apparebat, eam pro Liguria esse positam'.

29 On this topic: Ivaldi, 'Scheda per un "apparato" genovese', pp. 43–52; Sommariva, 'Coronationi'; Aliverti, 'Visits to Genoa', pp. 222–35; Stagno, 'L'hospitaggio', pp. 124–25.

30 ASG, AS, Cerimoniarum, 474, *Libro Primo delle Cerimonie*, c. 210v: 'Fu ordinato che se facesse un arco trionfale grande alla Pozzevera, e poi fu messo alla Linterna, poco discosto da quella casetta e loggia, che per far piazza fu buttata a terra, e dava più bella vista in quel prementorio a tutta la Città, designato da maestro Thadeo scarpellino e da messer Giacomo Mancino da Montepolciano'.

31 Stagno, 'L'hospitaggio', p. 124; Stagno, *Giovanni Andrea Doria*, p. 132.

32 The text is transcribed in its entirety by Aliverti (from a copy held at the Bibliothèque Nationale de France), in *Europa Triumphans*, pp. 310–28.

33 'Liguria in abito ninfale a sedere sopra uno scoglio tenendo nelle mani un arboro di nave con la gabbia e sarte, con veste dipinta a ricci marini, e coronata di vite'. Mancini, *Descrizzione dell'Arco Trionfale*, p. 12; Aliverti, *Europa Triumphans*, p. 314.

34 Mancini, *Descrizzione dell'Arco Trionfale*, p. 13. 'Genova pur con habito ninfale, havendo a' piedi la corona e scettro ducale, e sotto al braccio sinistro un delfino, e nella destra un timone'; Aliverti, *Europa Triumphans*, p. 316.

35 On the genesis of the new image: Borniotto, *L'identità di Genova*, pp. 29–39.

36 Ripa, *Iconologia*, pp. 249–50 ('Donna magra, di aspetto virile e feroce, sopra di uno scoglio o sasso, averà una veste succinta con ricamo d'oro, in dosso un corsaletto, et in capo un elmo. Terrà la destra mano aperta, in mezo della quale vi sarà depinto un occhio, e con la sinistra mano porgerà con bella grazia un ramo di palma, et appresso al lato destro vi sarà un timone, e dal sinistro uno scudo con due overo tre dardi').

37 Mâle, 'La Clef des allégories', p. 107. Among many studies concerning the importance and the role of the *Iconologia*, see *L'Iconologia di Cesare Ripa*. See also Maffei, *Le radici antiche dei simboli*; Maffei, *Cesare Ripa e gli spazi dell'allegoria*.

38 Beginning with the edition of 1546, Alciati's *Emblematum Libellus* includes an emblem showing a right hand – in which an eye is clearly discernible on the palm – with a garland of leaves at the wrist. The meaning attributed by Alciati to this emblem is twofold: prudence and sobriety. The later meaning of industry derives from Cesare Ripa himself, who used the same emblem as an attribute of the personification of Industry. See Borniotto, *L'identità di Genova*, pp. 29–37. On the symbolic meanings of the *manus oculata*, also in literary works, see Maranini, 'Col senno e con la mano', pp. 115–56.

39 Cesare Ripa was born around 1555 in Perugia; see Maffei, 'Introduzione', pp. VI-XXII.

40 Genoa, Musei di Strada Nuova, Gabinetto Disegni e Stampe di Palazzo Rosso, D. 3141; Boccardo, 'La Gloria di Colombo', pp. 35–44.

41 *Incoronatione*. For the iconography of the title page, see Borniotto, *L'identità di Genova*, pp. 45–48; Borniotto in *Luciano Borzone*, entry I, p. 62.

42 Borniotto, *L'identità di Genova*, pp. 55–56; Ruffini, 'Icones Ligusticae', pp. 18, 24.

43 Stagno, 'Turks in Genoese Art', p. 304. See also Ruffini, 'Icones Ligusticae', p. 18; Dagnino, '"Per la fabrica et ornamento della Cappella Reale"', p. 277, note 24; Borniotto, *L'identità di Genova*, pp. 57–60.

44 On Maria Elena Lusignani, see the chapter 'Pallade generata da Giano: Le dispute pubbliche di Maria Elena Lusignani dedicate alla città', in Borniotto, *L'identità di Genova*, pp. 63–82. Biographical information on the Genoese writer can be found in the work of the Franciscan friar Giovanni Franchini. See also Forlivesi, 'Materiali per una descrizione', pp. 252–79. Some interesting documents are also held at the ASG, AS, Cerimoniarum, 478.

45 ASG, AS, Cerimoniarum, 478, c. 171r; Franchini, *Bibliosofia e memorie letterarie*, p. 614.

46 See Maschietto, *Elena Lucrezia Cornaro Piscopia*.

47 On the last page of the volume by Maria Elena Lusignani, we read: 'Disputabuntur publice Genuae per tres dies successive, prima die in Aula Regia [Palazzo Ducale]; secunda, et tertia in Templo S. Francisci Anno 1695' (Lusignani, *Conclusiones*, p. 46).

48 Windsor Castle, RCIN 903766, first published (with an incorrect attribution to Marcantonio Franceschini) in Kurz, pp. 107–08. On the drawing (correctly attributed to Domenico Piola), see also Biavati, 'L'affresco che il Piola non dipinse', p. 18; Newcome, 'Prints after Domenico Piola'; Sanguineti, *Domenico Piola e i pittori della sua "casa"*, II, entry V.30, p. 497; Whitaker and Clayton, eds, *The art of Italy*, entry 152, pp. 400–01.

49 Lusignani, *Conclusiones*, p. 8.

50 On the book see Pedrol Aguilà, *Un écrivain méconnu*, pp. 700–04; Assereto, 'Storiografia e identità ligure', p. 69. The preparatory drawing by Anton Dieu is preserved in the BNF.

51 In many allegorical representations, the Lanterna serves as an immediately identifiable emblem of the city itself; on this topic, see Poleggi, *Iconografia*, pp. 45–61; Bertolucci and Leoncini, eds, *La città della Lanterna*.

52 For the following (and other) examples, see the website: https://www.oldmapsonline. org/map/mzk/2619270214 [2021/8/18], containing a large database of maps of Liguria, with high-resolution images.

53 To take only one example, in the drawing by Domenico Piola for the title page of *Li Scrittori della Liguria*, by Raffaele Soprani (1667), an unequivocal personification of Genoa – taken from Ripa's model – has been interpreted as Minerva (Bellini and Carter, eds, *The Illustrated Bartsch*, p. 238).

54 Puccio, 'Frescanti genovesi', pp. 113–30; Briano, Bruno and Righetti, *Palazzo Andrea Pitto*.

55 Borniotto, *L'identità di Genova*, pp. 83–84.

56 On the Chapel of Palazzo Ducale and its elaborate iconography: Biavati, 'La Cappella Ducale', pp. 391–93; Dagnino, '"Per la fabrica et ornamento della Cappella Reale"', pp. 270–77; Borniotto 'Gloria civica'; Borniotto, *L'identità di Genova*.

57 See for instance: Biavati, 'Il "concorso" del 1700', pp. 366–75.

58 Boccardo in *El Siglo de los Genoveses*, entry XIII.5, p. 380.

59 Biavati, 'L'affresco che il Piola non dipinse'; Biavati in *El Siglo de los Genoveses*, entries XIII. 1–2–3–4, pp. 376–79; Sanguineti, *Domenico Piola e i pittori della sua "casa"*, entries I.203 a-b-c, pp. 450–51; Borniotto, *L'identità di Genova*, pp. 98–106; Borniotto, 'Rinnovare la tradizione', pp. 225–28.

60 Marignoli and Drascek, 'The Bozzetto for Liguria Triumphans', pp. 35–47. The preparatory drawing of the personification is now preserved in Dusseldorf (Kunstmuseum, inv. 329). Other preparatory drawings by Gaulli (before the rediscovery of the sketch) were published by Graf, 'Liguria Triumphans', pp. 344–49.

61 Antetomaso, 'La decorazione del salone', pp. 110–21; Sommariva, 'Un'idea per il rifacimento del Real Palazzo', pp. 77–80; Davanzo, 'La committenza e le scelte iconografiche', pp. 135–44; Assini, 'Cronologia di una committenza', pp. 106–09.

62 Ratti, *Storia de' pittori*, p. 211v. 'In quel di mezzo figurò la Liguria che seco si tragge, avvinta a' piedi tra cattene la Fortuna. Sta essa su d'un maestoso carro guidato da due griffi e condotto dalla Libertà […]'.

63 'Un quadro da collocarsi nello spazio maggiore del volto del Salone del Gran Consiglio'. *Avvisi*, XIII, 30 March 1782, p. 97; the same information can also be found in the ASG, Giustiniani, 225bis, 30 March 1782. On the competition: Olcese Spingardi, 'Il concorso del 1782', pp. 27–34; Olcese Spingardi, 'Un mancato intervento', pp. 210–21; Borniotto, *L'identità di Genova*, pp. 119–40.

64 'In Heaven, Liguria seated on a Throne decorated with the characteristic Signs and Virtues'; 'nel Cielo la Liguria assisa in Trono adornato dalle distintive Insegne e Virtù caratteristiche'. The printed public announcement is preserved in the ASG, Giustiniani, 226, 26 September 1782.

65 Borniotto, *L'identità di Genova*, pp. 119–40.

66 *Avvisi*, XXXV, 28 August 1784, p. 285.

67 Olcese Spingardi, in *El Siglo*, entry XV.7, p. 420.

9

Sara Rulli

CONTINUITY AND RENEWAL OF THE CITY IMAGE

The Enhancement and Strengthening of Public Architecture and Infrastructure as an Instrument for Political Communication

As part of a policy aimed at relaunching the city and the Republic as a naval power and seeking military and political autonomy from the Spanish imperial system, the great public works carried out in Genoa between the 1720s and 1730s became literary and iconographic *topos*. Perceived by their contemporaries as the symbol of a renewed republican dignity and as proof of the implementation of a renewal programme that would ensure the recovery and autonomy of maritime traffic, they are in fact the fruit of a culture that combines ancient management skills with administrative and technological reflection. In this context, it is therefore of great interest to analyse the stringent unity that was created at this time between political thought, public works, the definition of urban space[1] and the renewal of the city's image.[2] In fact, a series of political and military events were radically transforming Genoa, persuading the most active members of its political class and, at the same time, a group of young intellectual aristocrats eager for a radical change in the political-economic line of the state,[3] to develop a renewal programme[4] capable of producing a different, new role for the city in the international sphere. The Franco-Piedmontese invasion of 1625, the cooling of relations with Spain – afflicted by the bankruptcy of 1627 and the consequent suspension of loan payments[5] – and, finally, the conspiracy of Giulio Cesare Vachero, bloodily repressed in 1628, made that coveted change increasingly indispensable, something that would necessarily have led the city – now internationally recognised as 'only' a financial centre of gravity – to be active once again as a mercantile and maritime centre and able to maintain a neutral role among the increasingly aggressive European potentates.[6]

It was in this context that the group of 'young' patricians – so called in contrast to the 'old' aristocrats, who were less inclined to pursue innovative political and economic strategies – gradually took on a fundamental role in the political culture of the time. Otherwise known as *novatori* ('innovators'), *navalisti* ('navalists') or *repubblichisti* ('republicans'), they became the protagonists of a project that, ideally, would have relaunched the Republic as a naval – and commercial – power, taking its glorious medieval past as an example;[7] a political programme that would have transformed the economic profile of the city, for too long tied to the fate of European finance, restoring its commercial and maritime independence.

These feelings and desires for renewal and relaunching were immediately intertwined with the by then 'ancient' debate on the naval rearrangement of the Republic: the desire for change and independence that aroused in the young seventeenth-century 'republicists' revitalised positions that were already clear in the mid-sixteenth century. Conditioned by the way in which, in 1528, Genoa had entered the Spanish sphere of influence,[8] the proposal to relaunch Genoa as a naval power for the purpose of political and military autonomy independent from the Hapsburg system had in fact found voice and strength in the *Dialogo della Republica di Genova*, published by Oberto Foglietta in Rome in 1559.[9] In this context, as Carlo Bitossi has pointed out,[10] if the supporters of the link with Spain never drew up their own political manifesto, their opponents were very prolific in this sense, reiterating over and over again the need to create an

9.3

Pieter Van der Aa, after Daniël Stoopendal,
Genua, capitale du même nom en Italie (detail), c. 1720.
Photo: Courtesy il Ponte Casa d'Aste.

'independent' fleet – made up of the so-called *galee di libertà* ('galleys of liberty') – the one and only thing that could guarantee the Republic and, more generally, the city, that ideal role that would be so dear to the seventeenth-century republican ideology.[11] The text of Foglietta – an authentic attack on the internal political structure of the Republic and a denunciation of the weakness of its fleet – in its shaping of the literary *topos* of the comparison between the glorious past of the city and the contemporary weakness and subordination would be widely taken up by the *novatori* ('innovators') of the following century. Anton Giulio Brignole Sale, in 1642 in the words of a 'Zealous Citizen living in Naples',[12] intent on celebrating the *Serenissimi Collegi* for having decided to rearm the Republic's navy:

> It is true that those times and those works cannot return, but they can return, and times and works in all respects similar to those, as long as we do not want to distinguish ourselves by stupidity from those ancestors, to whom we are very similar by nature, complexity, wit and heart.[13]

After all, just as in the previous century, 'Defence of the State, of the Reputation, of the Jurisdiction and of Liberty'.[14]

Led by Anton Giulio Brignole Sale and within the renewed *Accademia degli Addormentati*,[15] that same group of young people had in fact made explicit once again the objective of a necessary rearming of the Genoese fleet 'of the ancient centuries'[16] – now reduced 'to the number of six galleys'[17] – to support the naval policy of the Republic that would allow Genoa to play an autonomous role in the Mediterranean. They also invited, in 1638, the inhabitants of the Rivieras and Corsica to contribute with offers to the ambitious programme: an invitation that led many coastal towns to tax themselves in order to take part in the operation in the name of which Brignole himself launched the *Brignola* in April 1642.[18]

At the same time, efforts were made to make the city appear peaceful and harmonious from the outside, presenting that 'instability' typical of its citizens and so much criticised by detractors (first and foremost by the volume published by Agostino Mascardi in 1629 on the *Congiura del Conte Fieschi*)[19] as a quality necessary to adapt to the European political situation and to allow the Republic to remain equidistant from the major powers: 'Too well known is the nature of the Genoese, who resemble their climate in both instability and acuity, and who are just as unwavering in their perseverance

as they are fervent in their endeavours', stresses the *Cittadino zelante* Anton Giulio.[20]

The project of naval rearmament – explicitly and cunningly linked, by its promoters, to the feeling of self-promotion that had seen the Republic dress up as a king[21] – would allow the maintenance of a role of independence and neutrality among the European powers and, at the same time, would be the first step towards the more general renewal that the *novatori* ('innovators') were looking for: a renewal that would involve not only political actions but also, and above all, would launch a series of public works, the result of a broad and comprehensive programme, which would lead the city to erect new and mighty city walls, to build a new branch of the aqueduct, a new pier to protect the port arch and its commerce together with a whole series of maintenance works planned to keep the port of call efficient, which included, among other things, the expansion of the storage capacity for goods.[22] These were all major works that would help to relaunch Genoa's port system, supporting trade, guaranteeing security and autonomy for the city and restoring credibility, including international credibility, to the political institutions, which at the time were hard at work opposing the European powers that were threatening its independence and freedom.

The planned works would become the new reference points of the much hoped-for new historical course and, recognised by citizens and contemporaries as symbols of a regained republican dignity, would immediately appear in all those works (literary and graphic) intended to exalt the Republic and represent the city:[23] with reference to the building of the walls, Brignole Sale himself expressed the hope that 'the great work, so generously begun now […] with whose stones a whole city will be built, will be completed',[24] joining another man of letters of the time, Luca Assarino, who, albeit in a different tone and context, had already praised the grandiose undertaking in 1631 in his 'Discorso per le Nuove Mura di Genova'.[25] Giovan Bernardo Veneroso, a leading exponent of the *novatori* ('innovators') and *navalisti* ('navalists'), in 1650, in dedicating his *Genio Ligure Risvegliato* – a true manifesto of the so-called 'navalist movement' – 'to the Serenissimo Duce and Most Excellent Governors and Procurators of the Serenissima Republic of Genoa'[26] underlined how

> If they have been able to perpetually establish the ancient benevolence of their peoples by making peace flourish amidst fiery wars, by nesting security in the lap of the most dangerous

dangers, by bringing abundance from the depths of penury, & in the midst of the fiercest plagues, by maintaining continuous health: & beyond this, if they succeeded in making themselves admirable to foreigners, by making everyone see, in the most calamitous times for public and private fortunes, the most magnificent City with superb aqueducts, stronger with impregnable walls, more glorious with new naval armies and more illustrious with marvellous wharves in the depth of the unstable waves stably founded.[27]

The new fortifications and the well-protected port thus appeared immediately, with perfect precision and topographical correspondence, even in those drawings, paintings and prints that would promote the city's image abroad. Consolidated images that would be joined by the inventiveness of Domenico Fiasella who, while studying the image that would represent the city – now governed as a monarchy – outside its walls, raised the point of view with topographical and geometric precision. He may have taken as his model, in order to correctly delineate the coastal and port arch, the *Rilievo planimetrico e batimetrico del Porto di Genova*, which was probably carried out, as Ennio Poleggi notes, by the chamber architect Giovanni Battista Costanzo,[28] commissioned by the *Magistratura dei Padri del Comune* – thus updating the outdated view of 1616 by Gerolamo Bordoni[29] and depicting a city in all its orography, including the new city walls and the western pier. This iconography was an immediate success,[30] becoming a highly effective communicative model that would also represent the Genoese communities of Naples and Palermo.[31]

These images highlight the great seventeenth-century public works, first and foremost the *Mura Nuove*,[32] built between 1626 and 1632 to a design by the engineers and mathematicians Ansaldo De Mari – a 'praised inventor of military machines'[33] – and Giovanni Battista Baliani[34] – who was soon to be active in securing the port and extending the aqueduct, and who was active in the sphere of Galilean studies and the most up-to-date Jesuit environment in terms of scientific and technical progress, a friend of Giovanni Vincenzo Imperiale and Anton Giulio Brignole Sale[35] – under the coordination of the architect Bartolomeo Bianco.[36] The Molo Nuovo ('New Pier')[37] played the role of 'guiding image'. It was built between 1638 and 1644 after a long debate aimed at evaluating a series of works to protect the port from the violent attacks of the Libeccio,[38] and only in 1651 was it permanently anchored to the Lanterna cliff.[39]

The work, designed to guarantee protection to the Genoa basin from the western side, would enhance the shelter function offered by the Molo Vecchio ('Old Pier') which, extended to the east but seriously damaged by a storm in 1531, had recently been extended to a total length of 490 metres from the 446.5 metres of the medieval period.[40] The long planning debate that preceded the start of the work involved prominent figures such as Bernardo Strozzi,[41] but also Bianco himself, who was shortly afterwards put in charge of the building site for the walls. In 1622 he produced a plan, which was not pursued, that envisaged a semi-circular pier to be built immediately after the dock, near the San Tommaso area.[42] The final project, which well reflected the entrepreneurial spirit of the Genoese, was thus drawn up in 1638 under the guidance of Ansaldo De Mari who, after working on an initial proposal in 1626,[43] conceived a structure that would extend eastwards for a length of almost 450 metres.[44] The colossal and extremely costly[45] project was made possible thanks to an avant-garde construction technology derived from studies of wave motion, which involved the sinking of caissons full of lime and stones at a depth of 12.9 metres on a well-levelled bed of boulders to form an artificial trapezoidal reef.[46] Thus the port (as well as all the coves that could now be built in the western part of the inlet)[47] was finally protected from the storms, and it was possible to increase the number of anchorages for sugar, coffee and cocoa,[48] which were further secured from 1649, the year in which the port was joined to the Cape of Faro, closing the 124–metre gap left open ten years earlier (fig. 9.1).[49]

It was no coincidence that the work, as we shall see, was included in the new images of the city and, thanks once again to Domenico Fiasella's inventiveness, also in the frontispiece of a fundamental text for the *novatori* ('innovators'): *Il Genio ligure risvegliato* (fig. 2.3). This pier was a protagonist that would also be present – next to the new circuit of the walls, well in view at the crowning of the mountains that close the city to the north, and to the Molo Vecchio ('Old Pier') clearly recognisable in its extension – in the frontispiece of other books that, in this period, exalt the city and its politics. Among these is the work by Cornelis Bloemaert which, from a drawing by Giovanni Andrea Podestà, opens the *De Dominio Serenissimae Genuensis Reipublicae in Mari Ligustico* ('On the Domain of the Most Serene Republic of Genoa over the Ligurian Sea') published in a first edition in Rome by the publisher Dominmicus Marcianus in 1641. The text, divided into two books and

9.1

The Harbour of Genoa with the Project of the Molo Nuovo Studied by Ansaldo De Mari (Genoa, Archivio di Stato, Cartografia storica, Giunta di Marina, n. 73).

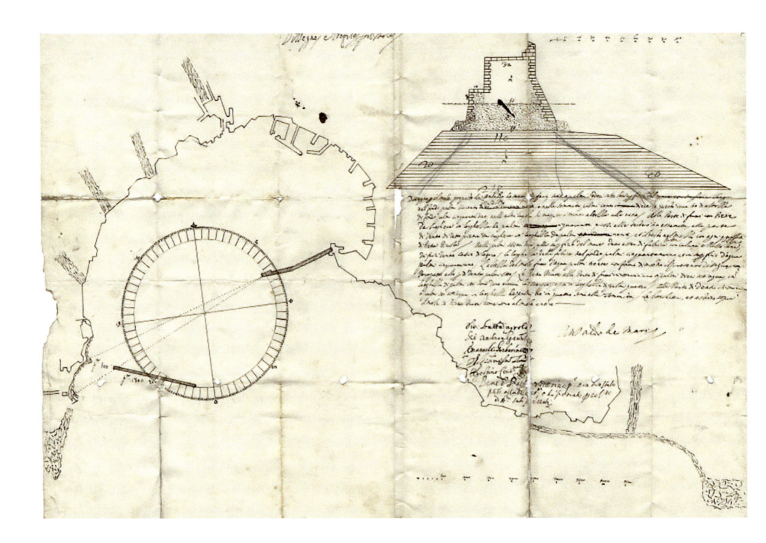

dedicated by the Genoese Pietro Battista Borgo to the legal foundations of Genoese dominion over the Ligurian Sea and freedom of trade at sea, to the power of Genoa and its magistracies,[50] opens with a dedication to the Doge, the Governors and Procurators of the Republic. The opening image of such an important work could not therefore fail to be promptly updated on the phases of the greatest city building works of the time. In this first edition, in fact, the pier is represented, correctly, not yet rooted to the promontory of the Lanterna, and this proves that the author of the drawing – or rather the commissioners, namely the Doges and the Magistrates of the Republic, dedicatees of the editorial propaganda work and direct financiers of the same – had referred, in both cases, to very precise project drawings (e.g. those of De Mari) or had in any case referred to the drawings of the Republic. The definitive anchorage of the pier does in fact appear in the second edition of the work, which opens with a new version of the frontispiece that skilfully retouches Bloemart's panel and depicts the pier during its last construction phase.

The great public undertaking that made it possible to secure the port is mentioned again in 1669 in the frontispiece engraved by Marcus Orozco for the *Real grandezza della Serenissima Repubblica di Genova*: this encomiastic work was produced for Luis de Góngora by Carlo Sperone and dedicated to the governing bodies of the Republic. It was intended to glorify a city with an extraordinary colonial past which, through Christopher Columbus, had 'doubled' the known world and now, having recovered from the demographic and economic crisis following the plague of 1657, was preparing to play the leading role for which it had been born.[51] In this case, the engraving once again takes Bloemart's graphic work from 1641 as a model, but still in its original version of 1657, i.e. without the reference to the definitive establishment of the quay. The harbour is also present in the opening of an important compendium promoted by the *Officio delle Compere di San Giorgio*, kept today at the State Archives of Genoa,[52] which aims to collect all the surveys and the consistency of the artefacts (warehouses and possessions) belonging to the *Magistratura del Sale* ('Salt Magistracy'), an integral part of the *Casa of San Giorgio* itself.[53] This rich documentation gives an accurate account of another important series of public works carried out in the first half of the seventeenth century by the Genoese government in parallel with the maintenance and safety of the port:[54] between 1615 and 1642, in fact, three more warehouses were added to the 22 that already existed (in the Prè and Darsena areas), which alone accounted for almost 15 percent of the total volume that the Republic had at that time for storing salt.[55] If the growth from the middle of the previous century is taken into account, the increase is almost 70 per cent.[56] The volume thus represents a not insignificant aspect of the good management of commercial port traffic, well represented by the Molo Nuovo ('New Pier') on the frontispiece, at a time when most of the goods handled were timber and foodstuffs, as well as some raw materials such as iron ore, building materials, wool, silk and silver.[57] According to the well-established 'rule' that having raw materials available meant guaranteeing the independence of the state even in times of famine or economic crisis, the Republic also did its best in this period to build other warehouses for storing, for example, cereals. In the period in question, to supplement the *Magazzini dell'Abbondanza* ('warehouses of abundance') built between 1564 and 1568 at the Molo ('Old Pier') but by then insufficient for seventeenth-century requirements, in 1606 the dedicated Magistrate began construction of four new buildings in the area of the Porta di San Tommaso, which were enlarged as early as 1622.[58] These warehouses were flanked by a whole series of new structures, specially rented or built, in which to store wine (in the area of San Marco al Molo, in the *contrada del Campo* and in the Darsena), oil and various goods, whose warehouse, between 1644 and 1645, was set up in the old hospital of San Lazzaro, or adjacent to the port.[59]

At the beginning of the seventeenth century, a decree issued by the Doge, Agostino Doria,[60] intensified efforts to deepen the port's waters by scheduling a series of extraordinary works and periodic maintenance and excavation operations, as well as increasing the number of vehicles and manpower, in an attempt to resolve an issue that had plagued the port for centuries.[61]

The last, but not least, work to be carried out was the construction of the branch of the aqueduct called *di Calzolo*[62] (otherwise known as *Cavassolo*): completed in 1623 and 18 miles long, it was developed mainly outside the city walls, along the valley of the Bisagno River, 'above mountain slopes'[63] thanks to the expertise of the architect Giovanni Aicardo, already an astute designer for the *Magistrato dell'Abbondanza* of the warehouses at the Porta di San Tommaso.[64] The work, an 'incredible expense and admirable artifice, but also an undertaking embraced by no one else but the Genoese',[65] and the complex technological solutions applied, allowed the rationalisation and strengthening of the ancient branches of the city's aqueduct which, from this moment onwards, would always be present in the iconography dedicated to the city, first and foremost in the great view by Alessandro Baratta, created in 1637.

The inhospitable mountain that had struck Petrarch was thus definitively tamed and made functional for the city, even beyond the urban outskirts, with the great public works represented by the hydraulic regulations and aqueduct, the walls and fortifications and the network of roads across the Apennines, which unlike the coastal road could not count on the easy alternative of the sea route. Entrusted to the direction of Genoa's greatest technicians and mathematicians, Giovanni Battista Baliani and Ansaldo De Mari, the new walls were not only to consecrate the fame of Genoa's great school of engineering in terms of their grandeur and modernity of conception, but also testified that Genoa was stronger than ever. As Claudio Costantini had already noted in 1976, the construction of the new walls also signified the Republic's commitment to 'do its own thing',[66] to rely mainly on its own forces for its defence. Public works found concreteness, therefore, in representations of the city: engraved and printed views which, on the one hand, are inspired by Michael Wolgemut's late fifteenth-century woodcut[67] with its medieval walls, wharves and lighthouses clearly visible and, on the other, extend their communication strategy by emphasising the presence of the Molo Nuovo ('New Pier') that was set up to protect the renewed commercial heart; the new city walls, a symbolic structure running along the ridges of Genoa's natural amphitheatre;

9.2

Alessandro Baratta, *La famosissima e nobilissima città di Genova cò le sue nuove Fortificazioni* (The Very Famous and Noble City of Genoa with its New Fortifications), 1637, detail. Photo: Wikimedia Commons (source: Bibliothèque Nationale de France). Public domain.

the aqueduct; and the roads, which often appear exaggeratedly wide and straight, as in Giovanni Domenico Rossi's work, published in 1640, which was to become a new prototype.[68] The first to depict the Molo Nuovo ('New Pier') not yet rooted to the Lanterna promontory, it took as its model, updating it, Alessandro Baratta's great view of 1637, in which the *Nuove Fortificazioni* ('New Fortifications') were present, but not yet the recent port infrastructure (fig. 9.2).[69]

From the Baratta/De Rossi prototype would also derive the city iconography of Daniël Stoopendal, whose engraving, produced, probably, in a year close to the end of the seventeenth century but printed and published by Pierre Vander in Leiden at the beginning of the following century, depicts *Genua, capitale du même nom en Italie* in an airy bird's-eye view with the Molo Nuovo ('New Pier') now rooted to the mainland and, as in the view presented by Baratta, the new sections of the aqueduct (fig. 9.3). These last views present a further novelty in the positioning of the point of view: until then positioned at the centre of the port arch, it is now moved towards the west and lowered with the sole purpose of magnifying the perception of the dimensions and the architecture, severe and 'resistant', of the new port infrastructure.

The new public works thus became not only cornerstones of the city's new iconography, but above all symbols of the renewal of the city's buildings, which until then had been centred solely on the palaces of Strada Nuova and Via Balbi

– thanks also to the extraordinary editorial work of Pietro Paolo Rubens, I Palazzi di Genova, published in a first edition in 1622 and in a second, enlarged, edition in 1652 in Antwerp – but which they flanked rather than replaced.[70] The public works give an account of a new common effort, which comes alongside, but does not replace, the wealth of the individual citizens, constituting and further strengthening the power of the government. The power of Genoa thus also became the power of the Genoese and was invoked as the basis of the Republic's right to use the wealth, prestige and skills of its private citizens for its own ends:[71] 'where there is unity there is strength', wrote Giovan Vincenzo Imperiale, commenting on the construction of the new walls, referring to the unity of the economic efforts – and therefore of the image – of both the institutions and the citizens 'and there is no fear of misery where there is fortress'.[72] It was no coincidence, in fact, that the Senate, from 1576 until 1664, in the absence of an adequate seat of representation, had started the system of public accommodation in the private residences of the Genoese aristocrats, specially commissioned and included in specific lists, the Rolli.[73]

This strategy of enlarging and magnifying not only the city within the seventeenth-century city walls but also the surrounding area with its villas was to be considered in literature as a further trait which, although belonging to the sphere of the private aristocracy, contributed – as we have seen – to making the city great on the international scene and to reinforcing its power, wealth and, above all, to conveying its image of independence.[74] It is worth noting how, both in Baratta's map and in the particularly interesting one by an anonymous author published by Pierre Mortier and dating back to a year after 1651,[75] in addition to exaggerating the width of the 'new streets', the villas outside the walls are in fact well highlighted: in the case of Sampierdarena, highlighting the 'Place of delights with beautiful Palaces and Gardens' directly on the beach (Baratta) or in the entries of the legend (Mortier).[76]

These characteristics would persist even when the image of the city was well established, as in the case of the view designed by Friedrich Werner and engraved by Johann Ringle in the mid-eighteenth century and the twin view of Probost, both dressed in 'German clothes'.[77]

It was then the works of Francesco Maria Accinelli in 1732 and Antonio Giolfi in 1769 that definitively consecrated the image of the city and its port, seen from the sea,[78] images which, in parallel with what was happening on an iconographic level, were also developing on a literary level where, within the vast production of the first half of the seventeenth century,[79] the work of Bernardo Morando stands out. He was a member of the Accademia degli Addormentati who, in Rosalinda, published in Piacenza in 1650, in line with the ideas of the novatori ('innovators') and alongside the exaltation of the concept of negotiatione (so different from the 'banal' mercatura), he presents, exalting them, other fundamental themes such as tranquillity and peace, the compactness and unity of the territory of a Republic that had by now overcome the particularisms of individuals, the power of the city and the architectural splendour and monumentality of its public and private works. Among these he does not fail to exalt those same villas and holiday districts that the cartographers and Vedutists had emphasised in their views of the city and that Anton Giulio Brignole Sale had already recalled, a few years earlier, by setting in the holiday district of Albaro – 'a very pleasant hill that imitating Alba with its name, comes to surpass it in vagueness'[80] – Le instabilità dell'ingegno, a real expedient for the celebration of a pacified city.[81] Thus, in the name of a rediscovered unity between public and private for the benefit of the Republic's power – as Giovan Vincenzo Imperiale himself underlined[82] – Rosalinda describes the extraordinary nature of Genoa's palaces, streets, churches and villas. The ideology guiding Rosalinda, in fact, is closely linked to the system of values pursued by the politics of the novatori ('innovators'): a vision that is continually reiterated through the repetition of the now customary key concepts, such as the nobility of trade, the tranquillity, unity and compactness of the republican territory, the power and freedom/independence of the State, its architectural splendour and the monumentality of its public works.

1 Grossi Bianchi and Poleggi, 'La strada del Guastato'.

2 Reference is made here to that broad strand of studies that includes the contributions on city iconography made by Ennio Poleggi and Lauro Magnani during the 1970s and 1980s: see, in particular: Poleggi, 'Uso dell'immagine urbana'; Poleggi, *Iconografia*; Poleggi, 'L'evoluzione storica dell'immagine di Genova'; Poleggi, *Paesaggio e immagine di Genova*; Poleggi, *Genova. Ritratto di una città*; Poleggi, 'Dalle mura ai saloni, un rinnovo segreto'; Magnani, *Il tempio di Venere*; Magnani, 'Apparati festivi e immagine della città tra Seicento e Settecento'; Magnani, 'Articolazione e immagine del sistema abitativo'; Magnani, 'Temporary architecture and public decoration'; Magnani, 'Novus orbis emergat'; Magnani, 'Sintesi iconografica e apparato per la città'. On this topic see also, in particular, the contributions of Nuti, 'The city and its image'; Giubbini, 'La città rappresentata'.

3 Bitossi, 'A Republic in Search of Legitimation'; Bitossi, '"Il dominio del mare e l'impero della terra"'; Costantini, 'La ricerca di un'identità'; the author, on p. 17, underlines, however, how this part was only an intellectual minority supporting an opposition battle and not a moment of identity of a power class.

4 Morando, 'La letteratura in Liguria tra Cinque e Seicento'.

5 Graziosi, *Lancio ed eclissi*, p. 1; Puncuh, 'Genova', p. 27; Lo Basso, 'Diaspora e armamento'; Bitossi, '"Il dominio del mare e l'impero della terra"'. For a more general picture of the city's political and economic history in the sixteenth and seventeenth centuries, see: Bitossi, *Il governo dei magnifici*; Grendi, *La Repubblica aristocratica*.

6 Bitossi, 'Il genio ligure risvegliato', p. 82.

7 Bitossi, '"Il dominio del mare e l'impero della terra"', pp. 9–13; Bitossi, 'Il genio ligure risvegliato', p. 82.

8 Bitossi, 'Il genio ligure risvegliato', p. 83.

9 Foglietta, *Dialogo della Republica di Genova*; Bitossi, '"Il dominio del mare e l'impero della terra"', p. 9; Bitossi, 'Il genio ligure risvegliato', p. 83.

10 Bitossi, 'Il genio ligure risvegliato', p. 83.

11 Bitossi, 'Il genio ligure risvegliato', p. 93 with cited bibliography. On this topic see also, in particular, the contribution by Costantini, 'La ricerca di un'identità', pp. 9–74.

12 'Cittadino zelante habitante in Napoli'.

13 Brignole Sale, *Congratulatione*, p. 17. 'Non possono tornar que' tempi, ne quell'opre stesse è vero, ma bene possono tornar, e tempi, ed opre in tutto à quelle somiglianti, purche non vogliamo noi per dapocaggine dissomigliarci da quegli antenati, a' quali siamo per natura, complessione, ingegno, e cuore somigliantissimi'.

14 Brignole Sale, *Congratulatione*, p. 17. 'La difesa dello Stato, della Riputazione, della Giurisdittione, e della Libertà' of the Republic of Genoa were at stake'; Bitossi, 'Il genio ligure risvegliato', p. 84.

15 Bitossi, '"Il dominio del mare e l'impero della terra"', p. 13; on the literary Brignole Sale, see, in particular: Costantini, Marini, Vazzoler, *Anton Giulio Brignole Sale*. On the *Accademia degli Addormentati* and its revival: Graziosi, *Lancio ed eclissi*, pp. 51–58; Morando, 'La letteratura in Liguria tra Cinque e Seicento', pp. 51–60;

16 Brignole Sale, *Congratulatione*, p. 4. 'De gli antichi secoli'.

17 Brignole Sale, *Congratulatione*, p. 4. 'Al numero di sei Galee'.

18 Bitossi, '"Il dominio del mare e l'impero della terra"', p. 12; Bitossi, 'Il genio ligure risvegliato', p. 90; Graziosi, *Lancio ed eclissi*, pp. 120–24.

19 Graziosi, *Lancio ed eclissi*, pp. 41–49.

20 Brignole Sale, *Congratulatione*, pp. 9–10. 'Troppo nota è la Natura de' Genovesi, che al loro Clima somigliano, sì nell'instabilità, come nell'acutezza, altrettanto sono men fermi nel perseverare, quanto fervidi nello intraprendere'.

21 Bitossi, '"Il dominio del mare e l'impero della terra"', p. 12; Bitossi, 'Il genio ligure risvegliato', p. 91.

22 Bitossi, 'Il genio ligure risvegliato', pp. 102–03.

23 Costantini, 'La ricerca di un'identità', pp. 65–66; Costantini, *La Repubblica di Genova*.

24 Brignole Sale, *Congratulatione*, pp. 26–27. 'Si doni compimento alla grande opra, tanto generosamente adesso incominciata […] co' cui sassi una Cittade intiera fabricherebbesi'.

25 As Simona Morando notes, the text was published a first time as *Discorso di Luca Assarino fatto in lode di Genova nell'occasione delle Nuove Mura, dedicato all'Illustriss. Sig. Andrea Mari* and a second time, to which reference is made here, as Assarino, 'Discorso per le Nuove Mura di Genova', p. 173. See the studies by Ruffini, *Sotto il segno del pavone*, p. 344 and by Morando, 'Luca Assarino, tra Genova e la modernità', note n. 11, pp. 248–49.

26 Veneroso, *Il genio ligure risvegliato*, p. a11. 'Al Serenissimo Duce et Eccellentissimi Signori Governatori, e Procuratori della Serenissima Repubblica di Genova'.

27 Veneroso, *Il genio ligure risvegliato*, p. 6. 'Only now the Serenissimi have been able to show everyone […] the most magnificent city with superb aqueducts, stronger with impregnable walls […] and more illustrious with marvellous piers founded in the depths of unstable waves' ('v v. ss. Serenissime se sono valse à perpetuamente stabilire l'antica benevolenza de loro popoli col far trà le guerre ardenti fiorir la pace, annidar la sicurezza in grembo alle più pericolose insidie, nascer l'abbondanza dall'infecondo seno delle penurie, & in mezzo alle contagioni più fiere mantenere una continuata salute: & oltre di ciò se loro è riuscito rendersi appò i stranieri ammirabili, col far, à ciascheduno vedere ne più calamitosi tempi per le pubbliche, e per le private fortune, la Città più magnifica co' superbi acquedotti, più forte con mura inespugnabili, più gloriosa con nuove armate Navali e più illustre con maravigliose moli nella profondità dell'onde instabili stabilmente fondate'). For an in-depth reading of the political message of the text read in the context of the moment, see Bitossi, 'Il genio ligure risvegliato'.

28 Poleggi, *Iconografia*, p. 100.

29 Poleggi, *Iconografia*, p. 119.

30 See George Gorse's contribution in this same volume.

31 See, most recently, the contributions of Di Fabio, 'Un'iconografia regia'; Borniotto, *L'identità di Genova*, pp. 244–64.

32 For a description of the grandeur, even technical, of the work, and the immediate prominence it had, see the contemporary chronicle by Capriata, *Dell'historia di Pietro Giouanni Capriata*, pp. 842–46.

33 Giuliani, *Prospetto cronologico*, p. 6.

34 For an in-depth profile of the Genoese technician and mathematician see: Costantini, *Baliani e i Gesuiti*; Faina, *Ingegneria portuale genovese*; Doldi, *Scienza e tecnica in Liguria*, pp. 36–42, 54–5; Natucci, 'Giovanni Battista Baliano'; Lavaggi, 'La scienza in Liguria'.

35 Lavaggi, 'La scienza in Liguria', pp. 506, 512–16.

36 On the work of Bianco, a master mason from Lombardy enrolled in Genoa in the *Arte dei Muratori Lombardi* from 1602 and involved, in the course of his career, in a dense series of works for the most important families in the Genoa area, see, in particular, the contributions by Profumo Müller, *Bartolomeo Bianco architetto*, pp. 1–127; Di Raimondo and Profumo Müller, *Bartolomeo Bianco e Genova*; on the role of Lombard master masons, see also Di Raimondo.

37 On the iconography of the city and its port in particular, see Podestà, *Il porto di Genova*, pp. 461–84; Faina, *Ingegneria portuale genovese*, pp. 79–199; Doria, 'La gestione del porto di Genova', pp. 147–50.

38 Faina, *Ingegneria portuale genovese*, p. 81; Doria, 'La gestione del porto di Genova', p. 148.

39 The opening was left in order to guarantee an opening to the basin that would avoid silting up the port and to allow small boats to enter directly from the west without 'circumnavigating' the quay. Faina, *Ingegneria portuale genovese*, pp. 172–73; Doria, 'La gestione del porto di Genova', pp. 150–67.

40 Doria, 'La gestione del porto di Genova', p. 148; on the work see also: Podestà, *Il porto di Genova*, pp. 212–15; Costamagna, 'La costruzioni del molo nuovo'.

41 The contribution of the painter, who in 1619 had studied and illustrated a solution for the securing of the moorings (preserved in the Genoa, State Archives), is illustrated in Faina, *Ingegneria portuale genovese*, pp. 53–59; Di Raimondo and Profumo Müller, *Bartolomeo Bianco e Genova*, pp. 172–73. The proposal has also been recently explored by Roberto Santamaria in the exhibition *Bernardo Strozzi e il Porto. Il Leonardo della Genova del Seicento*, held in Genoa, at Palazzo San Giorgio, from 26 November 2019 to 12 January 2020.

42 For the *Project for the works to be carried out in the port of Genoa to make it safe and avoid silting up*, kept in ASG, AS, n. 1653, see Di Raimondo and Profumo Müller, *Bartolomeo Bianco e Genova*, pp. 172–73; Faina, *Ingegneria portuale genovese*, pp. 59–63; Doria, 'La gestione del porto di Genova', p. 149.

43 Doria, 'La gestione del porto di Genova', p. 149; Faina, *Ingegneria portuale genovese*, p. 101.

44 The project is preserved in Genoa, State Archives, *Cartografia storica*, no. 73, *Disegno e profilo per il Molo*; Faina, *Ingegneria portuale genovese* pp. 108–13.

45 Giorgio Doria points out that the building site would have handled 453,000 cubic metres of stone and cost an initial estimate of 2 million lire, a sum covered by the simultaneous contribution of the Republic, the San Giorgio coffers and a number of private individuals, who subscribed to a 'life purchase' at 3.5 per cent interest (Doria, 'La gestione del porto di Genova', pp. 149–50).

46 Doria, 'La gestione del porto di Genova', p. 150; Faina, *Ingegneria portuale genovese*, p. 113.

47 Faina, *Ingegneria portuale genovese*, p. 81.

48 Piccinno, 'Il commercio marittimo e lo sviluppo del porto di Genova', pp. 20–21; Doria, 'La gestione del porto di Genova', pp. 150–51.

49 Doria, 'La gestione del porto di Genova', p. 167.

50 Castronovo, 'Borgo, Pietro Battista'.

51 Rotta, 'Fra Spagna e Francia', pp. 246–49; Rotta, 'Genova e il Re Sole', pp. 286–91.

52 ASG, *Cartografia storica*, nn. 3–5, *Piante et alzati delli magazzini e case che possiede l'Illustrissimo Officio delle compere di San Georgio della Serenissima Repubblica di Genova, cavato da D. Leonardo De Ferrari Genovese l'anno 1660* (1660 Dec. 20).

53 Doria, 'La gestione del porto di Genova', p. 153.

54 Piccinno, 'Il commercio marittimo e lo sviluppo del porto di Genova', pp. 21–25.

55 Doria, 'La gestione del porto di Genova', p. 154.

56 Doria, 'La gestione del porto di Genova', p. 154.

57 Doria, 'La gestione del porto di Genova', pp. 139–40.

58 Doria, 'La gestione del porto di Genova', pp. 154–55; Podestà, *Il porto di Genova*, pp. 62, 149; Costamagna, 'I magazzini del Magistrato'; Grossi Bianchi and Poleggi, 'La strada del Guastato', pp. 86–7.

59 Doria, 'La gestione del porto di Genova', pp. 155–58.

60 Doria, 'La gestione del porto di Genova', p. 146.

61 Doria, 'La gestione del porto di Genova', pp. 144–45; on this subject see also the contribution by Rebora, 'I lavori di espurgazione della Darsena'.

62 Temporelli, Cassinelli. For a more in-depth reading of the Genoese aqueduct system, see also Podestà, *L'acquedotto di Genova*.

63 Soprani, *Vite de pittori*, p. 334. 'Sopra falde de monti'.

64 Soprani, *Vite de pittori*, p. 334.

65 Soprani, *Vite de pittori*, p. 334.

66 Costantini 'La ricerca di un'identità', p. 48.

67 See Poleggi, *Iconografia di Genova e delle Riviere*, p. 71.

68 Rossi, *Nuova delineazione della nobilissima e famosissima città di Genova*.

69 Baratta, *La famosissima e nobilissima città di Genova*; Poleggi, *Iconografia*, pp. 76–80.

70 Costantini, 'La ricerca di un'identità', p. 47.

71 Costantini, 'La ricerca di un'identità', p. 47.

72 Imperiale, *De' Giornali di Gio Vincenzo Imperiale*, pp. 450–65. 'Ove è unione è forza', 'E non si tema di miseria ov'è fortezza'; Costantini, 'La ricerca di un'identità', p. 48.

73 On this topic see, most recently, the recent Rossi and Santamaria, eds, *Superbe carte*, with previous bibliography.

74 Magnani, 'Residenze di villa e immagini di giardino tra realtà e mito'; Magnani, 'Il giardino, spazio di realtà e spazio di illusione', pp. 29–31; Magnani, 'The Rise and Fall of Gardens in the Republic of Genoa'; Magnani, *Il tempio di Venere*, pp. 125–40; Magnani, 'Genoese Gardens between Pleasure and Politics'.

75 Poleggi, *Iconografia di Genova e delle Riviere*, p. 82. The dating is related to the presence of the complete Molo ('New Pier').

76 Poleggi, *Iconografia*, p. 83. 'Loco di delitie con bellissimi Palazzi e Giardini'.

77 Poleggi, *Iconografia*, p. 83. 'Panni tedeschi'.

78 Accinelli, *Genova*, engraved by F. Ganzinotto, 1732: see Poleggi, *Iconografia*, pp. 84–5; Antonio Giolfi, *Veduta della città di Genova*, engraved by Gian Lorenzo Guidotti, 1769: Poleggi, *Iconografia*, pp. 86–87; for Giolfi's graphic work on the city of Genoa, see: Poleggi, ed., *Genova nel Settecento*.

79 Morando, 'La letteratura in Liguria tra Cinque e Seicento', p. 59.

80 Brignole Sale, *Le instabilità dell'ingegno*, p. 1. 'Colle piacevolissimo che imitando l'Alba col nome, vien'à superarla in vaghezze'.

81 Graziosi, Graziosi, *Lancio ed eclissi*, pp. VII-VIII.

82 Costantini, 'La ricerca di un'identità', p. 48.

10

George L. Gorse

A 'ROYAL REPUBLIC'

The Virgin Mary as 'Queen of Genoa' in 1637

Through the triumphal façade of the Cathedral of San Lorenzo, down the long processional black-and-white marble nave, to the classical, illuminated domed crossing and scenic choir, from medieval commune to the Renaissance republic of Andrea Doria, dark into light, the Biennial Doge and 'Very Serene Colleges' presented a crown, sceptre, and keys to a portable, ceremonial, polychrome wood sculpture (fig. 10.1) of the Crowned Virgin Mary and Child in Heaven with scroll inscription, 'Et Rege Eos' ('And Rule Them'), from King David's *Psalms* (27: 8–9), on the high altar in a solemn state Mass on the feast day of the Annunciation, 25 March, 1637.[1] With this communal offering, a 'republic' became a 'monarchy' and a new civic iconography, a state ritual and representation were born, represented in the vital Genoese trading colony churches of Spanish Habsburg Naples and Palermo (fig. 10.2–10.3).[2]

Many scholars have interpreted this 'rededication' as a direct response to military, political and economic crises connected with the Savoy War of 1625–26, part of the devastating Thirty Years' War leading up to the Peace of Westphalia in 1648, and the building of the new city walls in 1626–37 to the mountaintops, enclosing and protecting the natural harbour city.[3] This paper adds two points or proposals to this analysis: first, that the crescent shape of Genoa, itself, represents the crescent or globe of the 'Immaculate Conception of the Virgin Mary', the state iconography of Spain and its world empire, to which Genoa was allied; and second, beyond the portals, the walls themselves represented the Sacred Belt ('La Sacra Cintura') of the Virgin Mary, protector of the 'royal Republic' of Genoa, now claiming equal status to rival principalities (Turin) and kingdoms.[4] The new walled city of Genoa embodied the Virgin Mary as 'Empress, Queen, and Governor of the Republic and of all its states', according to the rededication ceremony of 25 March, 1637.

During the fifteenth and sixteenth centuries, the theology of the Immaculate Conception of the Virgin Mary, rooted in the elevation of the Virgin Mary to 'Theotokos' ('Mother of God') at the Council of Ephesus in 431 under Byzantine

Emperor Theodosius II, and promoted by the Franciscans in the thirteenth century, became a state iconography of Spain, particularly in Seville in the south of Iberia in direct contact with its Muslim (lunar calendar) culture after the 'reconquista' in 1492.[5] A debate ensued whether the crescent moon should be upward or downward, in which Francisco Pacheco, Renaissance theorist and teacher of Velasquez and others, argued for the latter in his *Arte de la Pintura*, published in Seville in 1649:

> Especially with the moon I have followed the learned opinion of Father Luis de Alcazar, who says, 'Painters usually show the [crescent] moon upside down at the feet of this woman. But as is obvious to learned mathematicians, if the moon and sun face each other, both points of the moon have to point downward. Thus the woman will stand on a convex instead of a concave surface…' This is necessary so that the moon, receiving its light from the sun, will illuminate the woman standing on it.[6]

Like Artemis/Diana of Ephesus, the Virgin Mary on a crescent moon (a new beginning, after the new moon) faces and reflects the sun (Jupiter/Christ) theologically but also optically (and mathematically), according to Pacheco's Renaissance art theory. One can see this downward motion in a minority of the 'Inmacolada' ('Her Immaculate Birth'), which suggest a universal globe under her feet, as well.

With this in mind, it is suggestive to interpret the 'Madonna della Città' as a complex hybrid (but integrated) image of the Crowned Virgin and Child in Heaven over Genoa, her sacred royal entry city, and the 'Immacolata' with Genoa as the downward crescent moon or globe, incorporating her encyclopaedic iconography as divine ruler, protector and

10.4

Francisco de Zurbarán, *The Immaculate Conception.* Madrid, Museo Nacional del Prado, 1628–1630. Oil on canvas, 128 × 89 cm, Inv. P002992. Photo: © Photographic Archive Museo Nacional del Prado. Reproduced with permission.

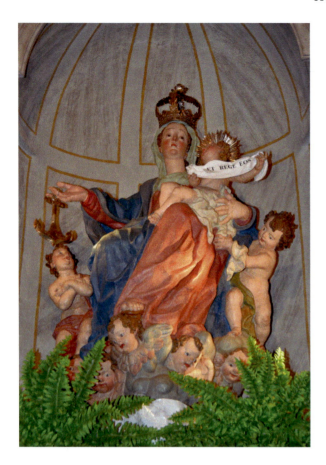

10.1
Giovanni Battista Bissoni after Domenico Fiasella, *Madonna of the Vow*. Fiorino (Genoa), Parrocchia di San Michele Arcangelo, 1637. Photo: Author. Reproduced with permission.

It is now embodied in the very fabric of a new walled 'Marian Genoa'—the *City as Body*.

This is a global iconography. An extraordinary example now resides in a private collection in Mexico City: a late sixteenth century Japanese lacquered wood and mother-of-pearl triptych, painted in Mexico ('New Spain') in the mid-eighteenth century, representing the miracles of indigenous peasant saint Juan Diego's visions in 1531.[9] We can also note the 'Virgin of the Andes' over crescent moon, representing the Tiwanacan-Incan Mountain Earth Goddess Pachamama intercessor (the Church), so familiar to medieval and Renaissance Genoa 'sacred foundation myths' as a major entry port city into Italy, 'Paradiso'.[7] In the case of Zurbarán (fig. 10.4), the Virgin Mary is, at once (from left to right, top to bottom): *Porta Coeli* ('Portal of Heaven') and 'Jacob's Ladder' ('Stairway to Heaven') at her head, which guard, open and ascend the firmament; at her heart, 'ivory tower' or 'closed temple' and 'spotless mirror' (*Speculum sine Macula*), which reflect her pure spiritual being; at her hips, *Stella Maris* (first morning star of the seas) and shadowy 'face of the moon' that guide the sublunar earthly realm. And like a 'predella' narrative altar frieze beneath her feet, the Virgin's role as 'protector of sailors' (i.e., pilgrims, seekers of faith, hope, salvation, journey of the soul, Ship of State or Church, *Navicella*) is represented by the caravel sailing across the serene waters (Divine Fortune) from Nature and landscape with palm tree of salvation to the fortified 'City of God' (Augustine's *Civitas Dei*) with entry gate, domed temple, and 'Tower of David' (*Turris David*, a guiding Lantern) above — a New Jerusalem. These repeat Her celestial attributes with other gendered virginal signs of 'Hortus Conclusus' ('closed garden') and 'living fountain' (*Fons Sapientiae* or 'Fountain of Divine Wisdom') of a New Celestial Jerusalem or Rome.[8] From Jacobus de Voragine to Petrarch and many others, this pagan to Christian iconography is woven into the very 'foundations' of medieval and Renaissance Genoa.

10.2
Domenico Fiasella, *Virgin and Child in Glory over Genoa*. Naples, Chiesa della Pietà dei Turchini, c. 1638. Photo: Wikimedia Commons. Public Domain.

10.3

Domenico Fiasella, *Madonna of the City*. Palermo,
Chiesa di San Giorgio dei Genovesi, c. 1640.
Oil on canvas, 314 × 195 cm. Photo: Giuseppe Oliveri.
Reproduced with Permission.

on Lake Titicaca (Island of the Sun) in Peru (modern Bolivia), part of the global gold and silver and slave trade across the Atlantic and Pacific Oceans.[10] From the Virgin of Guadalupe in Mexico City to the Black Virgin of Extremadura in Spain (without crescent moon but with dark 'Moorish' complexion), we find a crusading history from medieval *reconquista* to Renaissance global empire, *Plus Ultra* ('More Beyond'), and here I cannot resist including Montorsoli's monumental sculpture of Andrea Doria as a Roman admiral (a new Augustus over the Mediterranean, *mare nostrum*) with Emperor Charles V's 'Golden Fleece' (of 1531) on his breastplate over Michelangelesque bound slave with crescent moon on his breastplate.[11] This imperial iconography pervades the new civic iconography and ascent of the Virgin Mary over Baroque Genoa in the seventeenth and eighteenth centuries.

Ultimately, this all goes back to the 'Virgin of the Apocalypse' on crescent moon, triumphing over the 'Whore of Babylon' with the seven-headed dragon from St John the Evangelist's *Book of Revelation* (12: 1–9) – Salvation and Damnation at the Last Judgement – Eschatological Time.[12] In 1637, Alessandro Baratta published his monumental print view of Genoa with map of Liguria and Corsica ('il Regno' at lower left) to commemorate the completion of the new fortress walls (a radiant crown over the city) with 'royal court' of patron saints (at upper right): the luminous Crowned Virgin Mary and Christ on Crescent Moon, with medieval institutional patron saints Lawrence and John the Baptist, Crusading George over the Dragon, and penitent St Bernard of Clairvaux, embracing Instruments of the Passion, next to Fame's trumpet banderole 'Libertas', voted by the Republic as a new (French) patron saint in 1625 at the beginning of the Savoy War.[13] From then on, Bernard is everywhere, from the ceremonial staircase in the Palazzo Reale (formerly Palazzo Ducale) beneath the Michelangelesque/Carracci-inspired Trinity/Pietà fresco, triumphing over the Devil, lurking in the balustrade next to the Loggia degl'Alemanni (Loggia of German Guards); to the foundation medal of the new walls laid at the Lantern in a solemn procession on 7 December 1626, the day before the feast day of the Immaculate Conception on 8 December; to the *Immacolata* in ascent over patron saints on the monumental Albergo dei Poveri, built to 'crown' Genoa after the catastrophic plague of 1655–56, a fresco tympanum, now faded, but known through Giovanni Battista Carlone's contemporary oil painting of this magnificent Baroque ascent.[14] All of this was part of the change from 'civic' to 'royal' iconography after 1637, a watershed, reflected in Genoa's new 'royal' currency.

Two years later, in 1639, a Confraternity of the Sacred Belt of the Virgin Mary was formed at the church of St Agostino with a chapel and fresco dedicated to *La Sacra Cintura*, now lost.[15] The confraternity published a crowned civic history (with medieval guardian griffins) of the cult and relics with papal proclamations and privileges, dedicated to the 'Very Serene Doge, Most Excellent Governors, and Most Illustrious Procurators of the Genoese Republic' (just to highlight titles, which are paramount throughout this period).[16] On the second page, the Crowned Virgin Mary and Christ extend the Sacred Belt to kneeling Sts. Augustine and Monica below, originators of this sacred cult, who present a view of the Lantern at centre. In the dedication pages that follow, La Sacra Cintura protects this 'Real Città' from its enemies with enclosing walls (Cinta), fortress terminology, her sacred belt or mantle, embracing the harbour city, Her Realm.[17] One is reminded of Raphael's Ascension and Coronation of the Virgin Mary over her floral tomb with Sacred Belt held by St Thomas, flanked by Roman Sts Peter and Paul with John the Evangelist at right, for the Oddi family chapel in the Cathedral of San Francesco in papal Perugia of 1502.[18]

In Fiasella's paintings (fig. 10.2–10.3), the walls rise up to touch at their pinnacle the angels beneath the silver basin with crown, sceptre, and keys, offered to the Crowned Virgin and Child in Majesty, 'Et Rege Eos', over sacred mountains and enclosed harbour basin.[19] This is a 'royal sacred landscape' from God's perspective, straight down. The same 'divine' perspective is featured in the Carte Geografiche ('maps') of the Vatican Cortile del Belvedere in which the Italian peninsula is represented in classical ambulatio with major city views and plans with inscriptions and allegorical figures, displayed down the corridor, a kind of papal 'Grand Tour' between palace and villa, in which rival Genoa and Venice frame the end portal in three-dimensional flat-plan and bird's-eye views.[20] In 1633, Pope Urban VIII Barberini wrote to the Senate requesting two large paintings by Genoese artist Andrea Ansaldo di Voltri, one in plan and one bird's-eye, of the city and 'new walls' – a 'wonder' of modern fortifications.[21] The 'Nuove Mura' became iconic of the entrance port city and republic after the Savoy War. With their completion in 1637, not only were the monumental rustic church-like city gates, Porta Lanterna (west) and Porta Pila (east), dedicated to the Crowned Virgin Mary and Christ with inscription, 'Et Rege Eos', but the walls themselves, were 'La Sacra Cintura', a protector against Savoy cannon but also a 'corona' of her royal sovereignty.[22] They stood with the monastic Churches of Santa Maria della Guardia over Polcevera Valley to the west and Nostra Signora della Monte over Bisagno

to the east as flanking sentinels over the city, part of Marian worship throughout Liguria.[23] Now the Virgin Mary rose as the central figure in the Republic, axis mundi, embodying her royal character and status as a European capital in a world empire. And this is anticipated by Galeazzo Alessi's monumental domed church of Santa Maria Assuntà (1549–1602), a 'simulacrum' of St Peter's in Rome, for the new noble merchant-banking-cardinal Sauli family in their albergo in Carignano, defining the new 'Marian City'.[24]

One thinks of parallels in other Italian city-states, such as Siena. After the Battle of Montaperti over Florence in 1260, rival cults of the Virgin Mary and patron saints, relics and state rituals appeared, with Duccio's Maestà altar with (missing) central pinnacle panel of the Assumption of the Virgin Mary standing beneath Cimabue's stained-glass window in the Cathedral of Santa Maria Assuntà on the Bishop's acropolis of Città, while Simone Martini's Madonna and Child enthroned with patron saints presided over the Grand Council Chamber of Palazzo Pubblico on the Campo, in the valley, Her royal mantle and Roman theatre. We can also point to ex voto interventions to give thanks in times of crisis, such as Francesco di Giorgio's Biccherna (Treasury) cover after the earthquake of 1 January 1466 –'La Vergine della Misericordia' spreading her cloak over the city like the sky (Coelus) itself.[25] These all spring from Byzantine imperial relics and icons of the Virgin Mary and Child as protectors of (and on) the city gates and walls of Constantinople during the 7th century and Heraclius's defence of the capital and empire first against the Persians and then Islam.[26] This helps us to understand later Byzantine imperial icons of the Maestà and urban amphitheatre.

The 'Madonna della Città' defined the relationship between Genoa and its 'Regno' (Corsica) but also that with its trading colonies in other Mediterranean cities, in particular Naples and Palermo, key to the Spanish vice-regal empire, and its vital grain trade and military strategy.[27] In each city we find an altar dedicated to this Madonna. While these two altars are very similar, they differ in one significant way – the prominence given to the crown in Naples (fig. 10.2), like the new royal dogal crowns of Genoa, differed from the more subdued crown in Palermo (fig. 10.3), which might reflect the royal and colonial status of these two cities in the Kingdom of Naples and Sicily – a royal hierarchy in status (perhaps in the architecture too, on their respective harbour fronts).

With the coronation of Agostino Pallavicino as Doge in

10.5
Giovanni Battista Bianco, *Madonna, Queen of Genoa*.
Genoa, Cattedrale di San Lorenzo, 1652.
Photo: Genoa, Arcidiocesi. Reproduced with permission.

1637, the royal crown and sceptre of the Virgin Mary took precedence, in contrast to the coronation of Doge Iacopo Lomellino (Il Principe) at the beginning of the Savoy War, who was enthroned between Venus (Old Liguria) with her luxury and Minerva-Mars with foot on a bull's head (Torino), a Cato early Roman republican call to self-sacrifice on behalf of the *Patria* – a modern day 'Ulysses' triumphing over the Furies and Sirens of Circe (ANTICIRCE).[28] Throughout the coronation book of Agostino Pallavicino, given the sceptre by 'ancient founder' Janus and crowned by coral-crowned Corsica, 'il Regno', that gives the status of 'kingdom' to this 'republic', the panegyric orations dwell on the 'Augustan' connotations of 'Agostino's' name and his association with Pallas Athena (Minerva), Goddess of Reason and Wisdom, 'Palla-vicino'.[29] This represents a return to the 'Golden Age' iconography of Andrea Doria in the sixteenth century, 'Augustan' founder of the Republic and ruler of the Mediterranean, who 'refused' the dogal crown, but controlled the city from his imperial seaside villa and, through state portraiture, his 'reign'.[30] You see this throughout Agostino Pallavicino's patronage and his 'Augustan' promotion of royal iconography, sumptuous display and ceremony, from Cato to Augustus, a debate within the Republic, which might help us to understand his magnificent 1621 senatorial portrait by Anthony Van Dyck in the Getty Museum, Rubensian image of Genoese nobility as representative of the Republic at the coronation of Pope Gregory XV Ludovisi in Rome.[31]

In 1653, a bronze sculpture of the Crowned Virgin Mary and Christ with 'Et Rege Eos' scroll inscription over a Herculean tasselled lion-skin imprint of crescent-shaped Genoa was installed on the high altar of San Lorenzo, completing a sixteen-year odyssey from the portable wood sculpture by Bissoni (fig. 10.1) to the permanent bronze installation of Bianco (fig. 10.5).[32] Archbishop Stefano Durazzo refused to preside at the 'coronation' of the Virgin Mary as 'Queen of Genoa' in 1637, and was replaced by old noble Cardinal Giovanni Domenico Spinola, 'Protector of the Genoese Republic at the Papal Court of Urban VIII'.[33] The Pope and his Archbishop, as well as the French and even Spanish, resisted these claims to precedence, at the high altar or in statecraft, proclaiming that 'Monarchies come from God, Republics from the People', an extraordinary anticipation of the eighteenth-century Enlightenment and Age of Revolution.[34] Agostino Pallavicino was crowned in the Church of St Catherine of Genoa, to the northeast and near the Strada Nuova, residence of the Pallavicino old noble family palaces. The Bissoni 'Madonna della Città' was transported between San Lorenzo, Santa Caterina, and San Bernardo, a new church commissioned to the new patron saint after 1626 on Via San Bernardo, secularised and suppressed in the nineteenth century.[35] In the Ceremonial Books of the Genoese Republic (in the Archivio di Stato), the Jesuit Church of Sant' Andrea e Ambrogio to the east became a second 'state cathedral', physically attached by a bridge to the Palazzo Reale, for dogal ceremonies and feast-day celebrations, an indication of the central Jesuit role in this Counter-Reformation development.[36] 1653 institutionalised the Virgin Mary as 'Queen of Genoa', a 'royal republic' and contested iconography, where she presides today, recently restored magnificently in 'La Nuova Genova' of Renzo Piano.

* I first became aware of the 'Virgin Mary as Queen of Genoa in 1637' as part of the magnificent exhibition, curated by Piero Boccardo and Clario di Fabio, *El Siglo de Los Genoveses*, in the Palazzo Ducale in 1999. Since then, Naomi Sawelson-Gorse, a fellow art historian, has been an important collaborator on this project. We thank all our friends in Genoa for their help and the staffs of the Archivio di Stato di Genova, Biblioteca Civica Berio, Biblioteca Universitaria Genova, Istituto di Storia dell'Arte all'Università di Genova, Biblioteca di Storia dell'Arte a Palazzo Rosso, and Società Ligure di Storia Patria for their research assistance. This article is dedicated to the memory of Professor Ezia Gavazza, 'la nostra Regina di Genova, sempre'.

1 For the Coronation of the Virgin Mary as 'Queen of Genoa' on 25 March, 1637, see Lanzi, *Genova Città di Maria Santissima*, doc. A 6, pp. 32–34. An overview of this rich archival source on the ceremonial life of the Genoese republic of 1528 to Napoleonic suppression in 1797 can be found in Volpicella, 'I Libri dei Cerimoniali'; and for context, Di Fabio, ed., *La Cattedrale di Genova*; Aliverti, 'Visits to Genoa'.

2 Previous studies of this redefinition of republic and empire include: Veneruso, 'La "querelle" seicentesca'; Ravecca, 'Così Genova'; Di Fabio, 'Un' iconografia regia', 80–81; Bottaro Palumbo, '"Et rege eos"'; Lanzi, *Genova Città di Maria Santissima*; Di Fabio, 'La regina della Repubblica'; Schnettger, '*Principe Sovrano*'; Schnettger, 'Libertà e imperialità'; Zunckel, 'Tra Bodin e la Madonna'.

3 Schiaffino, *Memorie di Genova (1624–1647)*; Accinelli, *Compendio*, pp. 180–98; Vitale, *Breviario della Storia di Genova*, I, pp. 249–96; De Negri, *Storia di Genova*, pp. 697–726; Costantini, *La Repubblica di Genova*, pp. 245–417; Bitossi, 'Il blocco oligarchico'; Bitossi, *Il governo dei magnifici*, pp. 189–296; Rotta, 'Fra Spagna e Francia (1625–1637)'; Bitossi, 'A Republic in Search of Legitimation'.

4 Pollak, *Turin 1564–1680*; Osborne, *Dynasty and Diplomacy in the Court of Savoy*; Scott, *Architecture for the Shroud*; Symcox, *Victor Amadeus II*.

5 Graef, *Mary*; Warner, *Alone of All Her Sex*; Pelikan, *Mary through the Centuries*; Stratton, *The Immaculate Conception in Spanish Art*.

6 Stratton, *The Immaculate Conception in Spanish Art*, p. 92.

7 For descriptions of Genoa as an 'amphitheatre' and 'paradisal landscape' in late medieval Italy, see Petrarch and others in Petti Balbi, ed., *Genova medievale*, pp. 76–83; Beneš, ed., *A Companion to Medieval Genoa*, pp. 193–242.

8 Stratton, *The Immaculate Conception in Spanish Art*, pp. 92ff.

9 Oettinger Jr., ed., *San Antonio 1718*, p. 157, pl. 102 (triptych with 'paradisal landscape with animals' and 'H I S' with Cross on central tympanum): Artist unknown (Japan), *Travelling Altar with the Virgin of Guadalupe with the Four Apparitions*, Namban Travel Altar, lacquered wood decorated in gold, with mother-of-pearl applications; 17½ × 23¼ × 2 in. (44 × 59 × 5 cm). Artist unknown (New Spain), *Virgin of Guadalupe with the Four Apparitions*, oil on copper foil, embossed silver applications. Fundación Cultural Daniel Liebsohn, A.C., Mexico City. 'Attached to the back of this work is a 1786 manuscript stating that forty days of indulgence for the remission of sins are offered to persons who pray in front of this niche to the Virgin of Guadalupe'.

10 Annerino, *The Virgin of Guadalupe*; Damian, *The Virgin of the Andes*; Stagno, 'Immacolata India'.

11 Parma, Pesenti and Torrijos, 'Il secolo d'oro dei genovesi'; Boccardo, *Andrea Doria e le arti*, pp. 113–15; Pacini, *La Genova di Andrea Doria*; Gorse, 'Body Politics and Mythic Figures'.

12 *The New English Bible with the Apocrypha*, p. 326; Panofsky, *The Life and Art of Albrecht Dürer*, pp. 51–59.

13 Baratta, *La famosissima e nobilissima città di Genova*. Engraving in 10 plates, 72.5 × 247.5 cm. See Ennio Poleggi, *Iconografia*, pp. 76–80, no. 40; Schulz, 'Jacopo de' Barberi's View of Venice'.

14 For Domenico Fiasella's fresco of the Virgin with civic Saints John the Baptist, George, and Bernard interceding for the salvation of Genoa with the sacramental Trinity/Pietà (of 1625–30) over the grand exit staircase of the Palazzo Ducale: Boccardo and Di Fabio, eds, *El Siglo de Los Genoveses*, p. 250. For the foundation medal of the New Walls (dated 1626) with the haloed (not crowned) Madonna and Crowned Christ Child with civic Sts. Lawrence, Baptist, George, and Bernard over the Lantern: Pesce and Felloni, *Le monete genovesi*, p. 112; and new civic currency after the Coronation of the Virgin Mary as 'Queen of Genoa' in 1637: Pesce and Felloni, *Le monete genovesi*, pp. 118ff. On the ceremonial procession from the Cathedral of San Lorenzo to the Lantern for the laying of the foundation stone of the New Walls on 7 December 1626: Mulryne, Watanabe-O'Kelly, and Shewring, eds, *Europa Triumphans*, I, pp. 344–46. And Albergo dei Poveri: Parma, *Albergo dei Poveri*; Parma and Galassi, *La scultura a Genova*, II, fig. 156; De Marini, *Emanuele Brignole*; Guerra, Molteni and Nicolesi, *Il Trionfo della Miseria*.

15 For the chapel with fresco (now lost) to the *Sacra Cintura* in the church of Sant'Agostino, as well as a later monumental chapel and altar to the *Sacra Cintura* with Sts Augustine and Monica by sculptor Bernardo Schiaffino (1718) in the reformed Augustinian church of Nostra Signora della Consolazione, patronised by the Durazzo new noble family (in 1684–1706), now embedded in the Beaux Art, Parisian Haussmann-inspired-boulevard urban expansion of Via X X Settembre (in 1892): Prina, *Sant'Agostino a Genova*; Paolocci and Leonardi, eds, *La Liguria di Agostino*; Motta, ed., 'Nostra Signora della Consolazione'; Franchini Guelfi, 'Il Settecento', II, pp. 244–46.

16 Ferrari, *La Cintura Sacra*. Con Licenza de' Svperiori. Example in the B C B G, F. Ant. Gen. A. 27. See Niri, *La Tipografia*, p. 271, no. 769.

17 Ferrari, *La Cintura Sacra*, [dedication pages 1–3]: 'S E R E N I S S. S I G N O R I. Consacrarono le Signorie Vostre Serenissime gli anni adietro alla Gran' Madre di Dio lo Scettro, e la Corona di questo loro Regno, sottomettendo al di lei immortale Imperio l'vnico dono della publica Libertà; pegni al Figlio, & alla Madre così graditi, e cari, che giustamente credere possiamo, d'hauerne conseguito il premio della Protezzion' Diuina. E noi perciò, suoi sudditi, à ragione dobbiamo consacrare à v v. s s. Serenissime, nostri Principi, quello, che più di pretioso habbiamo. Sono obbligati i veri Sudditi ad immitare, e riuerire i loro Principi, e Signori. Onde se cinsero d'inespugnabili propugnacoli questa Real Città, per difenderla, e conseruarla dall'armi de'temporali nimici; e noi potendo, prouederle dobbiamo d'vna C I N T A, valeuole à difenderle da gl'insulti de' spirituali Auuersarij. Questa è la S A C R A C I N T V R A, che descritta in pochi fogli, le presentiamo, tutta guarnita di tante gemme, quante sono l'Indulgenze, e Priuilegi, da molti Sommi Pontefici, à chi se ne cinge; conceduti, come tesori di Paradiso, in essa epilogati. Per lo che ne gioua à sperare, che non isdegneranno le s s. v v. Sereniss. cortesemente accettandola, d'andarne cinte. Mentre anco sapranno, che la portorno la stessa Regina de gli Angioli il gran Patriarca, e Padre di cinquanta, e più Religioni approuate, S. Agostino, e Santa Monica sua Madre, con lungo stuolo d'innumerabili Santi, e Beati dell'Ordine Agostiniano. Restino pur seruite v v. s s. Sereniss. d'accettare il nostro diuoto dono, e di gradire l'affetto, con degnarci della loro disiderata Protezzione. Che noi non cesseremo giamai di supplicare quei celesti Numi, perche sempre le siano Assistenti al felice gouerno di questo Sereniss. Dominio, e Regno. Di Genoua li 3. Gennaio 1640. Di v v. s s. Sereniss. Humiliss. e Diuotiss. Serui. Il Gouernatore, e Confratelli della Compagnia de' Cinturati in S. Agostino di Genoua'.

18 Dussler, *Raphael*, pp. 31–32, 36–38, fig. 82–83; Jones and Penny, *Raphael*, pp. 88–92, 128–32.

19 Boccardo and Di Fabio, eds, *El Siglo de Los Genoveses*, pg. 265.

20 Poleggi, *Iconografia*, pp. 122–23, no. 63; Schütte, *Die Galleria*; Gambi and Pinelli, *La Galleria*; Courtright, *The Papacy*; Fiorani, *The Marvel of Maps*.

21 Poleggi and Cevini, *Le città nella storia d'Italia*, p. 133; Poleggi, 'Dalle mura ai saloni, un rinnovo segreto'. The contemporary chronicle of Agostino Schiaffino (*Memorie di Genova* (1624–1647), 1633, n. 6), records the strategic 'meraviglia' of these majestic city walls and the sharing of city views for papal benediction on which this cartographic representation was based: 'Il Senato fa dono al Pontefice [Urban VIII] di due quadri di capace grandezza ove era di colori dipinta la città colle nuove mura, in uno in pianta e nell'altro in lontananza, havendo esso Pontefice mostrato desiderio di vedere le sue fortificationi. Furono dipinti con gran diligenza et artificio da Andrea Ansaldo di Voltri, al quale perciò pagò il Publico L.2.000. Gli manda questi quadri chiedendogli che voglia benedire le nuove mura e la città per sua lettera data li 16 di aprile et il Pontefice risponde li 8 ottobre'. See Priarone, *Andrea Ansaldo 1584–1638*, pp. 64, 102–03, fig. 100; Zunckel, 'Tra Bodin e la Madonna', pp. 156, fn. 30 and 176, fn. 95.

22 Forti, *Le Fortificazioni di Genova*; Dellepiane, *Mura e Fortificazioni di Genova*; Motta, ed., *I Forti di Genova*.

23 Jane Garnett and Gervase Rosser have argued that medieval Genoa's state iconography was 'masculine' (i.e., a 'triad' of institutional St Lawrence, maritime St John the Baptist, and crusading St George), while the 'feminine' cult of the Virgin Mary was pervasive in miracle-making shrines and convent churches throughout the city and region of Liguria — a gendering of 'sacred landscape', of 'head and body'. See Garnett and Rosser, 'The Virgin Mary and the People of Liguria'; Garnett and Rosser, *Spectacular Miracles*; Rosser, 'The Church and Religious Life'. While the Virgin Mary as 'Queen of Genoa' became the high altar dedication in the Cathedral of San Lorenzo after 1653, as a 'state dogal cult', flanked by the consoling 'Madonna del Soccorso' chapel in the south apse and St Sebastian (plague saint) in the north apse, the Church of Santa Maria delle Vigne on the harbour front with its miracle-making altar of the Madonna and Child remained the 'popular cult' of the Virgin Mary in Genoa. See Motta, ed., 'Nostra Signora delle Vigne'; Garnett and Rosser, *Spectacular Miracles*, pp. 95–107; Zunckel, 'Tra Bodin e la Madonna'. Bernardi, 'Corpus Domini'. I thank Laura Stagno for making this key point between 'state and

popular devotions' during discussion after the presentation of this paper at the Genoese conference.

24 Heydenreich and Lotz, *Architecture in Italy 1400–1600*, pp. 287–90; Saginati, 'Ricerche nell'Archivio della Basilica di Carignano'; Motta, ed., 'Santa Maria Assunta in Carignano'; Gorse, 'Genova, Repubblica dell'Impero'; Gill, 'Conception and Construction'. For views of Genoa with Alessi's Santa Maria dell'Assunta as a *belvedere* towering over the port city on Carignano: Poleggi, *Iconografia*, pp. 36–37, 152–53, 156, 158–59.

25 White, *Duccio*, pp. 80–134; White, *Art and Architecture in Italy 1250–1400*, pp. 45–47, 51–54, 289–303, 495–506; Norman, ed., *Siena, Florence and Padua*.

26 Belting, *Likeness and Presence*; Cameron, 'Images of Authority'; Cameron, 'The Theotokos in Sixth-Century Constantinople'; Limberis, *Divine Heiress*; Mango, 'Constantinople as Theotokoupolis'; Vassilaki, ed., *Images of the Mother of God*; Pentcheva, *Icons and Power*. Meiss, *Painting in Florence and Siena after the Black Death*; and the Byzantine icons of the Madonna and Child Enthroned (Maestà) from Constantinople (circa 1250–80, National Gallery of Art, Washington, D. C.).

27 Chabod, *Storia di Milano nell'epoca di Carlo V*; Marino, *Becoming Neapolitan*; Dandelet, *Spanish Rome*; Herrero Sánchez and others, eds, *Génova y la Monarquía Hispánica*; Dauverd, *Imperial Ambition in the Early Modern Mediterranean*, pp. 188–94, 201–07.

28 For this complex allegorical state portrait of Biennial Doge Iacopo Lomellino (1626), based on Cesare Ripa's *Iconologia* (1603) and other textual sources: Borniotto, *L'Identità di Genova*, pp. 50–54. For the state portrait of Biennial Doge Agostino Pallavicino (1637), see Boccardo and Di Fabio, eds, *El Siglo de Los Genoveses*, p. 120, where a contemporary description helps to explain the iconography of Corsica, '[una] donna di aspetto rozzo […] in capo haverà una ghirlanda di fogli di viti [or coral], sarà armata & con la destra mano terrà una corsesca, dalla parte destra vi sarà un cane corso [growling and rebellious, but faithful]'. For Genoese dogal regalia and ceremony, Cataldi Gallo, 'Rosso, oro e nero'; Sommariva, '"Coronationi"'; Bruna Niccoli, 'Official Dress and Courtly Fashion in Genoese Entries'; Vazzoler, 'The Orations for the Election of the Doge'.

29 The 'royal' claims (acclamations) are directly stated in the title of this 'Oration Book': *Applausi della Liguria*. Biblioteca Civica Berio, Genova. For contemporary Medici iconography in Florence: Cox-Rearick, *Dynasty and Destiny in Medici Art*.

30 Parma, *Perin del Vaga*, pp. 73–152; Magnani, *Il Tempio di Venere*, pp. 27–47, 81–92, 115–24; Boccardo, *Andrea Doria e le arti*; Gorse, 'Between Empire and Republic'; Stagno, *Palazzo del Principe*; Gorse, 'Body Politics and Mythic Figures'; Zanker, *The Power of Images*.

31 Wheelock, *Anthony Van Dyck*, pp. 147–49, no. 25; Boccardo and Di Fabio, eds, *El Siglo de Los Genoveses*, pp. 180–82, 197.

32 Di Fabio, 'Un'iconografia regia', pp. 79–80, fig. 75; Parma and Galassi, 'Artisti e artigiani'; and recent restoration of the high altar: Montagni, ed., *Il Restauro dell'Altare Maggiore*. See the dogal chapel in the Palazzo Ducale, which also celebrated this royal iconography and medieval to Renaissance history: Dagnino, '"Per la fabrica et ornamento della Cappella Reale"'.

33 For this context between Rome and Genoa: Schnettger, 'Libertà e imperialità', pp. 129–44; Zunckel, 'Tra Bodin e la Madonna', pp. 145–91.

34 Ravecca, 'Così Genova', pp. 41–58; Bitossi, 'A Republic in Search of Legitimation', p. 240; Zunckel, 'Tra Bodin e la Madonna', p. 160.

35 Schiaffino, *Memorie di Genova*, 1625, n. 46. According to Accinelli (*Compendio*, pp. 182–3), in penitent celebration of Genoa's defence against the Savoyan invasion of Liguria to their city gates in 1625: 'Fece voto il Senato di far festa di precetto il giorno di S. Bernardo Protettore [August 20], e di fare solenne Processione alla sua Chiesa, di dar dote a dodici povere Figlie del Conservatorio di S. Genonimo della Carità, oggi di S. Maria della Providenza'. See Polonio, 'San Bernardo, Genova e Pisa'; Borniotto, *L'Identità di Genova*, pp. 244–64; Poleggi and Poleggi, eds., *Descrizione della Città di Genova*, p. 239.

36 Schiaffino, *Memorie*, 1638, n. 53: 'In questo mese [October] si fabricava dal Publico un ponte che mettendo piè nel Palazzo Ducale terminava nella chiesa del Giesù, havendo terminato il Senato di sentir le prediche in quella chiesa e non nel Domo'. See Magnani, 'Committenza e arte sacra'; Gavazza and Lamera, *Chiesa del Gesù*; Paolocci, ed., *I Gesuiti fra impegno religioso e potere politico*; Raffo, ed., 'I Gesuiti a Genova, see p. 254; Zunckel, 'Tra Bodin e la Madonna', p. 184, fn. 119; Bober, Boccardo, and Boggero, eds, *A Superb Baroque*.

Simona Morando

'VERA PACE GODESTE IN MEZZO ALL'ARMI'

The Commitment of Theatre and Literature in the Latter Half of the Seventeenth Century

As Claudio Costantini wrote in his historiographical masterpiece, the 'Giovani', 'the party of the Young of the early modern Genoese aristocracy adopted a sort of "armed neutrality" regarding Spain',[1] a political position which dissimulated an actual rebellion against the Spaniards by first of all disregarding the former pro-Spanish policy of the Republic of Genoa. In 1652, opposing this political view, Gaspare Squarciafico, a well-known member of 'i Vecchi', the Old party, dedicated a Pindaric ode to the newly elected doge Agostino Centurione expressing sorrow and anger for the loss of the glorious past of the Republic, its extinguished golden age, and for the squalor of present years, in which Genoa and its inhabitants live threatened by the Turks and among the corpses of other 'incadaverite monarchie' ('cadaverous monarchies'): among the ruins of Rome, of Mycenae, of Athens. The Ligurian people wandered dejected, drowning in the blood of other wounded countries.[2] The remarkable overpowering enemies of the allegory of a dispirited Genoa were explicitly mentioned as France and the Empire.

> The Golden Lilies [France]
> Bring forth paleness to your deaths.
> And on the other hand the Alemannic Eagle [Genoa] brings you
> The short days from Boote [the North].[3]

Consequently, the Old party regarded Agostino Centurione as its new Hercules in a land of decadence, a hero nonetheless destined to bow down to the Pope, who represented the only stable power in the Western World.

In 1650, only two years before Centurione's ode, in his novel *La Rosalinda* (fig. 11.1), Bernardo Morando identifies freedom as Genoa's first and most valuable gift. In those pages of historiographical and ekphrastic impetus, Genoa, 'in forma di teatro', imagined as a theatre, towers above all other cities and reigns because it possesses freedom, and freedom allows the country to remain at peace, even while turmoil was plaguing Europe and even with the internal discord, the dangerous conspiracies, of previous years:

> But the most beautiful kingdom she [Genoa, represented as a woman] owns is her Liberty, sustained with such rectitude and prudence, with such piety and valour, that in vain some of her citizens, who have become rebels and open enemies, have often tried with infernal devices to shake her up, to knock her down, to crush her; since she has always been preserved and protected by Heaven with the most evident patronage from internal snares and foreign insults. So now in the midst of the storms, among which Europe is swaying, she remains as calm and flourishing as ever she was, with the horn of richness full in her arms, and the olive trees of Peace greening at her temples.[4]

Morando represents Genoa as a sort of needle in the balance among wars and struggles. His idealistic stance, inspired by the construction of the new town walls, was bound to be overlooked by his contemporaries. Conversely, Squarciafico's more politically committed Pindaric ode was successful despite its low poetic quality, yet it will not be able to save its author from exile and embezzlement a few years later.

During the first years of his wandering, Squarciafico wrote a pamphlet titled *Le politiche malattie della Repubblica di Genova e loro medicine* ('The political diseases of the Republic of Genoa and their treatments'). Edoardo Villa, who edited the text in 1998 after the first edition in 1655, described it as a 'quadro ripreso dal vero',[5]

11.1
Frontispiece of Bernardo Morando, *La Rosalinda di Bernardo Morando nobile genouese. Spiegata in diece libri*, Piacenza, Giouanni Bazachi, 1650.
Photo: © Cambi Casa d'Aste 2024.

a painting taken from real life. The deep harshness that permeates those pages rages against many targets: both i Vecchi and i Giovani's political parties, the merchants, the confraternities – the so-called 'casacce' –, the artisans and all other social categories of the Republic. What's the cure for Genoa's sick body? Squarciafico uncovers an old recipe: setting up a Genoese fleet. Not exactly a new idea. And, especially, not a suggestion of peace. In the last pages of the book, Squarciafico refers to a war lexicon: victory, glory, strength. From his exile, he saw only a pale and old utopia, an unreachable lost image of a Republic that no longer existed.

For those who lived in the present and not in a wistful past, the Republic of Genoa was awaiting a decisive test. The crisis with Spain in 1654, caused by the position of the marquisate of Finale, had led to confiscations and a stalemate in international relationships. France tried to take advantage of the situation, without success.

In 1655 the restlessness of the Republic appeared for the first time on stage at the *Teatro del Falcone*, in an opera called *Ariodante*. Its author, Giovan Andrea Spinola (1627–1705), is one of the few Elisabetta Graziosi praises in her indispensable book *Da capitale a provincia. Genova 1660–1670*, a clear portrait of the ailing Genoese culture in the second half of the century. But a better context for Spinola's works is the birth of the *melodramma* in Genoa. As Lattarico notes, Genoa became a destination for the opera *tournées* around 1644–1645. *La Delia o sia la Sera sposa del Sole*, by Giulio Strozzi, was probably the first opera played in Teatro del Falcone, owned by the Adorno family.[6] Opera, in Venetian style, made its debut in Genoa. Some years later, the first Genoese author of *librettos*, Francesco Fulvio Frugoni staged *L'innocenza giustificata* (1653), dedicated to 'Serenissimi collegi della Repubblica di Genova'.

Spinola, however, meant to create a specifically Genoese style for his *drammi per musica*, far from the Venetian one, by inserting the dialect in *recitativi* ('recitatives'). After Anton Giulio Brignole Sale's comedy, *Due anelli* ('Two rings') Spinola was the first to put into his characters' mouth the typical Genoese language as a direct message of commitment to the social context of the Republic.[7] The main feature of Genoese literature is that it always alludes to internal politics, aristocratic relations and the preservation of the status quo, even when it speaks of something else. Spinola was not an exception. He's perfectly aware of this opportunity, and his *operas* are made to be performed for a Genoese public that can read the true message between the lines.

Spinola's *Ariodante*, inspired by an episode of Ariosto's *Orlando furioso*, shows an amorous plot at first glance, but this plot is also expected to be read as a political metaphor, a transposition of the unsettling picture of the relationship between the Republic of Genoa and Spain, and is not at all a claim of peace and of republican freedom.

It speaks about the alleged infidelity of Ginevra. Dalinda, dressed as Ginevra, is caught kissing Polisseno. This happens to be a trap set by Polisseno himself to deprive Ariodante, Ginevra's fiancé, of his place on the throne. An allegorical chariot appears at some point, carrying the Night and Deception, but the Sun will reveal it for what it really is. Likewise the noble knight Rinaldo will unmask Polisseno's plan, granting Ginevre the happy ending she deserved. Ariodante, believed dead by suicide, comes back, alive, under the guise of The Unknown Knight. All is well since it ends well, and spectators enjoy a marvellous play on stage, full of witty *a-parte* lines, powerful monologues and Arie that cunningly reveal suspicions, tricks, insincerities. Even the play's scenography, as the *Mutazioni* explain, shows a distant town, with ruined buildings, *galleries* and palaces: 'lontananza di case rotte con galerie di palazzo'. This destroyed town is Genoa and its ruins are the consequences of the immorality of its inhabitants. During the first performance in 1655, villains spoke in Genoese dialect, but they will speak Italian in the 1695 version. These villains are meant to be ridiculous, taken from the pastoral genre tradition, but they are surprisingly evil, ready to kill the innocent Ginevra. Furthermore, the Prologue is performed by Deception, 'Inganno', who is combatting the Herald of Truth. Deception triumphantly declares he doesn't know the Truth and that he's looking for Peace.[8] Meaningfully, then, the word 'Peace', is pronounced by Deception.

The character who represents the King of England is a symbol of weakness. He's ready to kill his daughter, but retracts when Rinaldo shows all his strength to defeat and execute Polisseno, the betrayer. The king knows no language, but that of violence. The political message is one of the bleakest: where are – ubi sunt, the classical commonplace – the ancient royal virtues? They're not to be found anymore. Only a tarnished Truth wins.

Ivaldi[9] first and then Lattarico studied the 1655 edition of *Ariodante* and particularly focused on the character of Polisseno's servant Trattugo, a local version of a 'bravo'. He seemed to bring *nostalgia* to the stage, thinking about the past of the Republic, the landscape of Genoa and Cornigliano, where Spinola had a villa. Trattugo's feelings are moderated in the final edition of 1695, found in the collected works titled *Il cuore in volta e 'l cuore in scena* ('The Heart on the Run and on Stage') (fig. 11.2). But the anti-Spanish controversy remains, or, as I suggest, a substantial negative judgement on power and on monarchies should be assumed, shouted by a writer that in the meantime witnessed the failure of the Republic. From 1670 to 1690 he was governor of Corsica, then of Savona and then ambassador in Madrid.

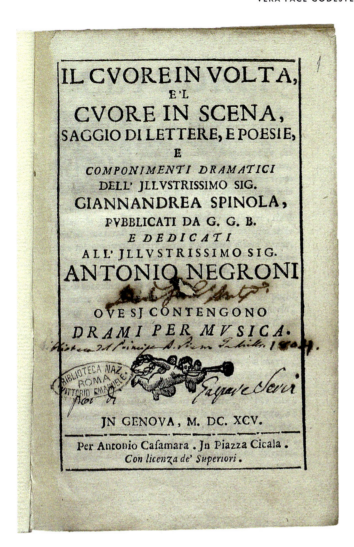

11.2
Title page of Giovanni Andrea Spinola, *Il cuore in volta, e 'l cuore in scena, saggio di lettere, e poesie, e componimenti dramatici*, Genoua, Antonio Casamara. Jn piazza Cicala, 1695. Photo: Rome, Biblioteca Nazionale Centrale 'Vittorio Emanuele II' (35. 4.H.15). Reproduced with permission.

In the first book of the collected works mentioned above, Spinola gathered letters sent to a huge number of Genoese nobles. It was a strategic move, a well-organised apology for himself and his political actions. Most of the letters referred to women – with gallant themes displaying a clear transition to the Arcadia literary system, but there's one that expresses how he labours over political issues as Governor of Corsica:

> It is true, I'm in charge of a Kingdom, but what shall be the point if power imprisons me thus? *He who has his heart in chains doesn't flatter himself with the Scepter because greatness has no charm to tame the passions of the soul.* In essence, even though I'm among porpoises, I'm an exile.[10]

In 1655 Spinola staged *Gli incanti di Ismeno*, musical intermezzos that quote Tasso's *Gerusalemme liberata*, especially c. XIII and the enchanted Saaron wood. Let's focus on the second *intermezzo*, scene 3, where the most ridiculous character of the play, the servant Delfido, is on stage. He's hunchbacked, he stammers, he is terrified by the enchantments. Suddenly, he breaks a branch off a tree – a clear allusion to Virgil and Dante – and seven different voices of men and women call out from the tree itself. Three of them belong to three ghosts: Spanish, German and French. The fourth ghost is Genoese. The effect of the whole scene must be 'macaronic'. It's hard to find sources for each voice: the French one surely sings a popular 'bacchica', a seventeenth-century song.[11] The German's line 'M'imbrigne Franze e Spagna' — literally: 'I don't care about France and Spain' — is one of the typical drunk catchphrases of the character of Lanzi in sixteenth-century Italian comedy. The last ghost, the Genoese one, scares the servant more and more, speaking nonsense,[12] but the most important line remains the one spoken by the German, which puts Spinola's political thought on paper.

Spinola's *dramma per musica* develops an effective political line of thought regarding the attempts of the Republic to find a new role in the European context. In 1660 he staged *Europa*, one of his most incisive and committed works, placed in part three of *Il cuore in volta*, after *Ariodante e Gl'incanti di Ismeno*. Beyond the mythological fable, Spinola wrote a sequel of Ovid's myth, a love story about the intrigues of power. Crete is governed by Neleo. Neleo's son Asterio suddenly comes back, unnoticed, from the hostile town of Tiro. Asterio falls in love with Europa and convinces her to run away with him disguised as a knight called Florindo. The pastoral scheme of the play, with comic scenes and roles, should not be read as a disengaged work. The prologue is pronounced by Peace, giving a solution for the troubles of the Old Continent. Here the reason behind the choice of the title character's name, obvious as it may be, emerges from its mythological context, and Europa is portrayed as the allegory of the actual continent at that historical moment:

> *The Peace*
> Behold! The Diva, to whose pleasing Name
> the threatening sound of weapons stops,
> to those who don't know who I am, I am the Peace,
> whose hair are adorned placid foliage,
> for me the rest is sweet, and the people have
> because of me the happiest hours of their life,
> since the hoarse rattling of warlike instruments
> do not importunate their peace anymore.
> Because of me the only sound you hear is that of festal hymns,
> highly sounding everywhere:
> because of me palm-trees and laurels wither,
> and only sprout olive-trees.

Upon the Ligurian scenes now I arrived
and happy events in noble web I warp;
while of Crete and Tyre together I unite
the two kingdoms finally reconciled,
of Agenor and Neleus the biting wrath,
with the 'Nozze d'Europa' here extinguished.
It is true that only Hymen is able
To unite the sceptres, to establish peace.
Ligurians, you, my deity friends
who enjoyed true peace in the midst of arms
rejoice now, to the sound of chants,
since you are going to enjoy the happy hours.[13]

Here lies the solution for Europa's troubles. Wedding stands as the only instrument of peace. The reference of the royal marriage of Louis XIV and Maria Teresa d'Asburgo, Philip IV's daughter, is crystal clear. Celebrated on 9 June 1660, the wedding not only legitimised the Treaty of the Pyrenees (1659) and hence the end of the war between Spain and France, but it even marked the beginning of the hegemony of France in Europe. A few months after the wedding, writers were ready to print their literary versions of the event, and that is the case for Spinola's *Europa*.

Despite the apparent outward focus in Europe as a whole, and the celebration of Spain and France's symbolic union, Spinola intended to remain politically committed to the Republic of Genoa, and not just by making his characters speak the Genoese dialect. He bluntly stated his opinion on Genoa's future role in the new European landscape. Genoa is, in Spinola's words, a weak Republic. There is no longer space for the self-isolating claim of freedom, as Bernardo Morando desired some few years before. Genoa is expected to take sides. The only space for freedom literature can claim is in the observation and judgement of power, such as monarchies, reigns, and the other forms of government the Republic had always refused to follow and accept. Strained by Fortune, by the Stars and even by God himself, King Neleo's soliloquy in *Europa* III.1 shows all the fragilities of his status: 'too miserable is the fate of a King' ('troppo misera sorte è d'un regnante').

The text utilises the commonplace of classical tragedy about a father and a son being in love with the same woman. However, instead of treating it as a family matter here, Spinola presents this tragedy as the lonely misfortune of those in power. Showcasing the actual restraint or loss of freedom of

a king, in marriage or in political discord, allows Spinola to show the frailty of a government run by one man, sacred but lonely, destined to a long soliloquy with his conscience. A republic, and Spinola's Genoese audience would agree, would therefore be the ideal government, where power is shared and where dialogue reigns sovereign. This thought emerges in a famous novel written by Luca Assarino, *I giuochi di Fortuna* ('The Games of Chance', 1656), but, whilst here tropes of misfortune and fortuity concerned human life from a philosophical point of view, Spinola gave a specifically political meaning to the same ideas. Spinola's message pushed Genoa to join the new political order by seeking connections with the other European republics, such as Venice, Holland and Switzerland, and authors such as Raffaele Della Torre were vocal in their support.

Spinola's exhortation was nonetheless ill-timed, with *Europa* being staged in 1660, in the midst of a plague outbreak on the continent. The resulting weakness of Genoa and the rest of the continent didn't allow for the fulfilment of any republican alliance, not with Venice or any other state. Even theatre had to face the new crisis and for that reason the trope of freedom subsisted in Spinola's dramaturgy, who staged, still in 1660, *La Perfidia fulminata da Sansone* ('The Perfidy Fulminated by Samson') and *Con le ruine del Tempio de' Filistei* ('With the Ruins of the Philistes' Temple'), published in the same year.

La Perfidia starts with a Prologue played by Vendetta (Revenge) and with a scene in which two slaves, Lisarda and Egeria, talk to Philistine soldiers. The fear of being subjugated and losing freedom inspired Spinola, and his spectators in Falcone Theatre had a chance to see the political crisis reenacted. Even the erotic subject of Samson and Delilah is read as a metaphor of power: Delilah is loved by two princes, Samson and Timante, and she has to choose between love and honour, between Samson, the enemy, the 'tyrant', and Timante, Prince of Gaza, and she's expected to kill Samson for *raison d'État*. From Samson's pitiful point of view, Delilah is a symbol of inconstancy, a betrayer like his servant Misia, who leaves him to serve Timante after Samson is defeated by him: 'One rises, the other falls', 'Un va su, l'altro giù', says Samson, pithily. Samson is defeated but the enemies have won without any glory. A *deus ex machina*, Revenge in person, flies down to punish the Philistines and ruin their temples and palaces. Victory is determined not by human beings, but by an invisible divine punishment.

11.3
Domenico Fiasella, *Samson and Delilah*. Genoa,
Musei di Strada Nuova – Palazzo Bianco, inv. PB 1402.
Reproduced with permission.

As Gavazza wrote,[14] in the Republic of Genoa subjects from the Bible were read in a new light: Domenico Fiasella painted Samson and Delilah (fig. 11.3), while Giovanni Andrea Ansaldo painted Samson killing the Philistines in one of the buildings owned by the powerful Brignole-Sale family. Some years after *Europa* came out, Bartolomeo Guidobono completed two big paintings for Spinola's villa in Cornigliano, one of which dealt with the subject of Samson and Delilah.[15] This specific episode of the Bible held a clear message for those who were planning to betray the Republic and its aristocracy. The same noble people who lived in marvellous palaces in the presence of those eloquent frescoes could meditate on the particular case of Samson being aided by Revenge at the theatre. Spinola was always very clear about his intentions, and he composed for Genoa, not for Venice, 'Ho composto per Genova, non per Venezia',[16] as he said, with obvious political undertones, while defending the formal structure of his *drammi per musica*. His *drammi* were much more sober than the Venetian ones and were linked to the first Florentine operas.[17]

In those years, Francesco Fulvio Frugoni, one of the most relevant Genoese writers, was banished and spent almost eleven years exiled from his country. In Venice, he wrote in

support of the Senate's position during the War of Candia.[18] But suddenly he was called back to Genoa, charged with writing a pamphlet against the House of Savoy, who were supposedly involved in the infamous conspiracy of Raffaele Della Torre in 1672. Frugoni chose to refuse the offer, preferring the punishment of four more years in exile rather than throwing himself into a politically entangled situation.

Spinola's last works, included in *Il cuore in volta* although without an indication of date or edition, show a drastic change in his approach to the European subject matter: they enact war. *Aspasia* treated the cruelty of war; *Amare e fingere o sia il Prasimene* ('Love and Pretence, or the Prasimene') enacts the struggle between Armenia and Media and the siege of Ismara. Specific wartime terminology helps to bring the audience into epic sieges and truces, with soldiers who form the chorus, all mixed with love stories and family conflicts. *Odoacre e Teodorico, la divisione del Regno d'Italia* announces already from its title the crucial and dramatic subject matter it enacts.

Aspasia, for which we have no known date, neither of composition nor of presentation, is based on a Spanish subject, as Spinola wrote in his preface. The pastoral scheme of the play includes a parodic character who speaks in Genoese dialect (Vespino), a spurned lover (Clorindo) who brings the 'arcadic' forest to the Court according to a pastoral commonplace. But in the middle of Act II war looms, announced by a messenger in a traditional style: People, weapons, disasters. / Infinite flags / are waving all around, / and armed battalions rush about and King Radamiro replies with a scream 'Who dares disturb the peace of my kingdom? / the unjust violence / of which enemy all of a sudden / chooses to assaults / an unprepared king?'.[19] The scenography represents an encampment with soldiers and the sea populated with the naval fleet (Act III, sc. x). The chorus of soldiers, the cries of vengeance, the commandments of war, the sight of prisoners, the drums and trumpets, the armed combat: any detail would be able to terrify the spectators of the *dramma* being performed on stage, serving as a cathartic ritual about the dramas of war. The opera's happy ending will certainly not reassure any spectator.

Based on historic sources, Spinola's last work, *Odoacre and Teodorico*, tells of the evil emperor Teodorico to whom the murders of Boezio and Simmaco are attributed. However, far from preserving the truths of history, Spinola fantasies that Odoacre, alive though believed dead, manages to obtain half of Italy and the crown of the Kingdom. The theme of power, despite the subtitle 'la divisione del Regno d'Italia', is not a priority. Spinola is more interested in the representation of a dark landscape, where violence and struggles in both politics and love remove any hope. One of the main scenes of Act III, the fifth, is performed in a prison, amidst knives and tortures; the ninth one is played by Teodorico dreaming about

Boezio and Simaco whom he had killed. Pressured by these events, Teodorico chooses to change his life. Hence goodness triumphs only because 'È la gloria d'un re vincer se stesso', a king's glory is to tame himself.

This final resolution resting on 'self-control' is something we can link to another author. *Odoacre e Teodorico* forms another chapter, indeed, of the long run that the Ostrogothsic and Gothic legends had in Italian literature, and of which Gabriello Chiabrera's 1582 poem *Gotiade* forms one of its most peculiar episodes.[20] Chiabrera died in 1638, but his works were rediscovered about thirty years later when his *Discorsi*, read at the *Accademia degli Addormentati* in 1629, were published by Alessandro Dego under Jesuits' protection in 1670.[21] Those lectures belonged to a different time of the Republic, but they represented the new key elements to underline the Republic's old virtues, such as 'Magnificenza', Richness and Nobility, which offered a positive memory and reinforcement for a present in an undoubted time of crisis. Chiabrera's *Discorsi* also serve another purpose: to reinforce a stoical and Christian philosophy that Genoa needed to face its decline. *Fortezza* ('Fortitude'), *Tribolazione* ('Tribulation'), weakness of Prudence, those were the tropes of the older Chiabrera's lectures, destined to find an echo of their severity in a brief book written by Spinola for his son, *Lo stoico cristiano*, published later in 1780. There is no space for political issues in this dialogue between father and son. Spinola, after a significant *cursus honorum*, writes a little *galateo* for the soul with a style noticeably distanced from the theatrical, which teaches internal freedom, sobriety, self-sufficiency and independence, extrication from passions: in a word, the rules of 'vivere indifferente', living unconcerned.[22] In spite of appearances, *Lo stoico cristiano* was not a surrender or the coming to terms with failure.

Spinola was instead proposing a way of preserving and developing aristocracy, richness, and power not so different from what Giovanni Vincenzo Imperiale's poem *Lo Stato rustico* had promoted almost seventy years before through the myth of the 'habitatore industre'. The industrious inhabitant of Genoa invests the profit of his mercantilist business and of his relationships with foreign countries in building a self-sufficient economy, a self-sufficient Republic. From this point of view and as Imperiale taught, *otium* and *negotium* are identical, and peace is not an international matter, but an individual one. When Spinola was in charge of the government of Corsica, he wrote a letter, which is included in the first tome of *Il cuore in volta*, to Paris Maria Salvago lamenting about the terrifying winds of war that would have driven him away from Genoa. The sonnet attached to the letter condenses the theme of war treated as a personal anguish in which the word 'Impero' is only another synonymous for his own troubled government activity:

What bloody Megera emerges from the earth
With her head crowned with serpents
Foretelling war on my happy thoughts?
A fierce storm
Does not break the hopes of a shepherd
As intensively
As this troublesome worry tortures my heart

I hoped to see an end
To the bitter affairs of the unwanted government
And turned my thoughts to my own good
Alas, mistaken hopes!
A new war has begun: let the way
To Heaven be opened at least
To those who wish to die amidst arms.[23]

1 Costantini, *La Repubblica di Genova*, p. 385.

2 Squarciafico, *Genova eterna*, p. 16.

3 Squarciafico, *Genova eterna*, p. 20. 'Quindi i Gigli dorati / inoltrano il pallor nelle tue morti. / E d'altra parte l'aquila alemana / ti reca da Boote i giorni corti'.

4 Morando, *La Rosalinda*, pp. 234–35. 'Ma il più bel Regno, ch'ella possiede, è la sua Libertà sostenuta con tanta rettitudine, e proddenza; con tal pietà, e valore; che invano han tentato più volte, con macchine infernali, alcuni de' suoi cittadini, fattisi suoi ribelli, non che Nemici aperti, di scuoterla, d'abbatterla, di conculcarla; posciaché sempre è dalle insidie interne, e dagl'insulti stranieri, con evidentissimo patrocinio fu preservata e guarentita dal Cielo. Onde hora in mezo delle tempeste, tra le quali ondeggia fluttuante l'Europa, ella mantiensi quieta, e florida, quanto mai fosse col corno della dovizia colmo tra le braccia, e con gli ulivi della Pace verdeggianti alle tempie'. But on the concept of freedom, see Costantini, *Politica e storiografia*, p. 96, who noticed the difference between Genoa and Venice and defined the Republic of Genoa as a woman who can love more than one man ('a questo e a quel signore') treating links with pure convenience. The historian Della Torre based on that difference his work *Lo squittinio della Repubblica di Venetia*.

5 Villa, *Genova al vaglio di un esiliato*, p. 8.

6 Lattarico, '"Questo è il gusto di Genova"', p. 31.

7 See Vazzoler, 'Letteratura e spettacolo nell'età della Repubblica aristocratica', p. 482.

8 Spinola, *L'Ariodante*, p. *4r. 'Verità non conosco, in queste selve / cerco pace, non Guerra'.

9 Ivaldi, 'Una polemica anti-spagnola', pp. 195–96.

10 Spinola, *Il cuore in volta, e 'l cuore in scena*, I, p. 61. 'È vero, sono al comando d'un Regno: Ma che mi giova? S'egli mi serve di carcere? Poco si lusinga de' Scettri chi sta col cuore fra le catene; che non hanno le grandezze incanto, che vaglia, per addormentare le passioni dell'animo. In somma, avvegnaché fra le porpore, non per tanto sono in esilio'.

11 Wackerlin, *L'ancienne chanson populaire en France*, p. 112.

12 Spinola, *Il cuore in volta, e 'l cuore in scena*, II, pp. 138–39: 'Albero. Vorrè favei da vui compà Lazà / Cose ha foeto ra Comà / Da merendà. / A l'ha foeto dri cori in ciò cà oilà, / ch'à no ne dà. / Solo a chi fa / Puinta, e carcagno, e balla chi sa'.

13 Spinola, *Il cuore in volta, e 'l cuore in scena*, II, pp. 141–42. 'Ecco la Diva, al cui gradito Nome / cessa de l'armi 'l minaccioso suono / che non sa, ch'io mi sia, la Pace io sono / che di placide frondi orno le chiome, / per me dolce è il riposo, e han le genti / per me del viver suo l'ore più liete: / né più turba importun la lor quiete / rauco fragor di bellici stromenti / solo s'ode, per me, d'inni festivi / rimbombar altamente ogni confine: / seccan palme, ed allori, e il mio crine / miransi solo germogliar gli ulivi. / Su le liguri scene ora io ne vegno / E lieti eventi in nobil tela ordisco; / mentre di Creta e Tiro insieme unisco / pacificati, e l'un e l'altro regno, / d'Agenore e Neleo l'ire mordaci, / co' le NOZZE D'EUROPA eccovi spente; / tant'è ver, ch'Imeneo solo è possente / a unir gli scettri, a stabilir le Paci. / Liguri voi, che del mio nume amici / vera pace godeste in mezo a l'armi / Lieti applaudete ora, ch'al suon de' carmi / si raggiran per voi l'ore felici'. Peace exhibits traditional iconography, crowned by a wreath of olive leaves. She announces her intentions of coming to Liguria and to show how peace is brought to Crete and Tiro through the marriage of the main characters of the play. 'Only Hymenaeus is mighty enough to establish peace', she sings.

14 Gavazza, 'Apparati decorativi', pp. 90–91.

15 See Spione, pp. 270–80.

16 Spinola, *Il cuore in volta, e 'l cuore in scena*, I, p. 63.

17 Lattarico, '"Questo è il gusto di Genova"', p. 44.

18 Marini, 'Francesco Fulvio Frugoni', p. 58.

19 Spinola, *Il cuore in volta, e 'l cuore in scena*, II, p. 402. 'Armi, genti, ruine. / Sventolano d'ogni intorno / Infinite bandiere, / E a danni del Regno / Corron per ogni parte armate schiere'; 'Chi del mio Regno osa turbar la pace? / Di qual oste nemica / Ingiusta violenza / Contro un re sproveduto / Muove assalti improvvisi?'.

20 We now have a new annotated edition: Chiabrera, *Guerra dei Goti*.

21 See Graziosi, *Da capitale a provincia*, p. 41. Chiabrera, *Discorsi*, pp. 3–7. The valuable book contained the autobiography *Vita di Gabriello Chiabrera*.

22 Spinola, *Lo Stoico cristiano*. See Graziosi, *Da capitale a provincia*, p. 31: the ideal of the Christian politician is argued in the same years by the books of the Genoese author Massola (*Il fasto della Corte cristiana*, 1674 and *La virtù nutrice e consigliera dei principi*, 1686).

23 Spinola, *Il cuore in volta, e 'l cuore in scena*, I, p. 81. 'Da nuovi motivi di guerra teme differito il ritorno'). 'Qual di serpi, e di ceraste il crine intesta / Sanguinosa Megera esce sotterra, / E, sonandomi al cor tromba funesta, / A' miei lieti pensier predice guerra? / Non così su'l fiorir fiera tempesta / Del pastorello le speranze atterra, / Come nel petto mio cura molesta / Scatena furie, e turbini disserra. / Già mi credea d'un abborrito Impero / Terminate veder l'aspre vicende, / Quindi al mio ben volgea tutto il pensiero. / Ahi speranze fallaci! Ecco si accende / Nuova guerra: fra l'armi ampio sentiero / Su s'apra almen a chi morir pretende'.

12

Giorgio Tosco

'I PIÙ SAVIJ POLITICHI DI TUTTE LE NAZIONI DEL MONDO'

The Political Use of the Dutch Model
in Seventeenth-Century Genoa

In his famous overview of the early modern history of the Republic of Genoa, Claudio Costantini titled a section 'the Dutch model' ('il modello olandese').[1] Costantini was describing the evolution of naval policy in the middle of the seventeenth century, and the gradual spread of the ideas of the so-called *repubblichisti*, the patrician faction that wanted to develop maritime trade and to strengthen the authority of the state. In order to achieve these aims, the Dutch Republic, which was then at the apex of its power, was apparently an example to follow. Costantini was not reading too much into the sources. Whoever browses the documents that the *repubblichisti* left behind in the Genoese archives and libraries cannot fail to notice the many references they made to the Netherlands.

The exact characteristics of this model, however, are much more elusive. Admiring a country is a rather different operation from identifying the roots of its success. In fact, the Genoese were not alone, as in that time many other observers across Europe noticed the prosperity of the Dutch Republic, and tried to imitate it.[2] The lessons they drew, however, were shaped by their own expectations and the debates they were addressing. There was not one single, obvious Dutch model, but many. This was true in Britain,[3] Switzerland,[4] and of course, in Genoa as well, as I will show.

In the Italian peninsula, attention to the Netherlands was primarily driven, at first, by its prolonged war against the Habsburgs. Those who supported Spanish hegemony in Italy viewed the Dutch as enemies, even though they could appreciate their bravery and determination at times. Conversely, those who had reasons to mistrust the Habsburgs saw their struggle in a more positive light.[5] In any case, understandably enough, both sides had a pro-Catholic bias. Even those who looked with favour at the Dutch rebels had no sympathy for their Calvinism, and they stressed the political, rather than the religious aspects of the conflict.[6]

If the Italian observers came from a republican environment, or had republican sympathies, it was only natural that they should reflect on the institutions of the rebels. Salvo Mastellone wrote that the Netherlands was a powerful political myth for the contemporary Italian bourgeoisie, and that it inspired the leaders of the Neapolitan Revolt of 1647–48.[7] In the seventeenth century, urban-based republics looked increasingly rare in a world of ascendant monarchies, and contemporaries had a clear perception that they shared some common characteristics.[8] Citizens of one republic, therefore, could draw useful lessons from the experience of the others.[9]

The admiration for the Netherlands could then convey both a republican identity and anti-Spanish sentiments. This made it particularly suited to be expressed in Genoa, where opposition to the extent of the alliance with Spain had been traditionally coupled with republican ideals.[10] According to Cees Reijner, this was already evident in the apparently pro-Spanish *Ragionamento sopra la triegua dei Paesi Bassi*, published in 1609.[11] Attention to the Netherlands would only increase in the following decades, as the twin issues of political reformation and decouplement from the Spanish alliance became more pressing.

In this work, I will try to flesh out the Dutch model that circulated in Genoa at that time. I will start by focusing on its preconditions, that is, the sudden rise of the Dutch mercantile presence in the Mediterranean. Among those who noticed it, there was Andrea Spinola, who exercised a strong influence on later *repubblichismo*. I will then analyse some texts from the middle of the century, the high point of *repubblichista* influence, and I will describe how they depicted the Dutch Republic. I

Detail of **12.1**
Aelbert Cuyp (circle of), *Senior Merchant with his Wife and an Enslaved Servant*, c. 1650–1655.

DOI 10.1484/M.DUNAMIS-EB.5.142041

12.1
Aelbert Cuyp (circle of), *Senior Merchant with his Wife and an Enslaved Servant*. Amsterdam, Rijksmuseum, c. 1650–1655. Photo: Public Domain.

will argue that the main element of the Dutch model that circulated was a particular interpretation of the Dutch trading companies, which were identified as the main asset of that country, and in any case the one that ought to be imported to Genoa.

The beginning of a Dutch presence and Andrea Spinola

'The Dutch swarmed into the Mediterranean like so many heavy insects crashing against the window panes'.[12] Fernand Braudel's account of the arrival of the Dutch merchant fleet in the Mediterranean between the end of the sixteenth century and the beginning of the seventeenth is justly famous, as it conveys the extent of their sudden presence. Later literature has painted this phenomenon in less dramatic tones, and stressed its gradual and unsteady character.[13] Nevertheless, in Genoa as elsewhere, their presence was inescapable.

As elsewhere in the region, their arrival was linked to the Mediterranean-wide famine of the early 1590s, which prompted merchants and authorities to import Baltic grain, carried on Dutch vessels.[14] The local Dutch-speaking community, so far almost indistinguishable among the larger 'Northern' (mostly German) one, became more numerous, also because of the contemporary wave of merchant migration started by the Eighty Years' War. The Dutchmen of Genoa connected the Genoese marketplace to the services provided by the Dutch ships, that continued to sail to the Mediterranean even after the end of the famine. These ships, besides carrying goods from Northern Europe, such as grain, timber and fish (and, soon, colonial products as well), sold freight to local operators.[15]

Their arrival was not always welcome. Already in 1613, a local commentator contrasted their relentless activity with the way Genoese nobles had pulled out of the shipping sector, leaving it in the hands of weaker merchants, who were unable to withstand Dutch competition.[16] Their presence could start looking threatening. Not so, however, for Andrea Spinola, who supported their presence wholeheartedly.

Andrea Spinola was one of the most influential thinkers in contemporary Genoa.[17] Known for his stern republican outlook and his dry realism, he spread his views in handwritten manuscripts that circulated among the Genoese nobility. Most notably, he collected his opinions on different topics in short notes, which were ordered like a dictionary (so

12.2
Reinier Nooms, *The Battle of Livorno*, Amsterdam,
Rijksmuseum, 1653–1664. Photo: Public Domain.

much so that his writings have been later labelled a *Dizionario storico-filosofico*, 'Historical-philosophical dictionary'). On the Dutch presence, he wrote that it had saved Genoa from the double danger of famine and exclusive dependence on Sicilian wheat.[18] Moreover, it had given rise to a thriving re-exportation trade, directed to the rest of Italy. As he pointed out, the Genoese should offer a couple of bottles of wine to every Dutch ship that arrived in port, 'faccendo loro conoscer con i fatti, che sono i benvenuti'.[19]

Spinola's positive attitude was visible in other areas as well: he sympathised with foreign sailors who happened to be harassed by Genoese authorities[20], and praised extensively the German trader Cristoforo Furtembach.[21] He even went as far as implying that Dutch people were morally better than the Genoese. After mentioning their joint-stock companies, he grimly remarked that the Genoese were not trustworthy enough to be able to operate them successfully.[22] As admirable as the Dutch were, and as welcome as their presence was, they were in any case too different to constitute a realistic policy model.

This was consistent with Spinola's conservative and pessimistic outlook. He did not think that Genoa could or should ever really become a significant military power on its own, and would have been satisfied with a stronger Republic, which would have remained nevertheless safely embedded within the Spanish imperial system. Later thinkers were much more ambitious.

The repubblichisti and the Dutch

The subsequent development in the Genoese political debate is well known, and has been at the centre of many historical reconstructions.[23] From the 1630s to the 1660s, the *repubblichista* ideas, first championed by a few intellectuals, became more widespread, and influenced actual policy-making. At their core, there was still a focus on the unification of the ruling élite, beyond factional and economic divisions, a development of republican virtues, and a strengthening of the state apparatus. Moreover, *repubblichisti* wanted to move away from a narrow specialisation on finance and galley-management, and to increase local shipping. In a radical departure from Spinola (though not from all previous thinkers), they also wanted to call into question, and renegotiate, the Genoese alliance with Spain, in order to pursue a more assertive and independent foreign policy.

The causes of this phenomenon were varied, and were in no way limited to purely intellectual debates. Decouplement from Spain started being widely considered a sensible option only after the financial and military setbacks of the Habsburgs. Starting from 1627, and especially in the 1640s and 1650s, investment in the Spanish public debt became riskier, and it was doubtful whether Madrid could effectively protect Genoese security. People looked for other investment opportunities, and the Republic had to seriously consider investing more for its own defence. In the end, most of the initiatives promoted by the *repubblichisti* did not lead to lasting results, and despite some diplomatic crises, Genoa remained a client state of Spain. However, the construction of a new galleon fleet protected the importation of silver, and fostered innovation in Genoese shipbuilding.[24]

The *repubblichisti* diffused their ideas through books, handwritten pamphlets, and policy proposals that circulated among the magistracies. One of their most famous pieces of propaganda was a book aptly called *Il Genio ligure risvegliato* (fig. 2.3), written by Giovanni Bernardo Veneroso, a man who pursued a successful military career, took part in all the initiatives promoted by his group, and lobbied for an intervention on the Venetian side during the War of Candia (1644–1669).[25] Other books were written by Tobia Pallavicini and Gaspare Squarciafico, young nobles who were involved in the internal political turmoil of the Republic (Squarciafico even died in exile).[26]

In all these works, the Dutch appeared as an example of military power, not just in Europe but also overseas, where they had conquered many countries in the Indies and in Africa.[27] They were all the more remarkable, as they came from a small, sandy and poor country, and their war of independence had been started by a few refugee rebels, fighting against Spain.[28] 'Never, from such humble beginnings, has such remarkable progress been seen', synthetised Pallavicini.[29] Their victories were coupled with economic success, which had turned them into a leading merchant nation, 'providers of every precious commodity to all European countries' (fig. 12.1–12.2).[30]

The link between commerce, power and navigation was at the core of the thought of these authors, and indeed of much strategical thinking of the time[31]. 'Il commercio del mare porge un largo campo, per esercitare i più grandi coraggi nel tempo della pace, perché il Commercio del mare è così bene una milizia, come un traffico' wrote Pallavicini[32]. Trading ships had to be ready to defend themselves against corsairs, or to switch to privateering themselves. In any case, ships and sailors alike could be mobilised in case of war, and constituted a strategic supply of materiel and personnel. This was true even if many of these people, like Veneroso, thought that actual fighting was mostly to be managed by purpose-built war galleys, because in any case trading vessels could provide logistical support.[33] Fostering navigation, in any case, would provide more 'experienced captains and brave soldiers'.[34]

The link between economic and military success rested on the basis of a well-managed republic, governed by virtuous people. Commerce had made the Dutch not just rich and brave, but also smart. Their intelligence caused them to be good citizens, who designed and enacted good policies. Overall, they could be considered 'the best spirits, and the wisest politicians among all the nations of the world'.[35]

The admiration for the Dutch was not, however, detached from considerations about Genoa itself. In fact, *repubblichisti* saw the Netherlands as a mirror for a possible future for their own city. The two countries were comparable, and the experiences of the United Provinces reflected the history of Genoa itself. For Veneroso, both countries were part of a long list of polities that had achieved power and wealth through navigation, and comprised, for example, Athens, Carthage and Venice (another model for Genoa).[36] The *repubblichisti* often presented medieval Genoa (or rather, a stylised version of it) as an example to be reproduced in the future, a powerful and wealthy state managed by virtuous citizens. The Netherlands were an equivalent version of the same political myth, that conveyed the same message.

The image of the Netherlands did not just lead to new actions and policies in Genoa, but influenced even how the Genoese themselves treated that country. Joseph Nye coined the term 'soft power' to describe how, in contemporary politics, a country can use its cultural influence to foster better relations with others.[37] The Dutch enjoyed a similar advantage at the time, and the *repubblichisti* sought to make Genoa collaborate with the fellow republic they so admired. This was, of course, valid before 1648, when Spain was at war with the Netherlands, and it was in the interest of whoever favoured a decoupling from the former to woo the latter. For example, in 1637 the Spanish fleet captured some Dutch merchant ships, loaded with grain and bound for Genoa. The Republic, which was then led by the *repubblichista* Doge Agostino Pallavicini, did not just fiercely protest to Madrid, but also took the unprecedented step of sending an embassy to The Hague.[38]

However, the same mechanism was also at work afterwards. In the 1650s the *repubblichisti* tried to reconcile their sympathies for the Dutch with those for another republic, the English Commonwealth.[39] Ugo Fieschi, a *repubblichista* naval officer and politician, described the two countries this way:

> They stand out so much for their greatness and exceptional force, and they have a regime which is favourable towards us, and laws according to it, so that they can promise us good understanding and a steady and stable friendship. They possess, with their formidable armies, the key to that traffic which – as I said before – is necessary not just for our wealth, but for our very existence.[40]

For Fieschi, then, a shared republican identity was supposed to create stable bonds of friendship and collaboration between Genoa, England and the Netherlands. The support of the great naval powers of the North Sea was also very useful for a small, commercial state like Genoa. This pan-republican solidarity was obviously little more than wishful thinking. Fieschi himself recognised that the two Republics of the North were then coming to loggerheads (the speech was probably made just before the beginning of the First Anglo-Dutch War, in 1652), and hoped that Genoa might mediate between the two, in the future.

Some form of collaboration with Dutch actors was in any case necessary, as the repubblichisti sought to renew Genoese shipbuilding and navigation along Dutch lines. These plans did not necessarily involve the public authorities of the United Provinces, however. The best-known example is perhaps the Genoese East India Company (CGIO), which was promoted by a Dutch merchant of Genoa, Hendrik Muilman, and bought its ships and recruited most of its personnel in the Netherlands. Their employment, however, violated the privileges of the VOC, the Dutch East India Company, which sequestered the Genoese ships when they reached Sumatra in 1649, even though it reimbursed the Genoese shareholders.[41]

A collaboration with individual Dutch merchants, in order to imitate the political economy of their country, could be actually detrimental to the interests of the Dutch state. A few years later, the Genoese also imported from the Netherlands their first squadron of galleons, along with the sailors and officers who were needed to man them.[42] Also in this case, relations with the Dutch authorities were not smooth (see below). In any case, some form of contact with that country was necessary, and Dutch merchants frequently collaborated with the initiatives of the repubblichisti.[43]

The rhetoric of republican collaboration could also be used both ways. That squadron of galleons was soon at the centre of a diplomatic crisis. In 1653, as the Netherlands faced the worst period of the war against England, the Admiralty of Amsterdam sequestered the new, state-of-the-art vessels that the Republic of Genoa had commissioned there. It offered to pay full reimbursement – and in any case the ships were duly delivered after the end of the war – but it asked not to pay any interest on its instalments, out of republican solidarity.[44] This time, it was the Genoese turn to dismiss their request, and to obtain all the money it was due.

To summarise, the admiration for the Dutch did not just remain on paper. The rhetoric of republican collaboration did not only derive from merely intellectual reasons, but also from the necessity to find some agreement with what was then the leading naval power in Europe, and a crucial source of skilled personnel and war matériel. It was a useful tool that could be deployed at times, even though both the Genoese and the Dutch knew that the interests of their respective states did not always coincide.

The Dutch companies

In many of the texts produced by the repubblichisti, the Dutch are first and foremost associated with proposals to establish joint-stock companies of trade. The link between the two concepts were the Dutch East and West India Companies. All over Europe, their accomplishments had impressed observers, who wanted to reproduce similar institutions in their own country.[45] Also in Genoa they were considered as a possible blueprint for similar projects, in spite of what Spinola had written, and actually, three joint-stock companies of trade were formed in this period.[46] The precedent of the Dutch companies was mentioned in the works of Veneroso, Pallavicini and Squarciafico.[47] It was also previously present in an anonymous project presented just after the first successful application of this institutional framework, in 1638.[48]

That year, the Compagnia di Nostra Signora di Libertà (CNSL), which drew its capital from a subscription raised by 520 people, was constituted with the purpose of manning galleys with free rowers, generally thought to be more efficient than the usual slaves.[49] The company ended soon, but it caught the attention of contemporaries. The investor I mentioned, who wanted to enlarge its structure, described it as 'with the form of the S. Giorgio company, and according to [the companies] of the Dutchmen'.[50] The joint-stock framework was actually one of the features that the Genoese Casa di San Giorgio shared with the Dutch India Companies, so it is not surprising that contemporaries noticed this similarity, just as later historians did.[51] What was more interesting, in the eyes of the Genoese, was not the propriety framework as such, but the purpose of the company.

The Casa di San Giorgio, multifold as its functions were, never worked as a company of trade, as the Northern European ones did. This was a rather original feature in the Genoese context, where commerce was usually managed by smaller enterprises. Later projects kept associating a primary trading purpose with a joint-stock framework and a reference to the Dutch. Its implications, however, were essentially political. Veneroso described them as such:

> The Dutch with the money of their merchants, and no expenses or damages for the United Provinces, increase their public and private revenues, and conquer new lands for their empire, as they did on the West African coast and in the East and the West Indies [...]. And they do so through two companies, in which

private citizens put as much money as they want, reap the benefits proportionally and build their armies.[52]

In this view, companies did not just provide wealth and military success, but they did so bypassing the public structures of the Dutch state: only those who desired so contributed to the costs of overseas expansion. Its benefits, however, reverberated through the whole country. These were not limited to larger customs revenues, but extended to foreign politics as well, as the 1638 commentator clearly noted:

> You would have greatness and reputation [in case a company is established], as a company would be armed by the Genoese, that is to say by the Republic. The same happens with the Dutch companies, whose glory is ascribed to the Dutch, even though the profits are private.[53]

This was bound to draw the attention of the *repubblichisti*. All over early modern Europe, attempts at building up naval and military power had to gather political support and resources from wide sectors of the society.[54] This problem was acutely visible in Genoa, where a large part of the political élite operated abroad or had business with foreign states, and where the structures of the Republic were designed to give them much leeway.[55] Not everyone needed or wished for a stronger Republic, with a more independent foreign policy. When the *repubblichisti* tried to restructure the Genoese state, they faced many entrenched interests, and this opposition eventually undid all their attempts.

Apparently, the Dutch had found a way to bypass this problem. A joint-stock company would allow the *repubblichisti* to start a policy change on their own, by drawing on the part of the patriciate that supported them, without waiting for the approval of the rest. Its fleet would provide public benefits, in terms of military potential and political prestige, and coordinate the private interests of the citizens without passing through the procedural bottlenecks of the Republic.

From this point of view, Dutch companies of trade shared another feature with the Casa di San Giorgio. Whereas foreign contemporaries often thought of San Giorgio as a private enterprise that controlled the state, reality was quite different. As the same social class, and often the very same people, controlled both the Republic and San Giorgio, the two institutions were running in parallel, even though, of course, there could be differences between them.[56] Private and public institutions enmeshed, as people moved seamlessly between the two, in Genoa as in many other early modern contexts.[57] In the eyes of the *repubblichisti*, joint-stock companies would be, like the Casa di San Giorgio, another institution that would compensate for the idiosyncrasies of their Republic.

Conclusion

The study of *repubblichismo* has sometimes tended to emphasise its distinction and originality from the way the state was actually managed in Genoa. Arturo Pacini once noted that, if we read only the sources the *repubblichisti* produced, we run the risk of producing a rather one-sided description of all the rest of the Genoese political environment, and of erasing the actual rationality of their choices.[58] More recently, Matteo Salonia even tried to reconstruct the ideas that informed the construction of the Genoese state into a full-fledged ideology, that stood in juxtaposition to the *repubblichista* line of thought. Allegedly, those thinkers departed radically from the existing local tradition.[59]

The study of how *repubblichisti* tried to import foreign ideas, however, offers a more nuanced picture. Their view of the Netherlands and its institutions was shaped by their local political environment, of which they were acutely aware. The Dutch companies could be assimilated and compared, for their structure, to the quintessentially Genoese institution of the Casa di San Giorgio. They could also perform a similar role as a semi-public institution, which could gather people and resources much more flexibly than the Republic could. In any case, they could be theoretically integrated within the local political system. As Pacini himself observed, once we look more closely and pay more attention to their actions, *repubblichisti* appear to be much more integrated in their environment than would seem otherwise.[60]

The construction of a Dutch model, then, was based on local requirements. Of course, some of its aspects could be shared with other European countries. The Dutch joint-stock companies formed a blueprint, often mediated by the transfer of actual merchants and sailors, for many other companies abroad.[61] It would be interesting to verify how in, say, France or Denmark, the intellectual components of their image differed from what happened in Genoa[62]. From this point of view, the role of joint-stock companies in state-building processes and projects needs further exploration, as they represented one of the ways modern states came into being.[63]

To summarise, the Dutch Republic and its people performed a very specific function in the Genoese political debate. It embodied a republican image that some part of the local élite wanted to reproduce in their own country, and a specific policy proposal (the establishment of companies), that eventually led to some actual initiatives. Even though this image was incomplete and partial, it was very significant, but it tells us more about the people who created it than about the people who were depicted.

1 'The Dutch model'. Claudio Costantini, *La Repubblica di Genova*, pp. 315–21.

2 Swart, *The Miracle of the Dutch Republic*; Van Ittersum, 'A Miracle Mirrored?'.

3 Speck, 'Britain and the Dutch Republic'.

4 Maissen, 'Inventing the Sovereign Republic'; Kapossy, 'Republican Futures'.

5 Belvederi, 'Genova e le Fiandre'; Reijner, 'Il mito dell'Olanda'. I have not been able to read Lamal, 'Italian Communication'.

6 Van Gelder, 'In Liefde En Werk Met de Lage Landen Verbonden'.

7 Mastellone, 'Holland as a Political Model'; Mastellone, 'I Repubblicani del Seicento'.

8 Durand, *Les républiques au temps des monarchies*; Conti, *Consociatio Civitatum*.

9 Zucchi, 'Republics in Comparison'.

10 Bitossi, 'Lo strano caso dell'antispagnolismo genovese'.

11 Reijner, 'Gesprekken in Genua'. On this work, see also Belvederi, 'Il "Ragionamento di Giovanni Costa"'.

12 Braudel, *The Mediterranean*, p. 634.

13 Lopez Martin, 'A Century of Small Paper Boats'; Fusaro, 'After Braudel'.

14 Gullino, 'Il network commerciale del Magistrato'.

15 Grendi, 'I nordici e il traffico del porto di Genova'; Engels, *Merchants, Interlopers, Seamen and Corsairs*, pp. 107–23; Tosco, 'Mediatori indispensabili'.

16 ASG, Manoscritti 632.

17 Bitossi, *Andrea Spinola*; Bitossi, 'Due Modelli Di Educazione Repubblicana'.

18 BUG, BVIII, 27, f. 265. 'La navigazione delle navi di Fiandra ha data la vita alla nostra Città havendola quasi assicurata da patir la fame, dove che soggiacendo per l'adietro dipendeva in gran parte delli grani di Sicilia et era ciò gran servitù per più versi'.

19 'To make them know, with deeds, that they are welcome'. BUG, BVIII, 27, f. 265.

20 BUG, BVIII, 26, f. 295.

21 BUG, BVIII, 26, f. 296.

22 Bitossi, *Andrea Spinola*, pp. 222–23.

23 Costantini, 'Politica e storiografia'; Bitossi, 'Navi e politica'; Kirk, *Genoa and the Sea*; Bitossi, 'Il genio ligure risvegliato'.

24 Calcagno, 'La navigazione convogliata a Genova'; Tosco, 'Importing the Netherlands'.

25 Pastine, 'Rapporti fra Genova e Venezia'. Bitossi, 'Il genio ligure risvegliato'.

26 Pallavicini, *Della navigazione e del commercio*; Squarciafico, *Le politiche malattie*. On Pallavicini, see Bitossi, *Il governo dei magnifici*, pp. 275–77.

27 Veneroso, *Il Genio ligure risvegliato*, p. 120.

28 Veneroso, *Il Genio ligure risvegliato*, p. 121.

29 'Non mai da principij così deboli si videro progressi così vantaggiosi'. Pallavicini, *Della navigazione e del commercio*, p. 57.

30 'Distributori d'ogni più preziosa mercadanzia agli altri stati d'Europa'. Pallavicini, *Della navigazione e del commercio*, p. 57.

31 Glete, *Navies and Nations*.

32 'Sea trade provides many opportunities to train bravery in times of peace, as it is a military exercise just as much as a form of commerce'. Pallavicini, *Della navigazione e del commercio*, p. 46.

33 Veneroso, *Il Genio ligure risvegliato*, p. 19.

34 'Esperimentati capitani e valorosi soldati'. Squarciafico, *Le politiche malattie*, p. 146.

35 'I migliori spiriti, ed i più savij politici di tutte le nazioni del mondo', Pallavicini, *Della navigazione e del commercio*, p. 74.

36 Veneroso, *Il Genio ligure risvegliato*, p. 121. On Veneroso's treatment of Venice, see also Assereto, 'Lo sguardo di Genova su Venezia'. and Zucchi.

37 Nye, *Soft Power*.

38 ASG, AS 2707E, 23rd September 1637.

39 Villani, 'La prima rivoluzione inglese'.

40 '[…] Giganteggiano sì mirabilmente di grandezza, e di sì immense, et impareggiabili forze, il regime de quali come simpatico al nostro, e le leggi del loro governo a questo conformi ben prometter ci possono, e facile la confomità di genij, e stabile e sicura la conservatione dell'amicitie, amicitie di quella gente, che sole con le loro formidabili armate posseggono per così dire le chiavi et il possesso di quel trafico, senza il quale come già dissi, non che il ben essere, ma nemmeno essere l'istesso mantener possiamo'. ASG, Manoscritti, 632. On this document, see Pastine, 'Genova e Inghilterra da Cromwell a Carlo II', pp. 312–15. On Fieschi, see Cavanna Ciappina, 'Ugo Fiesco'.

41 Subrahmanyam, 'On the Significance of Gadflies'. See also Tosco, 'In Pursuit of the World's Trade'.

42 ASG, AS 1667, 22nd March 1655. On this, see also footnote n. 24.

43 Tosco, 'Importing the Netherlands'.

44 ASG, AS 2335, 18 September 1653.

45 Holtz, 'The Model of the VOC'.

46 The Compagnia di Nostra Signora di Libertà (1638–?), the Compagnia Genovese delle Indie Orientali (1647–1653), and the Compagnia Marittima di San Giorgio (1653–1668). Ungari, *Statuti di compagnie e società azionarie italiane (1638–1808)*.

47 Veneroso, *Il Genio ligure risvegliato*, p. 120; Pallavicini, *Della navigazione e del commercio*, p. 93; Squarciafico, *Le politiche malattie*, p. 145.

48 ASG, AS 1654, 65 bis.

49 Lo Basso, *Uomini da remo*, pp. 252–66.

50 'Alla forma della compagnia di S. Giorgio in conformità di quelle de gl'olandesi'.

51 Taviani, 'La Casa de San Giorgio'.

52 '[I Neerlandesi] co i denari de' Mercatanti, e senza gravezza, ò danno pelle Province unite, accrescono le loro entrate pubbliche, e private, e sottomettono al loro Impero nuovi paesi, come hanno fatto nella costa d'Africa, nell'Indie Orientali et Occidentali […]. E questo fanno per mezzo di due loro compagnie, nelle quali, partecipando i privati in quella somma, che a ciascheduno piace, constituiscono le loro armate ad utile di essi secondo la proportione delle loro parti'. Veneroso, *Il Genio ligure risvegliato*, p. 120. See also Taviani, 'The making of the modern corporation.'

53 'La grandezza et riputatione vi è, perché [un'eventuale compagnia] sarà sempre armata de genovesi che tal è dire della Repubblica così segue delle compagnie d'Olanda che tutte l'imprese s'asiniano al nome degl'Olandesi, benché l'interesse sia de privati'. ASG, AS 1654, 65 bis.

54 Tilly, *Coercion, Capital, and European States*; Glete, *War and the State in Early Modern Europe*.

55 Bitossi, *Il governo dei magnifici*; Assereto, 'Comunità soggette e poteri centrali'.

56 Savelli, 'Tra Machiavelli e San Giorgio'; Cama, 'Banco di San Giorgio e sistema politico genovese'.

57 Grafe, 'On the Spatial Nature of Institutions'.

58 Pacini, 'Genova e il mare', p. 238.

59 Salonia, *Genoa's Freedom*.

60 Pacini, 'Genova e il mare', p. 240.

61 Antunes, Münch Miranda, and Salvado, 'The Resources of Others'.

62 For France, see Holtz, 'The Model of the VOC'.

63 Stern, *The Company-State*.

IV THE AGE OF CRISIS
1660–1700

13

Luana Salvarani

'NELLE VARIETÀ PROPRIE DELLA CITTÀ NOSTRA'

Giovan Francesco Spinola's Instruttione famigliare *Between Genoese Identity and the Renaissance Pedagogical Tradition*

In the realm of early modern educational thought, treatises generally known as *institutiones* have a central role in elaborating on the background of Renaissance pedagogy and in redesigning the pedagogical aims and priorities of a changing ruling class. A synthesis of such broad and articulated tradition clearly exceeds the aim of this article. Here it is worthwhile to recall a general evolutionary line, developing the pattern established in the early fifteenth century by the Humanist rediscovery of the pseudo-Plutarchean *De liberis educandis*, then making it more and more suitable to the needs of courtly life and increasingly refined diplomacy.[1]

In this framework, Giovan Francesco Spinola's *Instruttione famigliare* ('Family Education', written around 1650) represents both a turning point and a variant profoundly connected with the needs and circumstances of the places in which the work was conceived. On the local side, the book gives evidence of a peculiar, one-of-a-kind 'Genoese pedagogy' and carries the mark of the uncertainty and troubles of a declining republic still very proud of its manners and morals. From a more general perspective, the treatise stands as the most convincing testimony of the progressive dismissal of the educational model based on Humanism and the liberal arts, which was called on to include both the Genoese more practical approach and the impulse to specialised education brought about at the end of the sixteenth century by medical culture and the Spanish school of the *ingenio*.[2]

Spinola's *Instruttione* looks inconspicuous, both because of its rhetorically pared-down style and its unfinished structure, apparently lacking a second part. Carlo Bitossi has provided essential information on Spinola's *Instruttione*, convincingly identifying its author[3] as a nephew of the same Andrea Spinola who authored a short text 'Dell'educazione' in a large manuscript 'encyclopaedia' of Genoese civic culture

entitled (perhaps by librarians) *Il Cittadino di Republica*, like the well-known treatise published in 1617 by Ansaldo Cebà.

For all these reasons, the *Instruttione* comes from a network of cultural influences pinpointing the role of pedagogy for the conservation of the noble citizen and, most of all, of Genoese republican identity. It is therefore not surprising that the birth of his son Nicolò prompted in Giovan Francesco the idea of writing an educational text, from father to son, taking on both the role of the *pater familias* and of the preceptor, who in the Renaissance tradition wrote the works dedicated to the princely children. The author speaks in the first person, stating that the book aims to direct the action of his son according to 'civil and political prudence':

> In order to conform your actions to the rules arising from civil and political prudence, since you are born in a Republic – meaning a free city, which you must learn to serve as much as possible – and being crucial for that purpose the good government of your household, I decided to write for you an Instruction or Treatise, in two parts.[4]

The second part, which according to the Preface should have dealt with politics and the republican government, was never written, since Nicolò died prematurely in France, and the first part of the book, written in the 1650s-1660s, was published only in 1670, long after its composition and the abandonment of the project. The text was rediscovered thanks to

13.1
Quentin Metsys, *The Moneylender and his Wife*.
Paris, Musée du Louvre, 1514.
Photo: © RMN-Grand Palais (musée du Louvre) /
Gérard Blot. Reproduced with permission.

someone who thought the publication was useful, as mentioned in the foreword:

> But a pious hand, caring for the common good, rescued (the text) from the obscurity to which it was damned, when death closed prematurely the eyes to the noble boy to whom it was dedicated; just as the father should have buried, after his first offspring, also the second.[5]

It is impossible to discover the identity of the person who published the book under the transparent pseudonym 'Francesco Lanospigio', a syllabic anagram of the author's name. The choice to publish the booklet (88 pages), in a small practical format, among the avalanche of other small books printed in the flourishing market of Baroque Rome, indicates that the work was considered neither irrelevant nor out of fashion. However, in an educational context dominated by the institutions managed by the religious orders – most of all by the Jesuits, who had become the leaders in the field since the late sixteenth century – a treatise on private, household education probably could not attract much attention. Currently, the book is listed in the catalogues of only four Italian libraries: Braidense in Milan, Bobbio and Francone in Turin, and National Central Library in Rome (which owns a copy previously owned by the library of the Jesuit Collegio Romano and whose digitisation is freely available on the web). Therefore, it is plausible that the book did not exert significant influence. Nevertheless, it remains fascinating as a testimony on Genoese educational culture and, most of all, on the perception of a complex historical phase by a member of one of Genoa's governing families.

The 'Spinola model', between mercantile tradition, the humanities and the selection of talents

The *Instruttione* by Giovan Francesco Spinola, but also the *notoes on education* by his uncle Andrea Spinola, must be considered against the background of a rich, complex and competitive educational reality, where a variety of public and religious institutions and private contracts managed a demand for instruction driven by practical aims and not only by the self-legitimation of the aristocracy. Already in medieval Genoa, religious and secular institutions coexisted with teaching traditions such as the 'grammar for merchants' (*gramatica ad usum mercatorum*), taught from the fourteenth century onwards (beginning with Salvo da Pontremoli) by teachers privately appointed by the families.[6] This *gramatica* constituted a peculiarly Genoese complement to the *schola d'abaco*,[7] merging the technical side of the *abaco* with the teaching of 'applied humanities' in Latin and later in the vernacular (fig. 13.1–13.2). Following the evolution of

the educational landscape in the early modern age, Genoa hosted – like most Italian cities – several religious colleges and dozens of teachers and preceptors, paid by the municipality or privately, but never stopped calling for a curriculum whose practical utility must be straightforward at all social levels, a 'culture of necessity' (*ad necessitatem*) as defined by Enea Silvio Piccolomini in the fifteenth century.[8]

In the genre of 'instructions' from father to son, there are other examples in the Ligurian area, such as the *Instruttioni* by Francesco Maria Clavesana, whose aim is to give hints on how to govern the fief. Spinola's *Instruttione*, on the other hand, even in its unfinished form, has a much broader scope and tries to re-codify, in a fascinating manner, the Genoese tradition of practical studies in the framework of Humanist pedagogy, taking inspiration from sixteenth century landmark texts such as Alessandro Piccolomini's *De la institutione di tutta la vita de l'homo nato nobile e in città libera* (Venezia, 1542), explicitly quoted by Spinola, but also taking account of seventeenth-century court and political education.

This wide-angle approach is explicitly declared in the Chapter II of the *Instruttione*, 'Educatione de' figliuoli', where the author moves beyond the advice to be given to his son and takes on a general discourse on education:

> To secure the success of your sons in things that would be useful both to themselves and the household (as it seems today that the occupations of noblemen are reduced to three, i.e., Letters, War and Trade)[9]

While the importance of *Mercatura* ('trade') was nothing new in Genoese education, as we have seen before, the pairing with the two classical components of Renaissance education, *Lettere e Armi* ('letters and the art of war'), is undoubtedly a novelty. Both disciplines were the core of Renaissance education, at least beginning from Vergerius's *De ingenuis moribus*, one of the most influential Renaissance treatises on education, written in the early fifteenth century. The diptych of Letters and War was so typical that the addition of Trade at the same level with them amounts to a change of paradigm desired by the author, if not fully accomplished.

The aim seems to have been not so much to dignify trade – which did not need any legitimation in the Genoese context – but to legitimate the typical educational path of Genoese nobility, placing it in the same lineage of Humanist education based on the classics and the cultivation of moral philosophy.

However, Spinola also wants to distinguish Genoese education from the Humanist tradition, where it required an ideal profile of the learned prince that was substantially the same for everybody. Continuing the sentence quoted before, Spinola postulates the exigency of the examination of talents

13.2
Copy of Marinus van Reymerswaele, *Tax collectors*.
Warsaw, National Museum, first half of the
16th century. Photo by Piotr Ligier / National
Museum in Warsaw. Public Domain.

and the specialisation of curriculum, and does it by quoting Juan Huarte, the Spanish physician who authored of one of the most influential educational treatises of the late sixteenth century, the *Examen de ingenios*:

> I would appreciate if you do not apply them to one of these tasks based on your will, but that you take care to follow their talent: in doing that you cannot make something morally wrong, and you will also have the solace, when something wrong should occur, not to have acted out of your whim. A very learned Spanish author called Juan Huarte, in his Trial of Wits, says that human progress is hindered by the choices of the fathers, who decide for their sons without following their natural attitudes.[10]

While proposing an educational model based on a 'Genoese Humanism' and a triptych of basic disciplines, Spinola also highlights that the path to be followed must take account of individual talents. Therefore, the primacy in the curriculum of either letters, war, or trade must arise from a thorough examination of the pupil in order to achieve the best results with minimal effort. Juan Huarte based his theory on Galenic medicine and stated that talents are given at birth according to physical complexion. Thus, the main task of the educator is to assess individual skills and develop them through appropriate disciplines.[11]

Huarte's declared aim was to improve the Spanish educational system and provide appropriate functionaries for the State: the horizon of his theory was more public than private. Moreover, the same aim was shared by a key Genoese text, the already mentioned *Il cittadino di Republica* by Ansaldo Cebà, which was almost certainly known by Giovan Francesco Spinola and certainly well known by his uncle Andrea.

> Nevertheless, I see that for being a shoemaker or a tailor, one begins with a careful training; but, when it comes to managing the republic, very rarely it is prepared by appropriate civic discipline. [...] The legislators of the most famous cities have established how young people should be learned, so that the republic is well governed; and the philosophers, who are particularly advanced in these subjects, located in education all the substance of the good political government.[12]

Cebà's treatise focuses on the Republic. His ideas on the virtues necessary to preserve Genoese liberty were summarised in a book explicitly conceived for the common good. This intellectual and political attitude was shared by Andrea Spinola, as pinpointed by Simona Morando, in a common effort to improve the quality of the ruling class through their activity in the Accademia degli Addormentati.[13]

Despite this strong connection between Andrea Spinola and Ansaldo Cebà, the former, who probably shares the political views of Cebà, on the pedagogical side (in the few but dense pages of 'Dell'educatione') emphasised the role of education in the effective management of the family.

In continuity with his uncle, but with a broader scope, Giovan Francesco Spinola focused on the prosperity of the household and the political solidity of Genoese aristocracy, so that the selection of talents could help in optimising expenses for private teachers and maintaining the reputation of the family members in their diverse occupations.

Spinola sees a good examination of talents and choice of the preceptor as a wise investment that will produce a certain long-time income:

> Besides the ordinary household expenses, there are some expenses which occur rarely, and that can be defined accidental rather than continuous: but they are as necessary as the former, because they deal with our moral being and our most important actions. These are the expenses made for the education of sons, and for giving them good guidance; in providing good marriage for the daughters, in keeping good reputation, and in the defence of one's own life.[14]
>
> I remind that you must provide them with a teacher of good manners and culture, in choosing which you should not care for the price or other problems, accepting if necessary that your capital could be diminished; because a good education for your children could well substitute their share of heritage.[15]

When it is difficult to find a good preceptor, the abundance of religious colleges in Italy and abroad can offer a suitable education, with the added value of providing the student with experiences out of the family and establishing international connections:

> If finding a teacher with the right qualities is difficult, you can recur to the many colleges and universities founded in the main cities in Italy and Europe by learned clerics, in which one can learn, together with the sciences, piety and good manners. And being far from the household, they will obtain better results, according to Aristotle who says that man is like that sort of plants, which transplanted in a different soil become more productive.[16]

This positive attitude towards religious orders and institutions is one of the most important differences between the uncle and the nephew.[17] The reasons for Giovan Francesco's opening to the Jesuit college model are not only connected to the author's political experiences as a member of the Senate and candidate for the Dogate, and therefore as someone with a less radical perception of Genoese independence from the Papal See.

Here, the traditional educational path of the ruling nobility (from the preceptor, whose fidelity to the family was carefully supervised by the *pater familias*, directly to the court and the training for the functions of government) was changed from the beginning with the possibility to choose the *mercatura* according to the pupils' talents. Furthermore, it was also formally followed or replaced by the college experience, where young aristocrats could build connections and skills crucial to surviving in the world of international trade, and most of all in the network of an increasingly complex European diplomacy. In the years in which the *Instruttione* was presumably written, Genoa was facing a plague, the increasing instability of the Spanish debt and commercial decline (expressed by a decrease in the movement of goods through the harbour, as documented by Luisa Piccinno)[18]. The *Instruttione* gives a poignant account of this sense of insecurity:

> Besides the motives that we have already explained as a reason to increase the assets, there is the fact that when it does not increase, it will necessarily decrease and dissolve: in addition to the general fact, that nothing is sure in this world, our holdings in Genoa, which are founded on rents and debtors, are vanishing in our hands day by day; because, without finding another capital which replaces the extinguished one, or near to extinction, we will undoubtedly find us broke.[19]

While proudly and distinctively loyal to the Genoese ethos, Giovan Francesco has developed a perspective fit for difficult times. His educational model, fully aristocratic and therefore much broader in scope than the medieval tradition of *gramatica ad usum mercatorum*, aims at shaping less a venture capitalist than a very cautious investor, able to juggle the levers of politics and the connections with the church in order to protect himself from the uncertainties of the market. Moreover, among these abilities, the old *humanae litterae* did not suffice but remained an instrument of distinction necessary to build and preserve the image of the Genoese nobility outside Genoa.

The Instruttione *and the pedagogical tradition*

The structure itself of the *Instruttione* gives account both of the author's knowledge of the tradition of early modern educational treatises and his need for distinction and renewal of such tradition.

The first aspect that the reader can ascertain is the dismissal of the structure based on the coupling of liberal arts and moral philosophy, which had been consistently maintained for two centuries. Starting from Vergerius's *De ingenuis moribus et liberalibus studiis adulescentiae* (completed in 1402), this structure is to be found, for example, in François la Mothe le Vayer's *De l'Instruction de Monseigneur le Dauphin* (1640), even if written in French instead of Latin, and containing significant changes to the meaning and role of liberal arts in princely education. Spinola avoids the articulated structure of Alessandro Piccolomini's *Institutione di tutta la vita dell'homo nato*

nobile, e in città libera (1542), which discusses the supreme good before dealing with the liberal arts, the virtues and morals in a typical Aristotelian-Christian framework, even though he explicitly quotes the work.

On the contrary, Giovan Francesco Spinola reinvented the architecture of the genre completely, at least in the first part, and it is clear that the unwritten second part, which should have been exclusively about politics,[20] would not have dealt with liberal arts or moral philosophy at all. The summary clarifies that the traditional pillars of educational treatises are reduced to the bare minimum[21]. The liberal arts with the *trivium* and the study of history are compressed into six pages, in which Spinola also includes an invitation to the study of modern languages (French and Spanish),[22] in order to be able to read works prohibited by the Inquisition or not available in Italian, including Plutarch translated into French instead of Latin.

> Plutarch's works look to me the ones which should be chosen, and read continuously, if we had to choose only one book to read, especially his Lives of illustrious men; also Roman and Greek histories should be learned by heart, as they are the most important and contain important political and moral, almost Christian messages. Among the modern authors I have read, I liked a lot the Ministre d'Estat by Monsieur de Sillon, because his observations reveal an elevated and sincere mind. This author wrote in French, and you must be able to read in this language, because the Italian translation is prohibited. In order to read this book and others, like the Plutarch translation by Amyot which is better than the Latin one, it is good to learn French as well as Spanish, because there are many good books in these languages that are unavailable in Italian.[23]

This short chapter clearly states that the *studia humanitatis* must not be relinquished, but should be limited in time and space to leave room for more useful disciplines. Furthermore, the same can be said of the five-page chapter in which Spinola pays his debt to the realm of moral virtues at the end of the text, inviting the reader to look at Piccolomini and Giulio Landi for more information. It is not only a curricular question: the whole mentality postulating the superiority of the liberal arts because of their lack of direct practical aims (except for Rhetoric, whose utility is admitted from the beginning of this tradition) is entirely over, as it probably already was in the late sixteenth-century court culture, but times were not ripe for declaring this fact openly.

With the new structure proposed by Spinola, we have also the detachment from the palimpsest of almost all Renaissance educational treatises, i.e., the aforementioned Latin translation by Guarino Veronese of the pseudo-Plutarchean *De liberis educandis*, which has long opened, and still opens today, the *Moralia*. Spinola knows the text and makes indirect reference to it when he invites the reader to go to previous treatises on education, and quotes one of the best-known examples given in *De liberis*, the twin dogs educated by Lycurgus in different ways and therefore with different characters.[24] Quoting this example, Spinola both recognises the importance of a classical reference and highlights education's role in building a suitable ruling class.

However, his tribute to the tradition ends here. After the chapter on the education of children, where the reference to Plutarch is predictably contained, Spinola continues with the chapter on relatives, in which the devotion to the family, ordinarily crucial in aristocratic educational literature, is deemed suspicious and dangerous for the unity of the Republic. It is one of the main passages in the text where personal and household prosperity is considered a function and a requirement for a better collective good.

Another peculiarity of Spinola's *Instruttione* is the role of religion in the educational path. The educational tradition in Renaissance Europe had fully integrated Christianity into the system of classical virtues and conceived education mainly as the development of ability in controlling the passions and disciplining the body and instincts, hence the primacy of moral philosophy. As stated in *De liberis educandis*,

> Human intelligence found two sciences for taking care of the body: medicine and gymnastics; one protects health, the other improves the habits. However, there is only one science that heals from the pains and maladies of the soul, and this is philosophy.[25]

Especially in the difficult stages of adolescence, when heat and overflowing bodily fluids trigger irrationality and savage impulses (this tenet of Galenic medicine is recalled in *De liberis educandis* and only reinforced by the Huartian school in the late sixteenth century), moral philosophy is crucial in controlling the passions, and the Renaissance tradition adds religion as a necessary part of education. On this theme, the *Instruttione* is particularly clever in dismissing the importance of religion while celebrating it. As we have seen, devotion is the subject of the first chapter, three pages long, which is dedicated to highlighting the importance of inner devotion but, most of all, of not losing time and energy in going continuously to Mass, praying too much or doing other spiritual exercises, 'which could hinder the administration of the household':

> To this aim, you should learn the habit to dedicate every morning your action to the greater glory of God, and to scrutinise your conscience for a short time, so that you can employ your best attention and energy in manage your capital and take care of the family business: and you should also check all the members of the household and pay attention that everyone is rightly employed and not lacking resources, instead

of wasting time in attending many masses, making orations or devotional exercises, which could hinder in the administration of the household.[26]

Giovan Francesco Spinola, unlike his uncle Andrea, does not show any hostility to the educational and political power of the religious orders (the expression 'for the greater glory of God' is typically Jesuit), and the second part of the treatise would probably have contained precious statements on how to deal politically with the church authorities. Therefore, the scarce presence of religion in the *Instruttione* does not seem to have any ideological basis. Simply, religion is not considered as one of the essential tools with which a young Genoese aristocrat should be equipped, except for its role in accepting misfortune and moderating passions.

This fundamental scepticism regarding the formative role of religion is confirmed by the last (and likewise short) chapter of the *Instruttione* on moral philosophy, where religion is almost absent, and the classical system of civic virtues is only sketchily recalled. The chapter is indeed a celebration of the most political of all virtues, Prudence, seen as necessary so that the possible display of other virtues is made acceptable in the social context.

> This virtue, being the captain and the ruler of others, can be described with various names, according to the context in which it acts. If it concerns the past, it is called Experience; if the future, Providence; if the present, Discretion, but more in general Prudence, that means nothing else than the rule and measure to make perfect the use of reason.[27]

The definition of this core virtue as 'rule and measure to make perfect the use of reason' clarifies that Spinola does not conceive perfection in virtue as something spiritual, let alone supernatural. Moral virtue is a rational quality and can be perfected by cultivating prudence, i.e., experiencing society and attending courts, colleges and political institutions where knowledge of human nature can be improved and refined. The image of the Renaissance scholar, totally immersed in the study of the classics and in the almost monk-like discipline of the body (as recounted by Vittorino da Feltre's pupils), is quite far from the down-to-earth educational model proposed by the *Instruttione*. The central core of the text, with its considerations on trade, household management and real estate, has no antecedents in the pedagogical literature, and its sources must be sought in other genres. In this context, they strike the reader with their originality and the freshness of real advice, in a genre characterised by a high degree of conventional wisdom and overly repeated commonplaces.

Conclusions

With all its imperfections and somewhat rough prose, the *Instruttione* can be considered one of the most significant early modern educational treatises, especially among the highly conventional and often pedantic sixteenth century *Institutiones*. Its peculiarity lies in its attempt to re-encode Genoese tradition in the Renaissance pedagogy system, obtaining a new result in respect to both traditions.

The reasons for such an attempt could be found in the particular position of the Republic during the last decades before the French bombing and the long century of its decline. Giovan Francesco Spinola understood that a ruling class of skilled merchants could no longer govern the complexity of a large political chessboard and preserve the Republic's independence. His educational path could not be reduced to the essentials proposed by his uncle Andrea:

> As soon as they are twelve years old, without leaving aside the Latin language, they should have at home their master of abacus so that they begin soon to learn this science, without which here you cannot make any money. [...] Once they have learned and are able in accounting and book-keeping, I would advise sending them to the Piacenza fair for a couple of years to become experts in merchant society and negotiate, and can do it when necessary.[28]

For Andrea Spinola, this no-frills curriculum was the best guarantee of the conservation of Genoese culture with its peculiarities and ability to retain its identity despite being exposed to all sorts of influences. As Simona Morando has highlighted, the sixteenth century in Genoa was a time in which the princes did not protect the men of letters,[29] and intellectuals had to choose new paths instead of following the typical steps of the courtier.

Things were changing in the seventeenth century, and court culture was becoming more and more important. Giovan Francesco Spinola quotes Castiglione, Della Casa and Guazzo, giving evidence of his interest in renewing the Genoese curriculum with the best example of the courtly *institutiones*. Nevertheless, his Humanist redesigning of Genoese education did not seek to betray the republican tradition. Witnessing the sunset of the Republic, Giovan Francesco tries to give it a last opportunity to shine, reinforcing the mercantile tradition with a modicum of classical culture and a robust dose of new French and Spanish authors, including Juan Huarte's radically untraditional pedagogy.

Hence, it is not surprising that Giovan Francesco avoids the commonplace of education as moral preparation for the bad times. The fact that the Genoese noble citizens had to be rich was not new: Cebà himself stated it in his book.[30] Giovan Francesco says that the current situation of Genoa makes it more probable for the citizens to become poorer than wealthier. However, he affirms that he wants to educate to manage richness and fortune, not to withstand poverty and misfortune, because being virtuous in poverty is easier:

> Even if it is more probable, in the various fortunes typical of our city, that you become poorer than wealthier, I wanted to bring you reflections aimed to correct use of riches, more than to the toleration of adversities and to be able to react to misfortune without moral degradation. Because I agree with the author who said that it is easier to be virtuous in bad times, than to avoid corruption in good times.[31]

Therefore, the *Instruttione* proposes a pedagogy that, seeing the crisis approaching, decides to invest in preparing the young for the good management of future prosperity. In this perspective, its cautious investment in optimism appears to be a clever balance of Genoese peculiarities with the larger view required by an age of change.

1 See Quondam, '"Formare con parole"'; Vasoli, *La cultura delle corti*.

2 See Quintana Fernàndez, 'Los Orígenes de la "Tradición Espanola del Ingenio"'.

3 Bitossi, 'Due modelli di educazione repubblicana', p. 162.

4 [Spinola], *Instruttione famigliare*, Foreword [no page numbers]. 'Per ridur dunque le vostre Attioni a quelle regole, che sono effetti della prudenza Civile, e Politica, mentre siete nato in Republica, che vuol dire in Città libera, alla quale dovete rendervi atto a servire quanto sia possibile, e conferendo grandemente a questo il buon governo della propria casa, ho stimato a proposito formarvi una Instruttione, o sia Trattato che sarà diviso in due parti'.

5 [Spinola], *Instruttione famigliare*, Foreword [no page numbers]. 'Ma una mano zelante del publico Beneficio l'involò da quelle tenebre, alle quali fu egli dannato subito, che la morte chiude importunamente gli occhi a quel gran Giovanetto, a cui si era da principio destinato, quasi che il Genitore dovesse dopo la sepoltura del primo suo parto seppellire anche il secondo'.

6 Petti Balbi, 'La scuola medievale', pp. 19–20.

7 For the seventeenth-century situation of the *abaco* see Zanini, 'Abaco e aritmetica mercantile a Genova'.

8 Petti Balbi, 'La scuola medievale', p. 10.

9 [Spinola], *Instruttione famigliare*, p. 40. 'Per assicurar appresso la riuscita de' vostri figliuoli in cosa, che possa essere di giovamento a loro stessi, e di splendore alla Casa (parendo che hoggidì i trattenimenti, & impieghi delle persone nobili si riducano a tre, cioè alle Lettere, Armi, e Mercatura)'.

10 [Spinola], *Instruttione famigliare*, p. 40–41. 'Vi lodo a non applicarli ad alcuno di essi puramente per vostra volontà, ma che procurare di secondare il loro genio, la scorta del quale non potrete moralmente errare, oltre la soddisfazione, che vi rimarrà in qualunque sinistro accidente di non esservi regolato per proprio capriccio. Un Autor Spagnolo di molta dottrina nominato Iuan Vuarte nel suo Esame degli Ingegni assegna per cagione d'impedimento agli avanzamenti humani, le determinationi, che fanno i Padri nell'incaminamento de' figliuoli senza curare le loro naturali inclinationi'.

11 See Huarte, *Examen de ingenios*, and the commentary of the modern edition quoted in the References.

12 Cebà, *Il cittadino di Republica*, pp. 2–3. 'E nondimeno io veggo, che, per far il mestiero del calzolaio, o del sarto, si comincia sempre con la fatica d'una diligente institutione; e che, per maneggiar l'arte di governar la repubblica, s'antipon di raro la guida della disciplina civile […] E però stabilirono i legislatori delle città più famose, con quali dottrine s'avesse ad instituire la gioventù, perché ne fosse ben governata la republica; & i Filosofi, che sentirono più avanti un queste materie, riposero nell'institution de' giovani tutta la somma del buon reggimento politico'.

13 Morando, *La letteratura ligure*, p. 47.

14 [Spinola], *Instruttione famigliare*, p. 26. 'Oltre le spese concernenti l'uso ordinario domestico, alcune ve ne sono, l'occasione delle quali venendo di raro, si possono più tosto dire accidentali, che continue: ma non men necessarie delle prime, perché riguardano la sostanza del nostro essere morale, & il più importante delle nostre Attioni. Tali sono quelle, che s'impiegano nell'educazione de' Figliuoli, e nel dar loro incamminanti giovevoli, nel collocare in matrimonio le figliuole, nel conservare la riputazione, e nella difesa della propria vita'.

15 [Spinola], *Instruttione famigliare*, pp. 39–40. 'Vi ricordo il provederli di Persona non meno di costumi, che di lettere ornata, nell'election della quale non si deve guardar a spesa, né a qualunque altro incomodo, quando anche dovesse perciò diminuirsi il capitale delle vostre facoltà, poiché in tal caso una buona institutione di essi succederebbe degnamente in luogo di portione hereditaria'.

16 [Spinola], *Instruttione famigliare*, pp. 39–40. 'Alla difficoltà di ritrovare persona delle qualità suddette provede bastantemente l'erettione di varij Collegij, & Università nelle Città più principali d'Italia, e d'Europa sotto la disciplina di persone Religiose, e dotte, essendovi occasione di apprendere l'esercitio della pietà, e de' buoni costumi unito a quello delle Scienze. Et in tali luoghi lontani dalla Casa viene a conseguirsi quel beneficio di maggior profitto secondo il sentimento di Aristotele, che asserisce esser l'huomo, come quelle piante, che traspiantate dal nativo terreno più fecondamente producono'.

17 'Genova, lo sappiamo, stava già diventando, quando Spinola scriveva, una città dalla forte presenza gesuita. Il collegio dei gesuiti venne anzi a svolgere le funzioni di università, talché propriamente le origini dell'ateneo genovese vanno ricondotte all'ultimo quarto del Settecento, quando, secolarizzato e per così dire nazionalizzato il collegio, la repubblica pose mano, senza per altro riuscirvi, all'istituzione di uno studio statale vero e proprio. All'altezza del primo quarto del Seicento, dunque, Spinola difendeva un modello di clero e di rapporto tra clero e città decisamente pretridentino. Nessuna eco di questo atteggiamento nella Instruttione del nipote Gio. Francesco, che riflette un'adesione senza discussioni ai modelli religiosi prevalenti. Bitossi, 'Due modelli di educazione repubblicana', p. 166.

18 'Si può notare come nella prima metà del XVII secolo l'andamento dei traffici appaia relativamente stabile o in leggero rialzo, grazie soprattutto alla favorevole congiuntura granaria che evidenzia un culmine per le importazioni negli anni 1601–1639. Tuttavia, in conseguenza della peste del 1656–57 e di un'inversione di tendenza della congiuntura granaria, il trend favorevole muta e si evidenzia subito dopo una fase depressiva dei traffici che prosegue fino al 1675'. Piccinno, *Economia marittima*, p. 60.

19 [Spinola], *Instruttione famigliare*, p. 62. 'Oltre le ragioni, che si son dette per stimolo ad aumentar'il Patrimonio, vi è anche che non accrescendolo, è necessario si diminuisca, e si consumi; poiché oltre la proposition generale, che non sia alcuna cosa durevole nella mortalità: le facoltà nostre di Genova, che si riducono a rendite, & a debitori, habbiamo occasione di riconoscere giornalmente quanto ci svaniscono nelle mani, & in conseguenza, che non ritrovandosi alcun capitale che si possa sostituire all'estinto, o di brieve estinguendo, è necessario che ci riduchiamo al vuoto'.

20 'Spetterà in tutto al governo della Republica'. ([Spinola], *Instruttione famigliare*, Foreword, no page numbers).

21 The summary contains the following chapters: 'Del Timor di Dio' ('On fearing God'); 'Della liberalità verso i Poveri' ('On being charitable towards the poor'); 'Degli Esercitij scolastici e studij' ('On studies and training'). 'Delle buone Creanze, e Maniere del conversare' ('On good manners, and elegant conversation'); 'Delle compagnie, & amicizie' ('On good acquaintances and friendships'); 'Del vestire' ('On dressing appropriately'). 'Delle spese necessarie' ('On necessary expenses'); 'Delle spese superflue' ('On superfluous expenses'); 'Del Giuoco' ('On Gaming'); 'Del prender Moglie' ('On Marriage'); 'Della educazione de' Figliuoli' ('On the education of children'); 'De' Parenti' ('On Relatives'); 'Del Mantenimento, e Governo di Casa' ('On the management of the household'). 'Della supellettile di Casa' ('On domestic furniture'); 'Del Gouerno delle Facoltà' ('On the administration of patrimony); 'De' negotij di Mercatura' ('On trade'); 'Delle Rendite' ('On financial gain'); 'De' beni stabili' ('On real estate'); 'De' Feudi' ('On feudal rights'); 'Dell'esercitio delle Virtù morali' ('On moral virtues').

22 Cebà also included learning French and Spanish in *Il Cittadino di Republica* (p. 13).

23 [Spinola], *Instruttione famigliare*, p. 10. 'Le Opere di Plutarco mi paiono quelle, che quando si avesse a leggere un libro solo, si doverebbono tener continuamente tra le mani, e le Vite che ha fatte degli huomini illustri, oltre il ridur a memoria le Istorie Greche e Romane, che sono le più importanti e principali, contengono veramente sensi morali, e politici, e di pietà poco meno, che Christiana. Tra alcuni Autori moderni, che ho letti, mi è grandemente piaciuto il Ministro di Stato di Monsù di Silhon, perché le osservazioni, che fa, mi paiono di animo sollevato, e sincero. Questo Autore ha scritto in lingua Francese, nella quale dee leggersi, essendo la traduttione Italiana proibita. E per leggerlo, come anche la traduttione di Plutarco migliore della latina fatta da un Francese nominato Jacques d'Amiot, & altri che han fatto opere utilissime, vi lodo imparar la lingua, come anche la Spagnola, essendovi nell'una, e nell'altra libri di molta sostanza, che non si leggono nell'Italiana'.

24 [Spinola], *Instruttione famigliare*, pp. 38–39.

25 Plutarch [attr.], *De liberis educandis*, no page number [physical page 14]. 'Ad corporis quidem curam duplicem scientiam humana excogitavit industria: medicinam dico: atque gymnasticam: quarum alter sanitatem : altera bonam importat habitudinem.Animorum autem aegritudines atque làngores : sola est quae curet medeaturque philosophia'.

26 [Spinola], *Instruttione famigliare*, p. 2. 'Et a quest'effetto, con il buon habito procurerete di prendere per indirizzare particolarmente alla mattina tutte le vostre operationi a maggior gloria di Dio, e con l'applicazione di qualche poca parte di giorno al diligente Squitinio della vostra Coscienza, sarà più accertato che impieghiate la sollecitudine, e vigilanza in ciò che spetta alla conservatione delle facoltà, o cura de' Negotij domestici: come in contenere ogn'uno della famiglia ne' suoi esercitij, & avvertire, che non vi sia chi si assuma più del dovere, o a chi manchi il necessario, che in consumare il tempo in udire un gran numero di Messe, o fare altre Orationi, & Esercitij di divotione, i quali impediscano il sudetto governo di casa'.

27 [Spinola], *Instruttione famigliare*, p. 83. 'Questa virtù è quella, che essendo la conduttiera, e la maestra delle altre, è capace a descriversi con varie denominationi secondo le materie sopra le quali si aggira. Per lo che se riguarderà le cose passate il chiamerà Esperienza, se l'avvenire Providenza, se il presente Discretione, e più universalmente Prudenza, che altro non vuol dire che regola, e misura per ridurre a stato perfetto l'uso della ragione'.

28 Spinola, 'Dell'educatione', pp. 298–99. 'Compìti li dodici anni, non tralasciata la scuola del latino, si faccia venire a casa il mastro d'abbaco, acciò sin da putto si cominci ad imparare quella scienza, senza la quale qui non si guadagnan denari. Finito l'abbaco s'impari subito il modo di tener scrittura. […] Educati li figliuoli tra li detti essercizi, e divenuti pratichi dello far conti e tener scrittura, cominciarei a mandarli alle fere di Piacenza, continuando a farlo per un par d'anni, acciò fatti esperti di quel concorso di mercanti e di quel modo di negociare, sapessero come servirsene nelle occorrenze'.

29 Morando, 'La letteratura ligure', p. 29.

30 Cebà, *Il cittadino di Republica*, 34.

31 [Spinola], *Instruttione famigliare*, p. 88. 'E potendo più facilmente riuscire nelle varietà proprie della Città nostra, che il mediocre stato vostro si ristringa a tenuità, di chi si aumenti a ricchezze; nulladimeno io mi sia impiegato a proporvi considerationi più indirizzate all'uso delle sudette ricchezze, che alla tolleranza delle avversità, & allo schermirvi nelle percosse di contraria fortuna, per conservare l'animo illeso dalle bassezze. Per lo che dichiaro esser stato il senso mio assai conforme, a chi giudicò più facile il mantenere la pratica della virtù ne' contrasti calamitosi, che il preservarsi incorrotto tra le felicità'.

14

Emilio Pérez Blanco

NEUTRALITY IN QUESTION

Genoa, the Embassy of Spain,
and the Consequences of 1684

The historiography of relations between Spain and Genoa has received a considerable boost since the 1990s. This relationship was of such relevance and its consequences of such great weight for the economic, political and social development of the whole of the Hispanic Monarchy and Italy that the expression 'Century of the Genoese' is very accurate.[1] Fundamentally, the study of Genoese elites and their relations with the Monarchy and other agents, including cultural exchange, has attracted more attention than diplomatic relations, especially if we consider diplomacy towards the end of the seventeenth century. Many works have considered the year 1684 as a watershed for the Republic of Genoa,[2] but links with Madrid indicate continuity in the relations between Spain and the Genoese nobility like the Spinolas. They were totally inserted into the political and diplomatic system at the service of the King of Spain. Such was the case of the Marquises de Balbases, descendants of the famous general Ambrosio Spinola. Among those who stood out were the III and IV Marquis, the first as Counselor of State and ambassador of Spain in the negotiation of the Peace of Nijmegen in 1678 and the second as a soldier in the Nine Years' War and viceroy of Sicily during the War of the Spanish Succession.[3] Despite a certain distance marked by the suspension of payments of 1627 and the crisis of 1654, the truth is that Spain was able to guarantee the defence of the Republic in 1625 and 1684 and with it its much-loved freedom.

This dynamic of dependence on Spain, the competition of the maritime powers of Northern Europe and the double-edged sword drawn by Louis XIV of France with a singularly aggressive foreign and economic policy led to the apogee of navalist thought, whose origin is attested from the middle of the sixteenth century, a fundamentally neutral foreign policy but interventionist in the economic field with an ambitious programme of naval reconstruction, both military and civil, and an expansionist commercial policy.

The Nine Years' War and the economic demands that fell on the weak Royal Treasury of Carlos II of Spain had as a main consequence a worsening of relations between Spain and Genoa, since income had to be extracted from anywhere and even more from a republic of merchants whose transgressions were often ignored. Thus, the Nine Years' War constituted a real challenge as it concentrated multiple latent or old conflicts between the two states and raised new ones when Spain requested and planned the sending of convoys and squads from the United Provinces and England to the Mediterranean in order to blockade the French navy in Marseille and Toulon. Only the expertise of the ambassadors of the Spanish Monarchy and the intimate links of the Genoese elites with Madrid could prevent the situation from leading to a total division of paths within foreign policy in Europe at the end of the seventeenth century.

Repubblichisti *thought and*
the French bombardment of 1684

The Hispanic Monarchy ceased to be the greatest European power with the signing of the Peace of the Pyrenees of 1659. Since then in an increasingly multipolar Europe France managed to become the hegemonic power, taking advantage of the weakness of its great rival the Catholic Monarchy. In this context, Hispano-Genoese relations worsened considerably throughout the seventeenth century in a prolonged process that began with the suspension of payments in 1627 and extended throughout this century.[4] In the 1650s, specifically

Detail of **14.1**

Claude-Guy Hallé, *Reparations made to King Louis XIV by the Doge of Genoa in the Galerie des Glaces in Versailles, May 1685*, 1715. permission.

DOI 10.1484/M.DUNAMIS-EB.5.142043

in 1654, the tension became more evident. During this period Genoa tried to follow a new commercial and naval policy based on direct commerce with America and the East Indies. This policy was backed within the Republic by the *repubblichisti* or *navalisti* thought that had been developed since Uberto Foglietta published *Della Repubblica di Genova* in 1559. One of the axes of this work lay in the rearmament and distancing of Genoa from Spanish influence.[5] In 1650 the publication of *Il Genio Ligure Risvegliato* (fig. 2.3) helped to consolidate the *navalisti* thought. The aforementioned crisis that took place in 1654 brings together some common elements that will be repeated later during the Nine Years' War (1688–1697) and be mediated by the consequences of the bombing of the city in 1684. The crisis of 1654 took place as a result of the capture of several French ships by Finaline corsairs, vassals of the King of Spain in what Genoa considered to be its sovereign waters.[6] In the escalation of tensions that followed the incident, Genoa accelerated its rearmament plans and Spain seized the assets of the Genoese in Italy.[7] France even recognised the Genoese claim to opt for royal status, which opened the door to the full sovereignty of the Republic against the protection and subordination to the Spanish Monarchy that it had experienced until then.

Matters were just getting worse for Spain and Genoa when France, determined to maintain an independent commercial policy with the merchant republics of Europe, set out to defeat the Habsburgs of Madrid and Vienna to finally establish its hegemony in Europe. Genoa, in addition to its political and economic ties with Spain, was under Spain's protection, which meant that Genoa could not enjoy easily a full sovereignty that did not exist. It was also a key part of the Spanish defensive system in Europe, firstly because of the right of passage of Spanish troops and galley prisoners or *forzados* through Ligurian territory, and secondly because of the use of the ports of Genoa and Finale for the supply and overwintering of the King's armies and navies. Dealing a decisive blow to Genoa could seriously compromise the defence of the Spanish Monarchy and the integrity of its dominions.

In 1684, France discovered that Genoa was building four new galleys and that its government had accepted the credentials of the new ambassador Juan Carlos Bazán in February of the same year.[8] These credentials constituted a real diplomatic problem, as his predecessors Manuel Coloma and the Marquis de Villagarcía already experienced,[9] for the Republic did not accept the inclusion of the word 'protection' in the letters.

In fact, Manuel Coloma had to give up presenting the original credentials in 1678. Juan Carlos Bazán, on the other hand, managed to convince the Doge and the senators that 'no causaba perjuicio alguno a los derechos de su libertad' ('it did not cause any harm to his rights and liberty').[10] These two incidents, added to the interruption of the salt trade in Savona, were enough for France to carry out a direct armed intervention in Genoa. According to the French admiral Marquis de Seignelay's manifesto, Genoa had to destroy its four galleys, renounce the protection of the King of Spain, and commit itself to strict neutrality. The refusal to respond to the demands led to the bombing of the city for three days. The conflict culminated in the humiliating visit of the Doge of Genoa to Versailles (fig. 14.1) and the privilege granted to Louis XIV to be able to send an ambassador to the city, breaking the diplomatic monopoly that Spain had held until then. Although the Spanish Monarchy remained the official protector of Genoa and never recognised its sovereignty, Spain respected Genoa's autonomy and defended its integrity when it was in danger. 1684 is just one example, but we can find another one in 1625 when the II marquis of Santa Cruz came to Genoa's rescue, defeating an army of French and Savoyard troops.

After the bombing there appeared an anonymous account entitled *Ingenua y desnuda relación de lo sucedido en Génova en mayo de 1684* or *Naive and True Account of what happened in Genoua in May 1684*, probably printed in Milan with the help of Ambassador Juan Carlos Bazán. This account describes the origins of the conflict. During this crisis the role that the acceptance of the Spanish ambassador's credentials played in the bombing of the city was fundamental 'quando por medio del Nuevo embaxador español havian recientemente abrazado y admitido la declarada proteccion del rey católico' ('they had recently embraced and admitted the declared protection of the Catholic king').[11] In addition, the account asserted the role of Spain in Genoa as its protector and defended the subordinate role of Genoa with respect to Spain in Aristotelian terms referring to the association of the lunar and sublunar worlds where 'los dominios y principados se mantienen como los cuerpos sublunares por los mismos medios que se engendran infiriendo ser muy proporcionado que la Republica confiara la preservacion de su libertad a quien se la havia devido' ('the dominions and principalities are maintained as sublunar bodies by the same means that are engendered, inferring to be very proportionate that the Republic

14.1

Claude-Guy Hallé, *Reparations made to King Louis XIV by the Doge of Genoa in the Galerie des Glaces in Versailles, May 1685*. Versailles, Châteaux de Versailles et de Trianon, 1715. Photo: © RMN-Grand Palais (Château de Versailles) / Gérard Blot / Christian Jean. Reproduced with permission.

entrust the preservation of its liberty to the one who owed it').[12] Another interesting account that appeared in that year was an imagined dialogue between Genoa and Algiers (which suffered a French bombardment in 1683), *Dialogo fra Genova ed Algieri: città fulminate dal Giove Gallico*, attributed to Giovanni Paolo Marana and published in 1685 in Amsterdam. Here we find a humiliated Republic taking advice from an infidel city that suffered a French attack. The psychological impact was such that Genoa's policy towards France and Spain began to change course.

From 1684 Genoa committed itself to a more neutral policy with respect to Spain and France and also to a gradual disarmament, starting with the destruction of its four galleys and ending with the sale of its last galleon in 1689.[13] Again, and despite the signing of a defensive treaty with Spain in the autumn of 1684, Genoa had to yield to the Spanish intermediation in the Truce of Regensburg and to obey the terms of neutrality dictated by France. According to the instructions of the Genoese ambassador to Spain, the parallel agreement with Louis XIV had to be kept strictly in secret.

From then on, Genoa lived under constant fear of French retaliation such as the bombing or occupation of its territory by France whenever this power decided to attack Spain, a sentiment that the ambassadors of Spain knew how to recognise. From the time of the declaration of war by France against Spain in 1689 until 1697, the question of neutrality made Madrid fear a possible break with Genoa and the collapse of its defensive system in Italy.

The Spanish Monarchy and Genoa during the Nine Years' War

Despite these fears the Spanish Monarchy knew sometimes how to exert some control or show its power over Genoa. Spain forced Genoese neutrality on more than one occasion and tried to orient it towards 'benevolent neutrality' with Spain, despite the threat of the French armies in Savoy since 1690. In turn, the Genoese tried to assert their independence by appealing to its sovereignty and even by benefiting from it like other neutral countries through the commercial blockade imposed by the Allies (Spain, Great Britain, United Provinces, Savoy and the Empire) on France.[14] All in all, Genoa started this policy before war started. In 1686 Genoa denied Spain entry into the city of prisoners for the galleys of Spain, allowing it only in San Pedro de Arenas and not within the city as had been allowed until 1685. Genoa also refused to allow the mooring of navy ships except galleys, based on a precedent of 1683 that Manuel Coloma had to manage to secure together with Admiral Count of Aguilar. In that year, nevertheless, the dock for the galleys of the Duke of Tursi, of Genoese origin, continued to function at the service of the King of Spain.

However, in September 1692, Pedro Corbete's navy arrived at the port, an event to which, apparently, the Genoese government did not react at first. Corbete announced that he would enter the dock with the *Capitana* ship and four other ships that needed repair and supplies. The Republic accepted, but to its surprise, Corbete entered with the entire navy (16 ships). The protests of the Republic were such that the Marquis of Leganés had to go in person from Milan. The manoeuver coincided at a crucial moment with the expected arrival of the Anglo-Dutch navy in the Mediterranean to join that of Spain, and with the request of a dock for the galleys of France by this country and the conflict over the winter quarters. Spain asserted through this show of force its superiority at a difficult time during the war. On the other hand, although Genoa maintained the right of passage of Spanish troops through its territory, it did not grant said right some years. Although it was renewed in 1691, the next year Genoa changed its mind, interrupting until 1692 any type of movement towards the State of Milan. Again the question of winter quarters was behind this decision, and it is precisely this question that placed Genoese neutrality between a rock and a hard place during the Nine Years' War. For its part, Spain stopped using Genoa's dock, finding a substitute in Gaeta, in the Kingdom of Naples. In this way Spain avoided diplomatic *affairs* between Genoa and France. There were more ports like the *Presidios* of Tuscany, which defended the Tuscan Coast and the sea route to Naples and Sicily.

The question of the imperial quarters began at the end of 1691. The allies wanted to make Italy one of the main theatres of war and to achieve this Emperor Leopold I, at the request of Spain,[15] assigned large contingents of troops to Milan. Due to the lack of means to pay for the quarters of imperial troops in winter, Spain and the Empire agreed to charge the maintenance to the Italian states linked to the Holy Empire and the imperial fiefdoms of northern Italy; many of them belonged to the Genoese nobility. The payment of 92,000 escudos

fell on these families, but was soon refused by the Republic, encouraged this time by France, which tried to carry out a policy of threat and rapprochement towards Genoa. This policy consisted of threatening to declare war and bomb the city should the payment of the quarters exceed 30,000 escudos, at which time France would consider Genoese neutrality broken. In case of war with the Empire and Spain, France would offer all its support to Genoa.

To make matters worse, France tried to present itself, in the event of the outbreak of war with the Empire, as the protector of Genoa's liberty, thus replacing Spain. Thanks to the management of Juan Carlos Bazán and the Governor of Milan, Marquis de Leganés, it was agreed that the assets of the nobles in Milan, Naples and Sicily would be seized to pay the remaining 62,000 escudos. The so-called new nobility of Genoa had to assume this payment, which worried Juan Carlos Bazán, who in his final account as ambassador in 1693 would come to advise against the embargo method due to the damage it could do to the Spanish party, taking into account that some of the new nobility were considered to be pro-French and had their own French party.[16]

In 1695 a new ambassador to Genoa, Juan Antonio Albizu, was selected by the State Council as Francisco Moles's successor. The instructions that were given to him reveal the point of view that predominated in Spain regarding Genoese matters. These instructions reminded the new ambassador about the credentials experience in 1678 and 1684 and how the Republic valued its autonomy. In this document the State Council advised the new ambassador that he had to remind the doge that the Spanish Monarchy had always defended Genoa's interests and liberty. Moreover, the ambassador was ordered to remind the Genoese that the Republic would continue to enjoy the military protection of Spain in the same way as in 1684 even though Genoa did not fulfil its obligations as an ally after that event. The Spanish Monarchy was now fully concerned about the neutrality policy followed by Genoa and 'su contemplacion de aquel Rey [Louis XIV]' ('its contemplation of that King').[17] In order to respect the decision taken by Genoa of remaining neutral but on behalf of Spain, Juan Antonio Albizu had to maintain the links made with some notorious members of the Genoese aristocracy such as the Prince Doria and his house and, of course, the Duke of Tursi. The instruction stated 'Procurareis que la Republica vea en todas vuestas accionesla proteccion en que la tengo como lo ha manifestado la experiencia' ('You will ensure that the Republic sees in all our actions the protection in which I have it, as experience has shown')[18]. This protection would assure their 'liberty' and the Governor of Milan would help in case of need with the Lombardy Army.[19] In fact, Spain made some offers of alliance to Genoa during the war, but all of them were refused because of the alleged military weakness of the Spanish Monarchy.

Although Spain was not able to mobilise the same forces as in the times of Philip IV, that did not mean that it had lost its might. State Counsellors were very aware of this and explained to Albizu that although Genoa was making excuses on this point, he should always try to convince the Genoese that the Republic maintained a huge army in Milan and Piedmont and that the King's Navy and those of England and the United Provinces were in the Mediterranean 'aplicadas a la preservacion y defensa universal de todos los dominios de Italia' ('applied to the preservation and universal defence of all the dominions of Italy').[20] Here, Spain was just assuming the classic role of preserving the freedom of the whole of Italy, which was so appreciated by the small Italian states, threatened by France and an Empire with renewed forces.[21]

There was also the issue of commerce. As we have seen, commerce caused some of the most important problems in Spanish-Genoese relations whether it was related to corsairs, blockades or selling some products, and Genoa depended on it to survive. Spain knew that some Genoese merchants had arrangements with France and managed to gather many proofs. Most of this illegal commerce under the Blockade Agreement signed by Spain,[22] England and the United Provinces was localised in Cadiz, where many people were expecting the arrival of the galleons from the West Indies full of silver and gold. At the beginning of the war, in 1689 Spain counted 5 merchant ships under the Genoese flag, but in 1692–1695 this number had grown to 80. Genoa had benefited from neutrality, that was clear, and that increase in shipments was justified as one of the results of being neutral, but according to the Spanish Monarchy most of its commerce in the Mediterranean, not only in the Atlantic, benefited France indirectly for French merchants in neutral ports took advantage of neutrality to make profits. In the year 1691 the Spanish Monarchy put into practice a system of records and permits by which any ship that entered any port of the Hispanic Monarchy had to present the papers and records of the cargo it brought and be

visited and recognised by an official. Such a procedure had to be carried out also at the time of leaving the port. This practice had some success and soon attracted Genoese complaints, but given the circumstances that did not worry Madrid. The ambassadors to Genoa thought that it was more dangerous. There is no doubt that the blockade imposed by Spain and its allies had some effect in spite of its many faults and gaps, and the many letters written by Juan Carlos Bazán regarding the situation of Provence show that this French region was suffering from economic stagnation due to the blockade and the scorched-earth strategy applied by Duke Victor Amadeus II of Savoy and the allied army in 1692.[23]

What role did Genoa's politics play? The question of the old and new nobility as determining elements for the future of the neutrality of Genoa was already taken into account by the Spanish embassy. Moreover, it was linked to the world of the *repubblichisti*. Although the existence of a French party was suspected during the first years of the war, there was little proof, but at least the Durazzo family could be considered a member,[24] according to the Spanish embassy. In his account of 1693, Juan Carlos Bazán seems to contradict himself for he disavowed the rumours during the problems caused by the winter quarters that spoke of an inevitable inclination towards France on the part of the Genoese rulers, also motivated by the well-known cases of smuggling with France.[25] In reality they would be fully committed to neutrality, wrote Bazán. Genoese elites were just scared of being dragged into war by France or the Empire. Despite these misconceptions Bazán's, diagnosis was correct: Genoa feared a repetition of 1684, hence its apparently anti-Spanish attitude and the rejection of the allies was linked, according to his successor Francisco Moles, to the fact that the Anglo-Dutch army could end the trade with which the Genoese had prospered thanks to its neutrality maintained during the war. In one of his first letters as ambassador, Moles wrote that he found Genoa's inhabitants 'y de haver hallado en estos naturales una emocion de animo, dos son las causas el efecto referido: la una es por lo del sal del Final y esta despues de los sequestros de bienes' ('troubled over two causes that made this effect: the first one is due to the salt of Finale and later the embargo of property'). The second concern was the presence since 1694 of the Anglo-Dutch navy in the Mediterranean Sea.[26] The embassy knew of some rumours spread by French agents, or that was what the Spanish thought in 1693–1694.

Most of them talked about the malicious intentions of the British and Dutch ships, which were trying to exert new control over Mediterranean commerce and replace the Republic as a competitor. In any case, this fear did not cause more trouble. Some of the Spanish ambassadors thought that a French party was forming among those Genoese unsatisfied with Spain's most recent policies in Italy.[27]

The truth is that the Spanish embassy may have made a mistake when it came to assessing the Genoese nobility, since it recognised later the existence of a large third party called 'neutral', more inclined to Spain than to France, mentioning the navalists but without considering them a real threat around 1693. This is how Juan Carlos Bazán concluded his account, highlighting the intimate but fragile relationship between Spain and Genoa and underlining the role of Spain as protector of Genoa's freedom. In any case, as Juan Carlos Bazán stated, the offences committed by the Republic (mainly smuggling) should be understood not as malice or ties to France but as a sinful characteristic of a mercantile republic. The best strategy was to attract the neutral countries to commerce with Spain and observe carefully those families or individuals that could have ties with France or be more inclined to that nation. The same Durazzo family in spite of its past French ties, 'have some affectionate subjects to Your Majesty's Royal Service'.[28]

Conclusion

Despite Genoa's attempts to remain neutral, Spain's bond was still important enough not to be ignored. The evidence of asserting its independence navigated precisely in that direction, but always with a certain permissiveness on the part of Spain that, as we have seen, could make effective demonstrations of force to assert its primacy and condition many decisions taken in Genoa with a large amount of resources and guarantees that France could not provide. In any case, Genoa's policy of neutrality emerged from fear of a repetition of the bombing of 1684, which was still an even greater repetition of the one that took place in 1679 as a result of a conflict over salutes between Genoese and French ships. From the end of the Nine Years' War, Genoa still remained under the protective mantle of the Spanish Crown until the end of the War of the Spanish Succession. In any case, the question of sovereignty continued to be a subject of discussion in the modern age. The case of Genoa raises interesting questions when it is transferred to Spain itself, since in this same period the partition treaties of the Spanish Monarchy took place in 1698 and 1700 between France, England and the United Provinces, which paradoxically represented a violation of the sovereignty of the Crown of Spain. There is no doubt that in the society of the ancien régime, social schemes were also transferred to the treatment of nations in multiple ways and that republics occupied an inferior space compared to other political entities such as kingdoms.

This entailed numerous problems in the treatment of nations, including those concerning the figure of the ambassador, his credentials or greetings between ships. Genoa's sovereignty was constrained by the 1528 agreement, although that did not mean an end to its autonomy. In any case Genoa considered that Spain was preferable to France; the experience before Andre Doria's agreement with Spain in 1528 was a warning. Threats from France and the fact that the Ligurian territory was also linked to the Holy Roman Empire, like other Italian states, made things more complex. Thus we are faced with a world of political entities superimposed in theory and that, in practice, often play with state sovereignties. Spain, Austria and Poland experienced partition throughout the eighteenth century. Genoa suffered the loss of Corsica in 1768 and the French occupation of 1797 that saw the definitive end of this maritime Republic.

1 Sanz, *Los banqueros de Carlos* II. On the issue of cultural exchange Tagliaferro, *Rubens e Genova* and Boccardo, Colomer and Di Fabio, eds, *España y Génova*. Herrero Sánchez, *El acercamiento hispano-neerlandés*. This work contains some interesting and insightful findings on the change of orientation of the foreign policy of Spain and the United Provinces as well as the consequences it had for Genoa and the Mediterranean.

2 Bitossi, 1684. Kirk, *Genoa and the Sea*, this is an interesting work that is focused on navalisti thought and the commercial policy pursued by the Republic based on it until 1684 but it does not continue the study up to the end of the seventeenth century.

3 Álvarez-Ossorio and Herrero Sánchez, 'La aristocracia genovesa'. Álvarez-Ossorio, '¿El final de la Sicilia española?'.

4 Herrero Sánchez, 'La quiebra del Sistema hispano-genovés'.

5 Kirk, *Genoa and the Sea*, p. 121.

6 Kirk, 'La crisi del 1654'.

7 AGS, Estado, leg. 3607, doc. 52.

8 AGS, Estado, leg. 3620, doc. 149.

9 AGS, Estado, leg. 3636, doc. 250. García Pérez, 'Las embajadas italianas', p. 91.

10 AGS, Estado, leg. 3636, doc. 209.

11 BSB, Ital. 358, p. 6 (*Ingenua y desnuda relacion de lo sucedido en Genova en mayo de 1684*).

12 BSB, Ital. 358, p. 9.

13 Kirk, *Genoa and the Sea*, p. 120.

14 Genoa wanted to share the same benefits from neutrality enjoyed by other powers such as Sweden, Denmark or Portugal. The Allies imposed extreme measures in order to isolate France from certain revenues provided by commerce. AGS, Estado, leg. 3625, doc. 109.

15 Wilson, *The Holy Roman Empire*, p. 224. Other studies more precise and accurate see: Signorotto, ed., *L'Italia degli Austrias*; Cremonini, 'I feudi imperiali italiani' and Cremonini and Musso, eds, *I feudi imperiali in Italia*.

16 AGS, Estado, leg. 3633, doc. 203.

17 AGS, Estado, leg. 3636, doc. 212.

18 AGS, Estado, leg. 3636, doc. 212.

19 AGS, Estado, leg. 3636, doc. 212.

20 AGS, Estado, leg. 3636, doc. 212.

21 Bérenger, *Léopold (1640–1705)*, p. 384.

22 Despite all their efforts both Spain and England were unable to control the smuggling of French products in their respective countries. Ogg, *England in the reigns of James* II *and William* III, p. 300. But it is true that these embargoes and blockades were useful and in fact, Spain had been practising them throughout the seventeenth century with some success, according to Jonathan Israel. Israel, *Empires and Entrepots*, p. 129–30.

23 Symcox, *Victor Amadeus* II, p. 111. Symcox states that this campaign did not achieve anything, but Provence received a hard hit and Louis XIV's navy could not set sail. Moreover, France's fleet was defeated in La Hogue the same year. There is also a printed account which narrates this campaign: Anónimo, *Progressos maravillosos de las armas colligadas en el Piamonte*.

24 AGS, Estado, leg. 3633, doc. 203.

25 AGS, Estado, leg. 3643, 138. This document denounces the activities of English, Dutch and Genoese merchants in the ports of the Republic because many of them were related to smuggling.

26 AGS, Estado, leg. 3627, doc. 130.

27 AGS, Estado, leg. 3633, doc. 203.

28 AGS, Estado, leg. 3633, doc. 203. The Genoese ambassador to Spain wrote 'Lo stato odierno della Monarchia è così debole e fiacco, che se l'abuso della sua potenza ne' tempi prosperi non l'avesse resa altrettanto odiosa a principi quanto temuta, meriterebbe con ragione le affetuose dimostrazioni di un giusto e sincero compatimento' and, later in his memorial, he recommended not breaking ties with Spain as this would be terrible for the survival of Genoa, 'Connessione di interessi, vicinanza di Stati, rendite, feudi, traffico non altronde sperabile, o non così generale, che ne' regin del re Catolico, sono vincoli tanto tenaci, che altro non vale a scioglierli che l'imprudenza'. Ciasca, ed., *Istruzioni e relazioni*, p. 50.

15

Michael Paul Martoccio

TOURING 'THE PERU OF ITALY'

The Bank of Saint George and the Endurance of the Genoese Republic in the English, French, and German Press, 1684–1797

An unusual, telling account of greed, murder, penance, and redemption set in Genoa in the late eighteenth century can be found in a series of letters written by the British poet, travel writer and salon hostess, Anna Riggs, Lady Miller.[1] Stopping for a time in Genoa on her grand tour through Italy in the 1770s, Lady Miller recounted how one day she was strolling by the Basilica della Santissima Annunziata del Vastato to marvel at the 'profusion of marble, the lustre of which dazzles the sight' only to encounter on the steps of the immaculately white cathedral 'a very old man, poorly dressed, who licked [the steps] with his tongue' in the shape of crosses 'from one end to the other […] this he repeated every day at the same hour'. Curious to know why this man persevered in 'so singular and disgusting a penance', she approached the unusual penitent who proceeded to wow the noblewoman with his tale of woe. The old man had been a trained assassin in his youth responsible for at least a dozen murders, murder being, according to Lady Miller, 'no uncommon plan at Genoa; un *colpo di coltello* is seen in much the same light here, as the bruises' acquired by boxers back in England. Inquiring a bit more, the strange penitent, whom Lady Miller referred to as her *cicerone*, or local guide, recalled how, in a sad twist of fate, his son had himself fallen afoul of an assassin on the steps of that very same church only for the murderer, a local barber, to have escaped 'on board an English or Dutch ship for a short time; after which he reappeared and continued his business.[2] Unable to enact *vendetta* on his son's killer and with time finally catching up to him, the elderly *cicerone* had finally sought out a confessor 'who recommended to him the above humiliation of licking, with some scores of *Aves* and *Paters*'.

The story of Lady Miller's rather unusual *cicerone* captures the core theme of this essay: contemporary Northern European views of Genoa in the final century of the Republic's independence, from the French bombardment of 1684 to the collapse of the old aristocratic Republic in 1797. It argues that travellers to Genoa and news accounts originating from the city in the late seventeenth and eighteenth centuries reported two visions of the Republic at this time. On the one hand, many visitors and reporters envisioned the Republic in steep decline – a Genoa of murder, lawlessness, decadence, and superstition, full of *ciceroni* like the old man Lady Miller met. Indeed, until very recently, scholarship on Enlightenment Italy largely echoed Lady Miller's reports, with the Mediterranean's terminal decline generally and Genoa's specifically a subject of great interest.[3] Yet consider again the step-licking *cicerone's* story, especially the moment when his son's assassin hopped aboard the English or Dutch ship to evade capture. Read against the grain, another side to foreign accounts of Genoa in its last decades emerge, one of an internationalising city, of a city full of Dutch, English, Spanish, French, Danish, Swedish, German, Turkish, and Swiss merchants, travellers, soldiers, generals, spies, slaves, diplomats, financers, and transporters utilising Genoa as a centre for international commerce. If once the French bombardment of 1684 and Doge Giovan Francesco Imperiale-Lercari's subsequent painful, symbolic act the next year of travelling to Versailles in person could be seen as a sort of premature end to the Genoese Republic, and the remaining century a mere denouement, such a tidy narrative of decline seems less clear today. Rather than ending the Republic, a number of recent studies have shown how the French bombardment and subsequent demand that the Genoese maintain a form of 'rigorous neutrality' had the unexpected advantage of flooding the city with all manner of commercial activity: capital investments through private lenders and the public Bank of Saint George, orders for silks and velvet from the city's manufactures, and transshipping and storage in the newly-retrofitted Portofranco (free port) warehouses.[4] Beyond peacetime commerce, the city also leveraged

DOI 10.1484/M.DUNAMIS-EB.5.142044

15.1

Giovanni Lorenzo Guidotti after Giuseppe Torricelli, *View of the Banchi's square*. Engraving from *Description des beautés de Génes et de ses environs : ornée de differentes vuës, et de la carte topographique de la ville*, Génes, Chez Yves Gravier, 1773. Photo: Wikimedia Commons. Public Domain.

its neutrality to fund, supply, house, feed, clothe, and care for soldiers and sailors during the conflicts that battered Europe in these years: the Nine Years' War (1688–1697), the War of the Spanish Succession (1701–1714), the Second Morean War (1714–1718), the War of the Quadruple Alliance (1718–1720), the War of the Polish Succession (1733–1735), the War of Austrian Succession (1740–1748), and the Seven Years' War (1756–1763).[5] By examining two types of sources – travellers' accounts and political pamphlets – this essay aims to show how foreign visitors accounted for such new inflows of peacetime and wartime business into Genoa and, in doing so, assess more generally the continued vitality of the city and its Republic in its final century of independence.

Visions of Genoa in the literature of the Grand Tour (1684–1797)

With the significant increase in European tourism following the end of the Thirty Years' War, Genoa, with its richly decorated palaces of the Strada Nuova and Strada Balbi, had become a vital stop for Northern Europeans on the Grand Tour as one of the first Italian ports-of-call.[6] Foreign travellers to Genoa in its long eighteenth century followed well-scripted itineraries that circulated around Europe at the time. 'There are so many Descriptions of *Genoa* in our Language, that I shall take up the Reader's Time with those Things only that have been left unobserv'd by others', the British writer

John Durant Breval noted during his visit to the city in 1726, before, of course, going on to list all the places one would imagine a foreign visitor would comment on: the city's narrow streets, its *palazzi*, its civic monuments (fig. 15.1).[7] A telling list of typical topics for such sojourners appears as well in the Prussian officer and publicist Johann Wilhelm von Archenholz's 1786 *England und Italien* ('England and Italy'):

> Genoa: Government. Character of the Genoese. State oeconomy. Commerce. Capital funds. Parallel between Genoa and Hamburgh. Private Oeconomy. Parsimony. Sciences and arts. Works of Architecture. Ladies. Language. Gross ignorance. Acts of devotion. Brotherhoods. Solemnity with St Johns ashes. Constitution. Nobility. Genoa emancipated by the people in 1746. Army and navy. Harbour. Self-selling galley slaves. Commercial concerns of the Genoese nobles. Clifford. Bank of Genoa. Commerce oppressed. St Remo. Noli. Assemblies. Cicisbeat.[8]

Beyond offering a pre-set selection of art works, sights, and stereotypes, such itineraries structured as well what foreign visitors thought they would see during their trip. Following her visit to the Darsena, the city's ship arsenal, to examine the city's famed galley slaves, Lady Miller noted how 'upon the whole […] the idea I had acquired in England of the wretched situation of a galley-slave, was exaggerated, perhaps by my own imagination's forming a picture much too strong from what I had read or heard'.[9]

Like Lady Miller, many came expecting to see a city in steep decline, a narrative captured perhaps most starkly in descriptions of the republican seat of government, the Palazzo Ducale. The account of Johann Georg Keyßler, the German polymath, archaeologist, and Fellow of the Royal Society, can prove representative of such views. 'The doge resides in a palace belonging to the Republic, with his family and eight senators appointed for his council […] it is an old mean building', Keyßler wrote.[10] Beyond the official seat of government, travellers further commented on the nature of the Genoese Republic while visiting the city's many private Palazzi.

For many visitors undertaking the grand tour, the marvels of the Palazzi of the Strada Nuova and Strada Balbi not only formed an essential part of their accounts but offered them an opportunity to muse on the nature of the city's aristocracy, in particular Genoa's relationship with neighbouring powers. Commenting on the aristocracy's seeming poverty, the British Army captain and writer John Nothrall noted in his posthumous *Travels through Italy* how many of their subjects were in fact 'very rich, and have large estates in other dominions, particularly Naples and Spain; which is attended with great inconveniences, as throwing them into interests inconsistent with those of their own country',

while Anna Miller noted during her visit how the aristocracy's famed frugality explained the Republic's survival after 1684.[11]

> Weak in themselves, and unwarlike, they cannot resist any one power; but their safety has hitherto depended, and must always depend upon the interest others have, in their continuing a free state […] Besides, what bribe can Spain, Naples or even France offer to the Genoese nobility as an equivalent for their liberty? Can they, out of their own houses, see anything desirable in the palaces of Kings?[12]

As Miller's account suggests, travellers to Genoa in the eighteenth century bore witness to the Republic's system of government not only in formal spaces, but also informal, private ones. Visitors in particular assessed the health of the Republic on the city's narrow streets. Returning again to the well-received travelogue of Johann Georg Keyßler, the German traveller described the city's narrow streets as conveying a deep foreignness, likening the city to an Eastern metropolis with all the fears of oriental despotism attached to it.

> The want of coaches and other carriages conduces not a little to the cleanliness of the streets; besides the barrenness of the neighbouring soil requiring great quantities of manure, the dung of horses and mules is very carefully gathered up, what some oriental travelers inform us, that the Arabs do out of superstition with regard to those camels which have been in the Mecca Caravans, the poor people here do from necessity, carefully picking up all the horse and mule dung they meet with.[13]

Lady Anne Miller, perhaps with Keyßler's account in mind, took this analogy one step further, tying the cleanliness of the streets with Genoa's commercial success.

> How should a small strip of country, in itself wretched and barren, with but indifferent harbours, and a bigoted fanatical people, find, in their own miserable territory, those resources of wealth and prosperity, so visible in every quarter of this great city, did they not *manure this farm* with the produce of others.[14]

Northern European visitors to Genoa in the eighteenth century would appear to have cast a fairly dark image of the Republic as decadent and declining, even tipping towards oriental tyranny. But travellers also took note of the Republic's changing character following the 1684 French bombardment: the Republic's commitment to neutrality and its opening up to English, Dutch, French, and Austrian interests in the coming decades. Many commented for example on the influx of foreigners receiving care in the city's chief medical facility – L'Ospedale di Pammatone. 'The large hospital is another important establishment, where is received all the sick indifferently of whatever nation they may be,' reported the astronomer and writer Joseph Jérôme Lalande during his 1769 visit, a view shared by the British botanist Thomas Martyn, who added two decades later how the Ospedale 'receives the sick of all nations and religions.[15] 'The great Hospital is a glorious establishment for the Sick of all Nations, and likewise for Foundlings,' noted the British poet Mariana Starke, a distinction that marked off L'Ospedale di Pammatone from other civic or charitable institutions in the city. 'There is another Hospital of a smaller size, which receives the Sick of the Genoese nation only.[16] In addition to such plaudits, however, many travellers used their trip to L'Ospedale di Pammatone as an opportune moment to feed into decadent and violent stereotypes about the Genoese. 'Dr. Batt shewed us the great hospital, one of the largest and most superb in Europe. It is open to the sick of all nations and religions, and contains from 1200 to 2000 patients', applauded the botanist and founder of the Linnean Society John Edward Smith before adding darkly how 'about 700 women and 1200 men are admitted in the course of the year for wounds with knives or stilettos; a dreadful fact, almost sufficient to brand the national character with the general detestation of mankind'.[17] Travelling to Genoa three years later, the Anglican priest John Owen also merged the celebratory with the sadistic:

> [L'Ospedale di Pammatone] is an institution, which, in point of liberality, has no rival in Europe. Designed as a receptacle for distressed humanity, it receives under its protection the sick and maimed of every complexion, country, and religion. 'La sala de Feriti', or *Ward of the Stabbed*, was a sight which I knew not how to contemplate. This apartment was of considerable length; four ranks of beds, filled for the most part with miserable victims of assassination, variously wounded, and in different stages of suffering, was a spectacle full of horror.[18]

Popular, too, among visitors was Genoa's Porto Franco or *freeport*, the tightly regulated complex of bonded-free warehouses near the Molo Vecchio ('Old Pier') which the government had renovated in the wake of the French bombardment and opened up increasingly to foreign ownership.[19] 'The *franc* port, at Genoa, deserves to be noticed, as a commodious depositary and well-regulated office for […] customs', wrote Robert Gray, future Bishop of Bristol.[20] The warehouses possessed 'goods of every kind, lying by each other; heaps of verdigrease, and casks of sugar; marble and coffee; woods and linens; the productions of Asia, and the produce of the north. It is a scene of motion, activity, and affluence not to be imagined', noted Charles Dupaty, the enlightened *philosophe* who travelled in Italy in 1785.[21] Foreign goods kept in the Portofranco, sometimes for decades, could be particularly useful in times of war, something travelers and diplomats who visited the city during the War of the Spanish

Succession noted, for instance. '[Genoa] is the *place d'armes* for the French armies in Italy', sneered an English diplomat; 'their recruits, their armies, their ammunition, their money, their provisions, &c., are all landed at Genoa'.[22]

A further Genoese institution that attracted the attention of Northern European visitors was the Bank of Saint George. There was, of course, nothing novel about foreign writers commenting on the bank. A long literary-historical tradition dating back to Niccolò Machiavelli's 1526 *Istorie fiorentine* centred on the bank as an essential part of Genoa's republican constitution, and many Northern European visitors to Genoa in its long eighteenth century envisioned the Bank of Saint George in such terms.[23] The British poet and essayist Joseph Addison's description of the bank during a visit to the city in 1701 can provide a paradigmatic example. According to Addison, San Giorgio was a 'remarkable' part of the government of Genoa whose administrators took their offices 'for life', drew its funds 'partly in the hands of the chief citizens,' and exerted 'a powerful influence over the common people' acting as 'a second kind of senate':

> It distributes the power among more particular members of the republic, and gives the commons a figure: so that it is no small check upon the aristocracy, and may be one reason why the Genoese senate carries it with greater moderation towards their subjects than the Venetian.[24]

In much the same way, the Frenchmen Joseph Lalande likened the constitutional place of the bank to a chapel inside a larger cathedral. 'The Bank of St George forms a Republic of rich people and the great Council a Republic of politicians and Nobles'.[25] Yet increasingly Northern European travellers took note of the bank's international acclaim as a depository for foreign capital and a lender to foreign governments from the Habsburg dynasty to France to the Scandinavian countries to Russia.[26] Interested in finding some men of letters during a visit to Genoa in 1739, the French writer Charles de Brosses complained how he could not find any in Genoa due to the city's banking sector attracting so much capital:

> We wanted to look for men of letters: [there are] none. This is not the country, the merchants do not amuse themselves with trifles, and only know of the letters of the bills of exchange, of which they make the greatest trade of in the universe; and for that they have a public bank fund containing, they say, 300 million silver in effective cash.[27]

Brosses's countryman Charles Dupaty also marvelled at the international esteem of the bank. 'Here is kept shut up and secured under a hundred keys, the solution of that great and terrible enigma, whether the bank really possesses, or owes millions. This enigma constitutes the safety of the state, and in part, its riches'.[28] 'Its capital is immense, its credit universal, and the security as firm as the defenceless condition of Genoa will admit', echoed the Welsh churchman Thomas Watkins.[29] 'This decayed city […] is eminent for having some of the richest bankers in all Europe, and its profitable dealings in exchange', contributed Adam Anderson in his own travelogue in a passage that reminds us of how easily the imagery of decay could slip into such accounts.[30] Indeed, the image of the Bank of Saint George as both financially thriving and economically throttling is captured best in the work of the Prussian Johann Wilhelm von Archenholz.[31]

> People are accustomed to look upon Genoa as the Peru of Italy. The capital sums which this city has lent to kings, princes and towns, and still does lend, seem to confirm the idea of an inexhaustible treasure. The total decay of the trade of Genoa obliged the Genoese to lend out their capital funds by change. There are no warehouses, as in other commercial cities, stocked with the productions of different countries, and the trade of Genoa is entirely in money concerns. Money, however, being no wealth with respect to state-oeconomy, but only a token of wealth, ought to be looked upon here as a common article; for should it come to fail, the trade of the Genoese must cease forever, the country being quite destitute of natural productions.

As if needing to better make his point, Archenholz went on to compare Genoa to Hamburg, itself a major centre for foreign commercial and military loans, such comparisons being 'sometimes necessary to ascertain the proportion of one state, with respect to another'. According to Archenholtz, Genoese foreign loans 'amounted in June of 1780 to forty-five millions of rix-dollars', an amount that 'would not have been sufficient to maintain only for six months the English forces during the late American war'. Archenholtz's comments are a stark reminder that, even when seen in a positive light, Genoa's international position remained shaky at best, the Republic's neutrality always predicated on its perceived utility to other powers. Hester Lynch Piozzi – the Welsh-born diarist, author, art patron, and confidant of Samuel Johnson – provides just such a vision of the city. Approaching Genoa overland, she found soothing the sounds of the sea:

> Genoa la Superba stands proudly on the margin of a gulph crowded with ships, and resounding with voices, which never fail to animate a British hearer – the sailor's shout, the mariner's call, swelled by successful commerce, or strengthened by newly-acquired fame.[32]

Through the sea, Piozzi linked the Genoese to the British.

> One should not however speak unkindly of a people whose affectionate regard for our country shewed itself so clearly

during the late war: a few days residence with the English consul here at his country seat gave me an opportunity of hearing many instances of the Republic's generous attachment to Great Britain, whose triumphs at Gibraltar over the united forces of France and Spain were honestly enjoyed by the friendly Genoese, who gave many proofs of their sincerity, more solid than those clamorous ones of huzzaing our minister about wherever he went, and crying *Viva il General* Elliott; while many young gentlemen of high fashion offered themselves to go volunteers aboard our fleet, and were with difficulty restrained.[33]

In much the same way, the controversial literary critic, writer, poet, and linguist Giuseppe Marc'Antonio Baretti (known in England as 'Joseph Baretti') defended the Republic's neutrality in his own *Account of the manners and customs of Italy* (1768). Against 'a very large number of those despicable wretches who go in [Britain] under the appellation of the Grub-street writers' who belaboured the Genoese for being 'very wicked as to permit their artificers to build ships of war, and sell them to the French and Spanish', Baretti shot back that

> is it not a little surprising to hear the Genoese so often abused for doing what they have an indisputable right to do? Shipbuilding is a manufacture at Genoa […] and what foreign nation has any right to hinder the manufacturers […] from selling the products of their labour and ingenuity? When powder and ball are sold to the pirates of Algiers and Tunis, one would think that ships might also be sold to Spaniards and French without any danger of censure.[34]

It is to some of these very same Grub Street writers that we now proceed.

Genoa in the grub street press (1745–1748)

Turning away from travel accounts, the image of Genoa as an international military and commercial centre can be appreciated more fully by looking closely at a series of pro-Genoese political pamphlets produced in London during the War of the Austrian Succession (1740–48).[35] Fearful any change in Genoese neutrality could upset trade patterns in the broader Mediterranean, the British political class took a keen interest in the Republic's stance in the war, especially after 1745 when the Genoese shifted from neutral to openly hostile towards Britain and its allies, Austria and Sardinia, following news that the Austrian Empress Maria Theresa had promised the Genoese-controlled port of Finale to Savoy-Sardinia via the Treaty of Worms (1743). Thus, for the remainder of the war British eyes remained fixed on Genoa as the city first fell to Austrian troops in September 1746, subsequently revolted against the harsh Austrian rule three months later, and further resisted a second siege early the next year with the help of Spanish and French reinforcements.[36]

British political pamphlets bearing titles like *A Letter from a Genoese gentleman to a member of Parliament of Great-Britain, relating to that part of the treaty of Worms* (1744), *A Compleat and Authentick Account of the Late Revolution in Genoa* (1747), and *Seasonable Reflections on the Late Convention between the Courts of Vienna and Turin* (1747) served as vital propaganda tools, working to persuade parliamentary politicians to reconsider the British alliance with Savoy-Sardinia and Austria as well as to preserve Genoese independence and territorial integrity. As with many political pamphlets of the time, nearly all of these works were meant for quick reading, their authors using various anonymous pseudonyms: an English merchant residing in Livorno, a Genoese gentleman, or a member of parliament. While their authors (or, perhaps given their similar tone and topic, author) remain a mystery, we can know a bit about these works as many of the pamphlets shared a common publisher, the London-based Mary Cooper, who had inherited her husband Thomas's business at Paternoster Row in 1743 and remained active into the 1760s.[37] As a trade publisher, Cooper published for those who held the copyright, a practice done partly in order to conceal their identity, and her publications included works varying from early printed children's literature to controversial Enlightenment religious pamphlets to erotica to political pamphlets, the latter of which she brought to market during the Seven Years' War until her death in 1761.[38] These texts speak then less to the truth of the explosive events in Genoa in 1746–1747 and much more to the underlying assumptions the British political class held about Genoa and the Genoese at this delicate time.

As such, Genoa's role as a neutral military redistributive centre formed an essential part of British reports of the war. No work captured this view better than *A General History of the Late Revolution of Genoa*.[39] Said to have been published and written by the French adventurer, spy, gambler, journalist, serial pamphleteer, and scoundrel Ange Goudar, the *General History* is both a blow-by-blow account of the Genoese defence of their city in 1746–47 as well as a deliberate piece of pro-French propaganda and literary-historical memorial to Joseph Marie, Duke of Boufflers, the French commander who, 'like a tutelar god,' commanded Genoa's defence in 1747 and whom Goudar (allegedly) served as attaché.[40] And while much is still unknown about the text (least of all its publication during a time when Goudar was on a mission of industrial espionage in Portugal), the Genoese Republic that appears in the *General History* is one committed to neutrality and war-profiteering. Following the war's outbreak, the *General History* recounts a vigorous, fictionalised debate within the Genoese Senate during which its combatants tried to sway the Genoese

to their sides, the Franco-Spanish diplomats centring on the Republic's territorial integrity ('by this alliance you maintain your possession of Finale') while their Austrian enemies played on past grievances ('your palaces [are] still level with the ground by the fury of the [French]').[41] When at first sharp divisions between Franco-Spanish and Imperial parties deadlocked the deliberative body, a third faction emerged heralding neutrality. 'It is best for Genoa to declare for a strict neutrality in the present war, unless she would expose herself to the greatest calamities' declared an anonymous senator 'of the ancient nobility', marshalling in his defence numerous points: the natural proclivity of monarchies to repress republics, Finale's geopolitical deadlock, and, most importantly, the exhaustion of Genoese state finances following their long struggle against the rebellious Corsicans.[42]

> Besides, Gentlemen, suppose we had all the reason imaginable, to engage in the present war, where should we find funds to defray the expences? You all know how much the war of Corsica hath exhausted the republic [...] You further know, that the Bank of St George, so celebrated in the world for an immense treasure, has no other reality than the splendid reputation given it by foreigners; to us but a pure chimera [...] we employed [the Bank's funds] in the war of Corsica.[43]

But the war would provide a matchless economic boon if the Republic stayed neutral and handled the war business of both sides.

> But, gentleman, why should we be at a loss to choose a party? [...] Divine providence seems to send us this, to remedy the distress which the war of *Corsica* hath plunged us: you see numerous armies from all quarters just ready to enter Italy; they will soon be in want of every thing let us supply them with necessaries, without engaging in their quarrels; let us make an advantage of their divisions, and give our provisions in exchange for their gold; let our republic be the magazine of all provisions which they may want; by this we shall be serviceable to those foreign powers, and enrich ourselves. Let us shew to all Europe, that we understand our true interests, and how to make use of conjunctures. In short, let us redress the disorders in our finances; let us draw all the money from those foreign troops into the bosom of our state; let us accumulate their riches.[44]

Language similar to that of Goudar's fictionalised orator may be found in *A Letter from a Genoese gentleman to a member of Parliament of Great-Britain, relating to that part of the treaty of Worms*, an anonymous pamphlet which concerns itself with the inner workings of the aforementioned Austro-Sardinian treaty that would have seen the Genoese-controlled Marquisate of Finale pass into Sardinian hands. 'The Republick has observed as strict a Neutrality between the Crowns of Great Britain and Spain as is possible to conceive on the like occasion', the anonymous author noted, adding that any attack would reduce the Genoese use of English merchant vessels to ship their goods.[45] 'One would think, from the many Slips and Over-sights in this Treaty [of Worms], that it was negotiated over a Bottle, and sign'd on the Head of a Drum [...] Surely there were no Maps, but of Alsace and Lorrain, to be had at Worms', declared another tract on a similar topic.[46]

In spite of such calls for restraint, however, the Treaty of Worms went forward, and the Genoese joined the French and Spanish, a disastrous diplomatic error that led directly to the Austrian invasion of the city two years later. Yet despite the depths of Genoese suffering, British pamphleteer reports from the city at that time show a town still very much in the business of war, with the invading Austrians finding '700 sick Spaniards' in the city's *Lazaretto*, magazines in Sampierdarena stuffed with 'the immense [...] booty' of the retreating Fran-co-Spanish armies, 3,000 Austro-Sardinian deserters in the city given reprieve and rejoined to the 'augmentation of the Austrian forces', and, most notably, countless foreign punters desperate to draw their capital out of the Bank of Saint George before the Austrians extracted their steep cash demands from the Genoese following the Republic's capitulation in September 1746.[47] Goudar remarked:

> Many foreigners, who had part in the funds, being informed of [the Austrian payments], flew to Genoa to realize [lacuna], but found a considerable alteration. The paymasters of the bank had directions to pay off no bills till fresh orders, which caused a sort of bankruptcy. This novelty occasioned an alarm among these foreigners, who wrote to others concerned; so that in a short time the city of Genoa was crowded with people who had demands, and accused the Genoese of having made use of their funds.[48]

'No Prince, nor State in Italy in the most flourishing Circum-stances of that Country, since the Time of the Romans, was ever able to lay down so vast a Sum of ready Money', added the 50–page political pamphlet *The Case of the Genoese impar-tially stated*.[49]

According to the pamphlet's anonymous author(s), the Genoese, faced with 'the natural Impossibility' of raising the necessary war indemnities for the Austrians, which had 'com-pell'd this most serene Commonwealth to have Recourse to the last Remedy; the laying Hands on that sacred Deposi-tary, the Bank of St George, where was lodged not only the Cash of the subjects of this State, but that also of many other Nations'.[50] 'It [is] well known, that Foreigners were more deeply concern'd in the Bank of St George than the Geno-ese', the Austrian actions running contrary to 'what is handed down to us by History'.[51] 'This sacred Deposit of the Wealth of most Nations in Europe [e.g. the Bank], had been always regarded, and remain'd unviolated, during all the Convulsions

of the State', the *Case's* anonymous author(s) harangued. 'Even when the city of Genoa itself was given up by the Marquis of Pescara, in 1522, to be plundered by his Army, the Bank of St George was still untouch'd, by the impious Ravagers; so sacred was it held in those Days'.[52] Beyond foreign capital, other Aus-trian crimes targeted foreign goods in the city. Running short of food and fodder,

> some *German* officers arrogated to themselves, the Liberty of entering with an armed Force, and on Horse-back, into the *Porto-Franco* itself, to take a View of it; a Procedure which afforded the Worst of Omens to the Traders, who from that Time, justly apprehended, that the Merchandise, whether of the Genoses or Foreigners, were as little secure in this Asylum of *Porto-Franco*, as their Money in that of the Bank of St. *George*.[53]

We find similar reflections during the second siege of the city in spring 1747. Writing in May 1747 as Austrian and Sardin-ian troops once more besieged Genoa following their expul-sion the previous winter, the pamphlet *Seasonable reflections on the late convention, concluded the 3d of May last, between the courts of Vienna and Turin* argued that 'no event could more essen-tially affect the English Trade to the Mediterranean' than the feared partition of Genoa between Vienna and Turin, its anonymous author asserted.[54] Narrowing in, the pamphle-teer opposed any Austrian attempt to conquer and partition Genoa because of its effect on Genoese capital.

> Our Trade to Genoa would inevitably, and immediately dwindle to nothing, from the Inability of its Inhabitants to deal with us after they should be stript of all their *Specie*, which must be the certain Consequence of the Conquest by a Nation so greedy and necessitous as the Austrians.[55]

Recalling Genoa's role as centre for Bourbon cash remit-tances during the first half of the War of the Spanish Succes-sion (1701–14), *Seasonable Reflections* went on note how 'while the Spaniards bore Sway here' Genoa had been used as a key centre for the circulation of specie.[56]

> The Italians grew rich, and particularly while Lewis XIV supported the Interest of his Grandchild Philip V from 1701 to 1706. In that short Interval alone, the French brought above Eight Millions Sterling into Italy in weighty Louisdors, which had caused such a Circulation as was infinitely useful to the trading Nation of Europe, and to ours more than any,

only for all this money to be 'swept away to Germany by vari-ous methods' following the war.[57] The pamphleteer launched similar scathing accusations against Savoyard control of the *Riviera Ponente*: they would turn Savona into a freeport, dump cheap woollen goods on the Italian market, if left unchecked, grow into a maritime power in their own right liable at any time to 'dance to the Bourbon Pipe, however well inclined he may be to the Cause of Liberty in general, and to England in particular.'[58] Instead of a powerful Savoy, the author of *Seasonable reflections* preferred a neutral, subservient Genoa, which provided 'a new Nursery [...] for Seamen' 'capable of furnishing Sailors enough to carry on all the Trade of the Mediterranean' there being '20,000 Sea-faring Men to be found on the extended Coast from Nice to Genoa' alongside bills of exchange useful for commerce.[59] 'Except a few Velvets, and some Blocks of Marble, what Returns had we from *Genoa* but *Bills of Exchange*, which put the Balance of Trade considerably on our Side?' the pamphleteer asked.[60]

Here we see the Bank of Saint George, that most peculiar element of the Genoese constitutional order, stripped completely of its republican context and given a new one: as simply one small part of a European-wide capitalist system increasingly controlled by larger powers to Genoa's north. While foreign travellers to Genoa in the eighteenth century marvelled at the city and filled their accounts with what were by that time centuries-old tropes about the nature of the Genoese Republic, they also came to see the Republic as less an independent sovereign in its own right, and more a cog in a larger commercial or military machine.

---

* This paper draws on research conducted for the project *The European Fiscal-Military System, 1530–1870*, which is funded by the European Research Council (ERC) under the European Union's Horizon 2020 research and innovation programme (grant agreement No. 787504).

1 Miller, *Letters from Italy*, I, pp. 217–19.
2 On the figure of the *cicerone* see Tosi, *Language and the Grand Tour*, pp. 141–46.
3 This early view is captured best in Braudel's view of a 'northern invasion' of the Mediterranean. Braudel, *The Mediterranean*, I, pp. 615–42. See also Rapp, 'The Unmaking of the Mediterranean Trade Hegemony'. For a revision to these earlier claims see especially Greene, 'Beyond the Northern Invasion'; Heywood, 'The English in the Mediterranean'; Fusaro, *Political Economies of Empire*, pp. 83–84; Tazzara, *The Free Port of Livorno*, esp. pp. 166–201.
4 For a useful summary see Zanini, 'La Superba'.
5 Grech, 'Flow of Capital in the Mediterranean'; Pedemonte, 'Deserters, Mutineers, and Criminals'; Felloni, 'Genova e il capitalismo'; Martoccio, 'A Man of Particular Ability'; Martoccio, 'The Place for such Business'.
6 The literature on the Grand Tour is extensive. For Italy see especially: Sweet, *Cities and the Grand Tour*; and Ouditt, *Impressions of Southern Italy*.
7 Breval, *Remarks on several parts of Europe*, I, p. 275.
8 Archenholtz, *A Picture of Italy*, I, pp. 122–23.
9 Miller, *Letters from Italy*, I, p. 234.
10 Keyßler, *Travels Through Germany*, IV, p. 374.
11 Nothall, *Travels Through Italy*, p. 471.
12 Miller, *Letters from Italy*, I, p. 252.
13 Keyßler, *Travels Through Germany*, IV, p. 368.
14 Miller, *Letters from Italy*, I, p. 252.
15 Lalande, *Voyage d'un françois en Italie*, VIII, p. 492; Martyn, *A Tour Through Italy*, p. 48.
16 Starke, *Letters from Italy*, I, p. 190.
17 Smith, *Sketch of a Tour*, I, p. 240.

18 Owen, *Travels into Different Parts of Europe*, II, p. 181.
19 Piccinno and Zanini, 'Genoa: Colonizing and Colonized City?'.
20 Gray, *Letters*, p. 255.
21 Dupaty, *Travels Through Italy*, p. 53.
22 Hill, *The Diplomatic Correspondence*, I, p. 464.
23 Taviani, 'A Privatized State'.
24 Addison, *Remarks on Several Parts of Italy*, pp. 20–21.
25 Lalande, *Voyage d'un françois en Italie*, VIII, p. 283.
26 Felloni, 'Genova e il capitalismo'.
27 Brosses, *Lettres familières*, I, pp. 42–43. On the larger cultural place of bills of exchange in ancien régime Europe see Trivellato, *The Promise and Peril of Credit*.
28 Dupaty, *Travels Through Italy*, p. 53.
29 Watkins, *Travels Through Switzerland*, I, pp. 251–52.
30 Anderson, *An Historical and Chronological Deduction*, III, p. 492.
31 Archenholz, *A Picture of Italy*, pp. 127–28.
32 Piozzi, *Observations and Reflections*, I, p. 58. See also D'Ezio, 'The Advantages of "Demi-Naturalization"'.
33 Piozzi, *Observations and Reflections*, I, 61.
34 Baretti, *An Account of the Manners*, II, pp. 128–30.
35 For an overview of Austrian-British-Genoese relations in the war see: Anderson, *The War of Austrian Succession*, pp. 167–70; Hochedlinger, *Austria's Wars*, pp. 255–56; Pedemonte, 'Bombe sul dominio'.
36 For the best history of these events see: Bitossi and Paolocci, eds, *Genova, 1746*.
37 Schneller, 'Mary Cooper'; Schneller, 'Using Newspaper Advertisements'; Schneller, 'John Hill and Mary Cooper'; Harvey, *Reading Sex in the Eighteenth Century*, pp. 42–43. See generally McDowell, *The Women of Grub Street*.
38 Treadwell, 'London Trade Publishers 1675–1750'; Cardwell, *Arts and Arms*, p. 3.
39 Goudar, *A General History*.

40 Goudar, *A General History*, p. 183. Goudar's literary output was immense. See Mars, 'Ange Goudar'.
41 Goudar, *A General History*, pp. 3, 5.
42 Goudar, *A General History*, pp. 6, 8.
43 Goudar, *A General History*, pp. 9–10.
44 Goudar, *A General History*, pp. 11–12.
45 Anonymous, *A Letter from a Genoese Gentleman*.
46 Anonymous, *Free Thoughts*, p. 59.
47 Goudar, *A General History*, pp. 51, 53.
48 Goudar, *A General History*, pp. 70–71.
49 Anonymous, *The Case of the Genoese*, p. 35.
50 Anonymous, *The Case of the Genoese*, p. 11.
51 Anonymous, *The Case of the Genoese*, pp. 33, 50.
52 Anonymous, *The Case of the Genoese*, p. 33.
53 Anonymous, *The Case of the Genoese*, p. 15.
54 Anonymous, *Seasonable Reflections*, p. 7.
55 Anonymous, *Seasonable Reflections*, p. 10.
56 On Genoa in the War of Spanish Succession see Dellepiane and Piana, 'Le leve corse della Repubblica'; Assereto, 'La guerra di Successione spagnola'; Storrs, 'Negotiating the Transition'; and Martoccio, 'The Place for such Business'.
57 Anonymous, *Seasonable Reflections*, p. 12.
58 Anonymous, *Seasonable Reflections*, p. 43.
59 Anonymous, *Seasonable Reflections*, pp. 21, 33, 35.
60 Anonymous, *Seasonable Reflections*, p. 20.

LIST OF ABBREVIATIONS

AAV	Archivio Apostolico Vaticano
ADP	Archivio Doria Pamphilj, Roma
AGS	Archivio General de Simancas
AMAE	Archives du ministère des Affaires étrangères
ASCG	Archivio storico del Comune di Genova
MBS	Manoscritti Brignole Sale
ASF	Archivio di Stato di Firenze
ASG	Archivio di Stato di Genova
AS	Archivio Segreto
ASN	Archivio di Stato di Napoli
BAV	Biblioteca Apostolica Vaticana di Roma
BCBG	Biblioteca Civica Berio di Genova
BCBV	Biblioteca Civica Bertoliana di Vicenza
BNF	Bibliothèque National de France, Paris
BNM	Biblioteca Nacional de Madrid
BSB	Bayerische Staatsbibliothek, München
BUG	Biblioteca Universitaria di Genova
HHS	Haus-, Hof- und Staatsarchiv, Wien
KC	Kislak Center for Special Collections, Rare Books and Manuscripts, University of Pennsylvania,
MCV	Biblioteca del Museo Correr di Venezia
OSW	Österreichisches Staatsarchiv, Wien

BIBLIOGRAPHY

Accinelli, F. M., *Compendio delle Storie di Genova Dalla sua fondazione sino all'anno MDCCL* […], 2 vols (Lipsia [= Massa]: a Spese de' Benefattori, 1750).

Addison, J., *Remarks on Several Parts of Italy, &c. in the Years 1701, 1702, 1703* (London: J. and R. Tonson, 1767).

Airaldi, G., Parma, E., *L'avventura di Colombo. Storia, immagini, mito* (Genova: Carige, 2006).

Aliverti, M. I., 'L'ammiraglio, il gatto e l'orologio. La casa di Andrea Doria come teatro cerimoniale al tempo della visita di Filippo d'Asburgo (1548)', in *Il Palazzo del Principe, Genesi e trasformazioni della villa di Andrea Doria a Genova*, ed. by L. Stagno, *Ricerche di Storia dell'arte*, 82–83 (2004), pp. 87–116.

Aliverti, M. I., 'Visits to Genoa. the Printed Sources', in *Europa Triumphans: Court and Civic Festivals in Early Modern Europe*, ed. by J. R. Mulryne, H. Watanabe-O'Kelly and M. Shewring (London: Ashgate, 2004), pp. 222–35.

Alizeri, F., *Guida illustrativa del cittadino e del forestiero per la città di Genova e sue adiacenze* (Genova: Sambolino, 1875).

Alizeri, F., *Notizie dei professori del disegno in Liguria dalle origini al secolo XVI*, 6 vols (Genova: Sambolino, 1877).

Altavista, C., *La residenza di Andrea Doria a Fassolo. Il cantiere di un palazzo di villa genovese nel Rinascimento* (Milano: Franco Angeli, 2013).

Álvarez-Ossorio Alvariño, A, '¿El final de la Sicilia española? Fidelidad, familia y venalidad bajo el virrey marqués de los Balbases (1707–1713)', in *La pérdida de Europa. La guerra de Sucesión por la Monarquía de España*, ed. by B.J. García and V. León (Madrid: Fundación Carlos de Amberes, 2007), pp. 831–915.

Álvarez-Nogal, C., and Chamley, C., 'Debt Policy under Constraints: Philip II, the Cortes, and Genoese Bankers', in *The Economic History Review*, 67 (2014), pp. 192–213.

Anderson, A., *An Historical and Chronological Deduction of the Origin of Commerce, from the Earliest Accounts to the Present Time*, 4 vols (London: Walter, 1764).

Anderson, M.S., *The War of Austrian Succession, 1740–1748* (London: Longman, 1995).

Andreoli, I., 'Andrea Doria fra le righe: tre ritratti in due edizioni di una biografia tra Venezia e Genova', in *Argomenti di Storia dell'arte. Quaderno della Scuola di Specializzazione in Storia dell'arte della Facoltà di Lettere e Filosofia dell'Università di Genova. 1993–2003* (Recco: Microarts, 2004), pp. 27–37.

Annerino, J., *The Virgin of Guadalupe: Art and Legend* (Layton: Gibbs Smith, 2012).

Annuario Genovese. Guida amministrativa e commerciale. Anno V (Genova: Marro, 1889).

Anónimo, *Progressos maravillosos de las armas colligadas en el Piamonte, baxo el mando de su a[lteza] real de Saboya contra las armas de Francia, governadas por el general Catinat: sabidas por el correo de Milan, que llegò à esta ciudad de Zaragoça, á 24 de setiembre deste presente año de 1692* (Barcelona, 1692)

Anonimo Genovese, *Le poesie storiche. Testo e versione italiana a cura di Jean Nicolas* (Genova: A Compagna, 1983).

Anonimo Genovese, *Rime e ritmi latini a cura di Jean Nicolas* (Bologna: Commissione per i testi di lingua, 1994).

Anonymous, *A Letter from a Genoese Gentleman to a Member of Parliament of Great-Britain, Relating to That Part of the Treaty of Worms which Regards the Town and Marquisate of Final* (London: M. Cooper, 1744).

Anonymous, *Free Thoughts on the Late Treaty of Alliance Concluded at Worms by a Member of Parliament, in a Letter to his Friend in the Country* (London: M. Cooper, 1744).

Anonymous, *Seasonable Reflections on the Late Convention, Concluded the 3d of May last, Between the Courts of Vienna and Turin, for Partitioning Between them the Territories Belonging to the Republic of Genoa; Especially Shewing the Injurious Consequence to the British Trade, Should Savona and Final Be Annexed, in Virtue of Any Future General Peace, to the Dominions of the House of Savoy* (London: M. Cooper, 1747).

Anonymous, *The Case of the Genoese Impartially Stated; Wherein the Conduct of the People, the Austrians and Piedmontese, During the late Convulsions, is Candidly Examined* (London: L. Gillver).

Antetomaso, E., 'La decorazione del salone del Maggior Consiglio del Palazzo Ducale di Genova', in *Raro ed eccellente pittore, il restauro dei cartoni di Marcantonio Franceschini nelle collezioni demaniali in Orvieto*, ed. by G. Testa Grauso (Umbertide: Dream Service, 2002), pp. 110–21.

Antunes, C., Münch Miranda, S., and Salvado, J. P., 'The Resources of Others: Dutch Exploitation of European Expansion and Empires, 1570–1800', in *Tijdschrift Voor Geschiedenis*, 131, 3 (2018), pp. 501–21.

Applausi della Liguria nella Reale Incoronatione del Serenissimo Agostino Pallavicino, Duce della Republica di Genova (Genova: Pavoni, 1638).

Archenholtz, J. W., *A Picture of Italy: Translated from the Original German of W. De Archenholtz*, trans. Joseph Trapp, 2 vols (Dublin: W. Corbet, 1791).

Aretino, P., *Al Sacratissimo Re d'Inghilterra. Il secondo libro de Le Lettere* (Venezia: Marcolini, 1542).

Askew, P., 'Perino del Vaga's Decorations for the Palazzo Doria, Genoa', in *The Burlington Magazine*, 98 (1956), pp. 46–53.

Assarino, L., *Discorso di Luca Assarino fatto in lode di Genova nell'occasione delle Nuove Mura, dedicato all'Illustriss. Sig. Andrea Mari* (Genova: Pavoni, 1631).

Assarino, L., 'Discorso per le Nuove Mura di Genova', in *Diverse Lettere e Componimenti* (Venezia: per il Sarzina, 1639), pp. 173–92.

Assereto, G., 'Comunità soggette e poteri centrali', in *Le metamorfosi della Repubblica: saggi di storia genovese tra il XVI e il XIX secolo* (Savona: Elio Ferraris editore, 1999), pp. 77–96.

Assereto, G., *Le metamorfosi della Repubblica. Saggi di storia genovese tra il XVI e il XIX secolo*, (Savona: Ferraris, 1999), pp. 9–182.

Assereto, G., 'Lo sguardo di Genova su Venezia: odio, ammirazione, imitazione', in *La diversa visuale. Il fenomeno Venezia osservato dagli altri*, ed. by U. Israel (Roma: Edizioni di storia e letteratura – Centro tedesco di studi veneziani, 2008), pp. 89–114.

Assereto, G., 'Storiografia e identità ligure tra Settecento e primo Ottocento', in *Politica e cultura nel Risorgimento italiano. Genova 1857 e la fondazione della Società Ligure di Storia Patria*, ed. by L. Lo Basso, 48, 1 (2008), pp. 57–87.

Assereto, G., 'La guerra di Successione spagnola dal punto di vista genovese', in *Génova y la monarquía hispánica (1528–1713)*, ed. by M. Herrero Sánchez and others (Genova: Società ligure di storia patria, 2011), pp. 539–84.

Assini, A., 'Cronologia di una committenza: Marcantonio Franceschini e la famiglia Giustiniani', in *Raro ed Eccellente Pittore, il restauro dei cartoni di Marcantonio Franceschini nelle collezioni demaniali in Orvieto*, ed. by G. Testa Grauso (Umbertide: Dream Service, 2002), pp. 106–09.

Auer, L., 'The Role of the Imperial Aulic Council in the Constitutional Structure of the Holy Roman Empire', in *The Holy Roman Empire, 1495–1806*, ed. by R. H. W. Evans, M. Schaich, and P. H. Wilson (Oxford: Oxford University Press, 2011), pp. 63–76.

Baker-Bates, P., Pattenden, M., eds, *The Spanish Presence in Sixteenth-Century Italy: Images of Iberia* (Farnham Surrey: Ashgate, 2015).

Baratta, A., *La famosissima e nobilissima città di Genova cò le sue nuove Fortificazioni* (Roma: Giovanni Orlandi, 1637).

Baretti, G. M. A., *An Account of the Manners and Customs of Italy: with Observations on the Mistakes of some Travellers, with Regard to that Country* (London: Davis, 1768).

Bartoletti, M., 'Brusco, Paolo Gerolamo', in *La pittura in Italia. Il Settecento* (Milano: Electa, 1990), vol. 2, pp. 641–42.

Beck, C., 'Éléments sociaux et économiques de la vie des marchands génois à Anvers entre 1528 et 1555', in *Revue du Nord*, 64 (1982), pp. 254–55, 759–84.

P. Bellini and M. Carter Heach, eds, *The Illustrated Bartsch*, vol. 44, *Italian Masters of the Seventeenth Century* (New York: Abaris Books, 1983)

Belting, H., *Likeness and Presence: A History of the Image before the Era of Art* (Chicago: University of Chicago Press, 1994).

Beltrami, L., ed., *Leggi e ordini dell'Accademia degli Addormentati di Genova* (Manziana: Vecchiarelli, 2016).

Belvederi, R., 'Il "Ragionamento di Giovanni Costa, gentil'huomo genovese, sopra la triegua de' Paesi Bassi, conchiusa in Anversa l'anno MDCIX"', in *Genova, la Liguria e l'Oltremare fra Medioevo ed età moderna. Studi e ricerche d'archivio*, ed. by R. Belvederi (Genova: Università di Genova, Istituto di Scienze Storiche, 1981), pp. 275–360.

Belvederi, R., 'Genova e le Fiandre nella storiografia fra Cinquecento e Seicento', in *Atti del I Congresso Internazionale di Studi Storici: rapporti Genova – Mediterraneo – Atlantico nell'età moderna*, ed. by R. Belvederi (Genova: Università di Genova, Istituto di Scienze Storiche, 1983), pp. 505–46.

Ben Yessef Garfia, Y. R., 'Entre el servicio a la Corona y el interés familiar. Los Serra en el desempeño del Oficio del Correo Mayor de Milán (1604–1692)', in *Génova y la monarquía hispánica (1528–1713)*, ed. by M. Herrero Sánchez and others (Genova: Società ligure di storia patria, 2011), pp. 303–30.

Ben Yessef Garfia, Y. R, 'Mobilità e cooptazione delle élites al servizio della monarchia spagnola policentrica. Il caso del cardinale Antonio Maria Sauli (1587–1605)', in *Mélanges de l'École Française de Rome – Italie et Méditerranée modernes et contemporaines*, 133 (2021), pp. 51–64.

Ben Yessef Garfia, Y. R., *Los Serra entre la República de Génova y la Monarquía Hispánica* (Madrid: Consejo Superior de Investigaciones Científicas, 2022).

Beneš, Carrie E., ed., *A Companion to Medieval Genoa* (Leiden: Brill, 2018).

Bérenger, J., *Léopold (1640–1705). Fondateur de la puissance autrichienne* (Paris: PUF, 2004).

Beri, E., 'Accusation, Defense and Self-Defense: The Debate on the Action of Giovanni Andrea Doria in Lepanto', in *Lepanto and Beyond. Images of Religious Alterity from Genoa and the Christian Mediterranean*, ed. by L. Stagno and B. Franco Llopis (Leuven: Leuven University Press, 2021), pp. 157–70.

Bernardi, C., 'Corpus Domini: Ritual Metamorphoses and Social Changes in Sixteenth- and Seventeenth-Century Genoa', in *The Politics of Ritual Kinship: Confraternities and Social Order in Early Modern Italy*, ed. N. Terpstra (Cambridge: Cambridge University Press, 2000), pp. 228–42.

Bertolucci, S., Leoncini, L., eds, *La città della Lanterna. Iconografia di Genova e del suo faro tra Medioevo e presente* (Genova: De Ferrari, 2017).

Bettini, A., 'Americae Retectio: ricostruzione di un processo creativo', *Columbeis*, 3 (1988), pp. 191–201.

Biavati, G., 'L'affresco che il Piola non dipinse in Palazzo Ducale', in *Bollettino dei Musei Civici genovesi*, 2 (1980), pp. 5–54.

Biavati, G., 'La Cappella Ducale a Genova: immagini e simboli del potere oligarchico a metà del Seicento', in *Rapporti Genova-Mediterraneo-Atlantico nell'età moderna*, ed. by R. Belvederi (Genova: Istituto di Scienze Storiche, 1992), pp. 391–93.

Biavati, G., 'Il "concorso" del 1700 per il Salone del Maggior Consiglio', in *El Siglo de los Genoveses e una lunga storia di Arte e Splendori nel Palazzo dei Dogi*, ed. by P. Boccardo and C. Di Fabio (Milano: Skira, 1999), pp. 366–75.

Bitossi, C., *Andrea Spinola: scritti scelti* (Genova: Sagep, 1981).

Bitossi, C., '"Il piccolo sempre succombe al grande". La Repubblica di Genova tra Francia e Spagna, 1684–1685', in *Il bombardamento di Genova nel 1684. Atti della giornata di studio nel terzo centenario* (Genova: La Quercia edizioni, 1988), pp. 39–69.

Bitossi, C., 'Un lungo addio. Il tramonto del partito spagnolo nella Genova del '600', in *La Storia dei Genovesi* (Genova: Associazione Nobiliare Ligure, 1988), pp. 119–35.

Bitossi, 'Il blocco oligarchico nel decennio 1626–1637', in *Domenico Fiasella*, ed. by P. Donati (Genova: Sagep, 1990), pp. 47–59.

Bitossi, C., *Il governo dei magnifici. Patriziato e politica a Genova fra Cinque e Seicento* (Genova: ECIG, 1990).

Bitossi, C., 'Città, Repubblica e nobiltà nella cultura politica genovese fra Cinque e Seicento', in *La letteratura ligure. La Repubblica aristocratica* (Genova: Costa & Nolan, 1992), pp. 9–35.

Bitossi, C., 'Un oligarca antispagnolo del Seicento: Giambattista Raggio', in *Atti della società ligure di storia patria*, 36, 2 (1996), pp. 271–303.

Bitossi, C., Paolocci, C., eds, *Genova, 1746: una città di antico regime tra guerra e rivolta. Atti del Convegno di studi in occasione del 250° anniversario della rivolta genovese* (Genova: Associazione amici della Biblioteca Franzoniana, 1998).

Bitossi, C., 'Navi e politica nella Genova del Seicento', in *Atti dell'accademia ligure di scienze e lettere*, 5 (2000), pp. 261–83.

Bitossi, C., 'L'antico regime genovese, 1576–1797', in *Storia di Genova. Mediterraneo, Europa, Atlantico*, ed. by D. Puncuh (Genova: Società Ligure di Storia Patria, 2003), pp. 391–508.

Bitossi, C., 'Lo strano caso dell'antispagnolismo genovese', in *Alle origini di una nazione. Antispagnolismo e identità italiana*, ed. by A. Musi (Milano: Guerini e Associati, 2003), pp. 163–200.

Bitossi, C., 'A Republic in Search of Legitimation', in *Europa Triumphans. Court and Civic Festivals in Early Modern Europe*, ed. by J. R. Mulryne, H. Watanabe-O'Kelly and M. Shewring (Aldershot: Ashgate, 2004), pp. 236–46.

Bitossi, C., ' Il governo della Repubblica e della Casa di San Giorgio: i ceti dirigenti dopo la riforma costituzionale del 1576', in *La casa di San Giorgio: il potere del credito*, ed. by G. Felloni (Genova: Società Ligure di Storia Patria, 2004), pp. 91–107.

Bitossi, C., '"Il dominio del mare e l'impero della terra". Progetti di rilancio navale nella Genova del Seicento', in *Cristoforo Colombo nella Genova del Seicento*, ed, by F. Simonetti, G. Zanelli (Genova: San Giorgio, 2005), pp. 9–21.

Bitossi, C., 'L'età di Andrea Doria', in *Storia della Liguria*, ed. by G. Assereto and M. Doria (Roma: Laterza, 2007), pp. 61–78.

Bitossi, C., 'Il Genio ligure risvegliato: La potenza navale nel discorso politico genovese del Seicento', in *I linguaggi del potere nell'età barocca, I, Politica e religione*, ed. by F. Cantù (Roma: Viella, 2009), pp. 81–111.

Bitossi, C., 'Due modelli di educazione repubblicana nella Genova del Seicento negli scritti di Andrea Spinola e Gio. Francesco Spinola', in *Annali on Line Della Didattica e Della Formazione Docente*, 6 (2013), pp. 159–72.

Bitossi, C., *1684. La Repubblica sfida il Re Sole* (Roma: Editori Laterza, 2015).

Bitossi, C., 'La circulación de la información y el proceso de toma de decisiones en una República oligárquica: Génova entre Francia y España en 1679', in *Repúblicas Y Republicanismo En La Europa Moderna (Siglos XVI-XVII)*, ed. by M. Herrero Sanchez (Madrid: Fondo de Cultura Económica, 2017), pp. 371–94.

Bober, J., Boccardo, P., Boggero, F., eds., *A Superb Baroque: Art in Genoa 1600–1750* (Princeton and Oxford: Princeton University Press, 2020).

Boccalini, T., *Ragguagli di Parnaso e scritti minori*, 3 vols (Bari: Laterza, 1948).

Boccardo, P., *Andrea Doria e le arti. Committenza e mecenatismo a Genova* (Roma: Palombi 1989).

Boccardo, P., Colomer, J. L., and Di Fabio, C., eds, *España y Génova. Obras, artistas y colecciones* (Madrid: Centros de Estudios Europa Hispánica, 2003).

Boccardo, P., and others, eds, *Genova e la Francia: opere, artisti, committenti, collezionisti* (Cinisello Balsamo: Silvana, 2003).

Boccardo, P., *Andrea Doria e le arti. Committenza e mecenatismo a Genova nel Rinascimento* (Roma: Palombi, 1989).

Boccardo, P., Boggero F., eds., *Palazzi storici del Banco di Roma: Genova, De Ferrari* (Roma: La Meridiana, 1991).

Boccardo, P., 'La Gloria di Colombo: lo schizzo e il disegno di Giovan Battista Paggi', in *Bollettino dei Musei Civici genovesi*, 14 (1992), pp. 35–44.

Boccardo, P., Di Fabio, C., eds, *El Siglo de los Genoveses e una lunga storia di Arte e Splendori nel Palazzo dei Dogi* (Milano: Skira, 1999).

Boccardo, P., 'Michelangelo e Genova: il monumento ad Andrea Doria e la fallace "connoisseurship" dei Genovesi', in *Michelangelo divino artista*, ed. by C. Acidini Luchinat, A. Cecchi and E. Capretti (Genova: Sagep, 2020), pp. 108–17.

Bochius, J., *Descriptio Publicae Gratulationis, Spectaculorum, et Ludorum, in Adventu Serenissimi Principis Ernesti, Archiduchis Austriae […]* (Antwerp: Officina Plantiniana, 1595).

Bock, G., Skinner, Q., Viroli, M., eds, *Machiavelli and Republicanism* (Cambridge: Cambridge University Press, 1990).

Boggero, F., Simonetti, F., *L'argenteria Genovese del Settecento* (Genova: Carige, 1991).

Boggero, F., 'La produzione della grande argenteria sacra e profana. Maestri locali e "alemanni" nelle botteghe genovesi', in *Genova nell'età Barocca*, ed. by E. Gavazza and G. Rotondi Terminiello (Bologna: Nuova Alfa, 1992), pp. 341–61.

Boggero, F., 'Il cantiere di S. Agostino e l'equipe di Giovanni Andrea Doria', in *Giovanni Andrea Doria e Loano. La chiesa di Sant'Agostino*, ed. by F. Boggero and L. Stagno (Loano: Comune di Loano, 1999), pp. 61–76.

Boggero, F., 'Gli argenti', in *Il Palazzo Doria Spinola. Architettura e arredi di una dimora aristocratica genovese da un inventario del 1727*, ed. by R. Santamaria (Recco: Le Mani, 2011), pp. 323–44.

Bonfadio, J., *Gli annali di Genova dall'anno 1528 che recuperò la libertà, fino al 1550* (Genova: eredi di Gerolamo Bartoli, 1559).

Bongi, S., *Annali di Gabriel Giolito de' Ferrari, da Trino di Monferrato, stampatore in Venezia* (Roma: presso i principali librai, 1890).

Borghesi, ed., *Vita del Principe Giovanni Andrea Doria scritta da lui medesimo incompleta* (Genova: Compagnia dei Librai, 1997).

Borghesi, V., 'Doria, Giovanni Andrea [I]', in *Dizionario Biografico dei Liguri dalle origini ai nostri giorni*, vol. 7 (Genova: Consulta Ligure, 2008), pp. 105–21.

Borgo, P. B., *De Dominio Serenissimae Genuensis Reipublicae in mari Ligustico* (Roma: Domenico Marciano, 1641).

Borniotto, V., *L'identità di Genova. Immagini di glorificazione civica in età moderna* (Genova: Genova University Press, 2016).

Borniotto, V., 'Gloria civica come emblema di potere. Iconografia politica a Genova tra Palazzo San Giorgio e la Cappella Dogale', *Atti della Società Ligure di Storia Patria*, 128, 2 (2014), pp. 83–94.

Borniotto, V., 'Rinnovare la tradizione: sintesi, crasi e contaminazioni nei soggetti iconografici di Domenico Piola', in *Domenico Piola e la sua bottega. Approfondimenti sulle arti nel secondo Seicento Genovese*, ed. by D. Sanguineti (Genova: Sagep, 2019), pp. 216–29.

Borniotto, V., 'Ancient Relics, New Images and New Saints in Early Modern Genoa', in *Ikon*, 14 (2021), pp. 245–56.

Botero, G., *Della Ragion di Stato Libri Dieci* (In Ferrara: appresso Vittorio Baldini stampatore ducale, 1589).

Bottaro Palumbo, M. G., ed., *Genova e Francia al crocevia dell'Europa (1624–1642)*, 2 vols (Genova: Centro di Studi sull'Età Moderna, 1989).

Bottaro Palumbo, M. G., '"Et rege eos": la Vergine Maria Patrona, Signora e Regina della Repubblica (1637)', in *Genova e Maria. Contributi per la storia del Santuario di Nostra Signora della Guardia* (Genova: Associazione Amici della Biblioteca Franzoniana, 1991), pp. 93–109.

Bouza Álvarez, F., *'Corre manuscrito'. Una historia cultural del Siglo de Oro* (Madrid: Marcial Pons, 2001).

Bouwsma, W. J., *Venice and the Defense of Republican Liberty. Renaissance Values in the Age of the Counter Reformation* (Berkeley: University of California Press, 1984).

Bracco, R., *Il principe Giannandrea Doria: patriae libertatis conservator* (Genova: Scuola grafica Opera SS. Vergine di Pompei, 1960).

Brancaccio, G., *'Nazione genovese'. Consoli e colonia della Napoli moderna* (Napoli: Guida, 2001).

Braudel, F., *The Mediterranean and the Mediterranean World in the Age of Philip II* (London: Collins, 1972).

Breval, J., *Remarks on several parts of Europe relating chiefly to their antiquities and history*, 2 vols (London: H. Lintot, 1738).

Brevini, F., *La poesia in dialetto. Storia e testi dalle origini al Novecento* (Milano: Mondadori, 1999).

Briano, M., Bruno, M., and Righetti, C., *Palazzo Andrea Pitto già Centurione-Cambiaso* (Genova: Gruppo Casasco & Nardi, 2008).

Brignole Sale, A. G., *Le instabilità dell'ingegno, divise in otto giornate* (Bologna: Monti, 1637).

Brignole Sale, A. G., *Congratulatione fatta a' serenissimi collegi della Serenissima Republica di Genova, pe'l nuovo armamento delle galee, da un cittadino zelante habitante in Napoli* (Genova: Pier Giovanni Calenzani, 1642).

Brilli, C., *Genoese Trade and Migration in the Spanish Atlantic, 1700–1830* (New York: Cambridge University Press, 2016).

Brock, M., 'Le portrait d'Andrea Doria en Neptune par Bronzino', in *Les portraits du pouvoir. Collection d'histoire de l'art de l'Académie de France à Rome*, ed. by O. Bonfait, III (Roma: Académie de France, 2003), pp. 49–63.

Brosses, Charles de, *Lettres familières écrites d'Italie à quelques amis en 1739 et 1740*, ed. H. Babou, 2 vols (Paris: Didier, 1858).

Brown, J., Elliot, J. H., *A Palace for a King: the Buen Retiro and the Court of Philip IV* (London: Yale University Press, 2003).

Bouwsma, W. J., *Venice and the Defense of Republican Liberty. Renaissance Values in the Age of the Counter Reformation* (Berkeley: University of California Press, 1984).

Bussels, S., *Spectacle, Rhetoric and Power: The Triumphal Entry of Prince Philip of Spain into Antwerp* (Amsterdam: Rodopi, 2012).

Calabi, D., Camerino, U., Concina, E., *La città degli ebrei. Il ghetto di Venezia: architettura e urbanistica* (Venezia: Marsilio, 1991).

Calabrese, M. C., *Figli della città: consoli genovesi a Messina in età moderna* (Milano: Franco Angeli, 2018).

Calcagno, G. C., 'La navigazione convogliata a Genova nella seconda metà del Seicento', in *Guerra e commercio nell'evoluzione della marina genovese tra XVI e XVII secolo*, vol. 2 (Genova: Università di Genova, 1973), pp. 265–392.

Calcagno, P., '*La puerta a la mar*'. *Il Marchesato del Finale nel Sistema imperiale spagnolo (1571–1713)* (Rome: Viella, 2011).

Calvete de Estrella, J. C., *El Felicissimo Viaje del muy Alto y muy Poderoso Principe Don Phelippe, Hijo del Emperador Don Carlos Quinto Maximo […]* (Antwerp: Martin Nucio, 1552).

Cama, G., 'Banco di San Giorgio e sistema politico genovese: un'analisi teorica', in *La Casa di San Giorgio: il potere del credito : atti del convegno, Genova, 11 e 12 novembre 2004*, ed. by G. Felloni (Genova: Società ligure di storia patria, 2006), pp. 109–20.

Cameron, A., 'The Theotokos in Sixth-Century Constantinople: A City Finds Its Symbol', in *Journal of Theological Studies*, 29 (1978), pp. 79–108.

Cameron, A., 'Images of Authority: Elites and Icons in Late Sixth-Century Byzantium', in *Past and Present*, 84 (1979), pp. 3–35.

Canosa, R., *Banchieri genovesi e sovrani spagnoli tra Cinquecento e Seicento* (Roma: Sapere, 2000).

Capelloni, L., *Al vittorioso principe D'Oria* (Florence, Lorenzo Torrentino, 1550).

Capelloni, L., *La vita, e gesti di Andrea D'Oria* (Venezia: Gabriele Giolito De Ferrari e fratelli, 1562).

Capelloni, L., *Vita del prencipe Andrea Doria discritta da m. Lorenzo Capelloni con un compendio della medesima vita, e con due tauole; l'una delle cose più generali, & l'altra delle cose più notabili* (Venezia: Gabriel Giolito di Ferrari, 1569).

Cappelletti, G., *I Gesuiti e la Repubblica di Venezia* (Venezia: Grimaldo, 1873), pp. 169–72.

Capriata, P. G., *Dell'historia di Pietro Giouanni Capriata, Libri dodici. Ne' quali si contengono tutti i movimenti d'arme successi in Italia dal MDCXIII. Fino al MDCXXXIV.* (Genova: Pietro Giouanni Calenzano e Gio. Maria Farroni Compagni, 1638).

Cardim, P., and others, *Polycentric Monarchies: How Did Early Modern Spain and Portugal Achieve and Maintain a Global Hegemony?* (Brighton: Sussex Academic Press, 2012).

Carpentier, B., Priotti, J.-P., 'La forge instable d'une domination. Les Doria, Gênes et la monarchie hispanique (1560–1606)', in *Identités et territoires dans les mondes hispaniques XVIᵉ-XXᵉ siècle*, ed. by J.-P. Priotti (Rennes: Presses Universitaires de Rennes, 2015), pp. 75–96.

Cardwell, M. J., *Arts and Arms: Literature, Politics, and Patriotism during the Seven Years' War* (Manchester: Manchester University Press, 2004).

Carrió-Invernizzi, D., 'Génova y España en la pintura histórica del Palacio Real de Nápoles del s. XVII', in *Génova y la monarquía hispánica (1528–1713)*, ed. by M. Herrero Sánchez and others (Genova: Società Ligure di Storia Patria, 2011), pp. 753–74.

Caruso, C., 'History in a Painting: Sebastiano del Piombo's Portrait of Andrea Doria', in *Chivalry, Academy, and Cultural Dialogues: The Italian Contribution to European Culture*, ed. by S. Jossa and G. Pieri (Oxford: Legenda, 2017), pp. 192–209.

Castronovo, V., 'Borgo, Pietro Battista', *Dizionario biografico degli italiani*, vol. 12 (Roma: Treccani, 1971), p. 252.

Cataldi Gallo, M., 'Rosso, oro e nero: colori e simboli di potere nella Repubblica di Genova', in *El Siglo de Los Genoveses*, ed. by P. Boccardo and C. Di Fabio (Milano: Electa, 1999), pp. 78–87.

Cavalli, G. G., *Çittara zeneize di Gian-Giacomo Cavalli ricorretta, accresciuta e presentata al Serenissimo Lorenzo de Mari doge della Serenissima Repubblica di Genova …* (Genova: Franchelli, 1745).

Cavalli, G.G., *Ra cittara zeneize. Poesie scelte*, ed. by F. Toso (Alessandria: Edizioni dell'Orso, 2021).

Cavanna Ciappina, M., 'Ugo Fiesco', *Dizionario Biografico degli Italiani*, vol. 47 (Roma: Istituto dell'Enciclopedia Italiana, 1997), pp. 533–35.

Cebà, A., *Il Cittadino di Republica. Alla valorosa gioventù genovese* (Genova: Pavoni, 1617).

Ceccarelli, A., 'Tra sovranità e imperialità. Genova nell'età delle congiure popolari barocche (1623–1627)', in *Quellen und Forschungen aus italienischen Archiven und Bibliotheken*, XCIII (2014), pp. 251–82.

Ceccarelli, A., '*In forse di perdere la libertà*'. *La Repubblica di Genova nella riflessione di Giulio Pallavicino (1583–1635)* (Roma: Viella, 2018).

Ceribelli, A., 'La literatura italiana en la obra de Quevedo' (unpublished doctoral thesis, Universidade de Santiago de Compostela, 2020).

Chabod, F., *Storia di Milano nell'epoca di Carlo V* (Torino: Einaudi, 1971).

Chiabrera, G., *Discorsi fatti […] nell'Accademia degli Addormentati* (Genova: Anton Giorgio Franchello, 1670).

Chiabrera, G., *Guerra dei Goti*, ed. by V. Di Iasio (Milano: Ledizioni, 2021).

Chiarla, M., 'Schiappalaria, Stefano Ambrogio', *Dizionario Biografico degli Italiani*, 91 (2018).

Chiozza, E. M., *Guida commerciale descrittiva di Genova* (Genova: Carlo d'Aste, 1874).

Ciasca, R., 'Affermazioni di sovranità della Repubblica di Genova nel secolo XVII', in *Giornale storico e letterario della Liguria*, 14 (1938), pp. 81–181.

Ciasca, R., *Istruzioni e relazioni degli ambasciatori genovesi*, 7 vols (Roma: a cura dell'Istituto Storico italiano per l'età moderna e contemporanea, 1951).

Ciasca, R., 'La Repubblica di Genova "testa coronata"', in *Studi in onore di Amintore Fanfani*, vol. 4 (Milano: Giuffrè, 1962), pp. 289–319.

Cochrane, E. W., *Historians and Historiography in the Italian Renaissance* (Chicago: The University of Chicago Press, 1981).

Cieri Via, C., 'L'immagine del potere: il ritratto di Andrea Doria di Sebastiano del Piombo', in *Les portraits du pouvoir. Collection d'histoire de l'art de l'Académie de France à Rome*, ed. by O. Bonfait, vol. 3 (Roma: Académie de France, 2003), pp. 35–48.

Casero Cigala, B., *Ra chiù luxente gioia e ra chiù finna. Discorso in lingua genovese dopo l'elettione del Serenissimo Duce di Genova, il signor Antonio Cebà*, ed. by T. Hohnerlein-Buchinger (Recco: Le Mani, 2000).

Conti, V., *Consociatio Civitatum: le Repubbliche nei testi elzeviriani (1625–1649)* (Firenze: Centro Editoriale Toscano, 1997).

Copia di due lettere una publicata sotto nome della Republica di Genova alla Republica di Venetia. L'altra che contiene il parere sopra la medesima Lettera (Vicenza, 1607).

Costamagna, G., 'I magazzini del Magistrato del Sale e del Magistrato dell'Abbondanza', in *Il porto di Genova nella Mostra di Palazzo San Giorgio. Nel cinquantesimo del Consorzio Autonomo del Porto di Genova* (Milano: Alfieri, 1953), pp. 163–67.

Costamagna, G., 'La costruzione del molo nuovo ed il suo funzionamento', in *Il porto di Genova nella Mostra di Palazzo San Giorgio. Nel cinquantesimo del Consorzio Autonomo del Porto di Genova* (Milano: Alfieri, 1953), pp. 128–31.

Costamagna, P., 'Entre Raphaël, Titien et Michel-Ange: les portraits d'Andrea Doria par Sebastiano del Piombo et Bronzino', in *Les portraits du pouvoir. Collection d'histoire de l'art de l'Académie de France à Rome*, ed. by O. Bonfait, vol. 3 (Roma: Académie de France, 2003), pp. 25–33.

Costantini, C., *Baliani e i gesuiti: annotazioni in margine alla corrispondenza del Baliani con Gio Luigi Confalonieri e Orazio Grassi* (Firenze: Giunti, 1969).

Costantini, C., and others, *Dibattito politico e problemi di governo a Genova nella prima metà del Seicento* (Genova: La Nuova Italia Editrice, 1975).

Costantini, C., 'La ricerca di un'identità repubblicana nella Genova del primo Seicento', in *Miscellanea storica ligure*, 2 (1976), pp. 9–74.

Costantini, C., *La Repubblica di Genova nell'età moderna* (Torino: Utet, 1978).

Costantini, C., 'Politica e storiografia: l'età dei grandi repubblichisti', in *La letteratura ligure. La Repubblica aristocratica (1528–1797)*, II (Genova: Costa & Nolan, 1992), pp. 93–135.

Costantini C., Marini, Q. Vazzoler, F., eds, *Anton Giulio Brignole Sale: un ritratto letterario* (Genova: Universita, 1997).

Courtright, N., *The Papacy and the Art of Reform in Sixteenth-Century Rome: Gregory XIII's Tower of Winds in the Vatican* (Cambridge: Cambridge University Press, 2003).

Cox-Rearick, J., *Dynasty and Destiny in Medici Art: Pontormo, Leo X, and the two Cosimos* (Princeton: Princeton University Press, 1984).

Cozzi, G., *Paolo Sarpi tra Venezia e l'Europa* (Torino: Einaudi, 1979).

Cozzi, G., *Paolo Sarpi. Consulti*, ed. by C. Pin, 2 vols (Pisa-Roma: Istituto Italiano per gli studi filosofici, 2001).

Cremonini, C., 'I feudi imperiali italiani tra Sacro Romano Impero e monarchia cattolica (seconda metà XVI-inizio XVII secolo)', in *Annali dell'Istituto storico italo-germanico in Trento*, 17 (2006), pp. 41–65.

Cremonini, C., Musso, R., eds, *I feudi imperiali in Italia tra XV e XVIII secolo* (Bordighera: Bulzoni, 2010).

Croce, F., 'La letteratura dialettale ligure', in *La letteratura dialettale preunitaria*, ed. by P. Mazzamuto, vol. I (Palermo: Università degli Studi, 1994), pp. 413–69.

Crouzet-Pavan, É., *Venise: une invention de la ville, XIIIe-XVe siècle* (Seyssel: Champ Vallon, 1997).

Crouzet-Pavan, É., *Venise triomphante: les horizons d'un mythe* (Paris: Albin Michel, 1999).

Dagnino, A., '"Per la fabrica et ornamento della Cappella Reale". Storie di architettura e di arredo tra Medioevo ed età moderna', in *El Siglo de los Genoveses e una lunga storia di Arte e Splendori nel Palazzo dei Dogi*, ed. by P. Boccardo and C. Di Fabio (Milano: Skira, 1999), pp. 270–77.

Damian, C., *The Virgin of the Andes: Art and Ritual in Colonial Cuzco* (Miami Beach: Grassfield Press, 1995).

Dandelet, T., J., *Spanish Rome, 1500–1700* (New Haven: Yale University Press, 2001).

Dauverd, C., *Imperial Ambition in the Early Modern Mediterranean: Genoese Merchants and the Spanish Crown* (New York, NY: Cambridge University Press, 2015).

Davanzo, R., 'La committenza e le scelte iconografiche', in *Marcantonio Franceschini. I cartoni ritrovati*, ed. by G. Testa Grauso (Cinisello Balsamo: Silvana Editoriale, 2002), pp. 135–44.

Davidson, P., Van der Weel, A., 'Introduction: The Entry of Archduke Ernst into Antwerp in 1594 in Context', in *Europa Triumphans: Court and Civic Festivals in Early Modern Europe*, ed. by. J. R. Mulryne, H. Watanabe-O'Kelly and M. Shewring (London: Ashgate, 2004), pp. 492–96.

Davidson, B., 'Drawings by Perino del Vaga for the Palazzo Doria, Genoa', in *The Art Bulletin*, 4, 14 (1959), pp. 315–26.

De Franceschi, S. H., *Raison d'État et raison d'Église. La France et l'Interdit vénitien (1606–1607): aspects diplomatiques et doctrinaux* (Paris: Champion, 2009).

De Franchi, S., *Ro chitarrin ò sæ stroffoggi dra Muza de Steva de Franchi nobile patriçio zeneise dîto tra ri arcadi Micrilbo Termopilatide* (Zena: Gexiniana, 1772).

De Mailly, L., *Histoire de la République de Gênes depuis l'an 464 de la fondation de Rome jusqu'à présent* (Paris: Denys du Puis, 1696).

De Marini, A., *Emanuele Brignole e l'Albergo dei Poveri di Genova* (Genova: Stefano Termanini Editore, 2016).

De Negri, T., O., *Storia di Genova* (Milano: Martello, 1974).

De Sade, D. A. F., *Voyage d'Italie*, ed. by M. Lever (Paris: Fayard, 1995).

De Vivo, F., 'Historical Justifications of Venetian Power in the Adriatic', in *Journal of the History of Ideas*, 64 (2003), pp. 159–76.

De Vivo, F., *Information and Communication in Venice. Rethinking Early Modern Politics* (Oxford: Oxford University Press, 2007).

De Vivo, F., 'Francia e Inghilterra di fronte all'Interdetto di Venezia', in *Paolo Sarpi. Politique et religion en Europe* (Paris: Classiques Garnier, 2010), pp. 163–88.

Della Torre, R., *Lo squittinio della Repubblica di Venetia d'autore incognito squittinato da Raffaele Della Torre* (In Genova: per Benedetto Guasco, 1653).

Dellepiane, R., *Mura e Fortificazioni di Genova* (Genova: Nuova Edizione, 1984).

Dellepiane, R., Piana, G. P., 'Le leve corse della Repubblica di Genova: Dalla pace di Ryswick al Trattato di Utrecht (1697–1713)', in *Atti della società ligure di storia patria*, 36 (1996), pp. 427–46.

D'Ezio, M., 'The Advantages of "Demi-Naturalization": Mutual Perceptions of Britain and Italy in Hester Piozzi's Observations and Reflections Made in the Course of a Journey Through France, Italy and Germany', in *Journal for Eighteenth Century Studies*, 33, 2 (2010), pp. 165–80.

Di Fabio, C., 'Un'iconografia regia per la repubblica di Genova. La "Madonna della Città" e il ruolo di Domenico Fiasella', in *Domenico Fiasella*, ed. by P. Donati (Genova: Sagep, 1990), pp. 60–84.

Di Fabio, C., ed., *La Cattedrale di Genova nel Medioevo, secoli VI-XIV* (Milano: Cinisello Balsamo, 1998).

Di Fabio, C., 'La regina della Repubblica e la "Madonna della Città"', in *El siglo de los Genoveses*, ed. by P. Boccardo e C. Di Fabio (Milano: Electa, 1999), pp. 258–62.

Di Raimondo, A., Profumo Müller, L., *Bartolomeo Bianco e Genova. La controversa paternità dell'opera architettonica tra '500 e '600* (Genova: E.R.G.A, 1982).

Doldi, S., *Scienza e tecnica in Liguria dal Settecento all'Ottocento* (Genova: Ecig, 1984).

Dooley, B. M., and others, '1600 Experiment'. URL: https://www.euronewsproject.org/1600-experiment/ [2021/7/20].

Doria, G., 'La gestione del porto di Genova dal 1550 al 1797', *Atti della Società Ligure di Storia Patria*, 28, 1 (1988), pp. 137–97.

Doria, J., *La Chiesa di San Matteo in Genova descritta ed illustrata* (Genova: tip. del R.I. de' Sordo Muti, 1860).

Drelichman, M., and Voth, H. J., *Lending to the Borrower from Hell: Debt, Taxes, and Default in the Age of Philip II* (Princeton: Princeton University Press, 2014).

Du Val, P., *Le voyage et la description d'Italie montrant exactement les raretez et choses remarquables qui se trouvent es Provinces & en châques Villes, les distances d'icelles; Avec un dénombrement des Places & champ de battailles qui s'y sont données* (Paris: Nicolas Oudot, 1656).

Dupaty, C.-M.-J.-B. M., *Travels Through Italy In a Series of Letters; Written in the Year 1785, by the Abbé Dupaty. Translated from the French by an English Gentleman* (London: G.G.J. and J. Robinson, 1788).

Durand, Y., *Les républiques au temps des monarchies* (Paris: Presses Universitaires de France, 1973).

Dussler, L., *Raphael: A Critical Catalogue of His Pictures, Wall-Paintings and Tapestries* (London: Phaidon, 1966).

Edelmayer, F., *Maximilian II., Philipp II. und Reichsitalien. Die Auseinandersetzungen um das Reichslehen Finale in Ligurien, in Veröffentlichungen des Instituts für Europäische Geschichte Mainz 130: Abteilung für Universalgeschichte* (Stuttgart: Steiner, 1988).

Eisler, W., 'Perino del Vaga. Triumphal Arches for the Entrance of Charles V in to Genoa', in *Il Polittico di Sant'Erasmo di Perin del Vaga: rilevamento: una proposta didattica, problemi di restauro e di interpretazione*, ed. by L. Fagioli, G. Rotondi Terminiello and E. Gavazza (Avegno: Stringa, 1982), no pagination.

Eliav, J., 'Trident and Oar in Bronzino's Portrait of Andrea Doria', in *Renaissance Quarterly*, 73 (2020), pp. 775–820.

Engels, M.-C., *Merchants, Interlopers, Seamen and Corsairs: The 'Flemish' Community in Livorno and Genoa, 1615–1635* (Hilversum: Verloren, 1997), pp. 107–23.

Evelyn, J., *The Diary of John Evelyn* (London: Dent, 1906).

Fabris, A., 'Un caso di pirateria veneziana: la cattura della galea del bey di Gerba (21 ottobre 1584)', in *Quaderni di studi arabi*, 8 (1990), pp. 91–111.

Faina, G., *Ingegneria portuale genovese del Seicento* (Firenze: Giunti-Barbera, 1969).

Fasoli, G., 'I fondamenti della storiografia veneziana', in *La storiografia veneziana fino al secolo XVI. Aspetti e problemi*, ed. by A. Pertusi (Firenze: Olschki, 1970), pp. 11–44.

Favreau-Lilie, M.-L., 'Genua und das Reich am Ausgang des Mittelalters (14./15. Jh.)', in *Oriente e Occidente tra Medioevo ed Età Moderna. Studi in Onore di Geo Pistarino*, ed. by L. Balletto (Acqui Terme: Brigati, 1997), I, pp. 283–15.

Felloni, G., 'Stato genovese, finanza pubblica e ricchezza privata: un profilo storico', in *Scritti di storia economica*, 38 (Genoa: Atti della Società Ligure di Storia Patria, 1998), pp. 275–95.

Felloni, G., 'Ricchezza privata, credito e banche: Genova e Venezia nei sec. XII–XIV', in *Genova, Venezia, il Levante nei secoli XII–XIV*, ed. by G. Ortalli and D. Puncuh (Venezia: Istituto Veneto di Scienze Lettere e Arti – Società Ligure di Storia Patria, 2001), pp. 295–318.

Felloni, G., 'Genova e il capitalismo finanziario dalle origini all'apogeo (sec. X–XVIII)', in *Atti della Società Ligure di Storia Patria*, 56 (2016), pp. 71–90.

Ferrando, F., Zappia, A., Fioriti, F., eds, *Gli stranieri della repubblica. Controllo, gestione e convivenza a Genova in età moderna* (Saluzzo: Fusta, 2023).

Ferrari, G., *La Cintura Sacra della Beatissima Vergine, e del gran Patriarca S. Agostino, e M.S. Monica, Nobile, e Ricca D'Indulti, e Priuilegi Apostolici, Rinouati da Gregorio XV. Data a' Cinturati in Sant'Agostino di Genoua, Et à loro istanza, descritta dal P. M. F. Gregorio Ferrari, Varase Agostino. Al Serenissimo Dvce, Eccell. Governatori, et Ill.^mi Procvratori della Republica di Genoua* (Genova: per Gio: Maria Farroni, Niccolò Pesagno, & Pietro Francesco Barberi, 1639).

Ferrari, E., *Liguria trionfante delle principali nazioni del mondo* (Genova: Pier Giovanni Calenzani, 1643).

Fiorani, F., *The Marvel of Maps: Art, Cartography and Politics in Renaissance Italy* (New Haven: Yale University Press, 2005).

Firpo, L., ed., *Relazioni di ambasciatori veneti al senato. Tratte dalla migliori edizioni disponibili e ordinate cronologicamente* (Torino: Bottega d'Erasmo, 1965).

Florio, G., *Micropolitica della rappresentanza. Dinamiche del potere a Venezia in età moderna*, (Roma: Carocci, 2023).

Florio, G., Metlica, A., *Contending Representations II: Entangled Republican Spaces in Early Modern Venice* (Turnhout: Brepols, 2024).

Foglietta, O., *Della Republica di Genova* (Roma: Antonio Blado, 1559).

Foglietta, P., *Il barro*, ed. by M. Rosi, in *Atti della Società ligure di storia patria*, 25 (1892), pp. 219–535.

Forlivesi, M., 'Materiali per una descrizione della disputa e dell'esame di laurea in Età moderna', in *Dalla prima alla seconda Scolastica. Paradigmi e percorsi storiografici*, ed. by A. Ghisalberti (Bologna: ESD, 2000), pp. 252–79.

Forti, L. C., *Le Fortificazioni di Genova* (Genova: Stringa, 1971).

Franchini, G., *Bibliosofia e memorie letterarie di scrittori francescani conventuali ch'hanno scritto dopo l'anno 1585* (Modena: Eredi Soliani, 1693).

Franchini Guelfi, F., 'Il Settecento. Theatrum sacrum e magnifico apparato', in *La scultura a Genova e in Liguria* (Genova: cassa di risparmio di Genova e Imperia, 1988), II, pp. 244–46.

Fubini, R., 'The Italian League and the Policy of the Balance of Power at the Accession of Lorenzo de' Medici', in *The Journal of Modern History*, 67 (1995), pp. 166–99.

Fürttenbach, J., *Newes Itinerarium Italiae*, ed. by H. Foramitti (Hildesheim: Olms, 1971).

Fusaro, M., 'After Braudel: A Reassessment of Mediterranean Trade between the Northern Invasion and the Caravane Maritime', in *Trade and Cultural Exchange in the Early Modern Mediterranean: Braudel's Maritime Legacy*, ed. by M. Fusaro, C. Heywood, and M.-S. Omri (London: Tauris, 2010), pp. 1–22.

Fusaro, M., *Political Economies of Empire in the Early Modern Mediterranean: The Decline of Venice and the Rise of England, 1450–1700* (Cambridge: Cambridge University Press, 2015).

Gabriele, M., Galassi, C., and Guerrini, R., eds, *L'Iconologia di Cesare Ripa. Fonti letterarie e figurative dall'antichità al Rinascimento* (Florence: Olschki, 2013).

Gaeta, F., 'Venezia da "stato misto" ad aristocrazia "esemplare"', in *Storia della cultura veneta*, ed. by G. Arnaldi and M. P. Stocchi, vol. 2 (Vicenza: Neri Pozza Editore, 1983), pp. 437–94.

Galassi, M. C., 'The Permanence of Ephemera: a Rediscovered Fragment by Frans Floris', in *The Burlington Magazine*, 166 (2024), pp. 34–41.

Galasso, G., *Alla periferia dell'impero: Il Regno di Napoli nel periodo spagnolo (secoli XVI–XVII)* (Torino: Einaudi, 1994).

Galiñanes Gallén, M., 'Le poesie in lingua spagnola negli Applausi per l'elezione del serenissimo Agostino Pallavicino (1638)', in *Aspetti del plurilinguismo letterario nella Genova barocca*, ed. by F. Toso (Alessandria, Edizioni dell'Orso, 2022), pp. 33–57.

Gallucci, G., *Recitar cantando la libertà. Il dramma per musica nella Repubblica di Lucca (1636–1705)*, (Roma: Carocci, 2023).

Gambi, L., and Pinelli, A., *La Galleria delle carte geografiche in Vaticano* (Modena: Panini, 1994).

Garcia Garcia, B. J., Lo Basso, L., Mostaccio, S., *Ambrogio Spinola between Genoa, Flanders, and Spain* (Leuven: Leuven University Press, 2022).

García Montón, A., 'Trayectorias individuales durante la quiebra del sistema hispano-genovés: Domingo Grillo (1617–1687)', in *Génova y la monarquía hispánica (1528–1713)*, ed. by M. Herrero and others (Genova: Società Ligure di Storia Patria, 2011), pp. 367–84.

García Montón, A., *Genoese Entrepreneurship and the Asiento Slave Trade, 1650–1700* (New York: Routledge, 2022).

García Pérez, J. C., 'Las embajadas italianas del marqués de Villagarcía: correspondencia y noticias durante el período genovés (1672–1677)' (unpublished doctoral thesis, Universidad Complutense de Madrid, 2019)

Garnett, J., Rosser, G., 'The Virgin Mary and the People of Liguria: Image and Cult', in *The Church and Mary*, ed. R. N. Swanson (Rochester: Boydell & Brewer, 2004), pp. 280–97.

Garnett, J., Rosser, G., *Spectacular Miracles: Transforming Images in Italy from the Renaissance to the Present* (London: Reaktion Books, 2013).

Gavazza, E., 'Gli apparati per le entrate di Carlo V a Genova', in *Il Polittico di Sant'Erasmo di Perin del Vaga: rilevamento: una proposta didattica, problemi di restauro e di interpretazione*, ed. by L. Fagioli, G. Rotondi Terminiello and E. Gavazza (Avegno: Stringa, 1982), no pagination.

Gavazza, E., Lamera, F., *Chiesa del Gesù, Guide turistiche e d'arte* (Genova: Sagep, 1990).

Gavazza, E., Lamera, F., Magnani, L., *La pittura in Liguria: il secondo Seicento* (Genova: Sagep, 1990).

Gavazza, E., Rotondi Terminiello, G., eds, *Genova nell'età Barocca* (Bologna: Nuova Alfa, 1992).

Gavazza, E., 'Apparati decorativi e tematiche iconografiche nelle dimore dell'aristocrazia genovese dei secoli XVII e XVIII', in *Arte Lombarda*, 141, 2 (2004), pp. 88–96.

Gill, R. M., 'Conception and Construction: Galeazzo Alessi and the Use of Drawings in Sixteenth Century Architectural Practice', in *Architectural History*, 59 (2016), pp. 181–219.

Ginzburg, S., 'Perino del Vaga e la generazione di Salviati', in *Francesco Salviati "spirito veramente pellegrino ed eletto"*, ed. by A. Geremicca (Rome: Campisano Editore, 2015), pp. 41–52.

Girón Pascual, R. M., *Comercio y poder: mercaderes genoveses en el sureste de Castilla durante los siglos 16. y 17. (1550–1700)* (Valladolid: Ediciones Universidad de Valladolid, 2018).

Giubbini, G., 'La città rappresentata', in *Genova nell'età barocca*, ed. by E. Gavazza, G. Rotondi Terminiello (Bologna: Nuova Alfa Editoriale, 1992), pp. 32–38.

Giuliani, N., *Prospetto cronologico di un Nomenclatore Letterario Ligustico* (Genova: Tip. Lit. C. Marro e C., 1886).

Giustiniani, A., *Castigatissimi annali con la loro copiosa tavola della eccelsa & illustrissima Republica di Genoa* (Genova: Antonio Bellone, 1537).

Glete, J., *Navies and Nations: Warships, Navies and State Building in Europe and America, 1500–1860*, in *Acta Universitatis Stockholmiensis. Stockholm Studies in History, Stockholm Studies in History*, 48, 2 vols (Stockholm: Almqvist & Wiksell International, 1993).

Glete, J., *War and the State in Early Modern Europe: Spain, the Dutch Republic and Sweden as Fiscal–Military States, 1500–1660* (London: Routledge, 2002).

Gongora Alcasar, Y P. L., *Real grandeza de la serenissima republica de Genova* (Madrid: por Ioseph Fernandez de Buendia, 1665).

Gorse, G. L., 'The villa Doria in Fassolo, Genoa' (doctoral dissertation, Brown University, 1980).

Gorse, G. L., 'An Unpublished Description of the Villa Doria in Genoa During Charles V's Entry, 1533', in *The Art Bulletin*, 48 (1986), pp. 319–22.

Gorse, G. L., 'Between Empire and Republic: Triumphal Entries into Genoa During the Sixteenth Century', in *"All the world's a stage…": art and pageantry in the Renaissance and Baroque*, ed. by I. B. Wisch and S. Scott Munshower (Pennsylvania: State University, 1990), pp. 189–256.

Gorse, G. L., 'Entrate e trionfi: Cerimonie e decorazioni alla Villa di Andrea Doria a Genova', in *Disegni genovesi dal Cinquecento al Settecento* (Firenze: Edizioni Medicea, 1992), pp. 9–18.

Gorse, G. L., 'La "corte" di Andrea Doria a Genova', in *Arte, committenza ed economia a Roma e nelle corti del Rinascimento 1420–1530*, ed. by A. Esch and C. L. Frommel (Torino: Einaudi, 1995), pp. 255–71.

Gorse, G. L., 'Genova, Repubblica dell'Impero', in *Storia dell'architettura italiana: Il secondo Cinquecento*, ed. by C. Conforti and R. I. Tuttle (Milano: Electa, 2001), pp. 240–65.

Gorse, G. L., 'Augustan Mediterranean Iconography and Renaissance Hieroglyphics at the Court of Clement VII: Sebastiano del Piombo's Portrait of Andrea Doria', in *The Pontificate of Clement VII: History, Politics, Culture*, ed. by K. Gouwens and S. E. Reiss (Aldershot: Ashgate, 2005), pp. 313–17.

Gorse, G. L., 'A Question of Sovereignty: France and Genoa, 1494–1528', in *Italy and the European Powers. The Impact of War, 1500–1530*, ed. by C. Shaw (Leiden: Brill, 2006), pp. 187–206.

Gorse, G. L., 'Body Politics and Mythic Figures: Andrea Doria in the Mediterranean World', in *California Italian Studies*, 6, 1 (2016), pp. 1–28.

Goudar, A., *A General History of the Late Revolution of Genoa Containing What Happened in that Republick From the Death of Charles VI to the Raising of the Siege by the Germans* (London: Printed for the Author, 1752).

Graef, H. C., *Mary: A History of Doctrine and Devotion*, 2 vols (New York: Sheed and Ward, 1963–65).

Graf, D., 'Liguria Triumphans. Un capolavoro di Giovanni Battista Gaulli, mai eseguito', in *El Siglo de los Genoveses e una lunga storia di Arte e Splendori nel Palazzo dei Dogi*, ed. by P. Boccardo and C. Di Fabio (Milano: Skira, 1999), pp. 344–49.

Grafe, R., 'On the Spatial Nature of Institutions and the Institutional Nature of Personal Networks in the Spanish Atlantic', in *Culture & History Digital Journal*, 3, 1 (2014), pp. 1–11.

Gray, R., *Letters During the Course of a Tour Through Germany, Switzerland, and Italy, in the Year M.DCC.XCI, and M.DCC.XCII. With Reflections on the Manners, Literature, and Religion of Those Countries* (London: F. and C. Rivington, 1794).

Graziosi, E., *Da capitale a provincia. Genova 1660–1670* (Modena: Mucchi, 1993).

Graziosi, E., *Lancio ed eclissi di una capitale barocca. Genova 1630–1660* (Modena: Mucchi, 2006).

Grech, I., 'Flow of Capital in the Mediterranean: Financial Connections between Genoa and Hospitaller Malta in the Seventeenth and Eighteenth Centuries', in *International Journal of Maritime History*, 17 (2005), pp. 193–210.

Greene, M., 'Beyond the Northern Invasion: The Mediterranean in the Seventeenth Century', in *Past and Present*, 174 (2003), pp. 42–71.

Grendi, E., 'I nordici e il traffico del porto di Genova: 1590–1666', in *Rivista storica italiana*, 83, 1 (1971), pp. 23–69.

Grendi, E., *Introduzione alla storia moderna della repubblica di Genova* (Genova: Bozzi, 1976).

Grendi, E., *La Repubblica aristocratica dei genovesi: politica, carità e commercio fra Cinque e Seicento* (Bologna: Il Mulino, 1987).

Grendi, E., 'Le Società dei Giovani a Genova fra il 1460 e la Riforma del 1528', in *Quaderni storici*, 80 (1992), pp. 509–28.

Grendi, E., 'Doria, Andrea', in *Dizionario biografico degli Italiani*, vol. 41 (Roma: Istituto della Enciclopedia Italiana, 1992), pp. 264–74.

Grendi, E., *I Balbi. Una famiglia genovese fra Spagna e Impero* (Torino: Einaudi, 1997).

Grendi, E., *In altri termini. Etnografia e storia di una società di antico regime*, ed. by O. Raggio and A. Torre (Milano: Feltrinelli, 2004).

Grossi Bianchi, L., Poleggi, E., 'La strada del Guastato: capitale e urbanistica genovese agli inizi del Seicento', in *Dalla città preindustriale alla città del capitalismo*, ed. by A. Cracciolo, (Bologna: Il Mulino, 1975), pp. 81–93.

Grotemeyer, P., 'Eine Medaille des Andrea Doria von Christoph Weiditz', in *Centennial Volume of the American Numismatic Society*, ed. by Harald Ingholt (New York: The American Numismatic Society, 1958), pp. 317–27.

Guerra, A., Molteni, E., Nicoloso, P., *Il Trionfo della Miseria. Gli Alberghi dei Poveri di Genova, Palermo e Napoli* (Milano: Electa, 1995).

Gullino, S., 'Il network commerciale del Magistrato dell'Abbondanza genovese durante la crisi del 1590–91', in *Mediterranea ricerche storiche*, 17 (2020), pp. 577–98.

Haitsma Mulier, E. O. G., *The Myth of Venice and Dutch Republican Thought in the Seventeenth Century* (Assen: Van Gorcum, 1980).

Haitsma Mulier, E.O.G, 'Genova e l'Olanda nel Seicento: contatti mercantili e ispirazione politica', in *Rapporti Genova-Mediterraneo-Atlantico nell'età moderna*, ed. by Raffaele Belvederi (Genova: Istituto di Scienze Storiche, Università di Genova, 1983), pp. 429–44.

Hanss, S., '"Event and Narration". Spanish Storytelling on the Battle of Lepanto in the Early 1570s', in *Lepanto and Beyond. Images of Religious Alterity from Genoa and the Christian Mediterranean*, ed. by L. Stagno and B. Franco Llopis (Leuven: Leuven University Press, 2021), pp. 81–110.

Harvey, K., *Reading Sex in the Eighteenth Century: Bodies and Gender in English Erotic Culture* (Cambridge: Cambridge University Press, 2004).

Hermoso Cuesta, M., 'The Hall of Realms, a Space for Royal Magnificence', in *Magnificence in the Seventeenth Century. Performing Splendour in Catholic and Protestant Contexts*, ed. by G. Versteegen, S. Bussels and W. Melion (Leiden: Brill, 2020), pp. 89–112.

Herrero Sánchez, M., *El acercamiento hispano-neerlandés (1648–1678)* (Madrid: CSIC, 2000).

Herrero Sanchez, M., 'Génova y el sistema imperial hispánico', in *La Monarquía de las naciones. Patria, Nación y Naturaleza en la Monarquía de España*, ed. by A. Álvarez-Ossorio and B. García (Madrid: Fundación Carlos de Amberes, 2004), pp. 528–62.

Herrero Sánchez, M., 'La quiebra del sistema hispano-genovés', in *Hispania*, 65 (2005), pp. 115–51.

Herrero Sánchez, M., 'La red genovesa Spínola y el entramado transnacional de los marqueses de los Balbases al servicio de la Monarquía Hispánica en Bartolomé Yun Casalilla', in *Las redes del Imperio. Élites sociales en la articulación de la Monarquía Hispánica, 1492–1714*, ed. by M. Pons (Madrid: Marcial Pons, 2009), pp. 97–133.

Herrero Sánchez, M., Álvarez-Ossorio, A., 'La aristocracia genovesa al servicio de la Monarquía Católica: el caso del III marqués de Los Balbases (1630–1699)', in *Génova y la monarquía hispánica (1528–1713)*, ed. by M. Herrero Sanchez and others (Genova: Società Ligure di Storia Patria, 2011), pp. 331–66.

Herrero Sanchez, M., and others, eds, *Génova y la Monarquía Hispánica (1528–1713)*, 2 vols (Genova: Società Ligure di Storia Patria de Genova, 2011).

Herrero Sanchez, M., 'Republican Monarchies, Patrimonial RepublicsThe Catholic Monarchy and the Mercantile Republics of Genoa and the United Provinces', in *Polycentric monarchies: how did Early Modern Spain and Portugal Achieve and Maintain a Global Hegemony?*, ed. by P. Cardim and others (Brighton: Sussex Academic Press, 2012), pp. 181–96.

Herrero Sanchez, M., 'Introducción. Líneas de análisis y debates conceptuales en torno al estudio de las repúblicas y el republicanismo en la Europa Moderna', in *Repúblicas y republicanismo en la Europa moderna (siglos XVI–XVIII)*, ed. by M. H. Sánchez (Madrid: Fondo de Cultura Económica, 2017), pp. 17–89.

Herrero Sanchez, M., *Repúblicas y republicanismo en la Europa moderna (siglos XVI–XVII)* (Madrid: Fondo de Cultura Económica, 2017).

Herrero Sanchez, M., Albareda, J., eds, *Political Representation in the Ancien Régime* (London: Routledge, 2019).

Heydenreich, L., Lotz, W., *Architecture in Italy 1400–1600* (Baltimore: Penguin Books, 1974).

Heywood, C. J., 'The English in the Mediterranean, 1600–1630: A Post-Braudelian perspective in the "Northern Invasion", in *Trade and Cultural Exchange in the Early Modern Mediterranean: Braudel's Maritime Legacy*, ed. by M. Fusaro, C. J. Heywood and M.-S. Omri (London: I.B. Tauris, 2010), pp. 23–44.

Hill, R., *The Diplomatic Correspondence of the Right Hon. Richard Hill, Envoy Extraordinary from the Court of St. James to the Duke of Savoy, 1703–1706*, ed. by W. Blackley, I (London: 1845).

Hochedlinger, M., *Austria's Wars of Emergence War, State and Society in the Habsburg Monarchy, 1683–1797* (New York & Oxford: Routledge, 2013).

Holtz, G., 'The Model of the VOC in Early Seventeenth-Century France (Hugo Grotius and Pierre Bergeron)', in *The Dutch Trading Companies as Knowledge Networks*, ed. by S. Huigen, J. L. de Jong, and E. Kolfin (Leiden: Brill, 2010), pp. 329–35.

Huarte, J., *Essame degl'ingegni*, ed. by C. Casalini and L. Salvarani (Roma: Anicia, 2010).

Ieva, F., 'Il Principe di Piemonte nella guerra lampo del 1625', in *Genova e Torino. Quattro secoli di incontri e scontri*, ed. by G. Assereto, C. Bitossi and P. Merlin (Genova: Società Ligure di Storia Patria, 2015), pp. 81–97.

Imber, C., *The Crusade of Varna, 1443–45* (Aldershot: Ashgate, 2006).

Imperiale, G. V., *De' giornali di Gio. Vincenzo Imperiale dalla partenza dalla patria: anno primo / con prefazione e note di Anton Giulio Barrili* (Genova: Società Ligure di Storia Patria, 1898).

Incoronatione del Sereniss. Gio Giacomo Imperiale Duce di Genova (Venezia: Antonio Pinelli, 1618).

Infelise, M., *Prima dei giornali: alle origini della pubblica informazione, secoli XVI e XVII* (Roma: Laterza, 2002).

Interiano, P., *Ristretto delle historie genovesi* (Lucca: Busdrago, 1551).

Israel, J., *Empires and Entrepots: Dutch, the Spanish Monarchy and the Jews, 1585–1713* (London: Bloomsbury, 1990).

Ivaldi, A. F., 'Scheda per un "apparato" genovese del 1599. L'arco trionfale per il passaggio di Margherita di Spagna e Alberto d'Austria (Genova, 11–18 febbraio 1599)', in *La Berio*, 19, 3 (1979), pp. 43–52.

Ivaldi, A. F., 'Una polemica anti-spagnola: l'*Ariodante* di G. A. Spinola', in *Tradurre riscrivere mettere in scena*, ed. by M. G. Profeti (Firenze: Alinea, 1996), pp. 191–209.

Jones, R., and Penny, N., *Raphael* (New Haven: Yale University Press, 1983).

Kapossy, B., 'Republican Futures: The Image of Holland in the 18th-Century Swiss Reform Discourse', in *The Republican Alternative: The Netherlands and Switzerland Compared*, ed. by A. Holenstein, T. Maissen, and M. R. Prak (Amsterdam: Amsterdam University Press, 2008), pp. 279–300.

Keller, K., Molino, P., *Die Fuggerzeitungen im Kontext: Zeitungssammlungen im Alten Reich und in Italien* (Wien: Böhlau Verlag, 2015).

Keyßler, J. G., *Travels through Germany, Bohemia, Hungary, Switzerland, Italy, and Lorrain*, 4 vols (London: Linde, 1756).

Kirk, T. A., *Genoa and the Sea: Policy and Power in an Early Modern Maritime Republic, 1559–1684* (London: Johns Hopkins University Press, 2005).

Kirk, T., 'The Apogee of the Hispano-Genoese Bond, 1576–1627', in *Hispania*, 65, 219 (2005), pp. 45–65.

Kirk, T., 'La crisi del 1654 come indicatore del nuovo equilibrio mediterraneo', in *Génova y la Monarquía Hispánica (1528–1713)*, ed. by M. Herrero Sánchez, Yasmina Ben Yessef Garfia and Carlos Bitossi (Genova: Società Ligure di Storia Patria, 2011), pp. 527–38.

Kliemann, J., *Gesta dipinte. La grande decorazione nelle dimore italiane dal Quattrocento al Seicento* (Cinisello Balsamo: Silvana Editoriale, 1993).

Koenigsberger, Helmut G., 'Republicanism, monarchism and liberty', in *Royal and Republican Sovereignty in Early Modern Europe. Essays in memory of Ragnhild Hatton*, ed. by R. Oresko, G. C. Gibbs and H. M. Scott (Cambridge: Cambridge University Press, 1997), pp. 43–74.

Krefeld, T., 'La modellazione dello spazio comunicativo al di qua e al di là del territorio nazionale', in *Lingua, cultura e cittadinanza in contesti migratori. Europa e area mediterranea*, ed. by G. Berruto and others (Perugia: Guerra edizioni, 2009), pp. 33–44.

Kuyper, W., *The Triumphant Entry or Renaissance Architecture into the Netherlands: The Joyeuse Entrée of Philip of Spain into Antwerp in 1549. Renaissance and Mannerist architecture in the Low Countries from 1530 to 1630* (Alphen an den Rijn: Canaletto, 1994).

Kurz, O., *Bolognese Drawings of the XVII and XVIII centuries in the collections of Her Majesty the Queen at Windsor Castle* (London: Phaidon, 1955).

Lalande, J., *Voyage d'un françois en Italie, fait dans les années 1765 & 1766*, 8 vols (Genève, 1769).

Lamal, N., 'Le orecchie sì piene di Fiandra: Italian news and histories on the revolt in the Netherlands, 1566–1648' (unpublished doctoral thesis, 2014).

Lamal, N., *Italian Communication on the Revolt in the Low Countries*, Leiden: Brill, 2023.

Lane, F. C., *Venice: A Maritime Republic* (Baltimore: The Johns Hopkins University Press, 1973).

Lanzi, N., *Genova Città di Maria Santissima. Storie e documenti della pietà mariana genovese* (Pisa: Giardini Editore e Stampatore, 1992).

Lattarico, J-F., '"Questo è il gusto di Genova". À propos des Drammi per musica de Giovanni Andrea Spinola', in *Studi secenteschi*, 57 (2016), pp. 31–47.

Laubach, E., *Ferdinand I. als Kaiser. Politik und Herrscherauffassung* (Münster: Aschendorff, 2001).

Lavaggi, A., 'La scienza in Liguria dei secoli XVI e XVII: limiti, propensioni, individualità. Alcuni aspetti e considerazioni', in *Physis: Rivista internazionale di storia della scienza*, 42 (2005), pp. 501–19.

Lazzarini, I., *Communication and Conflict: Italian Diplomacy in the Early Renaissance, 1350–1520* (Oxford: Oxford University Press, 2015).

Lazzerini, L., 'Officina Sarpiana. Scritture del Sarpi in materia di Gesuiti', in *Rivista di storia della Chiesa in Italia*, 58, 1 (2004), pp. 29–80.

Leonardi, A., 'La committenza Doria tra Loano e Dolceacqua: sistemi di residenza "neofeudali" del Ponente ligure', in *Atlante tematico del Barocco in Italia. Residenze nobiliari. Italia settentrionale*, ed. by M. Fagiolo (Roma: De Luca Editori, 2009), pp. 111–21.

Leoncini, L., 'Deduzioni iconografiche, linguaggio geroglifico e uso dell'antico: il caso del Ritratto Doria', in *Il ritratto e la memoria. Materiali 2*, ed. by A. Gentili, Ph. Morel and C. Cieri Via, vol. 2 (Roma: Bulzoni, 1993), pp. 249–61.

Levin, M. J., *Agents of Empire: Spanish Ambassadors in Sixteenth-Century Italy* (Ithaca, N.Y.: Cornell University Press, 2005).

Limberis, V., *Divine Heiress: The Virgin Mary and the Creation of Christian Constantinople* (London: Routledge, 1994).

Lo Basso, L., *Uomini da remo. Galee e galeotti nel Mediterraneo in età moderna* (Milano: Selene, 2003).

Lo Basso, L., 'Diaspora e armamento marittimo nelle strategie economiche dei genovesi nella seconda metà del XVII secolo: una storia globale', in *Studi storici*, 1 (2015), pp. 137–56.

Lo Basso, L., 'De Curaçao a Esmirna. El armamento marítimo en las estrategias económicas de los genoveses en la segunda mitad del siglo XVII', in *Repúblicas y republicanismo en la Europa moderna (siglos XVI–XVIII)*, ed. by M. Herrero Sánchez (Madrid: Fondo de Cultura Económica, 2017), pp. 529–53.

Lo Basso, L., 'To Lose One's Honour: Ambrogio Spinola's Return to Italy, the Casale Affair, and the End of "Pax Hispanica" (1627–30)', in *Ambrogio Spinola between Genoa, Flanders, and Spain*, ed. by S. Mostaccio, Bernardo J. García García, l. Lo Basso (Leuven: Leuven University Press, 2022), pp. 177–210.

Lombardi, G., 'Sisto IV, Papa', in *Dizionario biografico degli italiani* (Roma: Istituto della Enciclopedia italiana, 2018).

Lopez Martin, I., 'A Century of Small Paper Boats. The Hispanic Monarchy, the United Provinces, and the Mediterranean' in *España y las 17 Provincias de los Países Bajos. Una Revisión Historiográfica*, ed. by A. Crespo Solana (Cordoba: Universidad de Cordoba, 2002), pp. 533–62.

Luccardini, R., *Carignano. Genova. Storia dell'espansione sulla collina* (Genova: Sagep, 2014).

Lucchini, E., 'Genova e Finale nella seconda metà del sec. XVI', in *Rivista ingauna e intemelia*, 34 (1979–1980), pp. 46–57.

Lucchini, E., *Dominio e Sopravvivenza. Genova nell'età di Filippo II* (Genova: Università di Genova, 1990).

Lünig, Johann Christian, *Codex Italiae diplomaticus [...]*, 4 vols (Frankfurt and Leipzig: Lankisch, 1725–1735).

Lusignani, M. E., *Conclusiones ex universa Theologia. Iuxta Subtilium Theologorum principis Ioannis Duns Scoti Inconcussam Doctrinam, quas sub auspiciis Serenissimae ac Inclytae Genuen. Reipublicae propugnandas exponit* (Genova: Antonio Casamara, 1695).

Machiavelli, N., *Istorie fiorentine*, ed. by F. Gaeta (Milano: Feltrinelli, 1962).

Mackenney, R., *The City-State, 1500–1700. Republican Liberty in an Age of Princely Power*, Studies in European History (London: Macmillan, 1989).

Maffe, S., *Le radici antiche dei simboli. Studi sull'Iconologia di Cesare Ripa e i suoi rapporti con l'antico* (Naples: La Stanza delle Scritture, 2009).

Maffei, S., ed., *Cesare Ripa e gli spazi dell'allegoria* (Napoli: La Stanza delle Scritture, 2010).

Maffei, S., 'Introduzione', in *Cesare Ripa. Iconologia*, ed. by S. Maffei (Torino: Einaudi, 2012).

Magnani, L., 'Sintesi iconografica e apparato per la città: la facciata dipinta di Palazzo S. Giorgio', in *Facciate dipinte conservazione e restauro* (Genova: Sagep, 1982), pp. 201–05.

Magnani, L., 'Committenza e arte sacra a Genova dopo il Concilio di Trento: Materiali di ricerca', in *Studi di storia delle arti*, 5 (1983–1985), pp. 133–84.

Magnani, L., *Il Tempio di Venere. Giardino e Villa nella cultura Genovese* (Genova: Sagep, 1987).

Magnani, L., 'Novus orbis emergat: iconografie colombiane per un arco trionfale', in *Columbeis*, 3 (1988), pp. 203–14.

Magnani, L., 'Committenti e architetture a Genova tra XVI e XVII secolo: l'edilizia religiosa e le scelte di Giovanni Andrea Doria', in *L'architettura a Roma e in Italia (1580–1621)*, ed. by G. Spagnesi (Roma: Centro di studi per la storia dell'architettura, 1989), pp. 141–49.

Magnani, L., 'Il giardino, spazio di realtà e spazio di illusione', in *Genova nell'età barocca*, ed. by E. Gavazza and G. Rotondi Terminiello (Bologna: Nuova Alfa Editoriale Libri, 1992), pp. 29–31.

Magnani, L., 'Residenze di villa e immagini di giardino tra realtà e mito', in *La scelta della misura. Gabriello Chiabrera: l'altro fuoco del barocco italiano*, ed. by F. Bianchi and, P. Russ (Genova: Costa & Nolan, 1993), pp. 467–86.

Magnani, L., 'I Doria e il Carmelo di Loano', in *Nicolò Doria. Itinerari economici, culturali, religiosi nei secoli XVI–XVII tra Spagna, Genova e l'Europa*, ed. by S. Giordano and C. Paolocci (Roma: Teresianum, 1996), pp. 407–22.

Magnani, L., 'The Rise and Fall of Garden in the Republic of Genova, 1528–1797', in *Bourgeois and Aristocratic Cultural Encounters in Garden Art, 1550–1850*, ed. by M. Conan (Washington: Dumbarton Oaks Research Library and collection, 2002), pp. 43–76.

Magnani, L., 'Temporary Architecture and Public Decoration: the Development of Images', in *Europa Triumphans: Court and Civic Festivals in Early Modern Europe*, ed. by J. R. Mulryne, H. Watanabe-O'Kelly and M. Shewring (London: Ashgate, 2004), pp. 250–60.

Magnani, L., 'Apparati festivi e immagine della città tra Seicento e Settecento', in *Il gran teatro del barocco. Le capitali della festa: Italia settentrionale*, ed. by M. Fagiolo (Roma: De Luca, 2007), pp. 116–39.

Magnani, L., 'Genoese Gardens between Pleasure and Politics', in Gardens, in *City Life and Culture*, ed. by M. Conan and C. Whangheng (Washington: Dumbarton Oaks Research Library and collection, 2008), pp. 54–71.

Magnani, L., 'Articolazione e immagine del sistema abitativo della nobiltà genovese tra spazio urbano e spazi di villa', in *Atlante tematico del barocco in Italia. Residenze nobiliari. Italia settentrionale*, ed. by M. Fagiolo (Roma: De Luca, 2009), pp. 70–96.

Magnani, L., Stagno, L., 'Il Carmelo di Loano nel quadro della committenza religiosa dei Doria. Le scelte delle iconografie e degli artisti: Paggi, Vanni, Passignano, Curradi', in *Monte Carmelo di Loano dal 1609. Una presenza carmelitana tra storia e attualità* (Cuneo: Agami, 2017), pp. 137–56.

Maissen. T., 'Inventing the Sovereign Republic: Imperial Structures, French Challenges, Dutch Models and the Early Modern Swiss Confederation', in *The Republican Alternative: The Netherlands and Switzerland Compared*, ed. by A. Holenstein, T. Maissen, and M. R. Prak (Amsterdam: Amsterdam University Press, 2008), pp. 125–51.

Maissen. T., 'Liberty and liberties in Europe's federal republics', in *Religious and constitutional liberties*, ed. by Q. Skinner and others (Cambridge: Cambridge University Press, 2012), pp. 235–55.

Maissen. T., 'Républiques et républicanismes en époque moderne. Théories et pratiques dans une perspective occidentale', in *Républiques et républicanismes. Les cheminements de la liberté*, ed. by O. Christin (Lormond: Le bord de l'eau, 2019), pp. 27–45.

Mâle, E., 'La Clef des allégories peintes et sculptées au XVIIe et au XVIIIe siècle', in *Revue des Deux Mondes*, 39 (1927), pp. 106–9, 375–94.

Manca, F., 'Ingerenze genovesi e spagnole nella prima rivolta dei finalesi contro Alfonso II del Carretto nel 1558', in *Atti dei convegni internazionali sulla storia del Finale, La Spagna, Milano ed il Finale. Il ruolo del marchesato finalese tra medioevo ed età moderna* (Finale Ligure: Bolla, 1994) pp. 245–61.

Mancini, G., *Descrizzione dell'Arco Trionfale fatto in Genova nel passaggio della Maestà della Regina Catolica e del Serenissimo Alberto, Arciduca d'Austria* (Genova: Giuseppe Pavoni, 1599).

Mango, C., 'Constantinople as Theotokoupolis', in *Mother of God: Representations of the Virgin in Byzantine Art*, ed. by M. Vassilaki (Milan: Skira, 2000), pp. 17–25.

Manzitti, A., ed., *Luciano Borzone. Pittore vivacissimo nella Genova di primo Seicento* (Genova: Sagep, 2015).

Maranini, A., 'Col senno e con la mano. Eyes, reason and hand in symbolic transmission', in *Glasgow Emblem Studies*, 12 (2007), pp. 115–56.

Maréchaux, B., 'Cultiver l'alternative au système philo-hispanique. Attraction, diffusion et appropriation du modèle vénitien dans la pensée républicaniste génoise du premier XVIIe siècle', in *Génova y la monarquía hispánica (1528–1713)*, ed. by M. Herrero Sánchez and others (Genova: Società Ligure di Storia Patria, 2011), pp. 657–94.

Maréchaux, B., 'Negociar, disuadir y comunicar para la conservación y reputación de la Monarquía: la República de Venecia en las estrategias de la Pax Hispánica bajo el valimiento de Lerma', in *El Arte de la prudencia. La Tregua de los Doce Años en la Europa de los pacificadores*, ed. by B. J. García García, M. H. Sánchez, and A. Hugon (Madrid: Fundación Carlos de Amberes, 2012), pp. 91–120.

Maréchaux, B., '"Non andare mai alla giustizia": conflictividad marítima, mediación y normas jurídicas comunes entre Venecia y el Imperio Otomano (1600–1630)', in *Repúblicas y Republicanismo en la Europa moderna (siglos XVI–XVIII)*, ed. by M. H. Sánchez (Madrid: Fondo de Cultura Económica, 2017), pp. 205–28.

Maréchaux, B., 'Los asentistas de galeras genoveses y la articulación naval de un imperio policéntrico (siglos XVI–XVII)', in *Hispania*, 80 (2020), pp. 47–77.

Maréchaux, B., (2023) 'Business Organisation in the Mediterranean Sea: Genoese Galley Entrepreneurs in the Service of the Spanish Empire (Late Sixteenth and Early Seventeenth Centuries)', in *Business History*, 65 (2023), pp. 56–87.

Marengo, E., 'Alfonso II Del Carretto Marchese di Finale e la Repubblica di Genova', in *Atti della Società Ligure di Storia Patria*, 46 (1917), pp. 3–141.

Marignoli, D. K., Drascek, M, 'The Bozzetto for Liguria Triumphans by Baciccio identified. New traces for the history of collecting in Friuli-Venezia-Giulia', in *Paragone Arte*, 143 (2019), pp. 35–47.

Marino, J., *Becoming Neapolitan: Citizen Culture in Baroque Naples* (Baltimore: Johns Hopkins University Press, 2011).

Marini, Q., 'Francesco Fulvio Frugoni', in *La letteratura ligure. La Repubblica aristocratica (1528–1797). Parte seconda* (Genova: Costa & Nolan, 1992), pp. 53–91..

Markey, L., 'Stradano's Allegorical Invention of the Americas in Late Sixteenth-Century Florence', in *Renaissance Quarterly*, 65 (2012), pp. 400–12.

Mars, F. L., 'Ange Goudar, cet inconnu (1708–1791): Essai bio-bibliographique sur un aventurier polygraphe du XVIIIe siècle', in *Casanova Gleanings*, 9 (1966), pp. 1–65.

Martínez de la Mata, F., *Memoriales y Discursos de Francisco Martinez de Mata* (Madrid: Editorial Moneda y Crédito, 1971).

Martini, E., 'Il Tasso istoriato. La Gerusalemme tra edizioni e affreschi a Genova tra XVI e XVII secolo', in *Le sorti d'Orlando. Illustrazioni e riscritture del Furioso* (Lucca: Pacini Fazzi, 2013), pp. 213–31.

Martyn, T., *A Tour Through Italy Containing Full Directions for Traveling in That Interesting Country… A New Edition* (London: Kearsley, 1791).

Martoccio, M. P., 'A Man of Particular Ability': A Jewish-Genoese Military Contractor in the Fiscal-Military System', in *Business History* 66, 3 (2024), pp. 625–52.

Martoccio, M. P., 'The Place for such Business': The Business of War in the City of Genoa, 1701–1714', in *War in History*, 29, 2 (2021), pp. 302–22.

Maschietto, F. L., *Elena Lucrezia Cornaro Piscopia (1646–1684): prima donna laureata nel mondo* (Padova: Antenore, 1978).

Massola, G. F., *Il fasto della Corte cristiana* (Genova: Franchelli, 1674).

Massola, G. F., *La virtù nutrice e consigliera dei principi* (Genova: Franchelli, 1686).

Mastellone, S., 'Holland as a Political Model in Italy in the Seventeenth Century', in *Bijdragen En Mededelingen Betreffende de Geschiedenis Der Nederlanden*, 98, 4 (1983), pp. 568–82.

Mastellone, S., 'I Repubblicani del Seicento ed il modello politico olandese', in *Il pensiero politico*, 18, 2 (1985), pp. 145–63.

Mazetti Petersson, A., *A Culture for the Christian Commonwealth. Antonio Possevino, Authority, History, and the Venetian Interdict* (Uppsala: Acta Universitatis Upsaliensis, 2022).

McDowell, P., *The Women of Grub Street: Press, Politics, and Gender in the London Literary Marketplace 1678–1730* (Oxford: Oxford University Press, 1998).

Meadow, M. A., 'Ritual and Civic Identity in Philip II's 1549 Antwerp Blijde Incompst', in *Hof-, Staats- en Stadsceremonies/Court, State and City Ceremonies*, ed. by R. Falkenburg, J. De Jong and M. A. Meadow (Zwolle: Waanders, 1999), pp. 37–67.

Meiss, M., *Painting in Florence and Siena after the Black Death: The Arts, Religion and Society in the Mid-Fourteenth Century* (Princeton: Princeton University Press, 1951).

Merli, A., Belgrano, L. T., 'Il palazzo del Principe d'Oria a Fassolo in Genova', in *Atti della Società Ligure di Storia Patria*, 10 (1874), pp. VII–XIII.

Metlica, A., 'Magnificence and Atticism in Seventeenth-Century Venice', in *Magnificence in the Seventeenth Century. Performing Splendour in Catholic and Protestant Contexts*, ed. by G. Versteegen, S. Bussels and W. Melion (Leiden: Brill, 2020), pp. 261–75.

Metlica, A., *Lessico della propaganda barocca* (Venezia: Marsilio, 2022).

Miller, A. R., *Letters from Italy, describing the manners, customs, antiquities, paintings, &c. of the country, in the years MDCCLXX and MDCCLXXI, to a friend residing in France. By an English woman. In three volumes*, 3 vols (Dublin: W. Watson etc., 1776).

Molà, L., 'Material Diplomacy: Venetian Luxury Gifts for the Ottoman Empire in the Late Renaissance', in *Global Gifts: The Material Culture of Diplomacy in Early Modern Eurasia*, ed. by Z. Biedermann, A. Gerritsen, and G. Riello (Cambridge: Cambridge University Press, 2017), pp. 56–87.

Montagni, C., ed., *Il Restauro dell'Altare Maggiore della Cattedrale di San Lorenzo in Genova* (Genova: Colombo Grafiche, 2008).

Morando, B., *La Rosalinda* (Piacenza: Giovanni Bazachi, 1650).

Morando, S., 'La letteratura in Liguria tra Cinque e Seicento', in *Storia della cultura ligure*, vol. 4 (2005), p. 27–64.

Morando, S., 'Luca Assarino, tra Genova e la modernità, verso i ragguagli di Cipro', in *I diversi fuochi della letteratura barocca: ricerche in corso* (Genova: Genova University Press, 2018), pp. 231–50.

Motta, P., ed., *I Forti di Genova, Guide di Genova* (Genova: Sagep, 1986).

Motta, P., ed., 'Nostra Signora delle Vigne', in *Chiese di Genova, Guide di Genova*, vol. 5 (Genova: Sagep, 1986), pp. 77–86.

Motta, P., ed., 'Santa Maria Assunta in Carignano', in *Chiese di Genova, Guide di Genova*, vol. 7 (Genova: Sagep, 1986), pp. 5–14

Motta, P., ed., 'Nostra Signora della Consolazione', in *Chiese di Genova, Guide di Genova*, vol. 7 (Genova: Sagep, 1986), pp. 15–24.

Mulryne, J. R., Watanabe-O'Kelly, H., and Shewring, M., eds, *Europa Triumphans: Court and Civic Festivals in Early Modern Europe* (London: Ashgate, 2004).

Musarra, A., *Genova e il mare nel Medioevo* (Bologna: Il Mulino, 2015).

Musarra, A., *Il Grifo e il Leone. Genova e Venezia in lotta per il Mediterraneo* (Bari: Laterza, 2020).

Muto, G., 'La presenza dei Genovesi dei domini spagnoli in Italia', in *Atti della Società Ligure di Storia Patria*, 43, 1 (2003), pp. 659–71.

Natucci, A., 'Giovanni Battista Baliano, letterato e scienziato genovese del secolo XVI', in *Atti dell'Accademia Ligure di Scienze e Lettere*, 17 (1960), pp. 13–27.

Newcome, M., 'Prints after Domenico Piola', in *The Burlington Magazine*, 124 (1982), pp. 609–18.

Newcome, M., ed., *Disegni genovesi dal XVI al XVIII secolo* (Firenze: Olschki, 1989).

Niccoli, B., 'Official Dress and Courtly Fashion in Genoese Entries', in *Europa Triumphans: Court and Civic Festivals in Early Modern Europe*, ed. by J. R. Mulryne, H. Watanabe-O'Kelly and M. Shewring (London: Ashgate, 2004), pp 261–73.

Niri, M. M., *La Tipografia a Genova e in Liguria nel XVII Secolo* (Firenze: Olschki, 1998).

Norman, D., ed., *Siena, Florence and Padua: Art, Society and Religion 1280–1400*, 2 vols (New Haven: Yale University Press, 1995).

Nothall, J., *Travels through Italy; Containing New and Curious Observations on that Country* (London: S. Hooper, 1766).

Nuti, L., 'The city and its image', in *Europa Triumphans: Court and Civic Festivals in Early Modern Europe*, ed. by J. R. Mulryne, H. Watanabe-O'Kelly and M. Shewring (London: Ashgate, 2004), pp. 242–49.

Nye, J. S., *Soft Power: The Means to Success in World Politics* (New York: Public Affairs, 2004).

Oddens, J., Moorman, G., Metlica, A., *Contending Representations I: The Dutch Republic and the Lure of Monarchy* (Turnhout Belgium: Brepols, 2023).

Oettinger Jr., M., ed., *San Antonio 1718: Art from Mexico* (San Antonio: Trinity University Press and San Antonio Museum of Art, 2018).

Oestmann, P., 'The highest courts of the Holy Roman Empire: Imperial Chamber Court and Imperial Aulic Council', in *Central Courts in Early Modern Europe and the Americas*, ed by A. M. Godfrey and C. H. van Ree (Berlin: Duncker & Humblot, 2020), pp. 225–86.

Ogg, D., *England in the reigns of James II and William III* (Oxford: Oxford University Press, 1984).

Olcse Spingardi, C., 'Il concorso del 1782 per la decorazione della volta di Palazzo Ducale: documenti d'archivio', in *Bollettino dei Musei Civici genovesi*, 44 (2000), pp. 27–34.

Olcese Spingardi, C., 'Un mancato intervento di Cristoforo Unterperger a Genova: vicende e retroscena del concorso del 1782 per la decorazione del Salone del Maggior Consiglio a Palazzo Ducale', in *Genova e L'Europa continentale*, ed. by P. Boccardo and C. Di Fabio (Genova: Carige, 2004), pp. 210–21.

Olivieri, A., *Monete, medaglie e sigilli dei principi Doria che serbansi nella biblioteca della regia Università* (Genova: Co' tipi del R. I. de' sordo-muti, 1958).

Oresko, R., 'The House of Savoy in search for a royal crown in the seventeenth century', in *Royal and Republican Sovereignty in Early Modern Europe*, ed. by R. Oresko, G. C. Gibbs and H. M. Scott (Cambridge: Cambridge University Press, 1997), pp. 272–350.

Ortalli, G., Puncuh, D., eds, *Genova, Venezia, il Levante nei secoli XII–XIV* (Venezia: Istituto Veneto di Scienze Lettere e Arti – Società Ligure di Storia Patria, 2001).

Osborne, T., *Dynasty and Diplomacy in the Court of Savoy: Political Culture and the Thirty Years' War* (Cambridge: Cambridge University Press, 2002).

Ouditt, S., *Impressions of Southern Italy: British Travel Writing from Henry Swinburne to Norman Douglas* (New York: Routledge, 2014).

Owen, J., *Travels into Different Parts of Europe, in the Years 1791 and 1792: With Familiar Remarks on Places, Men and Manners*, 2 vols (London: T. Cadell Jun and W. Davies, 1796).

Pacini, A., *La Genova di Andrea Doria nell'Impero di Carlo V* (Firenze: Bulzoni, 1999).

Pacini, A., 'Ideali repubblicani, lotta politica e gestione del potere a Genova nella prima metà del Cinquecento', in *Politica e cultura nelle repubbliche italiane dal Medioevo all'età moderna. Firenze, Genova, Lucca, Siena*, ed. by S. Adorni Braccesi and M. Ascheri, I (Roma: Istituto storico italiano per l'età moderna e contemporanea, 2001), pp. 189–236.

Pacini, A., 'El "Padre" y La "República Perfecta": Génova y La Monarquía Española En 1575', in *Espacios de Poder: Cortes, Ciudades y Villas (S. XVI–XVIII)*, vol. 2 (Madrid: Universidad Autónoma de Madrid, 2002), pp. 119–32.

Pacini, A., 'Genoa and Emperor Charles V', in *The World of Emperor Charles V*, ed. by W. Blockmans and N. Mout (Amsterdam: Royal Netherlands Academy of Arts and Sciences, 2004), pp. 161–99.

Pacini, A., 'Genova e il mare: Pacini legge Kirk', in *Storica*, 12, 35–36 (2006), pp. 229–41.

Pacini, A., '"Poiché gli stati non sono portatili": geopolitica e strategia nei rapporti tra Genova e Spagna tra Cinque e inizio Seicento', in *Génova y la monarquía hispánica (1528–1713)*, ed. by M. Herrero Sanchez and others (Genova: Società Ligure di Storia Patria, 2011), pp. 413–57.

Pacini, A., *I presupposti politici del 'secolo dei Genovesi'* (Genova: Società Ligure di Storia Patria, 1990).

Pacini, A., 'Pignatte di Vetro: Being a Republic in Philip II's Empire', in *Spain in Italy. Politics, Society, and Religion 1500–1700*, ed. by T. J. Dandelet and J. A. Marino (Leiden: Brill, 2007), pp. 409–35.

Pacini, A., *'Desde Rosas a Gaeta'. La costruzione della rotta spagnola nel Mediterraneo occidentale nel secolo XVI* (Milano: Franco Angeli, 2013).

Pallavicini, T., *Della navigazione e del commercio. Considerazioni politiche di Tobia Pallavicino del q. Fabrizio* (Genova: Benedetto Guasco, 1656).

Panofsky, E., *The Life and Art of Albrecht Dürer* (Princeton, NJ: Princeton University Press, 1971).

Paolocci, C., ed., *I Gesuiti fra impegno religioso e potere politico nella Repubblica di Genova*, in *Quaderni Franzoniani*, 5 (1992), pp. 5–364.

Paolocci, C., Leonardi, A., eds, *La Liguria di Agostino: architectura, iconografia, spiritualità: 750 anni di presenza sul territorio: mostra didattico-documentaria* (Genova: Editoriale tipografica, 2006).

Parker, G., *Imprudent King: A New Life of Philip II* (New Haven: Yale University Press, 2014).

Parma, E., 'Il palazzo del Principe Andrea Doria a Fassolo in Genova', in *L'Arte*, 10 (1970), pp. 12–58.

Parma, E., *Albergo dei Poveri*, Guide di Genova (Genova: Sagep, 1978).

Parma, E., 'Due Angeli di Giovannangelo Montorsoli', in *Studi in memoria di Teofilo Ossian De Negri*, vol. 1 (Genova: Carige, 1986), pp. 61–69.

Parma, E., *Perin del Vaga. L'anello mancante* (Genova: Sagep, 1986).

Parma, E., Pesenti, F. R., Torrijos, R. L., 'Il secolo d'oro dei genovesi: il Cinquecento', in *La scultura a Genova e in Liguria*, vol. 1 (Genova: Fratelli Pagano Editori, 1987), pp. 286–89.

Parma, E., Galassi, M. C., 'Artisti e artigiani del marmo dal Cinquecento al Seicento', in *La scultura a Genova e in Liguria dal Seicento al Primo Novecento*, vol. 2 (Genoa: Cassa di Risparmio, 1988), pp. 21–23.

Parma, E., Galassi, M. C., *La scultura a Genova* (Genoa: Cassa di Risparmio, 1988).

Parma, E., 'Tavarone, Lazzaro', in *La pittura in Liguria. Il Cinquecento*, ed. by E. Parma (Recco: Microarts, 1999), pp. 413–14.

Parma, E., ed., *Perino del Vaga tra Raffaello e Michelangelo* (Milano: Electa 2001).

Parma, E., ed., *Perino del Vaga. Prima, durante, dopo* (Genova: De Ferrari, 2004).

Parma, E., 'Genealogie Doria', in *Il Palazzo del Principe, Genesi e trasformazioni della villa di Andrea Doria a Genova*, ed. by L. Stagno (Roma: Carocci, 2004), pp. 55–74.

Pastine, O., 'Rapporti fra Genova e Venezia nel secolo XVII e Gio Bernardo Veneroso', in *Giornale Storico e Letterario della Liguria*, 14 (1939), pp. 190–266.

Pastine, O., 'Genova e Inghilterra da Cromwell a Carlo II: orientamenti politico–economici', in *Rivista storica italiana*, 66 (1954), pp. 309–47.

Pastore, A., 'Giulio II, Papa', in *Dizionario biografico degli italiani* (Roma: Istituto della Enciclopedia italiana, 2001).

Pattenden, M., 'Rome as a "Spanish Avignon"? The Spanish Faction and the Monarchy of Philip II', in *The Spanish Presence in Sixteenth-Century Italy: Images of Iberia*, ed. by P. Baker-Bates and M. Pattenden (Farnham Surrey: Ashgate, 2015), pp. 65–84.

Pavoni, R., 'I simboli di Genova alle origini del Comune', in *Civico Istituto Colombiano, studi e testi. Saggi e documenti*, 3 (1983), pp. 29–64.

Pedani, M. P., *La dimora della pace. Considerazioni sulle capitolazioni tra i paesi islamici e l'Europa* (Venezia: Cafoscarina, 1996).

Pedani, M. P., *Dalla frontiera al confine* (Roma: Herder, 2002).

Pedani, M. P., 'Between Diplomacy and Trade: Ottoman Merchants in Venice', in *Merchants in the Ottoman Empire*, ed. by S. Faroqhi and G. Veinstein (Leuven: Peeters, 2008), pp. 3–22.

Pedemonte, D., 'Bombe sul dominio: la campagna inglese contro la repubblica di Genova durante la Guerra di Successione Austriaca,' in *Mediterranea*, 27 (2013), pp. 109–48.

Pedemonte, D., 'Deserters, Mutineers, and Criminals: British Sailors and Problems of Port Jurisdiction in Genoa and Livorno during the Eighteenth Century', in *Law, Labour and Empire: Comparative Perspectives on Seafarers, c. 1500–1800*, ed. by M. Fusaro and others, (Palgrave, 2015), pp. 256–71.

Pedrol Aguilà, M., *Un écrivain méconnu entre Classicisme et Lumières: le chevalier de Mailly* (doctoral dissertation, Madrid, UNED, 2019).

Peirano, E., L., *Lettera della Repubblica di Genova, alla Repubblica di Venezia (28 Luglio 1606)* (Genova: tip. della Gioventù, 1868).

Pelikan, J., *Mary through the Centuries: Her Place in the History of Culture* (New Haven: Yale University Press, 1996).

Pentcheva, B. V., *Icons and Power: The Mother of God in Byzantium* (University Park: Pennsylvania State University Press, 2006).

Pesce, G., Felloni, G., *Le monete genovesi. Storia, arte ed economia nelle monete di Genova dal 1139 al 1814* (Genova: Stringa, 1975).

Pesenti, F. R., *La pittura in Liguria: artisti del primo Seicento* (Genova: Stringa, 1986).

Pesenti, F. R., 'L'Illuminismo e l'età neoclassica', in *La pittura a Genova e in Liguria*, 2, *Dal Seicento al primo Novecento* (Genova: Sagep, 1987), pp. 349–75.

Petitjean, J., 'Gênes et le bon gouvernement de l'information (1665–1670)', in *Cahiers de la Méditerranée*, 85 (2012), p. 215–31.

Petitjean, J., *L'intelligence des choses. Une histoire de l'information entre Italie et Méditerranée (XVIe-XVIIe siècles)* (Roma: BEFAR, 2013).

Pettegree, A., *The Invention of News: How the World Came to Know about Itself* (London: Yale University Press, 2014).

Petti Balbi, G., ed., *Genova medievale vista dai contemporanei* (Genova: Sagep, 1978).

Petti Balbi, G., 'La scuola medievale', in *Atti della Società Ligure di Storia Patria*, 45, 2 (2005), pp. 5–46.

Piccinno, L., 'Il commercio marittimo e lo sviluppo del porto di Genova tra Medioevo ed età Moderna', in *Quaderni di ricerca della Facoltà di Economia dell'Università degli Studi dell'Insubria*, 12 (2004), pp. 1–25.

Piccinno, L., *Economia marittima e operatività portuale. Genova, secc. XVII–XIX* (Genova: Società Ligure di Storia Patria, 2000).

Piccinno, L., Zanini, A., 'Genoa: Colonizing and Colonized City? The Port City as a Pole of Attraction for Foreign Merchants (16th-18th centuries)', in *Reti marittime come fattori dell'integrazione europea*, ed. by G. Nigro, (Firenze: Firenze University Press, 2019), pp. 281–96.

Piccolomini, A., *De la Institutione di tutta la Vita de l'Homo nato nobile e in città libera* (Venezia: Scotto, 1542).

Pierguidi, S., 'Perin del Vaga versus Pordenone, Beccafumi e Girolamo da Treviso nella decorazione delle facciate della villa di Andrea Doria a Genova', in *Arte Documento*, 26 (2010), pp. 166–75.

Piozzo, H. L., *Observations and Reflections Made in the Course of a Journey Through France, Italy, and Germany*, 2 vols (London: A. Strahan and T. Cadell, 1789).

Pizzorno, D., 'Il cannone e l'eversione. La minaccia sabauda nei primi tre decenni del Seicento', in *Genova e Torino. Quattro secoli di incontri e scontri*, ed. by G. Assereto, C. Bitossi, P. Merlin (Genova: Società Ligure di Storia Patria, 2015), pp. 81–97.

Pizzorno, D., *Genova e Roma tra Cinque e Seicento. Gruppi di potere, rapporti politico-diplomatici, strategie internazionali* (Modena: Mucchi, 2018).

Plutarchus [attr.], *De liberis educandis*, trad. By G. Veronese (Venezia: s.n., 1451–1475).

Pocock, J. G. A., *The Machiavellian Moment: Florentine Political Thought and the Atlantic Republican Tradition* (Princeton, NJ: Princeton University Press, 1975).

Podestà, F., *Il porto di Genova dalle origini fino alla caduta della Repubblica Genovese (1797)*, (Genova: Spiotti, 1913).

Podestà, F., *L'acquedotto di Genova, 1071–1879* (Genova: Fratelli Frilli, 2018).

Poleggi, E., Poleggi, F., eds., *Descrizione della Città di Genova da un anonimo del 1818* (Genova: Sagep, 1969).

Poleggi, E., *Iconografia di Genova e delle Riviere* (Genova: Sagep, 1977).

Poleggi, E., 'Uso dell'immagine urbana', in *Indice per i beni culturali del territorio ligure*, 10 (1978), pp. 2–6.

Poleggi, E., 'L'evoluzione storica dell'immagine di Genova', in *Prime ipotesi per un rilancio turistico della città di Genova*, (Genoa: Sagep, 1981), pp. 13–30.

Poleggi, E., Cevini, P., *Le città nella storia d'Italia: Genova* (Roma-Bari: Laterza, 1981).

Poleggi, E., *Paesaggio e immagine di Genova* (Genova: Sagep, 1982).

Poleggi, E., ed., *Genova. Ritratto di una città* (Genova: Sagep, 1985).

Poleggi, E., ed., *Genova nel Settecento e le vedute di Antonio Giolfi* (Milano: edizioni il Polifilo, 1986).

Poleggi, E., 'Dalle mura ai saloni, un rinnovo segreto', in *Genova nell'età Barocca*, ed. by E. Gavazza and G. Rotondi Terminiello (Bologna: Nuova Alfa Editore, 1992), pp. 18–28.

Pollak, M., *Turin 1564–1680: Urban Design, Military Culture, and the Creation of the Absolutist Capital* (Chicago: University of Chicago Press, 1991).

Polonio, V., 'San Bernardo, Genova e Pisa', in *San Bernardo e l'Italia*, ed. by P. Zerbi (Milano: Vita e Pensiero, 1993), pp. 69–99.

Possevino, A., *Lettera del Padre Antonio Possevino Giesuita al Padre Maestro Marc'Antonio Capello Minor Conventuale, con la risposta di detto padre* (Venezia: Cavalcaluppo, 1606).

Possevino, A., *Risposta del Sig. Paolo Anafesto all'avviso del Sig. Antonio Quirino, nobili venetiani, circa la scommunica della Santità di Papa Paolo V contro il Duce, et Senato di Venetia* (Bologna: Bartolomeo Cochi, 1607).

Priarone, M., *Andrea Ansaldo 1584–1638* (Genova: Sagep, 2011)

Prina, V., *Sant'Agostino a Genova* (Genova: Sagep, 1992).

Pro libertate status et reipublicae Venetorum Gallofranci ad Philenetum epistola (Paris, 1607).

Profumo Müller, L., *Bartolomeo Bianco architetto e il barocco genovese, Bollettino Centro Studi di Storia dell'Architettura*, 22 (Roma, Centro di Studi per la Storia dell'Architettura, 1968).

Puccio, L., 'Frescanti genovesi a Palazzo Centurione in Fossatello. Domenico Piola – Gregorio De Ferrari – Bartolomeo Guidobono', in *Bollettino Ligustico*, 21 (1969), pp. 113–30.

Pugliese, S., *Le prime strette dell'Austria in Italia* (Milano: Treves, 1932).

Puncuh, D., ed., *Storia della cultura ligure*, 4 vols (Genova: Società Ligure di Storia Patria, 2004–2005).

Puncuh, D., 'Genova. Mediterraneo, Europa, Atlantico', in *Atti della Società Ligure di Storia Patria*, 46, 1 (2006), pp. 9–29.

Quevedo, *Lince de Italia u Zahorí español*, ed. by I. Perez Ibanez (Pamplona: Ediciones Universidad de Navarra, 2002).

Quevedo, Francisco de, *La hora de todos y la Fortuna con seso*, ed. by L. Schwartz (Madrid: Classico Castalia, 2009).

Quintana Fernández, J., 'Los Orígenes de la «Tradición Española del Ingenio»', in *Revista de Historia de la Psicología*, 22, 3–4 (2001), pp. 505–15.

Quondam, A., '"Formare con parole": L'institutio del moderno gentiluomo', in *History of education & children's literature*, 1 (2006), pp. 23–54.

Raband, I., 'Printed Narrative: The Festival Books for Archduke Ernest of Austria from Brussel and Antwerp, 1594/95', in *Aspects of the Narrative in Art History*, ed. by K. Hiralawa (Kyoto: Kyoto University, 2014), pp. 17–32.

Raband, I., 'Staging Genoa in Antwerp: The Triumphal Arch of the Genoese Nation for the Blijde Inkomst of Archduke Ernest of Austria into Antwerp, 1594', in *Sites of Mediation. Connected Histories of Places, Processes, and Objects in Europe and Beyond (1450–1560)*, ed. by S. Burghartz, L. Burkart and C. Göttler (Leiden: Brill, 2016), pp. 46–70.

Raby, J., 'La Sérénissime et la Sublime Porte: les arts dans l'art diplomatique, 1453–1600', in *Venise et l'Orient, 828–1797*, ed. by S. Carboni (Paris: Gallimard-Institut du monde arabe, 2006), pp. 90–119.

Raccolta degli scritti vsciti fvori in istampa, e scritti a mano, nella cavsa del P. Paolo V co' Signori Venetiani. Secondo le stampe di Venetia, di Roma, & d'altri luoghi, 2 vols (Coira [Geneva]: Paul Marceau, 1607).

Raffo, G., ed., 'I Gesuiti a Genova nei secoli XVII e XVIII. Storia della Casa Professa di Genova della Compagnia di Gesù dall'anno 1603 al 1773', in *Atti della Società Ligure di Storia Patria*, 36, 1 (1996), pp. 153–403.

Ramirez de Arellano, F., and others, eds, *Colección de documentos inéditos para la historia de España*, XCVIII, (Madrid: Rafael Marco × Viñas, 1891).

Rapp, R. T., 'The Unmaking of the Mediterranean Trade Hegemony: International Trade Rivalry and the Commercial Revolution', in *Journal of Economic History* 35 (1975), pp. 499–525.

Ratti, C. G., *Storia de' pittori, scultori et architetti liguri e de' foresti che in Genova operarono, secondo il manoscritto del 1762*, ed. by M. Migliorini (Genoa: Istituto di storia dell'arte dell'Università di Genova, 1997).

Ravecca, P. R., 'Così Genova divenne "Città di Maria Santissima"', in *Studi Genuensi*, 8 (1990), pp. 33–58.

Rebora, G., 'I lavori di espurgazione della Darsena nel porto di Genova nel 1545', in *Atti della Società Ligure di Storia Patria*, 28 (1988), pp. 199–220.

Reijner, C., 'Gesprekken in Genua. Giovanni Costa over het Twaalfjarig Bestand', in *De Zeventiende Eeuw. Cultuur in de Nederlanden in interdisciplinair perspectief*, 30.1 (2014), pp. 76–96.

Reijner, C., 'Il mito dell'Olanda. Politiek en geschiedschrijving in vroegmodern Italië', in *Incontri. Rivista europea di studi italiani*, 30.2 (2015), pp. 41–55.

Riccomini, A. M., *Il viaggio in Italia di Pietro De Lama: la formazione di un archeologo in età neoclassica* (Pisa: ETS, 2003).

Rime diverse in lengua zeneise (Zena: s.n., 1575).

Rime diverse, in lingua genovese, le quali per la novità de' soggetti sono molto dilettevoli da leggere, di nuovo date in luce (Pavia: Bartoli, 1583).

Ripa, C., *Iconologia* (Roma: Lepido Faci, 1603).

Rose, W. S., *The Orlando Furioso Translated into English verse* (London: John Murray, 1858).

Rossi, G.D., *Nuova delineazione della nobilissima e famosissima città di Genova* (Roma: Gio Giacomo De Rossi, 1640).

Rospocher, M., *Il papa guerriero. Giulio II nello spazio pubblico europeo* (Bologna: Il Mulino, 2015).

Rosser, G., 'The Church and Religious Life', in *A Companion to Medieval Genoa*, ed. by C. E. Beneš (Boston: Brill, 2018), pp. 345–67.

Rossi, A., and Santamaria, R., eds, *Superbe carte. I Rolli dei Palazzi di Genova* (Genova: Paginaria, 2018).

Rotta, S., 'Fra Spagna e Francia', in *El Siglo de los Genoveses e una lunga storia di Arte e Splendori nel Palazzo dei Dogi*, ed. by P. Boccardo and C. Di Fabio (Milano: Electa, 1999), pp. 246–49.

Rotta, S., 'Genova e il Re Sole', in *El Siglo de los Genoveses e una lunga storia di Arte e Splendori nel Palazzo dei Dogi*, ed. by P. Boccardo and C. Di Fabio (Milano: Electa, 1999), pp. 286–91.

Ruffini, G., 'Icones Ligusticae: rappresentazioni simboliche della Liguria nel libro del Seicento', *I tempi della storia. Bollettino del Centro di Studi sull'Età Moderna*, 1 (1989), pp. 7–24.

Ruffini, G., *Sotto il segno del Pavone. Annali di Giuseppe Pavoni e dei suoi eredi 1598–1642* (Milano: Franco Angeli, 1994).

Ruffini, G., 'Entro serenissimi fogli. I volumi per le incoronazioni dei dogi', in *El siglo de los Genoveses*, ed. by P. Boccardo e C. Di Fabio (Milano: Electa, 1999), pp. 104–08.

Ruffini, G., *Cristoforo Zabata. Libraio, editore e scrittore del Cinquecento* (Firenze: University Press, 2014).

Ruffini, G., 'Tra Pallade e Marte: libri e letture alla corte dei Doria', in *Principi e Signori. Le biblioteche nella seconda metà del Quattrocento*, ed. by G. Arbizzoni, C. Bianca and M. Peruzzi (Urbino: Accademia Raffaello, 2010), pp. 363–75.

Saginati, L., 'Ricerche nell'Archivio della Basilica di Carignano', in *Galeazzo Alessi e l'architettura del Cinquecento*, ed. by W. Lotz (Genova: Sagep, 1975), pp. 333–47.

Salonia, M., *Genoa's freedom: entrepreneurship, republicanism, and the Spanish Atlantic* (Lanham: Lexington books, 2017).

Sanguineti, D., *Domenico Piola e i pittori della sua "casa"* (Soncino: Edizioni dei Soncino, 2004).

Sansovino, F., *Delle orationi volgarmente scritte da diuersi huomini illustri de tempi nostri… Raccolte già dalla felice memoria del signor Francesco Sansouino & hora in questa nostra vltima impressione arricchite di molte altre non più stampate. Con due tauole, vna delle orationi, & materie che trattano, l'altra delle cose notabili* (Venezia, Altobello Salicato: alla libraria della Fortezza, 1584).

Sanuto, M., *I Diarii*, LI (Venezia: Visentini 1898).

Sanz, A. C., *Los banqueros de Carlos II* (Valladolid: Universidad de Valladolid, 1989).

Sanz, A. C., *Los Banqueros y La Crisis de La Monarquía de 1640* (Madrid: Marcial Pons Ediciones de Historia, 2013).

Sanz, A. C., *Un banquero en el siglo de oro: Octavio Centurión, el financiero de los Austrias* (Madrid: La Esfera de los Libros, 2015).

Sanz, A. C., 'La triple red diplomática de la República de Génova en España y el entorno del duque de Lerma (1605–1608)', in *Identità nobiliare tra monarchia ispanica e Italia: lignaggi, potere e istituzioni (secoli XVI–XVIII)*, ed. by M. Aglietti, D. Edigati, S. Martinez Hernandez, and A. C. Sanz (Roma: Edizioni di Storia e Letteratura, 2019), pp. 31–46.

Sarpi, P., *Opere*, ed. by G. Cozzi and L. Cozzi (Milano: Ricciardi, 1969).

Savelli, R., *La Repubblica oligarchica. Legislazione, istituzioni e ceti a Genova nel Cinquecento* (Milano: Giuffrè, 1981).

Savelli, R., '"Honore e robba": sulla vita di Giovanni Andrea Doria', in *La Berio*, 29, 1 (1989), pp. 3–41.

Savelli, R., 'Doria, Giovanni Andrea', in *Dizionario Biografico degli Italiani*, XLI (Roma: Istituto della Enciclopedia Italiana, 1992), pp. 311–312.

Savelli, R., 'Tra Machiavelli e S. Giorgio. Cultura giuspolitica e dibattito istituzionali a Genova nel Cinque-Seicento', in *Finanze e ragion di Stato in Italia e in Germania nella prima età moderna*, ed. by A. de Maddalena and H. Kellenbenz (Bologna: Il Mulino, 1984), pp. 249–321.

Savelli, R., *Che cosa era il diritto patrio di una repubblica?*, in *Il diritto patrio, tra diritto comune e codificazione (secoli XVI–XIX)*, ed. by di I. Birocchi and A. Mattone (Roma: Viella, 2006).

SchedeL, H., *Liber chronicarum* (Nuremberg: Anton Koberger per Sebald Schreyer, Sebastian Kammermeister, 1493).

Schiaffino, A., *Memorie di Genova (1624–1647)*, ed. by C. Cabella, URL: www.quaderni.net [2024/5/13].

Schneller, B., 'Mary Cooper, Eighteenth Century London Bookseller, 1743–1761' (unpublished doctoral thesis, The Catholic University of America, 1987).

Schneller, B., 'Using Newspaper Advertisements to Study the Book Trade: A Year in the Life of Mary Cooper', in *Writers, Books, and Trade: An Eighteenth Century English Miscellany for Willam B. Todd* (New York: AMS Press, 1994), pp. 123–43.

Schneller, B., 'John Hill and Mary Cooper: A Case Study in Eighteenth-Century Publishing', in *Fame and Fortune: Sir John Hill and London Life in the 1750s*, ed. by C. Brant and G. Rousseau (London: Palgrave Macmillan, 2018), pp. 107–20.

Schnettger, M., 'Die Republik als König. Republikanisches Selbstverständnis und Souveränitätsstreben in der genuesischen Publizistik des 17. Jahrhunderts', in *Majestas*, 8/9 (2000–2001), pp. 171–209.

Schnettger, M., Verga, M., eds, *L'Impero e l'Italia nella prima età moderna.* (Bologna: Il Mulino, 2006).

Schnettger, M., *'Principe sovrano' oder 'Civitas imperalis'? Die Republik Genua und das Alte Reich in der Frühen Neuzeit (1556–1797)* (Mainz: Zabern, 2006).

Schnettger, M., 'Libertà e imperialità. La Repubblica di Genova e il Sacro Romano Impero nel tardo Cinquecento', in *Libertà e dominio. Il sistema politico genovese: le relazioni esterne e il controllo del territorio*, ed. by M. Schnettger and C. Taviani (Roma: Viella, 2011), pp. 129–44.

Schütte, M., *Die Galleria delle carte geografiche im Vatikan: Eine ikonologische Betrachtung des Gewölbeprogramms* (Hildesheim: Georg Olms, 1993).

Scott, J. B., *Architecture for the Shroud: Relic and Ritual in Turin* (Chicago: University of Chicago Press, 2003).

[Senckenberg, H. C. von], *Imperii Germanici Ius ac Possessio in Genua Ligustica eiusque ditionibus* [...] (Hannover: Förster, 1751).

Shaw, C., 'Concepts of Libertà in Renaissance Genoa', in *Communes and Despots in Medieval and Renaissance Italy*, ed. by J. E. Law and B. Paton (Aldershot: Ashgate, 2010), pp. 177–90.

Schobesberger, N., and others, 'European Postal Networks', in *News Networks in Early Modern Europe* (Leiden, Boston: Brill, 2016), pp. 19–63.

Schulz, J., 'Jacopo de' Barberi's View of Venice: Map Making, City Views, and Moralized Geography Before the Year 1500', in *Art Bulletin*, 60 (1978), pp. 425–74.

Signorot, G., ed., *L'Italia degli Austrias. Monarchia cattolica e domini italiani nei secoli XVI–XVII* (Mantova: Edizioni Centro Federico Odorici, 1993).

Sigonio, C., *De vita et rebus gestis Andreae Auriae* (Genoa: Girolamo Bartoli, 1586).

Sigonio, C., *Della vita et fatti di Andrea Doria principe di Melfi libri due tradotti dal latino di Carlo Sigonio nella nostra volgar lingua da Pompeo Arnolfini* (Genova: Pavoni, 1598).

Skinner, Q., *Liberty before Liberalism* (Cambridge: Cambridge University Press, 1998).

Smith, J. E., *Sketch of a Tour on the Continent in the Years 1786 and 1787*, 3 vols (London: J. Davis, 1793).

Sommariva, G., 'Coronationi e solenni esequie, visite e "segni d'allegrezza": il potere in scena alla corte dei dogi', in *El Siglo de los Genoveses e una lunga storia di Arte e Splendori nel Palazzo dei Dogi*, ed. by P. Boccardo and C. Di Fabio (Milano: Skira, 1999), pp. 130–37.

Sommariva, G., 'Un'idea per il rifacimento del Real Palazzo. Note in margine ai disegni di Marcantonio Franceschini nelle collezioni dell'Accademia Ligustica', in *Marcantonio Franceschini. I cartoni ritrovati*, ed. by G. Testa Grauso (Cinisello Balsamo: Silvana Editoriale, 2002), pp. 77–80.

Soprani, R., *Li scrittori della Liguria e particolarmente della maritima di Raffaele Soprani all'illustrissimo et eccellentissimo signor Marc'Antonio Saoli* (Genova: Calenzani, 1667).

Soprani, R., *Vite de pittori, scoltori et architetti Genovesi e de' forastieri, che in Genoua operarono con alcuni ritratti de gli stessi* (Genova: Bottaro e Tiboldi, 1674).

Speck, W., 'Britain and the Dutch Republic', in *A Miracle Mirrored: The Dutch Republic in European Perspective*, ed. by K. Davids and J. Lucassen (Cambridge: Cambridge University Press, 1995), pp. 173–95.

Spinola, G. A., *L'Ariodante, drama* (Genova: Benedetto Guasco, 1655).

Spinola, G. A., *Europa, drama per musica, rappresentato nel Teatro del Falcone di Genova. All'Illustrissimo Signore, mio Signore, il Signor Gio. Francesco Brignole* (Genova: Gerolamo Marino, 1665).

Spinola, G. A., *Il cuore in volta e 'l cuore in scena*, I and II, 2 vols (Genova: Casamara, 1695).

Spinola, A., *Scritti scelti*, ed. by C. Bitossi (Genova: Sagep, 1981).

[Spinola, G. F.], *Instruttione familiare di Francesco Lanospigio nobile genovese, a Niccolò suo figliuolo* (Roma: Tinassi, 1670).

Spione, G., '"…quel bel misto di colore che nelle primarie gallerie di Genova vien ammirato": i dipinti di Bartolomeo Guidobono della Galleria della Liguria', in *Nuove luci. Acquisizioni, donazioni e restauri Galleria Nazionale della Liguria 1958–2021*, ed. by A. Guerrini, G. Zanelli (Genova: Sagep, 2022), pp. 265–81.

Spiriti, A., 'Loano città imperiale e ideale: problemi di metodo e tipologie', in *I feudi imperiali in Italia tra XVI e XVIII secolo*, ed. by C. Cremonini and R. Musso (Roma: Bulzoni, 2010), pp. 318–38.

Squarciafico, G., *Genova eterna ode pindarica […] al serenissimo Agostino Centurione duce della Republica di Genova* (Roma: Stamperia d'Ignatio de' Lazari, 1652).

Squarciafico, G., *Le politiche malattie della Republica di Genova e loro medicine* (Genova: Costa & Nolan, 1998).

Stagno, L., 'Sovrani spagnoli a Genova: apparati trionfali e "hospitaggi" alla corte dei Doria', in *Genova e la Spagna. Opere, artisti, committenti, collezionisti*, ed. by P. Boccardo, J. L. Colomer and C. Di Fabio (Cinisello Balsamo: Silvana Editoriale, 2002), pp. 73–87.

Stagno, L., 'Due principi per un palazzo: I cicli decorativi commissionati da Andrea e Giovanni Andrea I Doria a Perino del Vaga, Lazzaro Calvi e Marcello Sparzo per Palazzo del Principe', in *Il Palazzo del Principe, Genesi e trasformazioni della villa di Andrea Doria a Genova*, ed. by L. Stagno (Roma: Carocci, 2004), pp. 9–32.

Stagno, L., 'L'hospitaggio a Genova di Massimiliano re di Boemia e di altri Asburgo della linea imperiale', in *Genova e L'Europa continentale*, ed. by P. Boccardo and C. Di Fabio (Genova: Carige, 2004), pp. 116–33.

Stagno, L., Di Marco Baffi, S., eds, *Il Palazzo del principe, genesi e trasformazioni della villa di Andrea Doria a Genova* (Roma: Carocci, 2004).

Stagno, L., *Palazzo del Principe. Villa di Andrea Doria* (Genova: Sagep, 2005).

Stagno, L., 'Immacolata india. L'immagine della Vergine di Guadalupe messicana a Genova e in Liguria', in *Immacolata nei rapporti tra l'Italia e la Spagna*, ed. by A. Anselmi (Roma: De Luca, 2008), pp. 379–96.

Stagno, L., 'Caravaggio a Genova: i rapporti con i Doria', in *Caravaggio e la fuga. Pittura di paesaggio nelle ville Doria Pamphilj*, ed. by A. Mercantini and L. Stagno (Cinisello Balsamo: Silvana Editoriale, 2010), pp. 23–25.

Stagno, L., 'Villa Centurione Doria a Pegli', in *Caravaggio e la fuga. Pittura di paesaggio nelle ville Doria Pamphilj*, ed. by A. Mercantini and L. Stagno (Cinisello Balsamo: Silvana Editoriale, 2010), pp. 31–47.

Stagno, L., 'La forza dell'effimero: apparati e rappresentazioni del potere a Genova', in *Il Teatro dei Cartelami. Effimeri per la devozione in area mediterranea*, ed. by F. Boggero and A. Sista (Genova: Sagep, 2012), pp. 62–69.

Stagno, L., 'Da Genova a Roma: collezioni e palazzi Doria Pamphilj; documenti, allestimenti, vicende', in *Collezionismo e spazi del collezionismo. Temi e sperimentazioni*, ed. by L. Magnani (Roma: Gangemi, 2013), pp. 193–230.

Stagno, L., 'Lorenzo Capelloni, la corte di Andrea Doria e l'immagine del Principe', in *Umanisti in Oltregiogo. Lettere e arti fra XVI e XIX secolo*, ed. by G. Ameri (Novi Ligure: Centro studi 'In Novitate', 2013), pp. 67–93.

Stagno, L., '"A honor e servicio di Dio utile di questo popolo et commodo delle loro case": Nostra Signora delle Grazie nella committenza di Giovanni Andrea I Doria', in *Restauri nella chiesa di Nostra Signora delle Grazie. Giovanni Battista Lama, Giovanni Battista Paggi. Cesare e Alessandro Semino*, ed. by G. Zanelli (Genova: Sagep, 2015), pp. 8–15.

Stagno, L., 'Triumphing over the Enemy: References to the Turks as Part of Andrea, Giannettino and Giovanni Andrea Doria's Artistic Patronage and Public Image', in *Il Capitale culturale*, 6 (2017), pp. 136–64.

Stagno, L., 'Turks in Genoese Art, 16th-18th Centuries: Roles and Images. A first approach', in *Jews and Muslims Made Visible in Christian Iberia and Beyond, 14th to 18th Centuries. Another Image*, ed. by B. Franco Llopis and A. Urquízar-Herrera (Leiden: Brill, 2019), pp. 296–330.

Stagno, L., 'Roman History Themes for Andrea Doria's Palazzo del Principe', in *Ikon*, 13 (2020), pp. 227–44.

Stagno, L., 'Celebrating Lepanto in the Republic of Genoa: Giovanni Andrea Doria's and Other Aristocrat's Patronage. Portraits, Paintings and Tapestries', in *Lepanto and Beyond. Images of Religious Alterity from Genoa and the Christian Mediterranean*, ed. By L. Stagno and B. F. Llopis (Leuven: Leuven University Press, 2021).

Stagno, L., *Giovanni Andrea Doria (1540–1606). Immagini, committenze artistiche, rapporti politici e culturali tra Genova e la Spagna* (Genova: Genova University Press, 2021).

Stagno, L., Franco Llopis, B., eds, *Religious Alterity from Genoa and the Christian Mediterranean* (Leuven: Leuven University Press, 2021), pp. 171–208.

Stagno, L., 'Prometheus in Palazzo del Principe', in *Il Capitale Culturale*, 27 (2023), pp. 353–76.

Starke, M., *Letters from Italy between the Years 1792 and 1798*, 2 vols (London: R. Phillips, 1800).

Stella, A., 'La riforma protestante', in *Storia di Venezia dalle origini alla caduta della Serenissima*, ed. by G. Cozzi and P. Prodi, VI (Roma: Istituto della Enciclopedia Italiana, 1994), pp. 341–63.

Stern, P. J., *The Company-State: Corporate Sovereignty and the Early Modern Foundation of the British Empire in India* (Oxford: Oxford University Press, 2011).

Stollberg-Rilinger, B., 'Honores regii. Die Königswürde im zeremoniellen Zeichensystem der Frühen Neuzeit', in *Dreihundert Jahre Preußische Königskrönung. Eine Tagungsdokumentation*, ed. by J. Kunisch (Berlin: Duncker & Humblot, 2002), pp. 1–26.

Stollberg-Rilinger, B., 'Einleitung', in *Konfessionelle Ambiguität. Uneindeutigkeit und Verstellung als religiöse Praxis in der Frühen Neuzeit, Schriften des Vereins für Reformationsgeschichte 214*, ed. by A. Pietsch and B. Stollberg-Rilinger (Gütersloh: Gütersloher Verlagshaus, 2013), pp. 9–26.

Storrs, C., 'Negotiating the Transition from Spanish to Austrian Habsburg Italy: Non-Spanish Italy and the War of the Spanish Succession (c. 1700–1713/14)', in *The War of the Spanish Succession*, ed. by M. Pohlig and M. Schaich (Oxford: Oxford University Press, 2018), pp. 131–57.

Stratton, S. L., *The Immaculate Conception in Spanish Art* (Cambridge: Cambridge University Press, 1994).

Strohmeyer, A., Edelmayer, F., eds, *Die Korrespondenz der Kaiser mit ihren Gesandten in Spanien, I, Der Briefwechsel zwischen Ferdinand I., Maximilian II. und Adam von Dietrichstein 1563–1565* (Wien: Verlag für Geschichte und Politik, 1997).

Subrahmanyam, S., 'On the Significance of Gadflies: The Genoese East India Company of the 1640s', in *Journal of European Economic History*, 17, 3 (1988), pp. 559–81.

Swart, K.W., *The Miracle of the Dutch Republic as Seen in the Seventeenth Century* (London: University College, 1969).

Sweet, R., *Cities and the Grand Tour: The British in Italy, c. 1690–1820* (Cambridge: Cambridge University Press,, 2012).

Symcox, G., *Victor Amadeus II: Absolutism in the Savoyard State 1675–1730* (Berkeley: University of California Press, 1983).

Taddei, E., Schnettger, M., Rebitsch, R., eds, *'Reichsitalien' in Mittelalter und Neuzeit* (Innsbruck: Studien Verlag, 2017).

Tagliaferro, L., *Rubens e Genova* (Genova: Palazzo Ducale, 1977).

Tagliaferro, L., '1882–1892. Riferimenti alla Galleria di Palazzo Bianco', in *Bollettino dei Musei Civici genovesi*, 7 (1986), pp. 49–88.

Tazzara, C., *The Free Port of Livorno and the Transformation of the Mediterranean World* (Oxford: Oxford University Press, 2017).

Taviani, C., 'A Privatized State: Discourses on the Casa di San Giorgio (1446–1562)', in *Languages of Power in Italy (1300–1600)*, ed. by D. Bornstein, L. Gaffuri, and B. Maxson (Turnhout: Brepols, 2017), pp. 49–62.

Taviani, C., 'La Casa de San Giorgio de Génova y los orígenes de las corporations europeas en la edad moderna', in *Repúblicas y republicanismo en la Europa moderna: siglos XVI–XVIII*, ed. by M. Herrero Sánchez (Madrid: FCE, Red Columnaria, 2017), pp. 507–27.

Taviani, C., "The Making of the Modern Corporation: The Casa di San Giorgio and its Legacy (1446–1720)", London and New York: Routledge, 2022.

The New English Bible with the Apocrypha (New York: Harper & Row, 1971).

Tilly, C., *Coercion, Capital, and European States, AD 990–1992* (Cambridge, Oxford: Blackwell, 1992).

Torriti, P., *Tesori di Strada Nuova. La via aurea dei Genovesi* (Genova: Sagep, 1970).

Tosco, G., 'In Pursuit of the World's Trade: Tuscan and Genoese Attempts to Enter Trans-Oceanic Trade in the Seventeenth Century' (unpublished doctoral thesis, European University Institute, 2020).

Tosco, G., 'Importing the Netherlands: Dutch influence on the Evolution of Genoese Shipping in the Middle of the Seventeenth Century', in *Tijdschrift voor Zeegeschiedenis*, 40 (2021), pp. 58–72.

Tosco, G., 'Mediatori indispensabili. La comunità neerlandofona di Genova a metà Seicento', in *Gli stranieri della repubblica. Controllo, gestione e convivenza a Genova in età moderna*, ed. by F. Ferrando, A. Zappia, F. Fioriti (Saluzzo: Fusta, 2023), pp. 243–70.

Tosi, A., *Language and the Grand Tour Linguistic Experiences of Travelling in Early Modern Europe* (Cambridge: Cambridge University Press, 2020).

Toso, F., 'Un modello di plurilinguismo urbano rinascimentale. Presupposti ideologici e risvolti culturali delle polemiche linguistiche nella Genova cinquecentesca', in *Città plurilingui. Lingue e culture a confronto in situazioni urbane. Atti del convegno internazionale di studi*, ed. by R. Bombi and F. Fusco (Udine: Forum 2005), pp. 491–530.

Toso, F., *La letteratura ligure in genovese e nei dialetti locali. Profilo storico e antologia* (Recco: le Mani, 2009).

Toso, F., 'Tra encomio privato e celebrazione pubblica: Balin ambasciao dri pescuei a ro Serenissimo Zorzo Centurion di Gian Giacomo Cavalli', in *Aspetti del plurilinguismo letterario nella Genova barocca*, ed. by F. Toso (Alessandria: Edizioni dell'Orso, 2022), pp. 107–28.

Treadwell, M., 'London Trade Publishers 1675–1750', in *The Library*, 4, 2 (1982), pp. 99–134.

Trivellato, F., *The Promise and Peril of Credit: What a Forgotten Legend about Jews and Finance Tells Us about the Making of European Commercial Society* (Princeton: Princeton University Press, 2019).

A True Relation of the Actions of the French Fleet Before Genova Together with the Messages that Passed Between the Said Fleet and the City' (London: Printed for William Cadman, 1664).

Tuleja, T. V., 'Eugenius IV and the Crusade of Varna', in *The Catholic Historical Review*, 35 (1949), pp. 257–75.

Ungari, P., *Statuti di compagnie e società azionarie italiane (1638–1808): per la storia delle società per azioni in Italia* (Milano: Giuffrè, 1993).

Van Gelderen, M., Skinner, Q., eds, *Republicanism: A Shared European Heritage*, 2 vols (Cambridge: Cambridge University Press, 2002).

Van Gelder, M., 'In Liefde En Werk Met de Lage Landen Verbonden: De Genuese koopman en literator Girolamo Conestaggio (ca. 1530–1614/15)', in *Internationale Handelsnetwerken En Culturele Contacten in de Vroegmoderne Tijd*, ed. by M. Van Gelder and E. Mijers (Maastricht: Shaker Publishing, 2009), pp. 27–42.

Van Ittersum, M. J., 'A Miracle Mirrored? The Reception of Dutch Economic and Political Thought in Europe in the Seventeenth and Eighteenth Centuries', in *BMGN – Low Countries Historical Review*, 127, 4 (2012), pp. 83–99.

Varchi, B., *Storia Fiorentina* (Augsburg: Paul Kuhzio, 1721).

Varchi, B., *Istoria fiorentina* (ed. by G. Milanesi, Florence, 1858).

Vargas Hidalgo, R., *Guerra y Diplomacia en el Mediterráneo: Correspondencia inédita de Felipe II con Andrea Doria y Juan Andrea Doria* (Madrid: Ediciones Polifemo, 2002).

Vasoli, C., *La cultura delle corti* (Bologna: Cappelli, 1980).

Vassilaki, M., ed., *Images of the Mother of God: Perceptions of the Theotokos in Byzantium* (Aldershot: Ashgate, 2005).

Vazzoler, F., 'Letteratura e spettacolo nell'età della Repubblica aristocratica', in *Atti della Società Ligure di Storia Patria*, 45, 2 (2005), pp. 471–92.

Vazzoler, F., 'The Orations for the Election of the Doge', in *Europa Triumphans: Court and Civic Festivals in Early Modern Europe*, ed. by J. R. Mulryne, H. Watanabe-O'Kelly and M. Shewring (London: Ashgate, 2004), pp 273–79.

Veneroso, G. B., *Il genio ligure risvegliato. Discorso* (Genova: Pieri, 1650).

Veneruso, D., 'La "querelle" seicentesca sulla gerarchia del potere internazionale: Un memoriale genovese per la corte di Spagna', in *Rapporti Genova-Mediterraneo-Atlantico nell'età moderna*, ed. by R. Belvederi (Genova: Università di Genova, 1989), pp. 447–86.

Viallon, M., and Dompnier, B., 'Le traité de la matière bénéficiale: le rapport à la France', in *Paolo Sarpi. Politique et religion en Europe*, ed. by M. Viallon (Paris: Éditions Classiques Garnier, 2010), pp. 209–55.

Villa, E., 'Genova, al vaglio d'un esiliato', in G. Squarciafico, *Le politiche malattie della Repubblica di Genova e loro medicine* (Genova: Costa & Nolan, 1998), pp. 5–19.

Villani, S., 'La prima rivoluzione inglese nel giudizio delle diplomazie veneziana e genovese', in *Repubblicanesimo e Repubbliche nell'Europa di Antico Regime*, ed. by E. Fasano Guarini, R. Sabbatini, and M. Natalizi (Milano: Franco Angeli, 2007), pp. 105–32.

Villari, R., *Elogio della dissimulazione. La lotta politica nel Seicento* (Roma: Laterza, 1992).

Viroli, M., *Repubblicanesimo* (Roma: Laterza, 1999).

Visceglia, M. A., 'Il cerimoniale come linguaggio politico. Su alcuni conflitti di precedenza alla corte di Roma tra Cinquecento e Seicento', in *Cérémonial et rituel à Rome (XVI–XIXᵉ siècle)* (Roma: École Française de Rome, 1997), pp. 117–76.

Vitale, V., *Diplomatici e consoli della repubblica di Genova* (Genova: Società Ligure di Storia Patria, 1934).

Vitale, V., *La diplomazia genovese* (Milano: Istituto per gli studi di politica internazionale, 1941).

Vitale, V., *Breviario della storia di Genova. Lineamenti storici ed orientamenti bibliografici*, 2 vols (Genova: Società ligure di Storia Patria, 1955), I, pp. 249–60.

Volpicella, L., 'I Libri dei Cerimoniali della Repubblica di Genova', in *Atti della Società Ligure di Storia Patria*, 49, 2 (1921), pp. 1–464.

Von Thiessen, H., *Das Zeitalter der Ambiguität. Vom Umgang mit Werten und Normen in der Frühen Neuzeit* (Köln: Böhlau, 2021).

Wackerlin, J. B., *L'ancienne chanson populaire en France* (Paris: Garnier, 1887).

Waldman, L. A., *Baccio Bandinelli and Art at the Medici Court. A Corpus of Early Modern Sources* (Philadelphia: American Philosophical Society, 2004).

Warner, M., *Alone of All Her Sex: The Myth and the Cult of the Virgin Mary* (New York: Vintage Books, 1983).

Watkins, T., *Travels through Switzerland, Italy, Sicily, the Greek Islands to Constantinople, Greece, Ragusa, and the Dalmatian Isles*, 2 vols (London: 1794).

Wheelock, A. K. Jr., and others, *Anthony Van Dyck* (Washington D.C.: National Gallery of Art, 1991).

Whitaker, L., Clayton, M., eds, *The art of Italy in the Royal Collection. Renaissance and Baroque* (London: Royal Collection Pubns, 2007).

White, J., *Duccio: Tuscan Art and the Medieval Workshop* (London: Thames & Hudson, 1979).

White, J., *Art and Architecture in Italy 1250–1400* (New Haven: Yale University Press, 1993).

Wilson, P., *The Holy Roman Empire. A Thousand Years of Europe's History* (London: Penguin Random House, 2017).

Wouk, E. H., *Frans Floris (1519/20–1570): Imagining a Northern Renaissance* (Leiden: Brill, 2018).

Zagorin, P., *Ways of Lying. Dissimulation, Persecution and Conformity in Early Modern Europe* (Cambridge: Harvard University Press, MA, 1990).

Zanini, A., 'Abaco e aritmetica mercantile a Genova nel XVII secolo: i manuali e la scuola di David Veronese', in *Atti della Accademia Ligure di Scienze e Lettere*, 6, 4 (2003), pp. 225–56.

Zanini, A., *Strategie politiche ed economia feudale ai confini della Repubblica di Genova (secoli XVI–XVIII). Un buon negotio con qualche contrarietà* (Genova: Società Ligure di Storia Patria, 2005).

Zanini, A., 'Feudi, feudatari ed economie nella montagna ligure', in *Libertà e dominio. Il sistema politico genovese: le relazioni esterne e il controllo del territorio*, ed. by M. Schnettger and C. Taviani (Roma: Viella, 2011), pp. 305–16.

Zanini, A., 'La Superba: Its Institutions and Fortune,' in *A Superb Baroque: Art in Genoa, 1660–1750*, ed. by J. Bober (Princeton: Princeton University Press, 2020), pp. 16–21.

Zanker, P., *The Power of Images in the Age of Augustus* (Ann Arbor: University of Michigan Press, 1990).

Zappella, G., *Il ritratto librario nel libro italiano del Cinquecento* (Milano: Editrice Bibliografica, 1988).

Zucchi, E., 'Alessandro Tassoni e i Politicorum libri di Justus Lipsius: citazione e contestazione', in *Parole rubate*, 24 (2021), pp. 171–93.

Zucchi, E., 'Repubblicanesimo antico e moderno. La Genova del Seicento alla prova della teoria della scuola di Cambridge', in *Studi Secenteschi*, 63 (2022), pp. 161–79.

Zucchi, E., 'Contesting the Spanish Myth: Republican Shaping of Ambrogio Spinola's Image in Genoese Literature (1608–52)', in *Ambrogio Spinola between Genoa, Flanders, and Spain*, ed. by B. J. Garcia Garcia, L. Lo Basso, S. Mostaccio (Leuven: Leuven University Press, 2022), pp. 251–70.

Zucchi, E., 'Repubblicanesimo antico e moderno. La Genova del Seicento alla prova della teoria della scuola di Cambridge', in *Studi secenteschi*, 43 (2022), pp. 161–79.

Zucchi, E., 'Republics in Comparison. Cross-cultural perspectives on Genoa, Venice and the United Provinces in Italian literature (1650–1699)', in *History of European Ideas*, 48 (2022), pp. 367–81.

Zunckel, J., 'Tra Bodin e la Madonna. La valenza della corte di Roma nel sistema politico genovese. Riflessioni sull'anello mancante', in *Libertà e dominio. Il sistema politico genovese: le relazioni esterne e il controllo del territorio*, ed. by M. Schnettger and C. Taviani (Roma: Viella, 2011), pp. 145–91.

NOTES ON CONTRIBUTORS

VALENTINA BORNIOTTO is Adjunct Professor of Visual Education and Postdoctoral Research Fellow in Art History at the University of Genoa.

GEORGE GORSE is Professor of Art History at Pomona College.

MANUEL HERRERO SÁNCHEZ is Full Professor of Early Modern History at Pablo de Olavide University in Seville.

WOUTER KREUZE is Scholarly Research Fellow at the Folger Shakespeare Library.

BENOÎT MARÉCHAUX is Assistant Professor of Early Modern History at the Complutense University of Madrid.

MICHAEL PAUL MARTOCCIO is Assistant Professor of History at the University of Wisconsin-Madison.

ALESSANDRO METLICA is Associate Professor of Comparative Literature at the University of Padua.

SIMONA MORANDO is Full Professor of Italian Literature at the University of Genoa.

EMILIO PÉREZ BLANCO is an independent scholar.

SARA RULLI is Adjunct Professor of History of Architecture at the University of Genoa.

LUANA SALVARANI is Full Professor of History of Education at the University of Parma.

MATTHIAS SCHNETTGER is Full Professor of Early Modern History at the Johannes Gutenberg University Mainz.

LAURA STAGNO is Full Professor of Early Modern Art History at the University of Genoa.

GIORGIO TOSCO is Postdoctoral Researcher at the University of Pavia.

FIORENZO TOSO († 2020) was Full Professor of General Linguistics at the University of Sassari.

ENRICO ZUCCHI is Researcher of Italian Literature at the University of Padova.